TAKING SIDES

Clashing Views in

American Foreign Policy

FOURTH EDITION

Clashing Views in

American Foreign Policy

FOURTH EDITION

Selected, Edited, and with Introductions by

Andrew Bennett
Georgetown University

George Shambaugh
Georgetown University

Contemporary Learning Series
2460 Kerper Blvd., Dubuque, IA 52001

Visit us on the Internet
http://www.mhcls.com

We dedicate this book to the men and women who have given their lives since September 11, 2001, in pursuit of a better life for all Americans.

Cover image:
DoD photo by Staff Sgt. Jacob N. Bailey, U.S. Air Force

Cover Acknowledgment
Maggie Lytle

Compositor: ICC Macmillan Inc.

Fourth Edition

123456789DOCDOC987

Library of Congress Cataloging-in-Publication Data
Main entry under title:
Taking sides: clashing views on controversial issues in American foreign policy/selected, edited,
and with introductions by Andrew Bennett and Geroge Shambaugh—4th ed.
Includes bibliographical references and index.
1. United States—Foreign policy. I. Bennet, Andrew, and Shambaugh, Geroge, *comp.*
327.73

MHID: 0-07-339722-9
ISBN: 978-0-07-339722-1
ISSN: 1536-3260

Printed on Recycled Paper

Preface

$\mathbf{A}$s of this writing, the United States finds itself with well over 100,000 troops deployed halfway around the world in a controversial conflict, trying to establish a democratic government capable of defending itself but facing daily guerilla-style attacks by opposing forces that take the lives of several Americans every day. It was not so long ago that a very different kind of foreign policy problem—a devastating surprise attack on U.S. territory—dominated public discussion, stimulated a far more assertive U.S. foreign policy, and ultimately led to the creation of vast new national security organizations to deal with a fundamentally changed international context.

The previous paragraph clearly describes the U.S. intervention in Iraq and the September 11, 2001, attacks on New York and Washington, but it could just as easily have been written in the early 1960s as the United States built up its forces in Vietnam and looked back to the surprise Japanese attack on Pearl Harbor that precipitated U.S. entry into World War II and that ultimately led to the creation of the Department of Defense, the Central Intelligence Agency, and the National Security Council in 1947.

These parallels, and many others that could be drawn as well to previous U.S. military interventions (in Somalia, Lebanon, Nicaragua, to name just a few) and previous surprise attacks on U.S. territory or forces (including terrorist bombings in the 1980s and 1990s in Lebanon, Yemen, and U.S. embassies in Africa), are a reminder that while the specific issues and countries that dominate U.S. foreign policy continually change, there is some continuity as well in both the foreign policy problems that the United States confronts and the ways in which Americans think about how to address them. True, the current situation in Iraq differs from Vietnam's in the 1960s in some ways that make Iraq a more challenging problem and in other ways that make it more amenable to America's influence. And the implications of the surprise attack on Pearl Harbor were very different from those of the 9/11 attacks. Even so, the study of recent foreign policies, with due attention to how they differ from the current context as well as the ways in which they resemble it, is extremely useful in clarifying the options the United States has as well as the likely costs and benefits of each alternative.

Thus, while much of this new edition focuses on the U.S. occupation of Iraq, readers should find it useful even if a U.S. withdrawal from Iraq is imminent or has already taken place. Whatever the outcome in Iraq, the United States will for the foreseeable future continue to confront the problem of autocratic states seeking, testing, or deploying weapons of mass destruction, including Iran and North Korea. Whether or not Osama bin Laden and other top al Qaeda leaders have been captured or killed by the time you read this book, the United States will continue to face a balancing act between giving law enforcement and intelligence officials a free hand to seek out terrorists and safeguarding civil liberties, and the monumental task of coordinating a vast bureaucratic machinery to protect tens of thousands of civilian and military sites that terrorists might target. These and other issues included in this volume will be with us in one form or another for many years to come.

This fourth edition maintains the philosophy of the *Taking Sides* series that debating vital issues is valuable and necessary and can push students and teachers alike to re-examine the assumptions behind their views. In a "fifty-fifty" nation in which each of the last two presidential elections was won by a narrow margin, it is essential to keep in mind that no party or individual is right all the time, ourselves included. It might seem at first glance that the format of this book—one reading on each side of an issue with an oversimplified label of "yes" or "no"—perpetuates the increasing polarization of our public political discourse. Readers will quickly discern, however, that each reading is far more subtle than the simple "yes" and "no" labels used as an organizing device, and the range of additional readings and Web sites suggested in each postscript present a still more diverse set of views.

This book follows a format that has proven successful in helping students come to terms with the complex challenges of American foreign policy. Each issue has two readings, one pro and one con. *Introductions* to each issue provide some background information on the essay authors and provide historical and political context for the debate in which they are engaged. The issues then conclude with *postscripts* that provide further avenues for exploration and suggest additional readings and Web sites. General Web sites are also listed under the heading *Internet References* for each part opener. At the back of the book is a listing of brief biographies for all the *contributors to the volume*. The contributors are a mix of scholars, journalists, practitioners, and noted political commentators.

Changes to the fourth edition   In the years between the third edition and the present volume, the basic issues confronting American foreign policy have not changed radically, but changing events have required the inclusion of more than 20 new essays. These include new essays on the issues of America's involvement in and leadership of world affairs, a potential U.S. withdrawal from Iraq, a potential partition of Iraq, U.S. policies toward Iran's nuclear program, the humanitarian crisis in Darfur, immigration, energy independence, climate change, terrorism and civil liberties, and U.S. relations with China, Israel, and Pakistan.

It is also worth noting a few of the many other important foreign policy issues that could not be included due to the need for keeping this book concise and staying within students' book budgets. We did not include essays on methods and means of addressing the proliferation of weapons of mass destruction other than military preemption, for example. We also included only a few of the many possible regional and bilateral issues important to U.S. foreign policy, omitting any dedicated essays on trans-Atlantic relations, Russia, Latin America, Africa, countries in Asia other than China and North Korea, and issues and countries in the Middle East other than Iraq and the Arab-Israeli conflict. Other important issues not included in this volume are those of illegal drugs entering the United States, the global threat of AIDS and other diseases, humanitarian aid and the International Criminal Court. Information on many of these issues is available through the Web sites listed in the part openers.

Note to instructors   A general guidebook, *Using Taking Sides in the Classroom*, which discusses methods and techniques for integrating the pro-con approach into any classroom setting, is available. An online version of this guidebook can be found at http://www.mhcls.com/usingts/index.mhtml.

Note for student readers   The debates in this book are not one-sided. Each author strongly believes in his or her position. If you read the debates with an open mind, you will find that each author makes cogent points that are hard to dismiss out of hand. Foreign policy involves trade-offs among competing values, and even when people agree on what values take priority, they may disagree about the best means of attaining them.

Yet to consider competing views with an open mind does not require that you remain neutral in the end. We hope these essays help clarify your own views and motivate you to put your views into action by writing to elected officials, working for candidates, and joining or creating organizations and political parties. Get involved, whichever side of an issue you are on!

Acknowledgments   We would like to thank the colleagues whose essays are reproduced herein. We would also like to thank Jill Peter and Susan Brusch of McGraw-Hill for their many helpful suggestions and hard work in producing this edition.

Andrew Bennett
Georgetown University

George Shambaugh
Georgetown University

Contents In Brief

Contents

Joseph Siegle, Douglas Dillon Fellow a the Council on Foreign Relations, argues that large numbers of countries are continuing to democratize and, because of the increase in accountability associated with democratization, they tend to experience economic growth as fast as, if not faster than, other countries in the same region. Tamara Cofman Wittes, research fellow in the Saban Center for Middle East Policy at the Brookings Institution, argues that U.S. efforts to promote democracy in Iraq and the Arab Middle East are likely to fail unless the U.S. government matches its rhetoric with a credible commitment to promote policies institutionalizing the forward movement of liberalism in Iraq and the region at large.

James Lacey, a journalist, argues that although there is evidence that Saddam Hussein did not have an inventory of weapons of mass destruction, he had the intent and the capability to produce such weapons on short notice and could easily have done so once UN inspectors departed had the United States not invaded Iraq. John B. Judis and Spencer Ackerman, respectively senior and associate editors at *The New Republic*, argue that the Bush administration greatly exaggerated intelligence information suggesting Iraq was a threat, particularly information suggesting ties between the Iraqi government and al Qaeda.

John McCain, U.S. Senator from Arizona and a veteran of the Vietnam War, argues that the withdrawal of U.S. troops from Iraq before stability is achieved there would lead to a bloody civil war, interference in Iraq by other states in the region, and a failed state that would become a haven for anti-American terrorists. William Odom, senior fellow at the Hudson Institute and former director of the National Security Agency, argues that all of the dire consequences predicted in the event of a U.S. withdrawal from Iraq—civil war, loss of American credibility, a haven for terrorists, and regional instability—have already taken place and will be made worse by a continuing U.S. military presence in Iraq.

Timothy Noah, author of the "Chatterbox" column of the online magazine *Slate*, argues that a managed partition of Iraq might be preferable to the ongoing conflict in that country. Rend al-Rahim, director of the Iraq Freedom Foundation and former representative of the Interim Iraqi government to the United States, argues that any attempt to draw lines of partition through the mixed regions of Iraq would intensify sectarian violence, lead to intervention by Iraq's neighbors, and bring about a radicalized Sunni regime in the middle of Iraq and a fundamentalist Shiite regime under Iranian influence in the south of Iraq.

UNIT 3   THE UNITED STATES AND THE WORLD: REGIONAL AND BILATERAL RELATIONS   109

Teresita Schaffer, director of the South Asian Program at the Center for Strategic and International Studies, notes man problems in Pakistan's domestic and foreign policies, but holds out the hope that Pakistan is getting more serious about cracking down on terrorists in Pakistan and pursuing peace in its troubled relations with India. Sydney Freedberg, a journalist for *The National Journal*, notes that Osama bin Laden and other top al Qaeda and Taliban leaders are widely believed to be hiding in northern Pakistan, and he details the difficulties of getting the Pakistani government, and even more importantly the tribes in the relatively lawless northern regions of Pakistan, to cooperate in capturing bin Laden and closing down military operations by al Qaeda and the Taliban.

Mario Loyola, a former consultant to the Department of Defense, argues that the United States needs to publicly retain the option of a preemptive military strike against Iranian nuclear facilities to give leverage to U.S. diplomatic efforts to get Iran to end its nuclear weapons program. Edward N. Luttwak, a senior adviser at the Center for Strategic and

International Studies, argues that the preemptive strikes on Iraq's nuclear facilities by the United States would alienate the Iranian public and lead Iran's government to retaliate against U.S. forces in Iraq and elsewhere in the Middle East.

Lawrence Kaplan, a senior editor at *The New Republic*, argues that the United Nations, the African Union, and NATO are unable or unwilling to intervene to stop genocide in Darfur, and that only a largely intervention by U.S. military forces can do so. David Rieff, a contributing editor at *The New Republic*, argues that although some form of international intervention in Darfur might eventually be necessary, a unilateral U.S. intervention would further damage U.S. relations with the Muslim world and would end up either with the secession of Darfur under a U.S. or UN protectorate or a Iraq-style counterinsurgency against the government of Sudan and the Janjaweed fighters it sponsors.

John J. Mearsheimer is the R. Wendell Harrison Distinguished Service Professor of Political Science and the codirector of the Program on International Security Policy at the University of Chicago. He argues that China's impressive economic growth will enable it to engage in an intense security competition with considerable potential for war. Dennis J. Blasko served as a military intelligence officer and foreign area officer specializing in China for the U.S. army and was army attaché in Beijing from 1992–1995 and in Hong Kong from 1995–1996. He argues the U.S. assessments of Chinese military modernization are biased to justify current U.S. policy and overstate the threat posed by China.

David C. Kang, associate professor of government at Dartmouth College, contends that the threat posed by North Korea is overblown because North Korea will continue to be deterred from acting aggressively and, consequently, that engagement offers the best strategy promoting economic, political, and military change. Victor D. Cha, associate professor of government and D.S. Song-Korea Foundation Chair in Asian Studies in the School of Foreign Service at Georgetown University and Asian director in the National Security Council of the U.S. government, argues that North Korea remains hostile and opportunistic. Engagement—if used at all—should be highly conditional, and the United States and its allies should remain prepared to isolate and contain North Korea if engagement fails.

Stephen Walt and John Mearsheimer, international relations scholars at Harvard University and the University of Chicago respectively, argue that the United States' unwavering support for Israel has undermined American interests in the Middle East. They assert that Israel is a strategic burden rather than an asset for the United States, and that the United States' policies toward Israel are largely driven by the political power of an "Israeli lobby" in the United States. Joseph Joffe, a leading German commentator on international affairs, maintains that if Israel had never existed, the United States would face many of the same problems it currently confronts in the Middle East. In his view, many of the challenges facing the United States are driven by problems within and between Arab states, rather than those between these states and Israel.

Tom Ridge, former security of homeland security, argues that the new department has made great progress in bringing together federal, state, and local security agencies and improving the coordination and information exchange among them to prevent terrorist attacks. Michael Crowley, senior editor of *The New Republic*, argues that the Department of Homeland Security is disorganized and underfunded and has not set the right priorities for best preventing new terrorist attacks.

Charles Krauthammer, *Washington Post* opinion columnist, argues that domestic spying and tough interrogation techniques are an important part of the United States' counter-terrorism policy and that their use helps to explain why the terrorists have not successfully hit the United States since 9/11/2001. Bob Barr, member of the House of Representatives from Georgia from 1995–2003, argues that President Bush's directive for the National Security Agency to spy on domestic citizens represents an abuse of presidential power and is contrary to the express and implied requirements of federal law as specified by the Fourth Amendment freedoms of the Constitution.

George W. Bush, president of the United States, argues that the United States can both be a law-abiding country with secure borders and a nation that upholds its tradition of welcoming immigrants. Mark Krikorian, executive director of the Center for Immigration Studies and a visiting fellow at the Nixon Center, argues that immigration reforms promoting guest workers or amnesty are unrealistic and prone to fraud and paralysis.

Murray Weidenbaum, the Mallinckrodt Distinguished University Professor of Economics at Washington University in St. Louis, asserts that opposition to economic globalization is based largely on 10 dangerous myths. Robert Kuttner, founder and coeditor of *The American Prospect*, argues that calls for virtually unchecked globalism are naïve, and he points out a number of problems that the trend toward globalism has revealed.

Edward Luce and Khozem Merchant argue that cost savings, labor flexibility, and the rising productivity of largely non-unionized youthful labor forces in India and elsewhere make offshore outsourcing beneficial to both U.S. firms, who can use their savings to retain higher skilled workers, and U.S. consumers, who benefit from access to low-cost, high-quality goods and services. Ronil Hira, who is the chair of the R&D Policy Committee for the Institute of Electrical and Electronics Engineers of the United States of America, argues that global outsourcing is leading to a loss of high-value/high-wage jobs in the natural sciences and engineering, which, in turn, undercuts U.S. innovation and leadership in the science, technology, and service sectors, attracts bright young people to countries other than the United States, and increases U.S. reliance on others for critical military and national security technologies.

William J. Clinton, former president of the Untied States, contends that global warming is real, that environmentally sound practices are economically feasible on personal and national levels, and that all peoples should work together to combat global warming. Jason Lee Steorts, deputy managing editor of *National Review*, argues data on global warming is not consistent and the fears of global warming are being fanned by politicians, the media, and some scientists.

Barack Obama, Democratic senator from Illinois, argues that America's high dependence on oil imports undermines its security by making it rely on unstable and often hostile governments. He argues that the United States can greatly reduce its reliance on oil imports by setting higher standards for auto fuel efficiency and promoting the use of biofuels like ethanol. Philip Deutch, director of Evergreen Solar and general partner of NGP Energy Technology partners, a private equity firm investing in energy technology companies, argues that U.S. oil imports are so high that it would be impossible to end them in the next few decades, and that U.S. energy use is likely to continue to grow, as will oil prices, even if energy efficiency and conservation increase.

Charles Krauthammer, *Washington Post* opinion columnist, argues the lives saved by information provided by those with information about terrorist incidents justify the use of torture to obtain that information. Andrew Sullivan, senior editor of *The New Republic*, argues against claims of the military utility and necessity of torture.

Kenneth Roth, executive director of Human Rights Watch, argues that while humanitarian intervention is extremely costly in human terms, it can be justified in situations involving ongoing or imminent slaughter, but that it should only be considered when five limiting criteria are met. Alan Kuperman, resident assistant professor of international relations at Johns Hopkins University, argues that the benefits of humanitarian intervention are much smaller and the costs much greater than are generally acknowledged because violence is perpetrated faster than interveners can act to stop it and the likelihood of humanitarian intervention may actually make some local conflicts worse.

Introduction

Just as economics generally involves competition over scarce resources, policymaking often involves competition over scarce values. Foreign policy decisions, in particular, are prone to debate because they affect multiple groups in the domestic and global arenas who often hold different values or have different sets of priorities. In the context of wars and crises, like the attacks on the World Trade Towers in New York and the Pentagon on September 11, 2001 or the attack on Pearl Harbor in 1942, the country tends to unify around the president and will give him or her extraordinary powers to shape the U.S. policy response. In the immediate aftermath of such events, U.S. national security is given precedence over other concerns. However, the rally-around-the flag effect does not last long. Within months of these events, other values— like the maintenance of civil liberties, the humane treatment of prisoners, the promotion of democracy abroad, the maintenance of good relations with allies, and concerns about the costs of conducting expansive foreign policy initiatives—begin to reassert themselves. Most people agree that maintaining national security, the preservation of liberty, and a healthy economy all matter all of the time. They are likely, however, to disagree about which issue takes precedence when policies designed to promote one goal potentially undermines the others.

How much security, liberty, or national wealth is enough? What takes precedence when strategies to enhance national security begin to undercut civil liberties at home or human rights abroad? What should we do when our desire to promote democracy abroad conflicts with the strategic or economic imperatives of maintaining good relations with authoritarian regimes? As always, there are compelling arguments for opposing answers to these questions.

In addition, even individuals or groups who share the same values can differ on what they think are the best strategies and tactics for attaining those values. When are diplomacy, foreign aid, trade, economic sanctions, or cultural exchanges called for, and when is force necessary? Under what conditions can the United States build and use international organizations and alliances, and when must it act unilaterally? Will raising the threat of a preemptive attack convince a potential adversary to stop working to obtain weapons of mass destruction, or will it only spur the country in question to accelerate its programs in the hope of acquiring weapons so deadly that the United States will be deterred from acting? There is no easy or universal answer to such questions regarding the widely shared goals of peace and prosperity.

Understanding all sides of an issue is one of the best ways to make a good decision. The contributors in this volume believe passionately in the views they put forth. They present cogent arguments that, when read in the absence of the competing point of view, are often very persuasive. Indeed, it is often easy to be seduced by the persuasiveness of a well-articulated argument and the use of a few illustrative examples—even if the argument is made in a 30-second election campaign commercial! To be an informed consumer, it is important to recognize and understand the viewpoints of those who are most likely to criticize the viewpoint you find most compelling. You might believe that their views are wrong, but do not dismiss them out of hand. You can become an informed consumer only by seeing various sides of an issue. Once you can see multiple sides to an issue, you will no longer be seduced by a flashy presentation. You may, however, be persuaded by a good one.

If, after seeing the issue from multiple perspectives, you still favor the argument that grabbed you in the beginning, so much the better. Now you can make your case stronger by anticipating and responding to those who would most likely challenge you. This will make your position stronger and your foreign policy choices more resilient. The Chinese strategist Sun Tzu once argued that to be successful you must know your enemy. By knowing your critics' arguments, you will better know yourself and be better able to defend your foreign policy position. Beyond the sheer fun of arguing, these are true benefits of a debate.

The debate format is intended to make you think, but it is not intended to neutralize your convictions. In fact, once you are informed, you *ought* to form convictions, and you should try to act on those convictions and to influence international policy to conform better with your beliefs. Ponder the similarities in the views of two very different leaders, a very young president in a relatively young democracy and a very old emperor in a very old country: In 1963, President John F. Kennedy, in recalling the words of the author of the epic poem *The Divine Comedy* (1321), told a West German audience, "Dante once said that the hottest places in hell are reserved for those who in a period of moral crisis maintain their neutrality." The very same year, while speaking to the United Nations, Ethiopia's emperor Haile Selassie (1892–1975) said, "Throughout history it has been the inaction of those who could have acted, the indifference of those who should have known better, the silence of the voice of justice when it mattered most, that has made it possible for evil to triumph."

The point is: Become informed. Then *do* something! Promoting democracy and civil liberties abroad have become centerpieces in U.S. foreign policy. For democracy to have meaning, informed individuals within democracies must act. Write letters to policymakers, donate money to causes you support, work for candidates with whom you agree, join an activist organization, or do any of the many other things that you can to make a difference. What you do is less important than that you do it.

Theories and Assumptions Behind American Foreign Policy

As will become evident as you read this volume, there are a number of ways to study American foreign policy. This reader is organized in terms of substantive topics, but it is important to remember that the competing views on these topics are informed by the theories and assumptions that each of the authors holds about how the world works. People in general tend to keep their theories and assumptions implicit until they are asked to justify why they think or feel the way they do about a particular issue. Academics are trained to be more explicit about the assumptions they make and the theories they use; yet they, too, often make judgments without acknowledging the foundations on which their judgments are made.

Since September 11, 2001, there has been a groundswell of debate about whether the world has fundamentally changed and, consequently, whether the assumptions and theories that we held about foreign policy and international affairs are still pertinent. If the content of this volume is compared to the previous editions, it becomes very apparent that many of the substantive issues are different—questions of the mistreatment of prisoners by U.S. soldiers and a preemptive war fought in Iraq are new. At the same time, the issues involved in this volume—the nature of sovereignty versus global governance, the costs and benefits of unilateralism versus those of multilateralism, the role of international norms and international law, the management of relations with allies and adversaries, the interaction of global forces and domestic politics in foreign policy, and tensions between security, economic, and environmental issues in the global arena—are all enduring. While the specific states, institutions, and individuals at the center of U.S. foreign policy may change, these issues will remain central. Thus, while they, too, may need to be tweaked to account for new players on the world scene, the basic concepts and theories that we use to explain and understand these issues remain pertinent as well.

American scholars who study international relations generally categorize the field into three theoretical approaches or schools of thought. The first is the "realist" school, which argues that states are the key actors in world politics and that they continually seek to increase their power as a means of ensuring their security and enhancing their prosperity. Realists also maintain that states balance against, or work to constrain, the other states that they find most powerful and threatening. In the process of seeking power and balancing against threats, military capabilities are the ultimate arbiter of which state will prevail at the negotiating table or on the battlefield. Realists believe that international institutions such as the United Nations do not truly constrain powerful states, because these institutions are created by the most powerful states to serve these states' interests, and these states will choose to ignore the institutions they create whenever they feel like it. Also, for realists, the domestic political structure of a state (democratic, authoritarian, communist, and so on) matters far less in determining its foreign policies than the level of military power the state has and the geographic threats and opportunities it faces. In terms of the history of American foreign policy, realism is most closely associated with President Nixon and his secretary of state, Henry Kissinger, while prominent scholars who are realists include Hans Morgenthau, Kenneth Waltz, Stephen Walt, and John Mearsheimer.

The "liberal" school of thought, which should not be confused with the term "liberal" in American politics despite some similarities, disagrees with the realists on several points. Liberals also see states as key actors focused on their own self-interests, but they believe states can use institutions to better serve those interests. In this view, states create international institutions, including formal organizations like the United Nations and the World Trade Organization and agreements like arms-control treaties, to help make international relations more transparent and provide mechanisms for sharing burdens to provide collective or public goods that benefit all states, such as a free trading system. Institutions, in other words, lower the "transactions costs" for states to cooperate on issues where they share goals by making it easier to identify which states have followed agreed-upon rules and which have not, and to punish the latter and reward the former. Liberals also believe that domestic politics greatly influence the foreign policies of states, and that democracies seldom if ever go to war against other democracies. In American foreign policy, Presidents Wilson and Carter are most clearly identified with the liberal approach. To the extent that they sought to maintain the U.S. role in existing multilateral military and economic institutions as a means of addressing U.S. foreign policy concerns, Presidents H. W. Bush and Bill Clinton fit in this category as well. Scholars who are associated with this approach include Immanuel Kant, Adam Smith, Michael Doyle, Robert Keohane, and G. John Ikenberry.

A third group, "constructivists," differs from both realists and liberals. Constructivists agree that states, for now, are key actors in world politics, but they emphasize that this was not always so and may not remain so. Constructivists are more attentive than liberals or realists to the roles of actors other than states, ranging from international corporations, to transnational human rights movements, to terrorist cells. For constructivists, both the actors in world politics and the principles (like sovereignty) that define them are *socially constructed*; that is, they are the result of social actors' behavior, not immutable entities created by the natural world. Such social structures, including formal and informal international institutions, rules, and patterns of behavior, are created and shaped by the interactions of various actors in world politics but, once created, these institutions also affect their behavior. International institutions in this view have not only intended consequences, which liberals emphasize, but also unintended consequences unforseen by their creators. Such institutions take on a life of their own and do not merely act on the orders of or in the interests of powerful states. Constructivists maintain that social structures, including both states and international institutions, are ideational as well as material. The military, economic, and political capabilities of states affect how other states view them, but so do the ideas, cultures, and values that they hold and that others hold about them. Among U.S. presidents, Theodore Roosevelt and Ronald Reagan best demonstrated an awareness of the importance of shaping ideas, images, and identities of the United States and others in the ways they exercised and promoted U.S. foreign policy in the domestic and global arenas. For example, President Reagan's success in identifying the Soviet Union as the "Evil Empire" was a key component in his foreign policy strategy, but once the reformist Soviet leader Mikhail Gorbachev began to show some success in changing the Soviet Union's identity and its way of government, Reagan moved to improve relations with the Soviet Union much more quickly than the realists in his administration. Scholars who are constructivists include Alexander Wendt and John Ruggie.

Table 1

	Realism	Liberalism	Constructivism
Intellectual Founders	Hans Morgenthau Kenneth Waltz	Adam Smith Immanuel Kant	Alexander Wendt John Ruggie
Academic Scholars	John Mearsheimer Randall Schweller Stephen Walt	Michael Doyle Robert Keohane G. John Ikenberry	Kathryn Sikkink Michael Barnet Martha Finnemore
Foreign Policy Personnel	Richard Nixon Henry Kissinger Colin Powell Condoleeza Rice	Woodrow Wilson Jimmy Carter George H. W. Bush Bill Clinton	Franklin Roosevelt Ronald Reagan

This table is adapted from Jack Snyder, "One World, Rival Theories," *Foreign Policy* (November/December 2004), p. 54.

These dominant approaches are summarized in Table 1. Each of these three approaches has something important to say about the post–9/11 world. Realism helps us understand why the United States has reacted so strongly to perceived threats, why it has largely acted with and through other states to address the problem of terrorism, and why, as the most powerful actor, it felt that it must and could intervene in Iraq even without a UN resolution specifically authorizing the use of force. Liberalism helps illuminate why even though the United States bypassed the UN on the question of a resolution authorizing force in Iraq, it still found the UN useful in setting up and monitoring elections in Iraq. Constructivism helps us understand the cultures and values that motivate not just terrorist groups but the many individuals around the world who do not themselves espouse terrorism but do express deep discontent in opinion polls about America's foreign policies.

Yet these three theoretical approaches only partially and imperfectly capture the schools of thought among the American public and American leaders on foreign policy. Four key questions have been the subject of continual debate through the history of American foreign policy: Should the United States take an active role in world affairs (internationalism), or can and should it confine its actions mostly to domestic matters (isolationism)? When it takes action abroad, should the United States work with and through international organizations and alliances (multilateralism), or should it work mostly through its own devices and avoid becoming entangled in the constraints inherent in working with others (unilateralism)? Should the United States rely heavily on strong military capabilities and the threat and use of force to achieve its ends, or should it emphasize diplomatic, economic, and political instruments? Finally, what relative emphasis should the United States place on preserving its immediate security, fostering democracies abroad, and advancing U.S. economic goals and the prosperity of U.S. businesses and citizens?

Some combinations of answers to these questions overlap fairly closely with the theoretical approaches outlined above. Foreign policy realists like Henry Kissinger are internationalist, multilateralist in terms of alliances but less so in terms of international organizations, willing to threaten and use force, and focused on security issues. Liberals like President Wilson are internationalist, multilateralist in terms of both institutions and alliances, reluctant to use force but willing to do so to defend the United States and democratic principles, and focused on building democracies abroad as a means of promoting American security as well as American values and economic interests.

Three important schools of thought in American foreign policy do not fall so easily within the three theoretical approaches above, however: Hamiltonians, Jacksonians, and neoconservatives.[1] Hamiltonians, who include to some degree George H. W. Bush, are internationalist and willing to use force for U.S. security and to protect U.S. businesses but less willing to do so to promote democracy abroad, and focused on the economic dimension of U.S. foreign policy. Jacksonians, like President Andrew Jackson, would prefer to focus on domestic matters and are skeptical of international institutions, but when provoked by threats to U.S. security, are highly motivated to use force decisively and victoriously; the Jacksonians' motto is "Don't tread on me."

Finally, neoconservatives are internationalist, deeply skeptical of international institutions and alliances and willing to act unilaterally, and are very focused on building democracies abroad and ready to use force for this purpose as well as for addressing direct threats to American security. This group agrees with the Wilsonians that it matters a great deal whether other states become democracies, and criticizes realists for ignoring this, but it disagrees with the Wilsonians' emphasis on international institutions and alliances and their hesitance to use force to help fledgling or endangered democracies. This neoconservative school of thought has received considerable attention recently because some characterize President George W. Bush's foreign policies as being neoconservative. Prominent current or former foreign policy officials in the Bush administration are widely identified as neoconservatives, including former Deputy Secretary of Defense and current World Bank president Paul Wolfowitz. Other top officials in the first and second terms of President George W. Bush, however, have been realists in their writings and public statements, including the first term Secretary of State Colin Powell and his second term successor, Condoleeza Rice. In any event, care must be taken in applying any such labels to individuals, as most of us have elements of all these approaches in our thinking. We provide these outlines of various schools of thought to provide a framework for thinking about and discussing foreign policy rather than a straightjacket to place on others or yourself.

Globalization, Domestic Politics, and Foreign Policy

In a vivid and dramatic stroke, the terrorist attacks of 9/11 shattered the illusion of American invulnerability to world events. Neither America's great economic or military resources nor the geographic benefits of being surrounded by large oceans and friendly countries could protect its citizens from the threats posed by nefarious individuals seeking to do them harm. In response to this

---

[1] The description of Hamiltonians and Jacksonians here is borrowed from Walter Russell Mead, *Special Providence: American Foreign Policy and How it Changed the World* (Routledge, 2002).

new global threat, the United States altered policies by promoting preemption (Issues 1 and 12) and invading Iraq.

Ironically, what these attacks demonstrated in the security arena has long been acknowledged in other areas: that U.S. foreign must anticipate, respond, and adapt to the actors and phenomena operating in a global context. In economic terms, the United States is more reliant upon trade and international financing than ever before (Issue 16). In health terms, the globalization of human and animal movements has increased the spread of new diseases—like AIDS, bird flu, and mad cow disease—and the resurgence of older diseases—like tuberculosis, malaria, and polio—which, though once eradicated, are again sickening many people in U.S. inner cities. In environmental terms, the activities of foreign actors have increasingly devastating effects on our land, people, and economy—through, for example, the depletion of commercial fish stocks by fishing trawlers operating in international waters or the degradation of our buildings, crops, and trees by acid rain produced by powerplants' emissions in other countries (Issue 18). In political terms, the inability of the United States to garner large-scale logistic, financial and military support for its invasion of Iraq suggests that gaining support for its foreign policy initiatives—even from its allies—requires consideration of their concerns.

As Peter Gourevitch argued in a seminal work in 1978 ("Second Image Reversed: International Sources of Domestic Policy," *International Organization,* Fall 1998), global actors and phenomena also influence the evolution of domestic institutions. For example, the creation of the Department of Homeland Security and the dramatic reorganization and centralization of U.S. intelligence services are both a direct response to the terrorist attacks of 9/11/2001 (Issue 13). Less obvious, but perhaps even more profound, the attacks led Congress to adopt the Patriot Act and modify other policies that have broad implications for civil and political liberties and social policy in the United States (Issues 14, 20). As was true following attacks on U.S. soil like the Japanese attack on Pearl Harbor in 1942 and the British invasion of Washington in 1812, Congress has also modified policies in other areas—like immigration and the treatment of prisoners—which have widespread domestic as well as international implications (Issues 15 and 20).

The reverse is also true—domestic politics often drive U.S. foreign policy with important consequences in the global arena. Matthew Evangelista ("Institution and Change," in Michael Doyle and G. John Ikenberry, eds., *New Thinking in International Relations Theory,* Westview Press, 1997) provides a useful review of this perspective on foreign policy. For example, domestic political pressure is driving part of the debate over the U.S. response to the Kyoto treaty (Issue 18) and the treatment of suspected terrorists under interrogation (Issue 20). It also drives much of U.S. policy toward the democratic Republic of China in Taiwan in ways that may run counter to U.S. strategic objectives regarding the People's Republic of China (Issue 10).

Furthermore, global actors and phenomena increasingly exert direct effects on domestic actors who, in turn, demand a compensatory response from their local and national governments. For example, the fear of job loss due to an increase in offshore outsourcing has led several labor groups to

Figure 1

Global Actors and Phenomena ⟷ U.S. Foreign Policy and Institutions ⟷ Domestic Actors and Politics

---

lobby the U.S. government to curb outsourcing. In anticipation of a policy backlash, the Indian government and Indian companies are engaging in a variety of strategies to highlight the benefits of outsourcing and calm the fears of those who may be hurt by it (Issue 17).

Thus, as represented in Figure 1, U.S. foreign policy decisions and the institutions in which those decisions are buffeted by competing pressures from global actors and phenomena are one hand, and domestic actors and domestic politics are on the other. Furthermore, domestic and global actors may influence each other directly and try to shape U.S. foreign policy and policy-making institutions accordingly.

Substantive Issues in U.S. Foreign Policy

Unit 1 (Issues 1–3) focuses on key aspects of the multifaceted question of what the overall role of the United States should be in the world. Michael Mandelbaum makes the case that active U.S. leadership in the world helps solve many collective action problems and bolsters peace, stability, and free trade, benefiting both America and its allies. Jack Snyder, in contrast, worries that American unilateralism is creating nationalist reactions against the United States around the world and leading to excessive American commitments around the world.

A related question is whether the United States should act preemptively to challenge threats to its vital interests and those of its allies. While the strategy of preemption is not new, its significance has grown sharply with the realization that terrorists, who are hard to deter, could attack the United States with weapons of mass destruction that may be difficult to detect before they are used. Ivo Daalder and Jim Lindsay differ with Bush administration officials on the question of whether such threats justify a strategy of preemption.

A third issue, promoting democratization abroad, has become a prominent long-term strategy for achieving Americas values and protecting its security. Yet democracy is not easy to achieve, especially from the outside. Joseph Siegle offers an optimistic assessment of democratization, whereas Tamara Wittes warns that democratization is not likely to be effective without enhanced and sustained American involvement.

Unit 2 (Issues 4–6) focuses on the issue of American security and the conflict in Iraq. Issue 4 addresses the question of whether the U.S. intervention in Iraq was justified, presenting differing views from James Lacey and John Judis and Spencer Ackerman. Issue 5 presents contrasting views on whether the United States should keep large military forces in Iraq, with Senator John McCain arguing in the affirmative and former head of the National Security Agency William Odom urging a near-term withdrawal of U.S. forces. Issue 7 concerns whether the United States should foster a partition of Iraq.

Timothy Noah maintains that a managed partition of Iraq into its three main ethnic groups might be preferable to the ongoing civil war in Iraq, while Rend al-Rahim argues that such a partition would only intensify sectarian violence and invite interventions by Iraqs neighbors.

Unit 3 (Issues 7–12) presents debates about American policies toward contries in strategically significant regions. Of particular concern today are the difficulties of allying strategically with countries whose practices or policies otherwise run counter to U.S. ideals. Issues 7–12 focus on the trade-offs involved in U.S. relations with Pakistan, Iran, Sudan/Darfur, the Peoples Republic of China, North Korea, and Israel. Regarding Pakistan (Issue 7), Teresita Schaffer points to progress in Pakistan's policies on terrorism and its relations with India, while Sydney Freedberg details the challenges of eliminating safe havens for Taliban and al Qaeda terrorists in northern Pakistan.

With respect to Iran (Issue 8), Mario Loyola argues that the United States should keep open the option of a preemptive strike against Iran's nuclear facilities, while Edward Luttwak cautions that a preemptive strike on Iran at this time would invite Iranian retaliation against U.S. forces in Iraq and alienate the Iranian public.

On the issue of Darfur (Issue 9), Lawrence Kaplan suggests that American intervention is the only option likely to stop genocidal violence in the region, but David Rieff maintains that a unilateral American intervention would further damage U.S. relations with the Islamic world and could lead to an insurgency against any U.S. troops deployed to Darfur.

Regarding China (Issue 10), John Mearsheimer warns that China's growing economic power will translate into a more assertive Chinese military posture in Asia, while Dennis Blasko suggests that such assessments of the "China threat" are greatly exaggerated.

Issue 11 addresses the problem of North Korea's nuclear weapons program and its first test of a nuclear bomb. David Kang argues that engagement with North Korea can be effective in changing its behavior, while Victor Cha, currently serving on the National Security Council, insists that the United States must be willing to use sticks as well as carrots to isolate and contain North Korea if its behavior does not change.

Issue 12 focuses on a perennial issue that has intensified in recent years, namely, U.S. relations with Israel. Stephen Walt and John Mearsheimer, international relations scholars at Harvard University and the University of Chicago, respectively, assert that America's strong support of Israel has undermined American interests in the Middle East. Joseph Joffe, a leading German commentator on international affairs, maintains instead that even if Israel had never existed, the United States would still confront many of the same problems it currently does within and between Arab states in the Middle East.

Unit 4 (Issues 13–21) addresses foreign policy issues that are closely intertwined with American institutions and domestic politics. In Issue 13, Tom Ridge, the first director of the Department of Homeland Security (DHS), debates the effectiveness of the DHS with Michael Crowley, who is critical of the organization. Issue 14 highlights the tradeoff between civil liberties and security, with Charles Krauthammer arguing that domestic spying and tough interrogation techniques are important and necessary tools in the fight against terrorism, and former Congressman Bob Barr argues that President Bush's directive on domestic eavesdropping violates the Constitution.

In Issue 15, President George W. Bush suggests that the United States can enforce its laws on immigration more rigorously while still upholding America's traditional openness to legal immigrants. Mark Krikorian, in contrast, argues that immigration reforms like those the president has proposed, including guest worker programs and elements of amnesty for illegal immigrants, are unrealistic and counterproductive.

Issues 16 and 17 turn to the issue of economic globalization. In Issue 16, Murray Weidenbaum asserts that globalization is on the whole good for most Americans, and that opposition to globalization is often based on misunderstandings of how the global economy works. Robert Kuttner, in contrast, argues that the costs of globalization are very real and that if the U.S. government does not address them, a backlash against international trade might result. On a related topic in Issue 17, Edward Luce and Khozem Merchant assert that outsourcing, or the production of goods or services overseas by American companies, is a natural and beneficial consequence of globalization. Ronil Hira disagrees, warning that outsourcing is causing the United States to lose high-wage and high-value-added jobs and could threaten America's lead in high technology.

In Issue 18, former President William Clinton contends that global warming is a very real problem and that economically and technologically feasible means exist to address this problem through sensible governmental and international policies. Jason Lee Steorts replies that data on global warming are not consistent and that the current flurry of attention on this issue is not justified.

Issue 19 addresses an issue Americans have been increasingly identifying as an important concern in recent public opinion polls: energy independence. Senator and candidate for the Democratic presidential nomination Barack Obama asserts that the United States can significantly reduce its dependence on foreign oil supplies by promoting energy conservation and increasing production of ethanol and other alternative renewable energy sources. In contrast, energy industry expert Philip Deutch contends that America's dependence on oil imports is so high that it is not likely to be substantially reduced in the next few decades even if energy conservation increases.

Issues 20 and 21 return to normative issues in American foreign policy. In Issue 20, newspaper columnist Charles Krauthammer insists that terrorists are not entitled to the protections afforded to enemy combatants under the laws of war, and that information obtained from terrorists through means of physical duress can save lives and is therefore justified. Andrew Sullivan argues that torture is not necessary or even useful in gaining information from captive terrorists, and that the use of torture is antithetical to American values and undermines respect for America in the world.

Finally, in Issue 21, Kenneth Roth argues that humanitarian intervention is justified in some circumstances, particularly when other approaches have proved fruitless. Alan Kuperman maintains instead that humanitarian intervention is often ineffective or even counterproductive, aggravating rather than resolving local conflicts.

All of the debates outlined above are critical because, regardless of which side of the argument you find more convincing, the norms and expectations of international behavior are changing as a result of U.S. policies. Although the United States cannot by itself define what the new norms will be, its actions as arguably the most powerful state in the contemporary world will clearly shape their evolution, with important implications for the prospects for achieving American values in the foreseeable future.

Internet References . . .

U.S. Department of State Web Site

The U.S. Department of State Web site reflects the department's view that the United States should be internationalist, should seek to play a very strong role in a wide range of international issues, and should usually take a multilateral approach and seek to work with other countries.

http://www2.etown.edu/vl

The WWW Virtual Library: International Affairs Resources

To understand U.S. foreign policy, it is important to also be able to explore the world beyond the territorial boundaries of the United States. The WWW Virtual Library is a fine resource to help that exploration. The site has over 1,750 annotated links on a range of international affairs topics.

http://www.etown.edu/vl

Foreign Policy in Focus

This site is a joint project of the Interhemispheric Resource Center and the Institute for Policy Studies and generally takes a liberal point of view. It is subdivided by topic.

http://www.fpif.org

Foreign Policy Home Page of the Heritage Foundation

To contrast the foreign policy slant of the Foreign Policy in Focus Web site, you can turn to the conservative views of the Heritage Foundation.

http://www.foreignpolicy.org

The Council on Foreign Relations

This site provides an independent and nonpartisan source of research and analysis on the world and the foreign policy choices facing the United States and other governments.

http://www.cfr.org

House Committee on International Relations and Senate Foreign Relations Committee

The House Committee on International Relations and the Senate Foreign Relations Committee are the primary bodies in which Congress debates and provides its input into U.S. foreign policy.

http://www.house.gov/international_relations

http://foreign.senate.gov/

The United States and the World: Strategic Choices

*T*he issues in this section all relate to the multidimensional question of what the role of the United States should be in the world. At its most fundamental, the issue is a debate between internationalists and isolationists over whether or not the United States should be strongly involved in world affairs. Given that the United States is involved, another question that must be addressed involves whether the United States should attempt to play a leading, or perhaps the leading, role on the world stage or whether it should be content to be just one among many actors. Whatever role the nation chooses to play, yet another matter that must be resolved is whether the United States should generally act unilaterally to promote its goals and ideals or whether it should modify its actions to work with others in the international community.

- Is American Hegemony Good for the United States and the World?

- Should the United States Have an Official Strategy of Preemption Against Potential Weapons of Mass Destruction Threats?

- Should Promoting Democracy Abroad Be a Top U.S. Priority?

ISSUE 1

Is American Hegemony Good for the United States and the World?

YES: Michael Mandelbaum, from "David's Friend Goliath," *Foreign Policy* (January/February 2006)

NO: Jack Snyder, from "Imperial Temptations," *The National Interest* (Spring 2003)

ISSUE SUMMARY

YES: Michael Mandelbaum, a professor of international relations at Johns Hopkins University, argues that most countries in the world benefit greatly from America's efforts to provide regional stability, limit proliferation of weapons of mass destruction, and maintain a free trading system. As a result, other countries are not responding to America's power by traditional power balancing.

NO: Jack Snyder, professor of international relations at Columbia University, argues that U.S. leaders have bought into the myths that entrapped imperial powers in the past, and that American unilateralism is creating nationalist backlashes against the United States, leading to a risk of imperial overstretch in which U.S. commitments would overburden American capabilities.

The Bush administration's policies after 9/11, and most notably the U.S. intervention in Iraq, have stimulated discussions in the United States and abroad on whether the United States has become an "empire," or perhaps more accurately a "hegemon," and if so, whether this is desirable. Few argue that the United States has become an empire in the traditional sense of a central power occupying many other lands and providing order and security but exacting tribute and suppressing political opposition. While some argue that the United States has become a new kind of "informal empire," it is probably more instructive to ask whether the United States is a hegemon, or an actor powerful enough to change the formal rules and informal practices of the international system all by itself.

There is no doubt that the United States, with the world's largest economy by a large margin and the only military force capable of projecting conventional forces or using nuclear weapons anywhere in the world, is the most powerful state in the international system. More controversial is whether the United States can, has, or should attempt to change the international "rules of the game" by itself. Those who emphasize the Bush administration's unilateralism point to the administration's rejection of the Kyoto Protocols on greenhouse gases, its lack of support for an International Criminal Court, and the U.S. intervention in Iraq in 2003 with far fewer allies and less United Nations support than the 1991 Persian Gulf War. Others note that the Bush administration has followed multilateral approaches on other important issues, including the occupation of Afghanistan, which is now a NATO operation, and participation in talks about North Korea carried out by a group of six countries, and that it sought U.N. approval and allied contributions on the intervention in Iraq.

There are sharply different views on whether it is beneficial to have a system in which one state is far more powerful than others, and how such a powerful state should conduct itself. Michael Mandelbaum expresses the most benign interpretation of American power, known as "hegemonic stability theory." In this view, international peace and free trade are "public goods," or goods that countries can benefit from whether or not they contribute to bringing them about. Because states can enjoy these goods whether or not they help provide them, there is a temptation to "free ride" and not assist in achieving these goods. This leads such public goods to be underprovided or scarce. A hegemon that is both willing and able to provide international public goods even when others ride free can solve this collective action problem.

A second view is that powerful democratic states like the United States find it in their interest to "self-bind," or tie themselves to international rules or institutions that actually reduce their freedom of action. The logic here is that in the absence of such self-imposed restraints, less powerful countries will challenge a powerful state because they fear that state will use its power in the future to exploit weaker states.

A third "preponderance of power" school maintains that the United States is so powerful that even a coalition of other great power states cannot effectively balance against the United States, and so they do not even try to do so. Scholars who make this argument, as Mandelbaum does, often add that because the United States is a democracy with no ambitions to permanently occupy other countries, other states have little incentive and limited capabilities to balance against the United States in the traditional military sense.

Arguing against these benign visions of America's exercise of power are those like Jack Snyder who argue that other states cannot and do not take such a complacent view of America's leading role in the world. Like many great powers in the past, Snyder argues, American leaders have convinced themselves of the "myths of empire" that have traditionally led to imperial overstretch, or a growing gap between commitments and capabilities. These include exaggerated fears of distant conflicts, excessive optimism about the effectiveness of preventive uses of force, and unrealistic expectations that adversaries will bandwagon with or bow down before America's power rather than balance against it. While most other countries are not building up their arms to balance against the United States as they did against great powers in the past, they are finding ways to constrain America's ability to act unilaterally.

3

YES ↩   Michael Mandelbaum

David's Friend Goliath

Everybody talks about the weather, Mark Twain once observed, but nobody does anything about it. The same is true of America's role in the world. The United States is the subject of endless commentary, most of it negative, some of it poisonously hostile. Statements by foreign leaders, street demonstrations in national capitals, and much-publicized opinion polls all seem to bespeak a worldwide conviction that the United States misuses its enormous power in ways that threaten the stability of the international system. That is hardly surprising. No one loves Goliath. What is surprising is the world's failure to respond to the United States as it did to the Goliaths of the past.

Sovereign states as powerful as the United States, and as dangerous as its critics declare it to be, were historically subject to a check on their power. Other countries banded together to block them.

Revolutionary and Napoleonic France in the late 18th and early 19th century, Germany during the two world wars, and the Soviet Union during the Cold War all inspired countervailing coalitions that ultimately defeated them. Yet no such anti-American alignment has formed or shows any sign of forming today. Widespread complaints about the United States' international role are met with an absence of concrete, effective measures to challenge, change, or restrict it.

The gap between what the world says about American power and what it fails to do about it is the single most striking feature of 21st-century international relations. The explanation for this gap is twofold. First, the charges most frequently leveled at America are false. The United States does not endanger other countries, nor does it invariably act without regard to the interests and wishes of others. Second, far from menacing the rest of the world, the United States plays a uniquely positive global role. The governments of most other countries understand that, although they have powerful reasons not to say so explicitly.

Benign Hegemon

The charge that the United States threatens others is frequently linked to the use of the term "empire" to describe America's international presence. In contrast with empires of the past, however, the United States does not control,

From *Foreign Policy*, January/February 2006, pp. 51–56. Copyright © 2006 by the Carnegie Endowment for International Peace. Reprinted with permission. www.foreignpolicy.com

or aspire to control, directly or indirectly, the politics and economics of other societies. True, in the post-Cold War period, America has intervened militarily in a few places outside its borders, including Somalia, Haiti, Bosnia, Kosovo, Afghanistan, and Iraq. But these cases are exceptions that prove the rule.

These foreign ventures are few in number and, with the exception of Iraq, none has any economic value or strategic importance. In each case, American control of the country came as the byproduct of a military intervention undertaken for quite different reasons: to rescue distressed people in Somalia, to stop ethnic cleansing in Bosnia, to depose a dangerous tyrant in Iraq. Unlike the great empires of the past, the U.S. goal was to build stable, effective governments and then to leave as quickly as possible. Moreover, unlike past imperial practice, the U.S. government has sought to share control of its occupied countries with allies, not to monopolize them.

One policy innovation of the current Bush administration that gives other countries pause is the doctrine of preventive war. According to this doctrine, the United States reserves the right to attack a country not in response to an actual act of aggression, or because it is unmistakably on the verge of aggression, but rather in anticipation of an assault at some point in the future. The United States implemented the doctrine in 2003 with the invasion of Iraq.

Were it to become central to American foreign policy, the preventive war doctrine would provide a broad charter for military intervention. But that is not its destiny. The Bush administration presented the campaign in Iraq not as a way to ensure that Saddam Hussein did not have the opportunity to acquire nuclear weapons at some point in the future, but rather as a way of depriving him of the far less dangerous chemical weapons that he was believed already to possess.

More important, the countries that are now plausible targets for a preventive war—North Korea and Iran—differ from Iraq in ways that make such a campaign extremely unattractive. North Korea is more heavily armed than Iraq, and in a war could do serious damage to America's chief ally in the region, South Korea, even if North Korea lost. Iran has a larger population than Iraq, and it is less isolated internationally. The United States would have hesitated before attacking either one of these countries even if the Iraq operation had gone smoothly. Now, with the occupation of Iraq proving to be both costly (some $251 billion and counting) and frustrating, support for repeating the exercise elsewhere is hard to find.

America the Accessible

The war in Iraq is the most-often cited piece of evidence that America conducts itself in a recklessly unilateral fashion. Because of its enormous power, critics say, the policies that the United States applies beyond its borders are bound to affect others, yet when it comes to deciding these policies, non-Americans have no influence. However valid the charge of unilateralism in the case of Iraq may be (and other governments did in fact support the war), it does not hold true for U.S. foreign policy as a whole.

The reason is that the American political system is fragmented, which means there are multiple points of access to it. Other countries can exert influence on one of the House or Senate committees with jurisdiction over foreign policy. Or countries can deal with one or more of the federal departments that conduct the nation's relations with other countries. For that matter, American think tanks generate such a wide variety of proposals for U.S. policies toward every country that almost any approach is bound to have a champion somewhere.

Even Sudan, which the U.S. government has accused of genocide, recently signed a $530,000 contract with a Washington lobbyist to help improve its image. Non-Americans may not enjoy formal representation in the U.S. political system, but because of the openness of that system, they can and do achieve what representation brings—a voice in the making of American policy.

Because the opportunities to be heard and heeded are so plentiful, countries with opposing aims often simultaneously attempt to persuade the American government to favor their respective causes. That has sometimes led the United States to become a mediator for international conflict, between Arabs and Israelis, Indians and Pakistanis, and other sets of antagonists. That's a role that other countries value.

The World's Government

The United States makes other positive contributions, albeit often unseen and even unknown, to the well-being of people around the world. In fact, America performs for the community of sovereign states many, though not all, of the tasks that national governments carry out within them. For instance, U.S. military power helps to keep order in the world. The American military presence in Europe and East Asia, which now includes approximately 185,000 personnel, reassures the governments of these regions that their neighbors cannot threaten them, helping to allay suspicions, forestall arms races, and make the chances of armed conflict remote. U.S. forces in Europe, for instance, reassure Western Europeans that they do not have to increase their own troop strength to protect themselves against the possibility of a resurgent Russia, while at the same time reassuring Russia that its great adversary of the last century, Germany, will not adopt aggressive policies. Similarly, the U.S.-Japan Security Treaty, which protects Japan, simultaneously reassures Japan's neighbors that it will remain peaceful. This reassurance is vital yet invisible, and it is all but taken for granted.

The United States has also assumed responsibility for coping with the foremost threat to contemporary international security, the spread of nuclear weapons to "rogue" states and terrorist organizations. The U.S.-sponsored Cooperative Threat Reduction program is designed to secure nuclear materials and weapons in the former Soviet Union. A significant part of the technical and human assets of the American intelligence community is devoted to the surveillance of nuclear weapons-related activities around the world. Although other countries may not always agree with how the United States seeks to prevent proliferation, they all endorse the goal, and none of them makes as significant a contribution to achieving that goal as does the United States.

America's services to the world also extend to economic matters and international trade. In the international economy, much of the confidence needed to proceed with transactions, and the protection that engenders this confidence, comes from the policies of the United States. For example, the U.S. Navy patrols shipping lanes in both the Atlantic and Pacific oceans, assuring the safe passage of commerce along the world's great trade routes. The United States also supplies the world's most frequently used currency, the U.S. dollar. Though the euro might one day supplant the dollar as the world's most popular reserve currency, that day, if it ever comes, lies far in the future.

Furthermore, working through the International Monetary Fund (imf), the United States also helps to carry out some of the duties that central banks perform within countries, including serving as a "lender of last resort." The driving force behind imf bailouts of failing economies in Latin America and Asia in the last decade was the United States, which holds the largest share of votes within the imf. And Americans' large appetite for consumer products partly reproduces on a global scale the service that the economist John Maynard Keynes assigned to national governments during times of economic slowdown: The United States is the world's "consumer of last resort."

Americans purchase Japanese cars, Chinese-made clothing, and South Korean electronics and appliances in greater volume than any other people. Just as national governments have the responsibility for delivering water and electricity within their jurisdictions, so the United States, through its military deployments and diplomacy, assures an adequate supply of the oil that allows industrial economies to run. It has established friendly political relations, and sometimes close military associations, with governments in most of the major oil-producing countries and has extended military protection to the largest of them, Saudi Arabia. Despite deep social, cultural, and political differences between the two countries, the United States and Saudi Arabia managed in the 20th century to establish a partnership that controlled the global market for this indispensable commodity. The economic well-being even of countries hostile to American foreign policy depends on the American role in assuring the free flow of oil throughout the world.

To be sure, the United States did not deliberately set out to become the world's government. The services it provides originated during the Cold War as part of its struggle with the Soviet Union, and America has continued, adapted, and in some cases expanded them in the post-Cold War era. Nor do Americans think of their country as the world's government. Rather, it conducts, in their view, a series of policies designed to further American interests. In this respect they are correct, but these policies serve the interests of others as well. The alternative to the role the United States plays in the world is not better global governance, but less of it—and that would make the world a far more dangerous and less prosperous place. Never in human history has one country done so much for so many others, and received so little appreciation for its efforts.

Inevitable Ingratitude

Nor is the world likely to express much gratitude to the United States any time soon. Even if they privately value what the United States does for the world, other countries, especially democratic ones, will continue to express anti-American sentiments. That is neither surprising nor undesirable. Within democracies, spirited criticism of the government is normal, indeed vital for its effective performance. The practice is no different between and among democracies.

Anti-Americanism has many domestic political uses. In many parts of the world, the United States serves as a convenient scapegoat for governments, a kind of political lightning rod to draw away from themselves the popular discontent that their shortcomings have helped to produce. That is particularly the case in the Middle East, but not only there. Former German Chancellor Gerhard Schröder achieved an electoral victory in 2002 by denouncing the war in Iraq. Similarly, it is convenient, even comforting, to blame the United States for the inevitable dislocations caused by the great, impersonal forces of globalization.

But neither the failure to acknowledge America's global role nor the barrage of criticism of it means that the officials of other countries are entirely unaware of the advantages that it brings them. If a global plebiscite concerning America's role in the world were held by secret ballot, most foreign-policy officials in other countries would vote in favor of continuing it. Though the Chinese object to the U.S. military role as Taiwan's protector, they value the effect that American military deployments in East Asia have in preventing Japan from pursuing more robust military policies. But others will not declare their support for America's global role. Acknowledging it would risk raising the question of why those who take advantage of the services America provides do not pay more for them. It would risk, that is, other countries' capacities to continue as free riders, which is an arrangement no government will lightly abandon.

In the end, however, what other nations do or do not say about the United States will not be crucial to whether, or for how long, the United States continues to function as the world's government. That will depend on the willingness of the American public, the ultimate arbiter of American foreign policy, to sustain the costs involved. In the near future, America's role in the world will have to compete for public funds with the rising costs of domestic entitlement programs. It is Social Security and Medicare, not the rise of China or the kind of coalition that defeated powerful empires in the past, that pose the greatest threat to America's role as the world's government.

The outcome of the looming contest in the United States between the national commitment to social welfare at home and the requirements for stability and prosperity abroad cannot be foreseen with any precision. About other countries' approach to America's remarkable 21st-century global role, however, three things may be safely predicted: They will not pay for it, they will continue to criticize it, and they will miss it when it is gone.

Jack Snyder

NO

Imperial Temptations

America today embodies a paradox of omnipotence and vulnerability. The U.S. military budget is greater than those of the next 14 countries combined and the American economy is larger than the next three combined. Yet Americans going about their daily lives face a greater risk of sudden death from terrorist attack than ever before. This situation has fostered a psychology of vulnerability that makes Americans hyperalert to foreign dangers and predisposed to use military power in what may be self-defeating attempts to escape their fears.

The Bush Administration's new national security doctrine, which provides a superficially attractive rationale for preventive war, reflects this uneasy state of mind.[1] In an open society, no strictly defensive strategy against terrorism can be foolproof. Similarly, deterring terrorist attack by the threat of retaliation seems impossible when the potential attackers welcome suicide. Bizarre or diabolical leaders of potentially nuclear-armed rogue states may likewise seem undeterrable. If so, attacking the sources of potential threats before they can mount their own attacks may seem the only safe option. Such a strategy presents a great temptation to a country as strong as the United States, which can project overwhelming military power to any spot on the globe.

In adopting this strategy, however, America risks marching in the well-trod footsteps of virtually every imperial power of the modern age. America has no formal colonial empire and seeks none, but like other great powers over the past two centuries, it has sometimes sought to impose peace on the tortured politics of weaker societies. Consequently, it faces many of the same strategic dilemmas as did the great powers that have gone before it. The Bush Administration's rhetoric of preventive war, however, does not reflect a sober appreciation of the American predicament, but instead echoes point by point the disastrous strategic ideas of those earlier keepers of imperial order.

Imperial Overstretch

Like America, the great empires of the 19th and 20th centuries enjoyed huge asymmetries of power relative to the societies at their periphery, yet they rightly feared disruptive attack from unruly peoples along the turbulent frontier of empire. Suspecting that their empires were houses of cards, imperial rulers feared that unchecked defiance on the periphery might cascade toward the

From *The National Interest*, Spring 2003. Copyright © 2003 by National Interest. Reprinted by permission.

imperial core. Repeatedly they tried the strategy of preventive attack to nip challenges in the bud and prevent their spread.

Typically, the preventive use of force proved counterproductive for imperial security because it often sparked endless brushfire wars at the edges of the empire, internal rebellions, and opposition from powers not yet conquered or otherwise subdued. Historically, the preventive pacification of one turbulent frontier of empire has usually led to the creation of another one, adjacent to the first. When the British conquered what is now Pakistan, for example, the turbulent frontier simply moved to neighboring Afghanistan. It was impossible to conquer everyone, so there was always another frontier.

Even inside well-established areas of imperial control, the use of repressive force against opponents often created a backlash among subjects who came to reassess the relative dangers and benefits of submission. The Amritsar massacre of 1919, for example, was the death knell for British India because it radicalized a formerly circumspect opposition. Moreover, the preventive use of force inside the empire and along its frontiers often intensified resistance from independent powers outside the empire who feared that unchecked, ruthless imperial force would soon encroach upon them. In other words, the balance of power kicked in. Through all of these mechanisms, empires have typically found that the preventive use of force expanded their security problems instead of ameliorating them.

As the dynamic of imperial overstretch became clearer, many of the great powers decided to solve their security dilemmas through even bolder preventive offensives. None of these efforts worked. To secure their European holdings, Napoleon and Hitler marched to Moscow, only to be engulfed in the Russian winter. Kaiser Wilhelm's Germany tried to break the allies' encirclement through unrestricted submarine warfare, which brought America's industrial might into the war against it. Imperial Japan, facing a quagmire in China and a U.S. oil embargo, tried to break what it saw as impending encirclement by seizing the Indonesian oil fields and preventively attacking Pearl Harbor. All sought security through expansion, and all ended in imperial collapse.

Some great powers, however, have pulled back from overstretch and husbanded their power for another day. Democratic great powers, notably Britain and the United States, are prominent among empires that learned how to retrench. At the turn of the 20th century, British leaders saw that the strategy of "splendid isolation"—what we would now call unilateralism—was getting the empire into trouble. The independence struggle of Boer farmers in South Africa drained the imperial coffers while, at the same time, the European great powers were challenging Britain's naval mastery and its hold on other colonial positions. Quickly doing the math, the British patched up relations with their secondary rivals, France and Russia, to form an alliance directed at the main danger, Germany. Likewise, when the United States blundered into war in Vietnam, it retrenched and adopted a more patient strategy for waiting out its less capable communist opponents.

Contemporary America, too, is capable of anticipating the counterproductive effects of offensive policies and of moderating them before much damage is done. The Bush team, guided by wary public opinion, worked through existing UN resolutions during the fall of 2002 to increase multilateral support for its threats of preventive war against Iraq. Moreover, the administration declined to apply mechanically its preventive war principles when North Korea renounced international controls on its nuclear materials in December 2002. Strikingly, too, a December codicil to the *NSS,* dealing specifically with the pro-liferation of weapons of mass destruction, never mentioned the option of pre-ventive attack.[2] A brief tour through the misguided strategic ideas of previous empires underscores the wisdom of such self-restraint.

Myths of Security Through Expansion

Every major historical instance of imperial overstretch has been propelled by arguments that security could best be achieved through further expansion— "myths of empire," I have called them.[3] Since many of these myths are echoed eerily in the Bush Administration's strategic rhetoric, it is worthwhile recalling how those earlier advocates of imperial overstretch tried to make their dubious cases. Eight themes deserve mention.

Offensive Advantage

The most general of the myths of empire is that the attacker has an inherent advantage. Sometimes this is explained in terms of the advantages of surprise. More often, it relies on the broader notion that seizing the initiative allows the attacker to impose a plan on a passive enemy and to choose a propitious time and circumstance for the fight. Even if the political objective is self-defense, in this view, attacking is still the best strategy. As the *NSS* says, "our best defense is a good offense."

Throughout history, strategists who have blundered into imperial over-stretch have shared this view. For example, General Alfred von Schlieffen, the author of Germany's misbegotten plan for a quick, decisive offensive in France in 1914, used to say that "if one is too weak to attack the whole" of the other side's army, "one should attack a section."[4] This idea defies elementary military common sense. In war, the weaker side normally remains on the defensive precisely because defending its home ground is typically easier than attacking the other side's strongholds.

The idea of offensive advantage also runs counter to the most typical patterns of deterrence and coercion. Sometimes the purpose of a military oper-ation is not to take or hold territory but to influence an adversary by inflicting pain. This is especially true when weapons of mass destruction are involved. In that case, war may resemble a competition in the willingness to endure pain. Here too, however, the defender normally has the advantage, because the side defending its own homeland and the survival of its regime typically cares more about the stakes of the conflict than does a would-be attacker. It is difficult to imagine North Korea using nuclear weapons or mounting a conventional artillery barrage on the South Korean capital of Seoul for purposes of con-quest, but it is much easier to envision such desperate measures in response to "preventive" U.S. attacks on the core power resources of the regime. Because the Bush Administration saw such retaliation as feasible and credible, it was deterred from undertaking preventive strikes when the North Koreans unsealed a nuclear reactor in December. Indeed, deterring any country from attacking is almost always easier than compelling it to disarm, surrender territory or change its regime. Once stated, this point seems obvious, but the logic of the Bush strategy document implies the opposite.

Power Shifts

One reason that blundering empires have been keen on offensive strategies is that they have relied on preventive attacks to forestall unfavorable shifts in the balance of power. In both World War I and II, for example, Germany's leaders sought war with Russia in the short run because they expected the Russian army to gain relative strength over time.[5] But the tactic backfired badly. Preventive aggression not only turned a possible enemy into a certain one, but in the long run it helped bring other powers into the fight to prevent Germany from gaining hegemony over all of them. This reflects a fundamental realist principle of the balance of power: In the international system, states and other powerful actors tend to form alliances against the expansionist state that most threatens them. Attackers provoke fears that drive their potential victims to cooperate with each other.

Astute strategists learn to anticipate such cooperation and try to use it to their advantage. For example, one of the most successful diplomats in European history, Otto von Bismarck, achieved the unification of Germany by always putting the other side in the wrong and, whenever possible, maneuvering the opponent into attacking first. As a result, Prussia expanded its control over the German lands without provoking excessive fears or resistance. Pressed by his generals on several occasions to authorize preventive attacks, Bismarck said that preventive war is like committing suicide from fear of death; it would "put the full weight of the imponderables . . . on the side of the enemies we have attacked."[6] Instead, he demanded patience: "I have often had to stand for long periods of time in the hunting blind and let myself be covered and stung by insects before the moment came to shoot."[7] Germany fared poorly under Bismarck's less-able successors, who shared his ruthlessness but lacked his understanding of the balance of power.

Because Saddam Hussein attacked Kuwait, the elder Bush enjoyed a diplomatic advantage in the 1991 war. That's why the coalition against Iraq was so large and willing. This advantage is vastly and inherently more difficult to achieve in a strategy of preventive attack, as the younger Bush has learned over the past year. Especially when an adverse power shift is merely hypothetical and not imminent, it hardly seems worthwhile to incur the substantial diplomatic disadvantages of a preventive attack.

Paper Tiger Enemies

Empires also become overstretched when they view their enemies as paper tigers, capable of becoming fiercely threatening if appeased, but easily crumpled by a resolute attack. These images are often not only wrong, but self-contradictory. For example, Japanese militarists saw the United States as so strong and insatiably aggressive that Japan would have to conquer a huge, self-sufficient empire to get the resources to defend itself; yet at the same time, the Japanese regime saw the United States as so vulnerable and irresolute that a sharp rap against Pearl Harbor would discourage it from fighting back.

Similarly, the Bush Administration's arguments for preventive war against Iraq have portrayed Saddam Hussein as being completely undeterrable from using weapons of mass destruction, yet Secretary of Defense Donald Rumsfeld said he expected that Iraq would not use them even if attacked because "wise Iraqis will not obey his orders to use WMD."[8] In other words, administration strategists think that deterrence is impossible even in situations in which Saddam lacks a motive to use weapons of mass destruction, but they think deterrence will succeed when a U.S. attack provides Iraq the strongest imaginable motive to use its weapons. The NSS says "the greater the threat, the greater is the risk of inaction"; but this is a rationale for preventive attack only if we accept a paper tiger image of the enemy.

Bandwagons

Another myth of empire is that states tend to jump on the bandwagon with threatening or forceful powers. During the Cold War, for example, the Soviet Union thought that forceful action in Berlin, Cuba and the developing world would demonstrate its political and military strength, encourage so-called progressive forces to ally actively with Moscow, and thereby shift the balance of forces still further in the favor of the communist bloc. The Soviets called this the "correlation of forces" theory. In fact, the balance of power effect far outweighed and erased the bandwagon effect. The Soviet Union was left far weaker in relative terms as a result of its pressing for unilateral advantage. As Churchill said of the Soviets in the wake of the first Berlin Crisis, "Why have they deliberately acted for three long years so as to unite the free world against them?"[9]

During the 1991 Gulf War, the earlier Bush Administration argued that rolling back Saddam Hussein's conquest of Kuwait was essential to discourage Arabs throughout the Middle East from jumping on the Iraqi bandwagon. Now the current Bush Administration hopes that bandwagon dynamics can be made to work in its own favor. Despite the difficulties that the United States has had in lining up support for an invasion of Iraq, the administration nonetheless asserts that its strategy of preventive war will lead others to jump on the U.S. bandwagon. Secretary Rumsfeld has said that "if our leaders do the right thing, others will follow and support our just cause—just as they have in the global war against terror."[10]

At the same time, some self-styled realists in the administration also argue that their policy is consistent with the concept of the balance of power, but the rhetoric of the NSS pulls this concept inside out: "Through our willingness to use force in our own defense and in the defense of others, the United States demonstrates its resolve to maintain a balance of power that favors freedom." What this Orwellian statement really seems to mean is that preventive war will attract a bandwagon of support that creates an *im*balance of power in America's favor, a conception that is logically the same as the wrongheaded Soviet theory of the "correlation of forces." Administration strategists like to use the terminology of the balance of power, but they understand that concept exactly backwards.

Big Stick Diplomacy

A closely related myth is the big stick theory of making friends by threatening them. Before World War I, Germany's leaders found that its rising power and belligerent diplomacy had pushed France, Russia and Britain into a loose alliance against it. In the backwards reasoning of German diplomacy, they decided to try to break apart this encirclement by trumping up a crisis over claims to Morocco, threatening France with an attack and hoping to prove to French leaders that its allies would not come to its rescue. In fact, Britain did support France, and the noose around Germany grew tighter.

How does the United States today seek to win friends abroad? The *NSS* offers some reassuring language about the need to work with allies. Unlike President Bill Clinton in the Kosovo war, President Bush worked very hard for a UN resolution to authorize an attack on Iraq. Nonetheless, on the Iraq issue and a series of others, the administration has extorted cooperation primarily by threats to act unilaterally, not gained it by persuasion or concessions. Russia was forced to accept a new strategic arms control regime on take-it-or-leave-it American terms. EU member states were similarly compelled to accept an exemption for U.S. officials from prosecution by the International Criminal Court. Germany was snubbed for resisting the war against Iraq. Multilateral initiatives on the environment were summarily rejected. Secretary Rumsfeld, in his personal jottings on strategy, has raised to the level of principle the dictum that the United States should "avoid trying so hard to persuade others to join a coalition that we compromise on our goals."[11] Either the administration believes allies are dispensable, or a powerful faction within it adheres to the Kaiser Wilhelm theory of diplomacy.

Falling Dominoes

Another common myth of empire is the famous domino theory. According to this conception, small setbacks at the periphery of the empire will tend to snowball into an unstoppable chain of defeats that will ultimately threaten the imperial core. Consequently, empires must fight hard to prevent even the most trivial setbacks. Various causal mechanisms are imagined that might trigger such cascades: The opponent will seize ever more strategic resources from these victories, tipping the balance of forces and making further conquests easier. Vulnerable defenders will lose heart. Allies and enemies alike will come to doubt the empire's resolve to fight for its commitments. An empire's domestic political support will be undermined. Above all, lost credibility is the ultimate domino.

Such reasoning has been nearly universal among overstretched empires.[12] For example, in 1898 the British and the French both believed that if a French scouting party could claim a tributary of the Upper Nile—at a place called Fashoda—France could build a dam there, block the flow of the Nile, trigger chaos in Egypt that would force Britain out of the Suez Canal, cut Britain's strategic lifeline to India, and thus topple the empire that depended on India's wealth and manpower. Britain and France, both democracies, nearly went to war because of this chimera. Similarly, Cold War America believed that if Vietnam fell to communism, then the credibility of its commitment to defend Taiwan, Japan and Berlin would be debased. Arguably, the peripheral setback in Vietnam tarnished American deterrent credibility only because we so often and so insistenly said it would.

Similar arguments, especially ones that hinge on lost credibility, have informed Secretary Rumsfeld's brief for preventive war against Iraq. In a nice rhetorical move, he quoted former President Clinton to the effect that if "we fail to act" against Saddam's non-compliance with inspections,

> he will conclude that the international community has lost its will. He will conclude that he can go right on and do more to rebuild an arsenal of devastating destruction. . . . Some day, some way, I guarantee you he will use that arsenal.[13]

Rumsfeld could have added (but didn't) that the Clinton Administration made the same argument even more strongly about the dire precedent that would be set by permitting the further expansion of North Korea's nuclear weapons capability. Ironically, the credibility of the United States is on the line in such cases mainly because of its own rhetoric.

And yet it may be that the threat of an American attack is all *too* credible. The main motivation for North Korea to break out of the 1994 agreement constraining its nuclear program was apparently its perceived need, in light of the Bush Administration's preventive war doctrine and reluctance to negotiate, for more powerful weapons to deter the United States.

A ubiquitous corollary of the domino theory holds that it is cheap and easy to stop aggressors if it is done early on. Secretary Rumsfeld has made this kind of argument to justify a preventive attack on Iraq. Between 35 and 60 million people died needlessly, he claimed, because the world didn't attack Hitler preventively: "He might have been stopped early—at minimal cost in lives—had the vast majority of the world's leaders not decided at the time that the risks of acting were greater than the risks of not acting." Apart from its questionable relevance to the case of Iraq, the historical point is itself debatable: Britain and France were militarily ill-prepared to launch a preventive attack at the time of the Munich crisis, and if they had, they probably would have had to fight Germany without the Soviet Union and the United States as allies. As Bismarck had understood, preventive war is bad strategy in part because it often leads to diplomatic isolation.

El Dorado and Manifest Destiny

Most of the central myths of empire focus on a comparison of the alleged costs of offensive versus defensive strategies. In addition, myths that exaggerate the benefits of imperial expansion sometimes play an important role in strategic debates. For example, German imperialism before World War I was fueled in part by the false idea that Central Africa would be an El Dorado of resources that would strengthen Germany's strategic position in the same way that India had supposedly strengthened Britain's. In debates about preventive war in Iraq, some commentators have portrayed an anticipated oil windfall as a comparable El Dorado. Astutely, the Bush Administration has refrained from rhetoric about this potential boon, realizing that it would be counter-productive and unnecessary to dwell on it. Such a windfall could turn out to be a curse in any event, since pumping massive amounts of oil to pay for an occupation of Iraq could undercut Saudi oil revenues and destabilize the political system there.

Sometimes the promised benefits of imperial expansion are also ideological—for example, France's civilizing mission or America's mission to make the world safe for democracy. In a surprising moment of candor, John Foster Dulles, a decade before he became Dwight Eisenhower's Secretary of State, wrote that all empires had been "imbued with and radiated great faiths [like] Manifest Destiny [and] The White Man's Burden." We Americans "need a faith", said Dulles, "that will make us strong, a faith so pronounced that we, too, will feel that we have a mission to spread throughout the world."[14] An idealistic goal is patently invoked here for its instrumental value in mobilizing support for the imperial enterprise.

The idealistic notes that grace the Bush Administration's strategy paper have the same hollow ring. The document is chock full of high-sounding prose about the goal of spreading democracy to Iraq and other countries living under the yoke of repression. President Bush's preface to the strategy document asserts that "the United States enjoys a position of unparalleled military strength", which creates "a moment of opportunity to extend the benefits of freedom across the globe. We will actively work to bring the hope of democracy, development, free markets, and free trade to every corner of the world." This sounds like insincere public relations in light of candidate Bush's warnings against the temptations of nation-building abroad. The theme of promoting democracy is rare in Secretary Rumsfeld's statements, which may turn out to be a better index of the administration's underlying views.

No Tradeoffs

A final myth of empire is that in strategy there are no tradeoffs. Proponents of imperial expansion tend to pile on every argument from the whole list of myths of empire. It is not enough to argue that the opponent is a paper tiger, or that dominoes tend to fall, or that big stick diplomacy will make friends, or that a preventive attack will help to civilize the natives. Rather, proponents of offensive self-defense inhabit a rhetorical world in which *all* of these things are simultaneously true, and thus all considerations point in the same direction.

The Bush Administration's strategic rhetoric about Iraq in late 2002 did not disappoint in this regard. Saddam was portrayed as undeterrable, as getting nuclear weapons unless deposed and giving them to terrorists, the war against him would be cheap and easy, grumbling allies would jump on our bandwagon, Iraq would become a democracy, and the Arab street would thank the United States for liberating it. In real life, as opposed to the world of imperial rhetoric, it is surprising when every conceivable consideration supports the preferred strategy. As is so often the case with the myths of empire, this piling on of reinforcing claims smacks of *ex post facto* justification rather than serious strategic assessment.

During the 2000 presidential campaign, Condoleezza Rice wrote of Iraq that "the first line of defense should be a clear and classical statement of deterrence—if they do acquire WMD, their weapons will be unusable because any attempt to use them will bring national obliteration."[15] Two years later, however, the possibility of deterrence has become unthinkable as administration rhetoric regarding Iraq has been piled higher and higher. "Given the goals of rogue states [and] the inability to deter a potential attacker" of this kind, says the *NSS*, "we cannot let our enemies strike first." Administration dogma left no room for any assessment of Iraq that did not reinforce the logic of the prevailing preventive strategy.

Why Are Myths of Empire So Prevalent?

In America today, strategic experts abound. Many are self-styled realists, people who pride themselves on accepting the hard reality that the use of force is often necessary in the defense of national interests. It is striking that many of these realists consider the Bush Administration's strategic justifications for preventive war against Iraq to be unconvincing. Indeed, 32 prominent international relations scholars, most of them realists, bought an ad in the *New York Times* to make their case against the Bush strategy. Included among them was the leading proponent of the "offensive realism" school of thought, John Mearsheimer, a professor at the University of Chicago.[16]

Proponents of the new preventive strategy charge that such realists are out of touch with a world in which forming alliances to balance against overwhelming U.S. power has simply become impossible. It is true that small rogue states and their ilk cannot on their own offset American power in the traditional sense. It is also true that their potential greatpower backers, Russia and China, have so far been wary of overtly opposing U.S. military interventions. But even if America's unprecedented power reduces the likelihood of traditional balancing alliances arising against it, the United States could find that its own offensive actions create their functional equivalents. Some earlier expansionist empires found themselves overstretched and surrounded by enemies even though balancing alliances were slow to oppose them. For example, although the prospective victims of Napoleon and Hitler found it difficult to form effective balancing coalitions, these empires attacked so many opponents simultaneously that substantial *de facto* alliances eventually did form against them. Today, an analogous form of self-imposed overstretch—political as well as military—could occur if the need for military operations to prevent nuclear proliferation risks were deemed urgent on several fronts at the same time, or if an attempt to impose democracy by force of arms on a score or more of Muslim countries were seriously undertaken.

Even in the absence of highly coordinated balancing alliances, simultaneous resistance by several troublemaking states and terrorist groups would be a daunting challenge for a strategy of universal preventive action. Highly motivated small powers or rebel movements defending their home ground have often prevailed against vastly superior states that lacked the sustained motivation to dominate them at extremely high cost, as in Vietnam and Algeria. Even when they do not prevail, as on the West Bank, they may fight on, imposing high costs over long periods.

Precisely because America is so strong, weak states on America's hit list may increasingly conclude that weapons of mass destruction joined to terror tactics are the only feasible equalizer to its power. Despite America's aggregate power advantages, weaker opponents can get access to outside resources to sustain this kind of cost-imposing resistance. Even a state as weak and isolated as North Korea has been able to mount a credible deterrent, in part by engaging in mutually valuable strategic trade with Pakistan and other Middle Eastern states. The Bush Administration itself stresses that Iraq bought components for the production of weapons of mass destruction on the commercial market and fears that no embargo can stop this. Iran is buying a nuclear reactor from Russia that the United States views as posing risks of nuclear proliferation. Palestinian suicide bombers successfully impose severe costs with minimal resources. In the September 11 attack, Al-Qaeda famously used its enemy's own resources.

In short, both historically and today, it seems hard to explain the prevalence of the myths of empire in terms of objective strategic analysis. So what, then, explains it?

In some historical cases, narrow interest groups that profited from imperial expansion or military preparations hijacked strategic debates by controlling the media or bankrolling imperial pressure groups. In imperial Japan, for example, when a civilian strategic planning board pointed out the implausibilities and contradictions in the militarists' worldview, its experts were thanked for their trenchant analysis and then summarily fired. In pre-World War I Germany, internal documents showing the gaping holes in the offensive strategic plans of the army and navy were kept secret, and civilians lacked the information or expertise to criticize the military's public reasoning. The directors of Krupp Steelworks subsidized the belligerent German Navy League before 1914, and then in the 1920s monopolized the wire services that brought nationalist-slanted news to Germany's smaller cities and towns. These were precisely the constituencies that later voted most heavily for Hitler.

In other cases, myths of empire were propounded by hard-pressed leaders seeking to rally support by pointing a finger at real or imagined enemies. For example, in the aftermath of the French Revolution, a series of unstable regimes found that they could increase their short-run popularity by exaggerating the threat from monarchical neighboring states and from aristocratic traitors to the Revolution. Napoleon perfected this strategy of rule, transforming the republic of the Rights of Man into an ever-expanding empire of popular nationalism.

Once the myths of empire gain widespread currency in a society, their origins in political expediency are often forgotten. Members of the second generation become true believers in the domino theory, big stick diplomacy and the civilizing mission. Kaiser Wilhelm's ministers were self-aware manipulators, but their audiences, including the generation that formed the Nazi movement, believed in German nationalist ideology with utmost conviction. In a process that Stephen Van Evera has called "blowback", the myths of empire may become ingrained in the psyche of the people and the institutions of their state.

Many skeptics about attacking Iraq suspect that similar domestic political dynamics are at the root of the Bush doctrine of preventive war. In particular, they think that the Iraq project echoes the plot of recent fictions in which a foreign war is trumped up to win an election. Some suggested that the day after the November 2002 election, the drumbeat of war would miraculously slacken and then disappear. Such rank cynicism deserved to be disappointed, and it was. Some members of Bush's inner circle have been spoiling for a rematch with Iraq for years, so clearly the convergence of its timing with the mid-term congressional election was a coincidence. Nonetheless, it probably did not hurt the hawks' cause in White House deliberations that the Iraq issue succeeded in pushing the parlous state of the economy off the front pages at a convenient moment.

A deeper reason for the prevalence of the myths of empire in contemporary debates is the legacy of Cold War rhetoric in the tropes of American strategic discourse. The Rumsfeld generation grew to political maturity inculcated with the Munich analogy and the domino theory. It is true that an opposite metaphor, the quagmire, is readily available for skeptics to invoke as a result of the Vietnam experience. But after the September 11 attack and the easy victory over the Taliban, the American political audience is primed for Munich analogies and preventive war, not for quagmire theories. Indeed, it is striking how many Senate speeches on the resolution authorizing the use of force in Iraq began with references to the effect of September 11 on the American psyche. They did not necessarily argue that the Iraqi government is a terrorist organization like Al-Qaeda. They simply noted the emotional reality that the attacks on the World Trade Center and the Pentagon had left Americans fearful and ready to fight back forcefully against threats of many sorts. In this sense, America is psychologically primed to accept the myths of empire. They "feel right"; but this is no way to run a grand strategy.

A final reason why America is primed to accept the myths of empire is simply the temptation of great power. As the German realist historian Ludwig Dehio wrote about Germany's bid for a hegemonic position in Europe, "since the supreme power stands in the solitude of its supremacy, it must face daemonic temptations of a special kind."[17] More recently, Christopher Layne has chronicled the tendency of unipolar hegemonic states since the Spain of Philip II to succumb to the temptations of overstretch and thereby to provoke the enmity of an opposing coalition.[18] Today, the United States is so strong compared to everyone else that almost any imaginable military objective may seem achievable. This circumstance, supercharged by the rhetoric of the myths of empire, makes the temptation of preventive war almost irresistible.

The historical record warrants a skeptical attitude toward arguments that security can be achieved through imperial expansion and preventive war. Moving beyond mere skepticism, we may consider a general prescription, one that might resonate with both liberals and realists alike.

Liberals might want to review a recent book by G. John Ikenberry, *After Victory*, which tells the story of attempts by the victors in global power contests to establish a stable post-conflict international order.[19] Ikenberry shows that democracies are particularly well suited to succeed in this because the transparency of their political institutions makes them trustworthy bargaining partners in the eyes of weaker states. As a result, strong and weak states are able to commit themselves to an international constitution that serves the interests of both. Realists should study this book, too, because it explains why even the strongest of powers has an incentive to lead through consensus rather than raw coercion.

President Bush's National Security Advisor, former Stanford political science professor and provost Condoleezza Rice, has recently advanced a much different view of the interplay of power-political realism and democratic

---

OF EMPIRE, POWER BALANCES AND PREVENTIVE WAR

To speak now of the true temper of empire, it is a thing rare and hard to keep; for both temper, and distemper, consist of contraries. . . . The difficulties in princes' business are many and great; but the greatest difficulty, is often in their own mind. For it is common with princes (saith Tacitus) to will contradictories, *Sunt plerumque regum voluntates vehementes, et inter se contrariae.* For it is the solecism of power, to think to command the end, and yet not to endure the mean. . . .

For their neighbors; there can no general rule be given (for occasions are so variable), save one, which ever holdeth, which is, that princes do keep due sentinel, that none of their neighbors do ever grow so (by increase of territory, by embracing of trade, by approaches, or the like), as they become more able to annoy them, than they were. And this is generally the work of standing counsels, to foresee and to hinder it. During that triumvirate of kings, King Henry the Eighth of England, Francis the First King of France, and Charles the Fifth Emperor, there was such a watch kept, that none of the three could win a palm of ground, but the other two would straightways balance it, either by confederation, or, if need were, by a war; and would not in any wise take up peace at interest. . . .

Neither is the opinion of some of the Schoolmen, to be received, *that a war cannot justly be made, but upon a precedent injury or provocation.* For there is no question, but a just fear of an imminent danger, though there be no blow given, is a lawful cause of a war. . . .

—Francis Bacon

idealism. (Once you have been a professor of international relations, it is evidently hard to get these debates out of your blood.) She argues that realism and idealism should not be seen as alternatives: a realistic sense of power politics should be used in the service of ideals. Who could possibly disagree? But contrary to what she and Bush once argued on the campaign trail about humility and a judicious sense of limits, Rice now believes that America's vast military power should be used preventively to spread democratic ideals. She has also said, speaking in New York this past October, that the aim of the Bush strategy is "to dissuade any potential adversary from pursuing a military build-up in the hope of surpassing, or equaling, the power of the United States and our allies." Today, no combination of adversaries can hope to equal America's power under any circumstances. However, if they fear the unbridled use of America's power, they may perceive overwhelming incentives to wield weapons of terror and mass destruction to deter America's offensive tactics of self-defense. Indeed, the history of the myths of empire suggests that a general strategy of preventive war is likely to bring about precisely the outcome that Bush and Rice wish to avert.

Notes

1.	Office of the President, *National Security Strategy of the United States* [hereafter *NSS*], September 2002.

2.	Office of the President, *National Strategy to Combat Weapons of Mass Destruction,* December 2002.

3.	See my *Myths of Empire: Domestic Politics and International Ambition* (Ithaca, NY: Cornell University Press, 1991). I used the term "empire" in the general sense of a powerful state that uses force to expand its influence abroad beyond the point at which the costs of expansion begin to rise sharply.

4.	Quoted in my *Ideology of the Offensive: Military Decision Making and the Disasters of 1914* (Ithaca, NY: Cornell University Press, 1984), p. 113.

5.	Dale C. Copeland, *The Origins of Major War* (Ithaca, NY: Cornell University Press, 2000).

6.	Gordon Craig, *Germany: 1866-1945* (New York: Oxford University Press, 1978), pp. 24–25; and Gerhard Ritter, *The Sword and the Scepter: The Problem of Militarism in Germany,* vol. 1 (Coral Gables, FL: University of Miami Press, 1969), p. 245, quoting Bismarck's Reichstag speech of February 6, 1888.

7.	Quoted in Otto Pflanze, *Bismarck and the Development of Germany: The Period of Unification, 1815-1871* (Princeton, NJ: Princeton University Press, 1963), p. 90.

8.	Testimony before the House Armed Services Committee, September 18–9, 2002.

9.	Speech at the Massachusetts Institute of Technology, March 31, 1949.

10.	Testimony before the House Armed Services Committee, September 18–9, 2002.

11.	Rumsfeld quoted in the *New York Times,* October 4, 2002.

12.	See Charles Kupchan, *The Vulnerability of Empire* (Ithaca, NY: Cornell University Press, 1994).

13.	Clinton quoted by Rumsfeld, Testimony before the House Armed Services Committee, September 18–9, 2002.

14. "A Righteous Faith for a Just and Durable Peace," October 1942, Dulles Papers, quoted in Ronald Pruessen, *John Foster Dulles: The Road to Power* (New York: Free Press, 1982), p. 200.

15. Rice, "Promoting the National Interest," *Foreign Affairs* (January/February 2000), p. 61.

16. *New York Times,* September 26, 2002. See also John J. Mearsheimer, "Hearts and Minds," *The National Interest* (Fall 2002), p. 15.

17. Dehio, *Germany and World Politics in the Twentieth Century* (New York: W.W. Norton, 1967 [1959]), p. 15.

18. Layne, "The Unipolar Illusion: Why New Powers Will Rise," *International Security* (Spring 1993).

19. See Ikenberry, *After Victory: Institutions, Strategic Restraint, and the Rebuilding of Order After Major Wars* (Princeton, NJ: Princeton University Press, 2000); and Ikenberry, "Getting Hegemony Right," *The National Interest* (Spring 2001).

POSTSCRIPT

Is American Hegemony Good for the United States and the World?

Many scholars have engaged in the debate over how the United States should exercise its preponderance of power. For more on Mandelbaum's views, see his book *The Case for Goliath: How America Acts as the World's Government in the Twenty-First Century* (Public Affairs, 2005). For other views on how the assertive use of American power can be good for both the United States and the world, see Robert J. Lieber, *The American Era: Power and Strategy for the 21st Century* (Cambridge, 2005) and Robert Kagan, "The Benevolent Empire," *Foreign Policy* (Summer 1998).

For a view that the United States is so powerful that even coalitions of other states are unlikely to balance against it, see William Wohlforth, "The Stability of a Unipolar World," *International Security* (Summer 1999). For a contrasting view that emphasizes balancing against the United States and eventual U.S. decline, see Charles Kupchan, *The End of the American Era: U.S. Foreign Policy and the Geopolitics of the Twenty-First Century* (Vintage, 2003).

For critiques of America's informal "empire," see Andrew Bacevich, *American Empire: The Realities and Consequences of U.S. Diplomacy* (Harvard University Press, 2002), Niall Fergusson, *The Price of Empire* (Penguin, 2004), and Robert W. Merry, *Sands of Empire: Missionary Zeal, American Foreign Policy, and the Hazards of Global Ambition* (Simon and Schuster, 2005).

For recommendations on how the United States can build institutions and use "soft power" (the appeal of American ideas and values) to better achieve its goals, see Joseph S. Nye, Jr., *Soft Power: The Means to Success in World Politics* (Public Affairs, 2004) and Richard Haass, *The Opportunity: America's Moment to Alter History's Course* (Public Affairs, 2005). For a discussion of the role of institutions and "self-binding," see G. John Ikenberry, *After Victory* (Princeton, 2000).

ISSUE 2

Should the United States Have an Official Strategy of Preemption Against Potential Weapons of Mass Destruction Threats?

YES: President George W. Bush, from "The National Security Strategy of the United States of America," *National Security Strategy* (September 20, 2002)

NO: Ivo H. Daalder and James M. Lindsay, from "Bush's Revolution," *Current History* (November 2003)

ISSUE SUMMARY

YES: President George W. Bush's official *National Security Strategy* argues that in an era in which "rogue" states and terrorists seek to obtain chemical, biological, and nuclear weapons of mass destruction, and in which terrorists have demonstrated a willingness and capability to attack the United States, the United States must be prepared to preemptively use force to forestall potential threats.

NO: Ivo Daalder, senior fellow at the Brookings Institution, and James Lindsay, director of studies at the Council on Foreign Relations, argue that the Bush doctrine does not distinguish between "preemption" and "preventive war," and that the war in Iraq, the first war waged under the new doctrine, has been costly and damaging to the United States' image and its relations with its allies.

Arguments over deterrence, containment, preemption, and preventive war have a long history in American foreign policy. Through the Cold War, as Bush's *National Security Strategy* notes, the United States relied on nuclear deterrence to prevent a nuclear missile attack by the Soviet Union. Deterrence relies on the ability to make a credible threat against an adversary that if they undertake an act against your interests, you will inflict a punishing attack that is more costly to them than any gain they could achieve by acting against you. During the Cold War, both the United States and the Soviet Union had a "triad" of land-based, aircraft-delivered, and submarine-launched nuclear missiles and bombs that their adversary could not confidently find and simultaneously strike, so if either side thought of attacking the other, it had to worry about a devastating retaliatory strike from its adversary. This state of affairs, known as "mutually assured destruction," was widely viewed as successfully deterring any direct U.S.-Soviet military conflict despite many Cold War crises. Strategists also believed that the possibility of a nuclear war helped prevent the Soviet Union from using its conventional military forces. Therefore, the United States was able to prevent any direct and large-scale Soviet aggression or expansion, a doctrine known as "containment."

Using force to prevent or disable an imminent attack by the adversary is known as "preemption." It is in this context that President Bush's *National Security Strategy* must be understood. The strategy argues that the strategic environment in the post–9/11 world is fundamentally different from that of the Cold War and thus requires a radically new approach. In the Cold War, Soviet leaders were interested in preserving their power, country, and lives. It would have been easy to identify any attack on the United States that came from the Soviet Union, and put U.S. forces on alert. Thus, the deterrent threat of a retaliatory nuclear strike was a credible and powerful disincentive to a Soviet attack. Terrorists, on the other hand, have proven willing to sacrifice their lives to inflict damage on the United States. They have announced and acted upon their intention of attacking American civilians and U.S. military forces with whatever weapons they can acquire, they might be hard to identify and locate after an attack, and they can attack at any time without an advance buildup or crisis. Thus, terrorists cannot be deterred or contained in the same way as the Soviet Union was during the Cold War.

After 9/11, these distinctions are not controversial with regard to U.S. policies against terrorists. Where the *National Security Strategy* ventures into controversy is in applying these arguments to rogue states, whose leaders, like Soviet leaders during the Cold War, are interested in surviving and staying in power and are relatively easy to locate. The *Strategy* rogue states might use or threaten to use weapons of mass destruction (WMDs) to prevent or disable the United States from acting to contain them, and they might thereby achieve their aggressive goals against their neighbors or the United States. The *Strategy* also suggests that such rogue states might provide WMDs to terrorist groups. In this view the United States might have to resort to preemptive strikes against rogue states before such threats materialize.

In the view of its critics, this strategy blurs the distinction between preemptive attacks to forestall imminent aggression by an adversary, which international law allows, and preventive war against an adversary that may or may not resort to force at some time in the future, which is not supported by international law. In addition to its questionable legitimacy, the critics argue, the strategy of preemption creates many practical problems. As Daalder and Lindsay note, the United States has ended up providing 80 percent of the troops in Iraq and bearing most of the human and financial costs of occupying the country. The *Strategy* states that force will not have to be used preemptively "in all cases," but it does not specify clear criteria for preemption. Many critics argued before the war in Iraq that it was possible to contain and deter Iraq by maintaining a capable military force in the region and engaging in intrusive or even coercive inspections of suspected Iraqi weapons sites.

YES ⤵   President George W. Bush

The National Security Strategy of the United States of America

Prevent Our Enemies from Threatening Us, Our Allies, and Our Friends with Weapons of Mass Destruction

"The gravest danger to freedom lies at the crossroads of radicalism and technology. When the spread of chemical and biological and nuclear weapons, along with ballistic missile technology—when that occurs, even weak states and small groups could attain a catastrophic power to strike great nations. Our enemies have declared this very intention, and have been caught seeking these terrible weapons. They want the capability to blackmail us, or to harm us, or to harm our friends—and we will oppose them with all our power."

President Bush
West Point, New York
June 1, 2002

The nature of the Cold War threat required the United States—with our allies and friends—to emphasize deterrence of the enemy's use of force, producing a grim strategy of mutual assured destruction. With the collapse of the Soviet Union and the end of the Cold War, our security environment has undergone profound transformation.

Having moved from confrontation to cooperation as the hallmark of our relationship with Russia, the dividends are evident: an end to the balance of terror that divided us; an historic reduction in the nuclear arsenals on both sides; and cooperation in areas such as counterterrorism and missile defense that until recently were inconceivable.

But new deadly challenges have emerged from rogue states and terrorists. None of these contemporary threats rival the sheer destructive power that was arrayed against us by the Soviet Union. However, the nature and motivations of these new adversaries, their determination to obtain destructive powers hitherto available only to the world's strongest states, and the greater likelihood that they will use weapons of mass destruction against us, make today's security environment more complex and dangerous.

The National Security Strategy of the United States of America by George W. Bush, September 20, 2002.

In the 1990s we witnessed the emergence of a small number of rogue states that, while different in important ways, share a number of attributes. These states:

- brutalize their own people and squander their national resources for the personal gain of the rulers;
- display no regard for international law, threaten their neighbors, and callously violate international treaties to which they are party;
- are determined to acquire weapons of mass destruction, along with other advanced military technology, to be used as threats or offensively to achieve the aggressive designs of these regimes;
- sponsor terrorism around the globe; and
- reject basic human values and hate the United States and everything for which it stands.

At the time of the Gulf War, we acquired irrefutable proof that Iraq's designs were not limited to the chemical weapons it had used against Iran and its own people, but also extended to the acquisition of nuclear weapons and biological agents. In the past decade North Korea has become the world's principal purveyor of ballistic missiles, and has tested increasingly capable missiles while developing its own WMD arsenal. Other rogue regimes seek nuclear, biological, and chemical weapons as well. These states' pursuit of, and global trade in, such weapons has become a looming threat to all nations.

We must be prepared to stop rogue states and their terrorist clients before they are able to threaten or use weapons of mass destruction against the United States and our allies and friends. Our response must take full advantage of strengthened alliances, the establishment of new partnerships with former adversaries, innovation in the use of military forces, modern technologies, including the development of an effective missile defense system, and increased emphasis on intelligence collection and analysis.

Our comprehensive strategy to combat WMD includes:

- *Proactive counterproliferation efforts.* We must deter and defend against the threat before it is unleashed. We must ensure that key capabilities—detection, active and passive defenses, and counterforce capabilities—are integrated into our defense transformation and our homeland security systems. Counterproliferation must also be integrated into the doctrine, training, and equipping of our forces and those of our allies to ensure that we can prevail in any conflict with WMD-armed adversaries.
- *Strengthened nonproliferation efforts to prevent rogue states and terrorists from acquiring the materials, technologies, and expertise necessary for weapons of mass destruction.* We will enhance diplomacy, arms control, multilateral export controls, and threat reduction assistance that impede states and terrorists seeking WMD, and when necessary, interdict enabling technologies and materials. We will continue to build coalitions to support these efforts, encouraging their increased political and financial support for nonproliferation and threat reduction programs. The recent G-8 agreement to commit up to $20 billion to a global partnership against proliferation marks a major step forward.

- *Effective consequence management to respond to the effects of WMD use, whether by terrorists or hostile states.* Minimizing the effects of WMD use against our people will help deter those who possess such weapons and dissuade those who seek to acquire them by persuading enemies that they cannot attain their desired ends. The United States must also be prepared to respond to the effects of WMD use against our forces abroad, and to help friends and allies if they are attacked.

It has taken almost a decade for us to comprehend the true nature of this new threat. Given the goals of rogue states and terrorists, the United States can no longer solely rely on a reactive posture as we have in the past. The inability to deter a potential attacker, the immediacy of today's threats, and the magnitude of potential harm that could be caused by our adversaries' choice of weapons, do not permit that option. We cannot let our enemies strike first.

In the Cold War, especially following the Cuban missile crisis, we faced a generally status quo, risk-averse adversary. Deterrence was an effective defense. But deterrence based only upon the threat of retaliation is less likely to work against leaders of rogue states more willing to take risks, gambling with the lives of their people, and the wealth of their nations.

- In the Cold War, weapons of mass destruction were considered weapons of last resort whose use risked the destruction of those who used them. Today, our enemies see weapons of mass destruction as weapons of choice. For rogue states these weapons are tools of intimidation and military aggression against their neighbors. These weapons may also allow these states to attempt to blackmail the United States and our allies to prevent us from deterring or repelling the aggressive behavior of rogue states. Such states also see these weapons as their best means of overcoming the conventional superiority of the United States.
- Traditional concepts of deterrence will not work against a terrorist enemy whose avowed tactics are wanton destruction and the targeting of innocents; whose so-called soldiers seek martyrdom in death and whose most potent protection is statelessness. The overlap between states that sponsor terror and those that pursue WMD compels us to action.

For centuries, international law recognized that nations need not suffer an attack before they can lawfully take action to defend themselves against forces that present an imminent danger of attack. Legal scholars and international jurists often conditioned the legitimacy of preemption on the existence of an imminent threat—most often a visible mobilization of armies, navies, and air forces preparing to attack.

We must adapt the concept of imminent threat to the capabilities and objectives of today's adversaries. Rogue states and terrorists do not seek to attack us using conventional means. They know such attacks would fail. Instead, they rely on acts of terror and, potentially, the use of weapons of mass destruction—weapons that can be easily concealed, delivered covertly, and used without warning.

The targets of these attacks are our military forces and our civilian population, in direct violation of one of the principal norms of the law of warfare. As was demonstrated by the losses on September 11, 2001, mass civilian casualties is the specific objective of terrorists and these losses would be exponentially more severe if terrorists acquired and used weapons of mass destruction.

The United States has long maintained the option of preemptive actions to counter a sufficient threat to our national security. The greater the threat, the greater is the risk of inaction—and the more compelling the case for taking anticipatory action to defend ourselves, even if uncertainty remains as to the time and place of the enemy's attack. To forestall or prevent such hostile acts by our adversaries, the United States will, if necessary, act preemptively.

The United States will not use force in all cases to preempt emerging threats, nor should nations use preemption as a pretext for aggression. Yet in an age where the enemies of civilization openly and actively seek the world's most destructive technologies, the United States cannot remain idle while dangers gather. We will always proceed deliberately, weighing the consequences of our actions. To support preemptive options, we will:

- build better, more integrated intelligence capabilities to provide timely, accurate information on threats, wherever they may emerge;
- coordinate closely with allies to form a common assessment of the most dangerous threats; and
- continue to transform our military forces to ensure our ability to conduct rapid and precise operations to achieve decisive results.

The purpose of our actions will always be to eliminate a specific threat to the United States or our allies and friends. The reasons for our actions will be clear, the force measured, and the cause just.

Ivo H. Daalder and
James M. Lindsay

NO

Bush's Revolution

George W. Bush had reason to be pleased as he peered down at Baghdad from the window of Air Force One in early June 2003. . . .

Bush could believe that he had become an extraordinarily effective foreign policy president. He had dominated the American political scene like few others. He had been the unquestioned master of his own administration. He had gained the confidence of the American people and persuaded them to follow his lead. He had demonstrated the courage of his convictions on a host of issues— abandoning cold war treaties, fighting terrorism, overthrowing Saddam Hussein. He had spent rather than hoarded his considerable political capital, consistently confounding his critics with the audacity of his policy initiatives. He had been motivated by a determination to succeed, not paralyzed by a fear of failure. And, while he had steadfastly pursued his goals in the face of sharp criticism, he had acted pragmatically when circumstances warranted. In the process, Bush had set in motion a revolution in American foreign policy.

This revolution continues today, even in the face of growing challenges and criticism. It is a revolution not in America's foreign policy goals, but in how to achieve them. In his first 32 months in office, Bush has discarded or redefined many of the key principles governing the way the United States should act overseas. He has relied on the unilateral exercise of American power rather than on international law and institutions to get his way. He has championed a proactive doctrine of preemption and de-emphasized the reactive strategies of deterrence and containment. He has promoted forceful interdiction, preemptive strikes, and missile defenses as means to counter the proliferation of weapons of mass destruction, and he has downplayed America's traditional support for treaty-based nonproliferation regimes. He has preferred regime change to direct negotiations with countries and leaders that he loathes. He has depended on ad hoc coalitions of the willing to gain support abroad while ignoring permanent alliances. He has retreated from America's decades-long policy of backing European integration and instead exploited Europe's internal divisions. And he has tried to unite the great powers in the common cause of fighting terrorism while rejecting traditional policies that sought to balance one power against another. By rewriting the rules of America's engagement in the world, the man dismissed throughout his political career as a lightweight has left an indelible mark on politics at home and abroad.

From *Current History* by Ivo H. Daalder and James M. Lindsay, pp. 367–376. Copyright © 2003 by Current History, Inc. Reprinted by permission.

Nevertheless, the revolution that might have seemed promising at its start has with time proved problematic. Even as he peered out the window of Air Force One to look at Baghdad, there were troubling signs of things to come. American troops in Iraq were embroiled in what had all the makings of guerrilla war. Anger had swelled overseas at what was seen as American arrogance and hypocrisy. Several close allies spoke openly about how to constrain the United States rather than how best to work with it. As the president's plane flew home, Washington was beginning to confront a new question: Were the costs of the Bush revolution about to swamp the presumed benefits?

Making the World Safe for America

What precisely is the Bush revolution in foreign policy? At its broadest level, it rests on two beliefs. The first is that in a dangerous world the best—if not the only—way to ensure America's security is to remove the constraints imposed by friends, allies, and international institutions. Maximizing America's freedom to act is essential because the unique position of the United States makes it the most likely target for any country or group hostile to the West. Americans cannot count on others to protect them because countries inevitably ignore threats that do not involve them. Moreover, formal arrangements restrict the ability of the United States to make the most of its primacy. Gulliver must shed those constraints that he helped the Lilliputians weave.

The other belief is that an America unbound should use its strength to change the status quo in the world. Bush's foreign policy does not propose that the United States keep its powder dry while it waits for dangers to gather. Instead, the Bush philosophy turns John Quincy Adams on his head and argues that the United States should aggressively go abroad to search for monsters to destroy. That was the logic behind the Iraq war, and it animates the administration's efforts to deal with other rogue states.

These fundamental beliefs have important consequences for the practice of American foreign policy. One consequence is a decided preference for unilateral action. Unilateralism is appealing because it is often easier and more efficient, at least in the short term, than multilateralism. Contrast the Clinton administration's 1999 Kosovo war, where Bush and his advisers believed that the task of coordinating the views of all NATO members greatly complicated the war effort, with the U.S. war in Afghanistan under Bush, in which Pentagon planners did not have to subject any of their decisions to foreign approval. This is not to say that Bush flatly rules out working with others. Rather, his preferred form of multilateralism—to be indulged when unilateral action is impossible or unwise—involves building ad hoc coalitions of the willing, or what Richard Haass, an adviser to Colin Powell, has called "à la carte multilateralism."

Second, preemption no longer is a last resort of American foreign policy. In a world in which weapons of mass destruction are spreading and terrorists and rogue states are readying to attack in unconventional ways, Bush argues that "the United States can no longer solely rely on a reactive posture as we have in the past.... We cannot let our enemies strike first." Indeed, the

United States should be prepared to act not just preemptively against imminent threats, but also preventively against potential threats. Vice President Dick Cheney was emphatic on this point in justifying the overthrow of Saddam on the eve of the Iraq War. "There's no question about who is going to prevail if there is military action. And there's no question but [that] it is going to be cheaper and less costly to do now than it will be to wait a year or two years or three years until he's developed even more deadly weapons, perhaps nuclear weapons."

Third, the United States should use its unprecedented power to carry out regime change in rogue states. The idea of regime change is not new to American foreign policy. The Eisenhower administration engineered the overthrow of Iranian Prime Minister Mohammed Mossadegh in the 1950s; the CIA trained Cuban exiles in the 1960s in a botched bid to oust Fidel Castro; Ronald Reagan channeled aid to the Nicaraguan contras in the 1980s to overthrow the Sandinista government; and Bill Clinton helped Serb opposition forces to remove Slobodan Milosevic in 2000. What is different in the Bush presidency is the willingness, even in the absence of a direct attack on the United States, to use U.S. military forces for the express purpose of toppling other governments. This was the gist of both the Afghanistan and the Iraq wars. Unlike proponents of rollback, who never succeeded in overcoming the argument that their anti-communist policies could lead to World War III, Bush bases his policy on the belief that no one can push back. . . .

The National Security Strategy

The fullest elaboration of Bush's strategy for defeating the terrifying combination of terrorism, tyrants, and technologies of mass destruction came in the *National Security Strategy,* a document that the White House issues annually at the behest of Congress. Bush released the strategy on September 20, 2002, just as the domestic and international debate on Iraq was heating up. . . .

The strategy document asserts that, after 9-11, there can be no doubt that terrorists and the rogue states that support them will stop at nothing in their attempts to strike America again. "Today, our enemies see weapons of mass destruction as weapons of choice. For rogue states these weapons are tools of intimidation and military aggression against their neighbors." Such weapons could enable them "to blackmail the United States and our allies to prevent us from deterring or repelling the aggressive behavior of rogue states." Deterrence by threatening retaliation is less likely to work "against leaders of rogue states more willing to take risks, gambling with the lives of their people, and the wealth of their nations." And, of course, "deterrence will not work against a terrorist enemy whose avowed tactics are wanton destruction and the targeting of innocents."

This is why America might have to act preemptively, the strategy argues. "The United States has long maintained the option of preemptive actions to counter a sufficient threat to our national security. The greater the threat, the greater is the risk of inaction—and the more compelling the case for taking anticipatory action to defend ourselves, even if uncertainty remains as to the time and place of the enemy's attack." Of course, force will not have to be used "in all cases to preempt emerging threats, nor should nations use preemption as a pretext for aggression. Yet in an age where the enemies of civilization openly and actively seek the world's most destructive technologies, the United States cannot remain idle while dangers gather." . . .

The New Sparta

The Bush strategy represents a profound strategic innovation—less in its goals than in the way Bush proposes to achieve them. This is why the doctrine of preemption has become the focal point of discussions about the strategy at home and abroad. After all, Bush has effectively abandoned a decades-long consensus that put deterrence and containment at the heart of American foreign policy. "After September the 11th, the doctrine of containment just doesn't hold any water, as far as I'm concerned," Bush explained in early 2003.

Critics have leveled four complaints against the preemption doctrine. First, many question why the administration decided to make a public statement about something that has long been a U.S. policy option and, in some instances, an actual policy. "It is not clear to me what advantage there is in declaring it publicly," said Brent Scowcroft, national security adviser during the Ford and first Bush administrations. "It has been common knowledge that under some circumstances the United States would preempt. As a declaratory policy it tends to leave the door open to others who want to claim the same right. By making it public we also tend to add to the world's perception that we are arrogant and unilateral." In other words, there is much to lose and little to gain by making the doctrine public—or even turning an option into a policy.

Scowcroft's comment touched on a second objection to the preemption argument: countries may use it as a cover for settling their own national security scores. Days after the strategy's publication, Russia hinted that it might have to intervene in neighboring Georgia to go after Islamic terrorists allegedly hiding in the Pankisi Gorge. India embraced preemption as a universal doctrine. "Every nation has that right," Finance Minister Jaswant Singh said on a visit to Washington days after the strategy's publication. "It is not the prerogative of any one country. Preemption is the right of any nation to prevent injury to itself." But, as Henry Kissinger has suggested, "it cannot be in either the American national interest or the world's interest to develop principles that grant every nation an unfettered right of preemption against its own definition of threats to its security." The strategy recognizes this problem by warning nations not to "use preemption as a pretext for aggression." But the administration has not identified what separates justifiable preemption from unlawful aggression. Without a bright line that can gain widespread adherence abroad, the administration runs the risk that its words will be used to justify ends that it opposes.

Third, critics argue that the Bush strategy suffers from considerable conceptual confusion, which has real policy consequences. Most important, it conflates the notion of preemptive and preventive war. *Preemptive* wars are initiated when another country is clearly about to attack. Israel's decision to go to war in June 1967 against its Arab neighbors is the classic example. *Preventive* wars are launched by states against others before the state being attacked poses a real or imminent threat. "What made war inevitable," the ancient Greek historian Thucydides wrote about the Peloponnesian War, "was the growth in Athenian power and the fear this caused in Sparta." The purpose of initiating war in these circumstances is therefore to stop a threat before it can arise. Israel's strike against Iraq's Osirak reactor in 1981 was one example of preventive war. Cheney's argument that Iraq needed to be struck before it acquired nuclear weapons is another. Much of the Bush rhetoric—including its justification for the Iraq War—is consistent with the notion of preventive war, not preemption. The problem is that, while preemptive wars have long-recognized standing in international law as a legitimate form of self-defense, preventive wars do not. Not surprisingly, a resort to preventive war in the case of Iraq has proved highly controversial.

For all the criticism of the Bush strategy's core innovation, the real debate has been a practical one about Iraq rather than a doctrinal one about preemption. In part this reflects the fact that, the rhetoric surrounding the doctrine notwithstanding, Iraq was the driving force behind its promulgation. For all the talk about an axis of evil, it was clear that the administration at least initially would focus squarely on Baghdad. Just two weeks after the president warned about the axis, Secretary of State Colin Powell told Congress, "There is no plan to start a war with these nations," referring to Iran and North Korea. "We want to see a dialogue. We want to contain North Korea's activities with respect to proliferation, and we are going to keep the pressure on them. But there is no plan to begin a war with North Korea; nor is there a plan to begin a conflict with Iran." Yet neither Powell nor any other official had anything reassuring to say about Iraq. On the contrary, Bush left no doubt that he wanted Saddam gone—and sooner rather than later. When U.S. forces, aided by small numbers of British and Australian troops, invaded Iraq in March 2003, they did so over the objections of many key allies and without explicit United Nations authorization. . . .

The Revolution's Results

. . . Are Americans better off with or without the Bush revolution?

The president is hardly alone in understanding that America possesses unrivaled power—especially military power. What makes him revolutionary is his willingness to use it, even over the strenuous objections of America's friends and allies. In the war on terrorism, he has used American power to set the international agenda. In the war against Iraq, he has used it to compel others to follow—or at least to accept—his chosen course. In America's policies toward the Middle East, he has used it to sideline leaders whom America preferred not to deal with, from Mullah Omar and Saddam to Yasir Arafat. In these and other instances, Bush has moved decisively to take the initiative. Rather than debate issues endlessly, he has chosen to act. And his decisions more often than not have reflected his convictions, rather than Washington's conventional wisdom.

Even so, while Bush understands that American muscle can shape events, he has overestimated what the unilateral exercise of its power can achieve. America is not omnipotent. To achieve most of its goals it still requires the cooperation of others. Washington's ability to rally allies to its side depends on identifying and pursuing common interests, not just national ones. Yet, since Bush became president, people around the world have lost trust in the United States, doubting that it has much interest in them or their problems. They fear that an America unbound has taken the tyrant's motto as its own: *Oderint dum metuant*—"Let them hate as long as they fear." And they have become more reluctant to cooperate with Washington. America suddenly faces the possibility that it will end up standing all alone, a great power unable to achieve its most important goals.

From the start, Bush has insisted that the rest of the world be measured by America's standard, not the other way around. This attitude infuses Bush's language, his polite but cursory treatment of other world leaders, and his lack of concern for their interests and their advice. Bush's approach strikes many as an arrogance born of power, not principle. And they resent it deeply.

Since September 11, Bush has painted the world in black and white, while others, particularly overseas, still paint it in shades of gray. He has distinguished between those who are "evil" and those who are "good," between those who are "for us" and those who are "against us," between those who "love freedom" and those who "hate the freedom we love." The war on terrorism is a "crusade." Osama bin Laden had to be found "dead or alive." And Bush was "sick and tired" of the games Saddam played. This rhetoric initially helped galvanize Americans to support the president's assertive and often audacious policies abroad. But it is alien to most foreigners, who, because of America's unquestioned supremacy, comprise as much a part of Bush's audience as the American people do. Not accustomed to the blunt language and locutions of west Texas, many people outside the United States see Bush's words as proof that their views do not matter.

Bush and his advisers have not tried to dispel such perceptions. Instead, they frequently express their contempt for opinions different from their own. When Gerhard Schröder used his opposition to a war against Iraq to squeeze out a narrow reelection victory in Germany, Bush refused to place the customary congratulatory phone call. National security adviser Condoleezza Rice spoke of the "poisoned" state of U.S.-German relations.

Rumsfeld has a particular knack for twisting a knife in open wounds. He dismissed France and Germany as "old Europe" for failing to support the war against Iraq. . . .

After 9-11, Bush also made clear that only a country's support for the war on terror mattered much to the United States. Just as he has reoriented America's foreign policy agenda to focus single-mindedly on defeating terrorism, so the president expects every other country to reorient its foreign policy as well. At the same time, the Bush administration acts as if the world has entered a post-diplomatic age, in which making speeches or issuing ultimatums takes the place of give-and-take negotiations. Once America's position is clear, others are expected to follow.

The Arrogance of Power

"If we're an arrogant nation, they'll resent us," Bush observed about other countries during his second presidential debate with Al Gore. "If we're a humble nation, but strong, they'll welcome us." It was a wise observation that Bush and much of his administration somehow forgot. Resentment, not respect, best characterizes how most other countries have reacted to the Bush revolution. Early evidence came during the 2002 elections in Germany and South Korea. In both countries, the results turned on opposition to U.S. policy. . . .

Although Bush's imperious style has entailed great costs for American foreign policy, it is not the only shortcoming in his revolution. To be sure, Bush would be wiser to show what the Declaration of Independence called "a decent respect to the opinions of mankind." But more grace by itself would not be enough to allay the fears of friends and allies. The deeper problem is that the fundamental premise of the Bush revolution—that America's security rests on an America unbound—is mistaken.

This premise might be right if the unilateral exercise of American power could achieve America's major foreign policy goals. But the most important foreign policy challenges that America faces—whether defeating terrorism, reversing weapons proliferation, promoting economic prosperity, safeguarding political liberty, sustaining the global environment, or halting the spread of killer diseases—cannot be solved by Washington alone. They require the active cooperation of others.

The question is how best to secure that cooperation. Bush maintains that, far from impeding cooperation, unilateralism will foster it. If the United States leads, others will follow. They will join with America because they share its values and interests. To be sure, some countries might object to how Washington intends to lead. But Bush is convinced they will come around once the benefits of American action become clear.

The flaw in this thinking has become painfully obvious in Iraq. No doubt many countries, including all members of the U.N. Security Council, shared a major interest in making sure that Iraq did not possess nuclear and other horrific weapons. For most, however, that common interest did not translate into active cooperation in a war to oust Saddam from power—or even into support for such a war. A few countries actively tried to stop the march to war; many others simply sat on the sidelines.

Little has changed since the toppling of Saddam's statue in Firdos Square. Although many countries believe that stabilizing postwar Iraq is vitally important—for regional stability, international security, and their own national safety—they have not rushed to join the reconstruction effort. In September 2003, American troops constituted more than 80 percent of all forces supporting the Iraq operation—at an annual cost to the American taxpayer of more than $50 billion. Britain provides nearly half of the other forces. The remaining foreign contributions are insignificant. Hungary, for instance, is to provide 133 truck drivers. In many cases, countries have agreed to contribute troops only after Washington said it would help pay for them.

Not Following the Leader

The lesson of Iraq, then, is that sometimes when you lead, few follow. This, ultimately, constitutes the real danger of the Bush revolution. America's friends and allies might not be able to stop Washington from doing as it wishes, but neither will they necessarily be willing to come to its aid when their help is most needed. Indeed, the more that others question America's power, purpose, and priorities, the less influence America will have. If others seek to counter the United States and delegitimize its power, Washington will need to exert more effort to reach the same desired end—assuming it can reach its objective at all. If others step aside and leave Washington to tackle common problems as it sees fit, the costs will increase. This prospect risks undermining not only what the United States can achieve abroad but also domestic support for its engagement in the world. The American public, always wary of being played for a sucker, might balk at paying the price of unilateralism. Americans might rightly ask, if others are not willing to bear the burdens of meeting tough challenges, why should they? In this respect, an unbound America is a less secure America.

But Bush's way is not America's only choice. In fact, Washington has chosen differently before. When America emerged from World War II as the predominant power in the world, it could have imposed an imperium commensurate with its power—and no one could have prevented it. But Franklin Roosevelt and Harry Truman chose not to. They recognized that American power would be more acceptable and thus more effective and lasting if it were folded into alliances and multilateral institutions that served the interests and purposes of many countries. So they created the United Nations to help ensure international peace and security, set up the Bretton Woods system to help stabilize international economic interactions, and spent vast sums to help rebuild countries (including vanquished foes) that had been devastated by the war. It was not just America's victory in war, but also its magnanimity in peace, that made the twentieth century the American century.

Throughout the cold war, international institutions provided a crucial means to exert America's authority. They bound everyone else into a U.S.-run world order. They in effect constituted what a British journalist called "America's secret empire." Bush has preferred to build his empire on American power alone rather than on the greater power that comes from working with friends and allies. His reliance on military power has proved extraordinarily effective in routing foes, but far less effective in building a lasting basis for peace and prosperity. The United States could decisively defeat the Taliban and Saddam, but rebuilding Afghanistan and Iraq would be better accomplished by working with others. The lesson is clear. Far from demonstrating the triumph of unilateral American power, Bush's wars have demonstrated the importance of basing American foreign policy on a blend of power and cooperation. . . .

POSTSCRIPT

Should the United States Have an Official Strategy of Preemption Against Potential Weapons of Mass Destruction Threats?

Because it is driven by long-term political and technological developments in the threats the United States faces, the debate over whether and when preemptive use of force is justified is likely to endure for many years, much as debates on how best to achieve nuclear deterrence raged throughout the Cold War. The outcome of this debate at any given time is likely to reflect America's ongoing experiences in the world, the behavior of so-called rogue states toward their neighbors and toward terrorism, and America's capacity to carry out preemptive strikes against potentially threatening states.

The doctrine of preemption may well have already reached its high point with the initiation of the war in Iraq. Concern over the continuing possibility of terrorist attacks on the United States was sufficiently high at the time that the Congress voted in the fall of 2002 to authorize the use of force against Iraq if it failed to comply with United Nations resolutions on weapons inspections. The long and costly nature of the war in Iraq, however, unexpected as it was to the war's proponents, has likely diminished the willingness of Congress and the public to support any new preemptive use of force without strong evidence that a potential adversary is likely to attack the United States or its allies or transfer WMDs to terrorists.

The ongoing behavior of rogue states matters as well. While both North Korea and Iran have supported or sponsored terrorist attacks over the years, they have been largely directed at regional adversaries (South Korea and Israel, respectively) rather than the United States. Even so, any ongoing support for terrorist acts by these states is of great concern in itself, and is additionally worrisome in that it raises the concern that later acts of terrorism might be directed at the United States; the terrorists in al Qaeda, after all, honed their capabilities in attacks in other countries before targeting the United States. Meanwhile, attempts by North Korea and Iran or other states to acquire WMDs cut both ways: if the location of these weapons and the means of their production can be reliably located by the United States, the temptation for preemption will be high. But if states have already acquired WMDs and means to deliver them, and have at the same time been able to hide and disperse these capabilities, the United States may be deterred from acting.

For the immediate future, as long as the United States has over 100,000 troops serving in Iraq and others deployed in the region, America's capability to undertake large-scale preemptive attacks elsewhere is substantially constrained. Few now argue, as some did early in the war in Iraq, that U.S. success in Iraq might put pressure on Iraqi neighbors such as Syria and Iran to democratize. More ominously, to the extent that the war in Iraq constrains the ability of the United States to raise the prospect of preemptively using force to destroy weapons programs or attack terrorists and those who support them, the leverage of U.S. diplomatic action against weapons proliferation and terrorism is diminished, whether or not the United States has an official doctrine of preemption.

For more on President Bush's grand strategy and the issue of preemption, see Robert Jervis, "The Compulsive Empire," *Foreign Policy* (July/August 2003), Melvyn Leffler, "Bush's Foreign Policy," *Foreign Policy* (September/October 2004), John Lewis Gaddis, "A Grand Strategy of Transformation?" *Foreign Policy* (November/December 2002), and Philip Zelikow, "The Transformation of National Security," *The National Interest* (Spring 2003).

ISSUE 3

Should Promoting Democracy Abroad Be a Top U.S. Priority?

YES: Joseph Siegle, from "Developing Democracy: Democratizers' Surprisingly Bright Development Record," *Harvard International Review* (Summer 2004)

NO: Tamara Cofman Wittes, from "Arab Democracy, American Ambivalence," *The Weekly Standard* (February 23, 2004)

ISSUE SUMMARY

YES: Joseph Siegle, Douglas Dillon Fellow at the Council on Foreign Relations, argues that large numbers of countries are continuing to democratize and, because of the increase in accountability associated with democratization, they tend to experience economic growth as fast as, if not faster than, other countries in the same region.

NO: Tamara Cofman Wittes, research fellow in the Saban Center for Middle East Policy at the Brookings Institution, argues that U.S. efforts to promote democracy in Iraq and the Arab Middle East are likely to fail unless the U.S. government matches its rhetoric with a credible commitment to promote policies institutionalizing the forward movement of liberalism in Iraq and the region at large.

President George H. W. Bush responded to the dramatic increase in the number of countries pursuing democracy in the early 1990s by calling for a "a new world order" in which "nations recognize the shared responsibility for freedom and justice." Since then over 80 previously non-democratic countries have made progress toward democratization. As a result, over two-thirds of the countries in the world practice some form of democratic rule today.

Promoting democracy became a central component of U.S. foreign policy under President Bill Clinton, and it remains so today under President George W. Bush. The core motivation for this rests on the "Democratic Peace proposition" that democracies tend not to fight with one another and instead are generally highly integrated economically and politically with one another. While some vocal dissenters exist, a large amount of political science research in the

1990s suggests that democracies have historically been less likely to fight wars with other democracies. Promoting democracy is, therefore, seen as a means of increasing stability, peace, and economic prosperity in the international system.

Arguments for why this pattern exists generally emphasize the pacifying effect of constraints that democratic institutions impose on their leaders; the legal, social and political norms shared by democratic states; and the relatively high level of interdependence among democratic states. Democratic institutions—including open public debate as well as legal and constitutional constraints on the executive—help promote peace by limiting the ability of the executive to act rashly or without consultation. Furthermore, the desire to get reelected is presumed to make politicians less willing to engage in risky foreign policies. Shared norms further decrease the likelihood of conflict by providing a common basis of understanding that enhances trust and reduces the likelihood of misinterpreting one another's actions to be aggressive. Finally, market-based economic systems tend to be more prevalent in—though not exclusive to—democracies, and the interdependence they generate creates incentives to maintain peaceful and mutually beneficial international relationships.

The process of democratization is not always smooth. When, for example, elections take place before legal systems are solidified or before realistic plans for sustained economic growth are established, public expectations can outpace the newly elected government's ability to deliver positive changes. The result may be a political backlash against democracy, the rise of corruption, or other forms of political or economic instability. Research in international relations has demonstrated that while established democracies are less prone to engage in risky behavior, states undergoing the process of democratization are more prone than others to do so. Thus, while a world populated by democracies is likely to be more peaceful than others, a world of countries going through the process of democratization may be more unstable and conflict-prone.

Given these risks, many scholars and politicians have argued that perhaps economic liberalization should take place before political liberalization (as in Singapore or the People's Republic of China) or that political elections in the absence of a strong independent judiciary will simply empower former elites and promote corruption (as in Russia following the fall of the Soviet Union). Joseph Siegle argues that despite these concerns, countries that are truly democratizing have developed faster than their non-democratic counterparts. Tamara Cofman Wittes argues that the transition to democracy is difficult and likely to fail in the Arab Middle East unless the United States dedicates itself to creating the institutions necessary to make it work over the long haul.

YES

Joseph Siegle

Developing Democracy: Democratizers' Surprisingly Bright Development Record

The past 25 years have seen an astonishing advance in the number of democracies around the world. Some 87 previously nondemocratic countries have made discernible advances towards democracy during this time. Of these democratizers, 70 have per capita incomes below US$4,000, making this a largely developing country phenomenon. Today, two-thirds of all countries live under some form of self-governance—a reversal from just 15 years ago.

Despite this tectonic shift in global governance patterns, the sentiment that a poor country must first develop economically before it can democratize persists. The stellar growth of autocratic Singapore, China, and Vietnam as well as the experiences of South Korea, Taiwan, and Chile are trotted out as justification for this seemingly hard but true reality. Low income countries that do start down a democratic path are bound to fail or at least take a sharp economic hit in the process, according to this view. Indeed, authoritarian governments throughout the Middle East, the former Soviet Union, and elsewhere are quick to cite this concern when deflecting growing pressure to democratize.

A closer look at the development track record tells a different story, however. Most of the 87 contemporary democratizers have realized economic growth as fast as, if not faster than, the norm for their respective regions over the past five years. That is, democratizers such as Poland, Hungary, Bulgaria, the Baltic states, Mexico, Senegal, and Mozambique are typically growing more rapidly than countries with autocratic governments such as Syria, Saudi Arabia, Uzbekistan, North Korea, Cuba, Zimbabwe, Togo, and Gabon. The pattern holds up for the entire 25-year period of the contemporary democratization era. This is so despite the fact that a full quarter of (typically underperforming) autocratic governments do not publicly report their economic data and therefore are not even factored into these comparisons.

The differences are even more striking when we consider indicators of well-being such as life expectancy, illiteracy, and access to clean drinking water. Low-income democratizers enjoy demonstrably better living standards than autocracies. Consider infant mortality rates, an indicator many development experts consider the best all around measure of social welfare progress.

Autocratic countries with per capita incomes below US$2,000 averaged 79 infant deaths per 1,000 live births during the 1990s. Democratizers in the same income category and time period typically experienced 62 infant deaths. Given that many of these countries still rely on their agricultural sectors for the bulk of their employment and income, democratizers' track record of posting agricultural yields that are on average 25 percent superior to those of developing country autocracies is similarly noteworthy.

Simply put, democratic governance is good for development. This is not to say that there are not exceptions; clearly, there are. However, the pattern of superior developmental performance among countries that are on a demo-cratic path is robust. The traditional view that political liberalization inevitably precipitates populist economic policies and economic contraction has not been demonstrated in practice when compared to autocratic countries in the same regions or income groups.

In many ways, this is intuitive—what is government but a mechanism by which a society orders its priorities? The more representative, transparent, and accountable this process, the more balanced the outcomes will be com-pared to a system that is narrowly based and lacking incentives for responsive-ness to citizen interests.

Why Do Some Democratizers Do So Much Better?

Given that democratizers more than hold their own when it comes to develop-ment, the more interesting question is why some democratizers do so much better than others in their development efforts? That is, if democracy is a plus for development, why aren't all democratizers thriving?

A significant degree of this difference can be explained by the extent to which democratizers have established institutional mechanisms of shared power, or what I refer to as "accountability institutions." These include checks on the chief executive (for example, a legislature that can initiate legislation and block egregious policies pursued by the executive branch), the separation of political party influence from state structures (evidenced by a merit-based civil service), the separation of economic opportunity from political authority as seen through an autonomous private sector, an independent judiciary, and a free press.

Democratizing states that move to establish and strengthen these institu-tions of shared power tend to develop more rapidly. Specifically, looking at the experience of democratizers over the last 25 years, it is apparent that annual per capita growth rates for democratizers in the top quartile of a com-posite measure of these accountability institutions grew, on average, more than a full percentage point faster than democratizers in the bottom quartile of these accountability rankings—2.2 percent versus 1.0 percent. So, demo-cratizers as diverse as Botswana, South Africa, Senegal, Slovenia, Estonia, Czech Republic, Chile, Dominican Republic, and Thailand that have estab-lished comparatively stronger institutional mechanisms protecting against the arbitrary use of power have realized substantially more economic growth than other democratizers such as Algeria, Cameroon, Burkina Faso, Guinea, Tajikistan, Kazakhstan, and Georgia, where restraints on political monopolization have been weak. Analogous growth differences hold across income levels.

Similar differentials are apparent on measures of social progress. Democratizers with stronger institutions of accountability score, on average, 15 to 25 percent higher on indicators of life expectancy, access to medical service, and primary school enrollment among others. Countries in the top quartile of accountability scores for all low income (that is, below US$2,000 per capita) democratizers typically have had infant mortality rates of 37 per 1,000 live births in the 1990s compared to a 79 per 1,000 mortality rate for democratizers in the lower quartile of the accountability rankings. The disparities only widen when the under US$1,000 income category is considered. Understanding the development advantage of democratizers thus involves assessing the extensiveness of their checks and balances on power—as distinguished from those that may solely adopt some of the symbols of democracy, such as elections. Countries that democratize in deed and not just name tend to develop more rapidly.

Progress on any of the individual accountability dimensions tends to improve development outcomes. Thus, strengthening the independence of the judiciary, the civil service, or the private sector each has positive effects for development. In practical terms, however, it is rare for a country to distinguish itself on a sole accountability element. A society commonly makes progress across a number of fronts simultaneously. This suggests that a shift in norms and expectations regarding the limits of political power occurs. A "culture of accountability" begins to take root. And it is the cumulative effect of these enhanced norms that is most important for transferring political change into development improvements. Such a shift occurred in Kenya following the election of President Mwai Kibaki in late 2002, representing the first transfer of power between political parties in Kenyan history. Having campaigned on an anti-corruption platform, upon taking office Kibaki instituted new standards of transparency and disclosure for conflicts of interest among senior government officials. Acting on this cue, ordinary Kenyans began refusing to pay the ubiquitous bribes demanded by Kenyan police. In some cases, incensed crowds would chase bribe-seeking police officers straight off their beats. Government contracts awarded under questionable circumstances, previously accepted as the norm, were increasingly challenged in the courts by the general public. Corrupt judges have been forced to resign. While Kenya still has a way to go, the indirect benefits to the Kenyan economy, in terms of reduced transaction costs, time saved, and improved economic efficiency resulting from the higher level of accountability, are surely substantial.

To the extent that any single accountability factor determines development progress, an independent media stands out. Of all 87 democratizers considered, only Cambodia and Angola have realized economic development in the late 1990s at a rate faster than their regional norm without also establishing at least an intermediate degree of press freedoms. Therefore, while a free press is often invoked for its importance in strengthening democracy, its contribution to material progress may be equally relevant.

More informed deliberation prior to the adoption of a policy, heightened scrutiny and pressure to rectify policies producing poor results, and strengthened market confidence created by the greater transparency fostered by a free press all contribute to this phenomenon. In other words, an independent media creates an environment in which democracy's self-correcting mechanisms can come into play. The end result of this is a more pragmatic set of development policies.

A free press may also be indispensable to the realization of the other accountability structures. Consider the rule of law. Without the transparency and scrutiny fostered by independent media, the scope for misuse of public monies by government officials is substantially greater. This, in turn, affects the prospects for a competitive private sector. The recent experience of the petroleum industry in India is indicative of this phenomenon. Only after an investigation by the newspaper *Indian Express* was it discovered that in state after state, the bulk of licenses for gas stations were going to members of the governing Bharatiya Janata Party and their friends and relatives. The scandal forced Indian Prime Minister Atal Bihari Vajpayee to cancel the allotments for more than 3,000 gas stations, resulting in greater economic competition and lower prices for consumers. In short, it was the transparency generated by the independent media that invigorated the rule of law.

Accordingly, Vladimir Putin's systematic efforts to disembowel an independent media in Russia will likely be self-defeating. His effort to control the flow of information diminishes the rule of law, the autonomy of the private sector, and checks on the executive branch. While he certainly enjoys additional maneuverability under a state-owned media, this advantage is destined to be fleeting. In the process, he is inexorably undermining his stated priority of establishing a strong foundation for Russia's sustained economic growth. As tales of government extortion and intimidation of entrepreneurs increase, foreign direct investment will dwindle further.

Pseudo-Democratizers

The realization that democratizers with relatively stronger institutions of shared power tend to grow more rapidly raises important issues over how we categorize democratizers. The classic litmus test—holding multi-party elections—is increasingly unsatisfactory. With the evolving international norm of according legitimacy only to those leaders that have been democratically elected, heads of authoritarian states have craftily attempted to co-opt the language and trappings of democracy so as to make the grade without ever seriously intending to share power. President Hosni Mubarak's Egypt is the prototypical case. Presidential elections are held every six years and opposition parties, a civil society, and a free press are ostensibly allowed. However, these democratic processes are heavily circumscribed. Political opponents are frequently harassed, licenses of civil society organizations critical of the government are regularly rescinded, and strict self-censorship is imposed. Political power comfortably remains within the hands of Mubarak.

Similarly, Rwanda went through an electoral charade late last year in order to anoint Paul Kagame as president. Opposition parties were allowed but were frequently prevented from holding rallies or appearing on state-sponsored television. Not only were supporters afraid to show up at opposition rallies but, intimidated by government threats, opposition candidates themselves would at times preemptively cancel planned gatherings. Some recent examples of autocrats trying to masquerade as democrats in order to attain a degree of international credibility include Azerbaijan's transition of power from father to son in the guise of elections, Robert Mugabe's manipulation of democratic procedures in Zimbabwe, Iran's Guardian Council (representing the unelected clerical hierarchy) barring of 2,400 moderate candidates from running in parliamentary elections, and General Pervez Musharraf's elaborately staged national referenda in Pakistan, to name a few.

This more sophisticated class of "pseudo-democratizers" has learned that they can often avoid international scrutiny so long as they maintain some of the more visible rituals of democratic governance. And to a large extent, they are right. In addition to setting fuzzy and embarrassingly low standards, the international community has yet to figure out how to deal with authoritarian states dressed up in democratic regalia. Arguments for constructive engagement, patience for the slow pace, and a misguided focus on the "glass half-full" argument continue to be convincingly made. The neo-authoritarians have played on this ambiguity to suggest real change is taking place, when all the while, they are, in fact, tightening their grip on power. Unsurprisingly, the democratizer-growth relationship for electoral democracies is only one quarter as strong as when the extent of a democratizer's accountability structures is taken into consideration.

Including this collection of pseudo-democratizers in the broader class of countries undergoing genuine political change, predictably obscures our understanding of the democratizers' development track record. The challenge to the international community is to match the sophistication of the democratic charlatans by devising methods to better discriminate which states are making real, if incremental, progress towards greater political participation and power sharing. Assessing the extent to which accountability institutions have been created provides a potential lens to do so.

Democracy and Accountability

As one would expect, democracies and countries on the road to democracy generally have stronger systems of accountability in place than autocratic states. This creates the self-correcting processes that allow political institutions to moderate and facilitate positive economic and social welfare outcomes. Those democracies and democratizers with relatively stronger accountability institutions within their respective income or regional cohort have typically excelled in their developmental outcomes. Interestingly enough, the same principle applies when we look at groupings of authoritarian countries. Those authoritarian regimes with relatively stronger accountability structures have realized more rapid growth. In other words, the pattern of strong accountability institutions and steady economic development is consistent regardless of whether a country is democratic, democratizing, or authoritarian. It is just that democracies have a considerably higher likelihood of creating such accountability structures.

Understanding the relationship between accountability and development thus sheds light on a couple of missing pieces in the democracy-development puzzle. First, it is widely recognized that almost all of the world's prosperous states are democracies. The real debate has always been about how poor countries get there from where they are starting. That is, how do we reconcile the outstanding record of the industrialized democracies with the checkered results generated by democratizers? Focusing on the depth of accountability institutions, a common trait of both the industrialized democracies and democratizers that have grown more rapidly, provides at least part of the answer. Poor countries that started down the democratization path and established strong accountability structures have generally grown rapidly; democracy and development do go together. The prescription of a prolonged period of authoritarian purgatory before enjoying democratic redemption is unwarranted. For that matter, formerly low-income countries like Malta, Mauritius, Botswana, and post-Pinochet Chile have grown so rapidly and steadily that they have made considerable headway in closing the prosperity gap with the industrialized democracies. While at varying stages in the process, Thailand, Poland, Hungary, the Baltic countries, Mozambique, and the Dominican Republic are recent democratizers also on a development fast track. Democratizers that have moved less cogently to establish institutions that constrain political and economic monopolization have generally grown less quickly.

Second, one of the perplexities to the democracy-development debate has been the stellar economic performance of a selected number of authoritarian countries, most notably in East Asia. How have these exceptional autocratic growers bucked the trend? Their strength of accountability institutions has something to do with it. This category of rapidly-growing autocrats, controlling for income, scores 20 to 40 percent better on the various categories of accountability compared to other authoritarian countries. In short, economically vibrant autocracies are clear-cut outliers.

This helps us to understand the anomalous nature of the fast-growing authoritarians. Yes, they do exist but they are far from representative and therefore a poor basis on which to guide development policy. Specifically, over the past 25 years there have been eight authoritarian countries that have enjoyed rapid economic growth for over a decade: Bhutan, China, Egypt, South Korea, Singapore, Taiwan, Tunisia, and Vietnam. This compares to the roughly 60 other authoritarian governments that experienced stagnant growth during this time period. In other words, it is not the authoritarian character of the fast-growing states that explains their remarkable development. The wait for development in low accountability states such as Turkmenistan, Azerbaijan, Belarus, Sudan, Cameroon, Burma, Haiti, and Syria before the promotion of democracy will be a long wait indeed.

Policy Implications

At present, development funding to low-income democracies, as a share of GDP, is no greater than that to authoritarian states. To better reduce poverty and propel economic growth, this should change. International investors and development agencies should instead identify countries undertaking genuine political reform and target resource flows to them with the aim of accelerating their economic growth and material development. The track record suggests that the impact and returns from such investment will be maximized. Directing capital flows to these countries, coupled with the enhanced economic progress these democratizers would experience, accentuates incentives for other developing countries to initiate democratic political reform in earnest.

The United States' recently inaugurated Millennium Challenge Account is a potentially important instrument for such a democracy-focused development strategy. While substantially scaled-back from US President George Bush's original proposal, this US$1 billion annual fund for countries deemed to be ruling democratically, investing in their populations, and to be establishing basic economic rights could facilitate a marked shift in development outlays towards democratizers. To be effective and to ensure that the incentive structure of this program clearly resounds throughout the developing world, however, robust democratic governance standards should be maintained in selecting eligible countries. This would signal to non-democratic countries that hope to participate in the program that the prospect of gaining access to increased development funding is linked to their pursuit of genuine democratic reforms. The humanitarian instinct to loosen the standards, thereby allowing more countries to qualify for this new pot of resources, would inadvertently undercut the distinctive purpose of this program and should therefore be resisted.

Pursuing a democracy-centered development strategy recognizes that political orientation is a central feature to development, not just one other desirable objective. Such a perspective requires better integration into the foreign policies of the industrialized democracies. It is not a matter that can be solely relegated to their development agencies. In the United States, for example, it requires greater harmonization of the policies of the State, Treasury, and Commerce Departments—and in an age of shifting security threats, the Defense Department and Central Intelligence Agency. What is required is no less than a coherent foreign policy toward the developing world—something that has not existed in the United States for decades. Within agencies whose primary mission is development, such as the US Agency for International Development, better integration of experts dealing with democracy and development issues is needed. Despite their evident complementarities, there remains substantial stove-piping among specialists in these fields. Given the close relationship between democratic governance and positive development outcomes, this compartmentalization is a handicap.

Recognizing the central role that accountability institutions play in development also provides a framework for more effectively targeting development resources. While moving towards a "culture of accountability" and the adoption of political institutions that facilitate shared power and ensure checks and balances are ultimately up to the society in question, certain external efforts can assist this process. Perhaps most important is holding countries claiming to be democracies to international standards of openness, shared power, and political participation. By enforcing a high bar for international democratic legitimacy—with the diplomatic and capital market benefits this branding entails—the international community is ensuring that an incentive structure is in place to propel international reforms, which in turn have a better chance of being sustained. Meanwhile, internal efforts should focus on enhancing the capacity of democratizing countries' institutions of accountability: strengthening the caliber of the civil service, the judiciary, the oversight of the executive branch, and the autonomy of the private sector from political influences. Particular attention should be paid to the establishment of independent media. A free press augments the ability of other institutions, including civil society, to exert the checks and balances against centralized control so critical for sustained development. Mechanisms by which the general public can become better informed of policy debates, actions of public officials, management of public finances, and the functioning of markets will enhance transparency, efficiency, and pressure for corrective action. International efforts can help develop a cadre of trained journalists and media institutions with a clear understanding of their roles and responsibilities. Technical support for the management and marketing skills needed to run regional and national newspapers, television, and radio stations can also better ensure the financial and technological independence of these ventures over time. Notably, these efforts should not be limited to the public sector. Mobilizing private investment into media enterprises, most viably with local partners, further enhances prospects for their sustainability.

There is a compelling case for encouraging democratization in the developing world. Most countries that pursue political reform do economically better. They are not destined to political instability and economic stagnation as established thinking would have us believe. This, of course, is on top of the many moral and justice-based advantages of democracy. However, the policy indecisiveness bred by the conventional view risks unnecessarily propping up dictatorial or neo-authoritarian governments to the detriment of their populations and the world at large. Waiting for a country to develop economically before promoting democratic reform is a *non sequitur* in nearly all cases. Rather, what is needed is an increasingly sophisticated strategy on the part of the world's leading democracies to delineate genuine democratizers from those that are simply going through the motions—and then to ensure that adequate levels of financial and political support are available to foster their success.

Countries undertaking the difficult steps of political liberalization are engaged in one of the most challenging and important political processes of our time. In aggregate, they are shaping global political norms for the 21st century. It is incumbent on the established democracies to better understand this process so as to effect a more decisive and consistent influence.

Tamara Cofman Wittes

→ **NO**

Arab Democracy, American Ambivalence

Over the past year, the goal of democratizing the Arab Middle East has been elevated from wooly-headed ideal to national security imperative and a key part of the war on terrorism. The Bush administration judged that political dysfunction and failing, corrupt autocracies were making Muslims, and particularly Arabs, especially vulnerable to the appeal of radical Islamist ideologies. America's longtime rationale for supporting Arab autocrats was their promise of stability. But as the president recognized in his landmark speech at the National Endowment for Democracy in November, the price was high and the stability was deceptive. Hence the new "generational commitment" to promote democracy in the Arab world.

In pursuit of this commitment (and other worthy goals), the administration has already taken one enormously large and costly action: It has launched regime change in Iraq, an endeavor on which the U.S. government has lavished considerable blood and treasure, and in which it cannot afford to fail (though fail it might).

It has also done smaller things—and promised in the loftiest rhetoric to do a great many more such things in the decades ahead—to spur democratic development across the entire Middle East. In what the president calls a "forward strategy of freedom," the administration has vowed to reorient U.S. diplomacy and U.S. aid so as to lend moral and material support to pro-democracy forces throughout the Arab world. Its instruments to this end include the Middle East Partnership Initiative, just over one year old; a Middle East Free Trade Area; and a proposed doubling of the budget of the National Endowment for Democracy, a bipartisan grant-giving organization funded by the U.S. government to support the growth of democracy. In addition, at a series of summits this year with the G-8, NATO, and the European Union, Washington reportedly plans to enlist other advanced democracies to endorse reform principles for the Greater Middle East.

Where does this ambitious venture stand at the end of its first year? It is too early, of course, to offer any verdict as to outcomes. But this is clear: For the endeavor to succeed, many within the U.S. government must overcome their own misgivings about it. Only then will Washington convince the Arab world's lonely liberals of the seriousness of its commitment to the goal of "a democratic peace—a peace founded upon the dignity and rights of every man and woman." What's more, given the complexity and scope of the endeavor, its announced centrality to our national security, and its inevitable consequences for our standing in the world, it is none too soon to clarify underlying assumptions, question priorities, and point out pitfalls.

Why, after all, should Arab democrats believe us? Both "anti-imperialist" Arab intellectuals and American analysts note the credibility gap we confront in preaching democracy to the Middle East. Acknowledging our past support for autocrats, as President Bush did in November, is a start. But actually overcoming the credibility gap and building an effective democratization program requires a firmness of purpose the Bush administration has thus far not displayed. Whether it can and will do this remains to be seen.

To be sure, the administration has taken an irrevocable step with the invasion of Iraq. Having committed many billions of dollars to the democratization program there, America must make its success our first priority. One obvious reason is that if democracy takes hold in Iraq, it really might provide a powerful demonstration effect to the neighborhood.

Less obvious is the fact that America's current problems in Iraq—especially the insistence in Washington on a timetable and procedure for transferring sovereignty driven more by our own needs than Iraqis'—are right now providing a powerful *negative* demonstration effect to the neighborhood. The more repressive governments in the region are tightening their domestic controls, confident that we are distracted. Skeptical Arab commentators point out that American liberation has seemingly brought Iraqis nothing but chaos and death. Because President Bush linked the American democracy project in Iraq to reform in other Arab countries, the fate of democracy activists elsewhere in the Arab world now hangs on the success of the new Iraq. If the United States leaves Iraq's political reconstruction half-finished, Washington will have hung Arab democrats out to dry.

Some Arabs doubt President Bush's staying power on behalf of Iraqi democracy, but even more, they doubt that was ever his goal. This deeper skepticism is, sadly, justified by America's historical ambivalence about Arab democracy, an ambivalence that undermines even the new initiatives that are part of the forward strategy. America's error of "excusing and accommodating the lack of freedom in the Middle East," as the president put it, was compounded in 1992, when the U.S. government acquiesced in a military coup in Algeria designed to forestall a victory by the radical Islamic Salvation Front in the country's first free parliamentary elections. The "Algeria problem"—famously defined by veteran diplomat Edward Djerejian as "one man, one vote, one time"—still haunts American policymakers: the fear that free elections in the Arab world will bring to power Islamist governments that can claim democratic legitimacy but are anti-American and ultimately anti-democratic.

Add to this Washington's worry that assertive democracy-promotion in the Arab world will exacerbate tensions with Arab states whose cooperation on other issues is highly valued in the State Department and the Pentagon. The United States has little to lose by calling for a democratic transformation in states like Libya and Syria, but the Middle East is full of regimes America has worked closely with for years, and whose cooperation it desires on a variety of security and economic matters, not least the war on terrorism. In the past, the U.S. government has typically subordinated its concerns about governance and human rights to cooperation on defense, the Arab-Israeli peace process, and other core issues.

Because of these longstanding concerns, American democratization efforts in the Arab world have traditionally been modest, undertaken in consultation with the region's governments, and aimed at delivering technical assistance rather than altering the distribution of political power. Despite the new imperative driving the president's strategy, the policies devised to implement it so far—setting aside the unique case of Iraq—have not escaped these constraints.

In effect, the Bush administration has embraced the Arab regimes' own survival strategy of *controlled liberalization*. Most of the 22 Arab states themselves recognize their systemic failures, and seek to reform in ways that improve government and economic performance without changing the distribution of political power. While a few forward-leaning regimes have placed some power in the hands of their peoples through constitutional and electoral reforms, many others are trying to create just enough sense of forward motion and participation without power to alleviate the building public pressure for change at the top.

The premise underlying America's embrace of this gradual approach is that we can avoid the risk of Islamist victories and minimize bilateral tensions if we help existing governments reform, even if they resist opening up political competition and sharing power. In theory, our new assistance under the Middle East Partnership Initiative and the National Endowment for Democracy is also supposed to identify liberal forces within civil society, give them funding and training, and help them grow to the point where they can bring about velvet revolutions. This gradualist strategy assumes that, over time, liberalization will take on such momentum that the regimes will no longer be able to avoid devolution of power.

But that is an uncertain assumption: If existing regimes do lose control and chaos ensues, there is no guarantee that long-repressed liberals will win out. Indeed, the top-down "liberalization" underway in many Arab states has not relaxed state controls sufficiently to enable any third political force to organize, beyond the state and the Islamist opposition. The Islamists have the mosque as their forum for organizing, but freedom to organize outside the mosque—to talk politics and form parties—is still heavily restricted. So the regimes maintain control, and the Islamists remain the only alternative— as well as the excuse the regimes give Washington for deeming truly free politics too dangerous.

The larger the Algeria scenario looms in American policymakers' minds as the nightmare to be avoided at all costs, the more our policy is paralyzed; recalcitrant Arab leaders are quick to see this. But that's not the worst of it. The longer the U.S. government rewards regimes that "liberalize" without allowing new political forces to develop, the more the Islamists benefit from such limited political openings as exist. The more entrenched the Islamists become as the political alternative to the status quo, the more the language of Islamism becomes *the* language of protest politics, and other voices are marginalized. As an Arab official told me recently, "The only institution expressing freedom [to criticize the government] in the Arab world today is the mosque. That's why they're popular." The net effect of gradual "liberalization," then, may be not to drain the swamp of extremism, but to expand it.

For liberalization to have real meaning, the regimes themselves must change. No matter how many small-bore grants the U.S. government gives to improve parliamentary effectiveness, judicial independence, or the rule of law, the legislature and judiciary in most Arab countries will remain subordinated to their executives—until those executives give up emergency laws and restrain security forces. And no matter how much training the National Endowment for Democracy sponsors for women candidates or liberal politicians, they will not be able to compete in the political marketplace until their governments allow freedom of expression and association.

America can constrain the power of Arab autocrats and help create space for the emergence of liberal alternatives only by putting political pressure on the regimes and, at the same time, developing partnerships with indigenous reformers both in and out of government. To succeed, America must dovetail its assistance with the needs of Arab activists on the ground. This requires American officials to get outside their embassies and cultivate Arab allies. It also requires U.S. assistance programs to abandon familiar but ineffective approaches such as relying on international "trainers" and placing our funds at the service of governments with a different agenda.

This hasn't happened yet. In its first fiscal year, the Middle East Partnership Initiative spent just under $28 million. Only about $2 million of it went directly to local Arab nongovernmental organizations to help them expand their work, all of it in less controversial areas such as family law, literacy, and anticorruption campaigns. This meager involvement of the nongovernmental sector is largely the result of the Americans' working within, and not pushing, the bounds set by Arab governments: Nongovernmental organizations are tightly controlled in most Arab countries, and in many they are barred from receiving foreign funding. As a result, roughly one-quarter of the money for political, educational, and economic reform is spent through Arab governments or on training for government officials.

What did the reform programs do? In the political area, they trained the newly elected members of Morocco's feeble parliament ($600,000); assisted the elections commission in Yemen's de facto one-party state ($325,000); convened a group of Arab judges, whose courts are plagued by corruption and government interference, to discuss "judicial procedure, independence, ethics, appointments, and training" ($1,425,000); and so on. Economic reform projects include funding the translation of government documents, under the rubric of helping Arab states join the World Trade Organization and negotiate free-trade agreements with the United States. Education programs include "English in a Box" for Jordanian and Moroccan teachers ($400,000), Internet connections for Yemeni high schools ($1.5 million), and a "child-centered education program" for North Africa and the Gulf ($1.1 million). None of these programs is intrinsically bad. But as catalysts for tangible political change, they don't stand a chance.

Yet even as American aid programs fail to challenge autocratic regimes from below by supporting local activists, the administration—despite the president's fine words—is failing to challenge the regimes from above. Yet surely the United States must press Arab regimes to reform their politics, not just their political process. The United States should press a consistent message in the region: that controlled "liberalization" that creates quasi-democratic institutions with no power is not democratization. Elections are important, of course, but as Algeria taught us, they are not the primary need. Even more basic are the protections that enable a variety of citizens and groups to speak and organize and operate effectively in politics: freedom of the press, freedom of association, the right to peaceably assemble, and the legalization of political parties and advocacy groups. Some or all of these are absent in most Arab states.

Forcing governments to withdraw their control over the public square and give power to participatory institutions is necessary if non-Islamist political forces are to organize, formulate agendas, and press their case against the state in competition with the Islamists. In Kuwait—where the emir loosened controls under American prodding after the Iraqi occupation of the country in 1991—a decade of freedom of expression, the abolition of state security courts, and the election of parliaments with meaningful oversight over executive policy-making have enabled the emergence of a liberal political movement, with representatives in parliament, as a real alternative to the Islamists and the monarchy. While the Islamists are still the principal opposition, the liberals are viable competitors in the political arena. Even more significant, liberals in Kuwait occasionally ally themselves with Islamists to argue for political freedoms, just as they ally themselves with liberal factions within the royal family to try to contain Islamist initiatives. This embryonic coalition politics is the first evidence that a healthy political pluralism can develop in an Arab society and may be able to prevent liberalization from leading to "one man, one vote, one time." With these ingredients of democracy in place, it seems inevitable that those advocating the vote for women will soon succeed.

But in other states where political expression and the ability to organize are still severely restricted, non-Islamist social groups have a large gap to overcome before they can mount an effective challenge in the marketplace of ideas, much less in the political arena. In Saudi Arabia, for example, there is a group of intellectuals who are essentially liberal reformers. But since political parties and political meetings are outlawed and the press is controlled, they have no means of organizing themselves, no way of demonstrating their base of support within society, and no way to lobby the government beyond open letters to the crown prince.

The U.S. government must also do a better job of coordinating its assistance programs for civil society with its diplomatic agenda. To give one example, funds from the Middle East Partnership Initiative are currently flowing to Internews, an international nonprofit organization, to train journalists across the region—but this program is not accompanied by any noticeable pressure on regimes to relax their controls on the media. Saudi journalists are participating in the Internews program, but abstract discussions of journalistic independence are less relevant to their daily reality than the fact that several Saudi journalists lost their jobs or their columns last year after they questioned the influence of extremist clerics in politics and the exclusion of women from public life. When the United States fails to speak up for those who challenge the system, others have little incentive to try, and activists who would like to take President Bush's words seriously and look to America for support feel betrayed.

In order to build credibility with Arab democrats, American foreign policy must communicate to Arab governments that states that are actually changing the distribution of political power will enjoy better relations with the United States than those that talk about reform but fail to implement it. America has powerful carrots to offer. If we cared to work at devising targeted incentives for real reform we would discover a panoply of underused tools at our disposal. The president's proposal for a Middle East Free Trade Area, in particular, was conceived mainly as a means of integrating Arab economies into world markets and creating wealth, on the general assumption that economic liberalization over time encourages democracy. But opening trade negotiations could be made conditional on political progress. While the United States does not typically insert human rights clauses into trade agreements, it could certainly use trade talks with Arab nations to promote liberal change (notably in such areas as transparency and rule of law). What the United States must *not* do is direct even more money to Arab governments as a reward for limited reform. This, unfortunately, appears to be part of the "Helsinki" plan currently being discussed with the Europeans.

Finally, the United States must trust that shared interests with its Arab interlocutors will mediate the tensions that an effective democratization effort is bound to create. Many in the diplomatic establishment argue that a more aggressive approach to democratization will necessarily cost Arab cooperation with America's other regional goals. A broader perspective is essential.

America's relations with key states are grounded in a web of longstanding mutual interests and benefits. Such relationships can withstand tensions. Riyadh and Washington share interests in the strategic defense of the Gulf and stability in the price of oil, and they still would, even if the United States were to push Saudi Arabia harder on political reform. And in 2002, when Washington threatened to withhold additional aid to Egypt over the imprisonment of democracy activist (and dual U.S. citizen) Saad Eddin Ibrahim, it sent a strong message to the Egyptian government, and did no significant damage to bilateral relations. Although Ibrahim was released by a court ruling, local activists fear he received special treatment because of his dual nationality. The United States should make clear that its handling of his case is to be seen not as an outlier but as a precedent for U.S. policy toward our Arab friends.

If the administration means it when it calls Arab democracy necessary to American security, then we must build a policy to match and back it with political will. We cannot shrink from the tradeoffs required to achieve success, but must accept them and develop ways to manage both the costs for bilateral relations and the risks of undesired outcomes. It must be a policy that combines the assistance to indigenous liberals that the Middle East Partnership Initiative is supposed to provide but is not now structured to succeed at, with consistent, high-profile diplomatic and economic pressure and incentives to induce states to allow political freedom and to shift power away from the central executive.

America cannot promote democracy in the Arab world unless its strategy is credible. That requires staying the course in Iraq. Equally, it requires a carefully calibrated and robustly supported set of policies institutionalizing the forward strategy of freedom for the long haul. Otherwise, President Bush's powerful rhetoric on the universality of liberal values will prove to be a dead letter, and the cost to the United States, and to the peoples of the Arab world, will be immense.

POSTSCRIPT

Should Promoting Democracy Abroad Be a Top U.S. Priority?

Promoting democracy abroad was a cornerstone of foreign policy under both President Clinton and President George W. Bush. The means by which they pursued this objective, however, varied dramatically. While President Clinton sought to promote democratization through the bolstering of existing international agreements and institutions, President Bush has done so in a more unilateral fashion, often bypassing existing institutions and reinterpreting existing international agreements and practices. Thus, while President Clinton sought to promote political liberalism through politically liberal and institutional means, President Bush has sought to promote political liberalism through more politically realist means unconstrained by existing norms. While the latter strategy has contradictory elements within it, recent elections in Afghanistan, Palestine, and Iraq suggest that it is bearing fruit. The official U.S. position on promoting democracy can be found on the White House Web site at http://www.whitehouse.gov/news/releases/2003/11/20031106-11.html. For a useful debate on U.S. policy and the prospects for democracy in the Middle East, see Marina Ottaway and Thomas Carothers, "Middle East Democracy," *Foreign Policy* (November/December 2004).

The theory of democratic peace dates back to the work of Immanual Kant in the eighteenth century, but gained prominence in political science and the policy arena in the 1990s. For a summary of the contemporary debate, see Michael Brown, Sean Lynn-Jones and Steve Miller, eds., *Debating the Democratic Peace* (Cambridge University Press, 1996). For a discussion of the dangers associated with countries undergoing shifts to democracy, see Edward Mansfield and Jack Snyder, "Democratization and the Danger of War," *International Security* (Summer 1995) and Patricia Weitsman and George Shambaugh, "International Systems, Domestic Structures and Risk," *Journal of Peace Research* (2003).

Additional evidence on the link between democratization and economic development is available in Joseph Siegle's book, *The Democracy Advantage: How Democracies Promote Prosperity and Peace* (Routledge, 2004). Representing another dimension to this debate, the Center for Democracy and the Third Sector (CDATS) at Georgetown University provides training, research, and outreach on the relationship between democratic governance and those parts of civil society that are neither government nor business, including associations, non-governmental organizations, non-profit organizations, advocacy groups, citizen groups, and social movements, as well as the cultures, norms, and social values that enable these social phenomena. Links to this information is available on the Web site at http://www.georgetown.edu/centers/cdats/.

Internet References . . .

War, Peace, and Security Guide

An invaluable resource for general inquiries into global national security—the context within which American defense issues must be set—is this Web site maintained by the Information Resource Centre, Canadian Forces College.

http://wps.cfc.dnd.ca

DefenseLINK

The Department of Defense (DoD) provides an impressive array of information about virtually all aspects of the U.S. military establishment.

http://www.defenselink.mil

Center for Strategic and International Studies

Like all the other agencies and policy analysis centers that relate to defense, the Center for Strategic and International Studies (CSIS) has added extensively to its information on terrorism in the aftermath of the attacks on the United Sates in September 2001.

http://www.csis.org

The Homeland Security Institute

The Homeland Security Institute was involved in collecting and disseminating information and opinions about terrorist threats to the United States before the attacks in September 2001. This site contains links, suggested readings, and other valuable information.

http://www.homelandsecurity.org

U.S. National Security Issues

*F*or nearly a half-century, extending from the end of World War II into the early 1990s, the Cold War provided a context within which a great deal of American foreign policy was formulated. The primary policy goal was to guard against the dual dangers of communist ideology and the military might of the Soviet Union, China, and other communist countries. Now the Soviet Union is gone, and China, while still politically communist, has become a major player in the global market economy. In the aftermath of attacks by foreign terrorists on 9/11/ 2001, U.S. foreign policy has been dominated by concerns about terrorism, weapons of mass destruction, and a war in Iraq that was justified in part as a means of reducing these threats.

- Was the War in Iraq Justified?

- Should the United States Stay in Iraq?

- Should the United States Foster a Partition of Iraq?

ISSUE 4

Was the War in Iraq Justified?

YES: James Lacey, from "The Threat Saddam Posed: A Dictator and His WMD," *National Review* (April 2006)

NO: John B. Judis and Spencer Ackerman, from "The Selling of the Iraq War: The First Casualty," *The New Republic* (June 30, 2003)

ISSUE SUMMARY

YES: James Lacey, a journalist, argues that although there is evidence that Saddam Hussein did not have an inventory of weapons of mass destruction, he had the intent and the capability to produce such weapons on short notice and could easily have done so once UN inspectors departed had the United States not invaded Iraq.

NO: John B. Judis and Spencer Ackerman, respectively senior and associate editors at *The New Republic,* argue that the Bush administration greatly exaggerated intelligence information suggesting Iraq was a threat, particularly information suggesting ties between the Iraqi government and al Qaeda.

Iraq's alleged ties to the al Qaeda terrorist group were one of the main justifications the Bush administration offered for going to war against Iraq. While it is widely agreed that Iraq had ties to groups carrying out terrorist attacks against Israel, particularly Hamas, the extent and nature of any ties between Saddam Hussein's government and al Qaeda are hotly disputed. Although public opinion polls have shown that at various times as much as two-thirds of the public has believed that Saddam was involved in the 9/11 attacks, top Bush administration officials, including the president, the vice president, and Secretary of Defense Donald Rumsfeld, have never directly argued this. Instead, these leaders have argued that Iraq had various general ties to al Qaeda that suggest some level of common interest and perhaps cooperation between the two.

The case for ties between Iraq and al Qaeda rests on several points. First, although Saddam and Osama bin Laden disagreed on many issues, they shared a common interest in reducing the influence of the United States in the Middle East. Second, there is evidence, noted in the 9/11 commission report, that bin Laden sought assistance from Iraq in meetings with a senior Iraqi intelligence officer during his time in Sudan. Third, Saddam is widely believed to have offered a safe haven for bin Laden in Iraq in late 1998 or early 1999.

The skeptics of close ties between Iraq and al Qaeda are in a difficult position in the sense that it is difficult to prove a negative; that is, what evidence would definitively show the absence of close links between the two? Yet they dispute the evidence and logic of any operational ties between Iraq and al Qaeda. First, although Saddam and bin Laden both hoped to undermine America's role in the Middle East, Saddam had good reason to be wary of a messianic terrorist who had called him an "infidel" and whose desire to attack the United States, if acted upon and traced back to Iraq, could easily lead to an American attack on Iraq. Indeed, as it turned out, even the mere suspicion of ties between Iraq and al Qaeda proved sufficient to provoke the United States into removing Saddam from power. Second, as the 9/11 Commission Report notes, there is no indication that Iraq provided the weapons or training camps that bin Laden requested when he met with an Iraqi agent in Sudan in 1993. There is also no evidence that al Qaeda received any material, intelligence, or operational support from Iraq in the 9/11 attacks or any of its other attacks. Nor is there any sign that al Qaeda would have needed outside assistance, as its attacks required considerable patience and organization but were inexpensive, demanded only limited training, and did not rely upon any equipment not readily available on the black market or even the open market. Judis and Ackerman report that many CIA and FBI officials remain unconvinced of strong ties between Iraq and al Qaeda, and that these officials felt pressured by top Bush administration leaders, particularly Vice President Cheney, to slant the evidence in favor of concluding that an important connection existed between the two.

The second major rationale for intervening in Iraq was the Bush administration's claim that Iraq possessed a variety of weapons of mass destruction (WMD) and was seeking to build other weapons, including nuclear weapons. On this point, four years into the American occupation of Iraq, after an intensive search of the country and interrogation of Iraqi military officers and political officials, no evidence has been found that Iraq possessed significant WMD or was close to being able to build a nuclear weapon. This does not by itself entirely end the debate over whether the war was justified, however; one could still argue, as Lacey does, that Saddam Hussein had the intent to build such weapons if the United States had not invaded. Moreover, the Bush administration had to decide in 2003 whether to invade Iraq in the face of uncertain and ambiguous evidence on whether Iraq possessed WMD, and there is now evidence that Saddam Hussein intentionally exaggerated his weapons capabilities to deter regional adversaries, maintain his domestic support, and embolden his military forces. As much research on the causes of war demonstrates, asymmetries of information, and incentives to bluff or to misrepresent privately held information, are an important cause of wars. The contemporary debate over whether the war in Iraq was justified thus centers on whether the Bush administration knowingly or inadvertently exaggerated the evidence on the potential threat Iraq posed, above and beyond the inevitable uncertainties that attend any international conflict.

YES ↵

James Lacey

The Threat Saddam Posed

For almost three years, the anti-war protesters have kept up the drumbeat: "Bush lied and people died." Because weapons of mass destruction (WMD) were not found in Iraq, an endless stream of commentators continues to declare that Saddam Hussein was not the serious threat the administration claimed him to be. The critics usually go even further, and assert that sanctions and the destruction of WMD facilities by U.N. investigators had done so much damage to WMD infrastructure that it would have taken Saddam years to rebuild it even to a minimal capacity.

But these claims ignore huge amounts of contrary evidence; and most of this evidence can be found in the final report of the Iraqi Survey Group (ISG)—the very same report that many critics hold up as proof positive that Iraq was not a WMD threat. The evidence found by the ISG (an investigative commission set up by the Bush administration after the invasion of Iraq) confirms that Saddam was preparing to rapidly reconstitute his WMD program the moment he broke out of sanctions, which—given the frayed state of the coalition against him—would inevitably have happened. Not only did Bush not "lie"; the critics themselves are guilty of selectively citing evidence and of ignoring facts inconvenient to their argument. The ISG report, as well as the other evidence that continues to come to light, demonstrates that Saddam couldn't be trusted with the apparatus of a modern state, which he would have turned quickly back to producing WMD as soon as circumstances allowed.

Consider just one datum: According to the report, Saddam had the capability to start anthrax production within one week of making the decision to do so, and thereafter to produce *over ten tons* of weaponized anthrax a year. If even 1 percent of that amount—200 pounds—were released into the air over Washington, D.C., Congress's Office of Technology Assessment estimates that up to 3 million people would die.

How did Saddam keep such a massive capability from being discovered by the inspectors? Simply by hiding it in plain sight. For instance, at a facility called al-Hakam, Dr. Rihab Rashid Taha al-Azawi maintained a production line that produced ten tons of biopesticides for agricultural use each year. These biopesticides were produced in powder form and milled to 1 to 10 microns in size—but bio agents milled this finely are absolutely useless for agricultural purposes. Farmers found the biopesticide Dr. Rihab was sending them almost impossible to use, as it had to be handdropped one plant at a time or it would disappear. When they followed her recommendation to mix it with water and spray it, all they got was a thick slurry that clogged spray nozzles.

Though such finely milled powder may be useless for agricultural work, it is the perfect size for an inhalation bioweapon. (To be effective, anthrax must be milled at less then 10 microns.) Experts estimate that weaponized-anthrax spores that infect the skin will kill 50 percent of untreated patients; inhaled anthrax will kill 100 percent of untreated victims and 50 percent of those receiving immediate treatment. Simulations prior to Desert Storm estimated that an anthrax attack would kill over 25 percent of Coalition forces, as many as 200,000 men. In the hands of terrorists, this would be a weapon of incalculable value.

Dr. Rihab, the supposed agricultural scientist, is better known to U.S. intelligence agencies as "Dr. Germ," the head of Saddam's biological-warfare program for most of the decade immediately preceding the invasion. A 1999 Defense Intelligence Agency report called her the most dangerous woman in the world, and others have testified that she used political prisoners to test her bioweapons when she began to doubt she was getting accurate data from infected donkeys and dogs. When questioned by U.N. inspectors about al-Hakam, she claimed it was a chicken-feed plant. (Charles Duelfer, deputy executive chairman for the U.N. inspection team, later told reporters, "There were a few things that were peculiar about this animal-feed production plant, beginning with the extensive air defenses surrounding it.") According to the 1999 DIA report, the normally mild-mannered Rihab exploded into violent rages when questioned about al-Hakam, shouting, screaming, and, on one occasion, storming out of the room, before returning and smashing a chair.

In 1995, the U.N. inspectors showed Rihab documents obtained from the Israelis that demonstrated that Iraq had purchased ten tons of growth media from a British company called Oxoid. Shown this evidence, Rihab admitted to the inspectors that she had grown 19,000 liters of botulism toxin; 8,000 liters of anthrax; 2,000 liters of aflatoxins, which can cause liver cancer; clostridium perfringens, a bacterium that can cause gas gangrene; and ricin, a castor-bean derivative that can kill by impeding circulation. She also admitted conducting research into cholera, salmonella, foot-and-mouth disease, and camel pox. Neither the U.N. nor later inspectors were able to certify that all of this lethal cornucopia was ever destroyed.

In fact, in a document declassified just recently, there are indications that these deadly organisms—and the infrastructure to create them—were *not* destroyed. According to this document, persons at the highest levels of the regime were convinced that Iraq had eliminated its entire biological-weapons program: In a mid-1990s conference of Saddam's Revolutionary Command Council, Iraqi deputy prime minister Tariq Aziz told Saddam Hussein that he expected to resolve all biological issues with U.N. inspectors very quickly, because the program no longer existed. But Aziz was immediately contradicted by Saddam's son-in-law, who reminded Saddam that not everything had been disclosed, not even to supposedly trusted members of the regime's inner circle:

> Some teams work and no one knows of them. Sir, they [U.N. investigators] do not know all of the methods or all of the means nor all of the scientists nor all of the places. Frankly, yes, some activities were discovered . . . Sir, what they have discovered in the biological file is the least and most insignificant concern. The 17 tons [the amount of biological growth medium imported into Iraq] are not the problem, but the thousands of tons we have not accounted for or told how they were produced or how they were used . . . Sir, I would like to go back to this subject [biological weapons]: Do we have to reveal everything? If we continued with the silence and if the meeting took this line, I must say that it is in our interest not to reveal anything.

It is clear from the remainder of this transcript—a document captured by U.S. forces—that Tariq Aziz is both startled and angry to discover that Saddam has been keeping him in the dark about continuing WMD programs even as he tries to convince U.N. inspectors that no such programs still exist. It was not until Saddam's son-in-law defected in August 1995 that the U.N. was alerted to the fact that Iraq's biological program was far greater than they believed. But by this time Saddam was close to throwing the inspectors out—before they could uncover and dismantle the program in its entirety.

The ISG report goes out of its way to understate its WMD findings, but the underlying facts are duly alarming. For instance, the report goes on at great length about Iraq's attempts to import super-high-quality aluminum tubes in 2001–2003. At the time, this was cited by Western intelligence agencies as evidence that Saddam was trying to reconstitute his WMD program. The agencies claimed that the tubes were intended to be used to build centrifuges for nuclear enrichment. The Iraqis maintained, however, that the tubes were for 81mm rockets and had nothing to do with WMD. The ISG report accepts this explanation, even though it notes that Iraq was producing 50 lower-quality tubes a day for its 81mm rockets, and had no need for the expensive higher-quality imported tubes. The report also states that an Iraqi general, Husam Muhammad Amin, became worried about repeated attempts to purchase aluminum tubes that were subject to U.N. nuclear controls and took his concerns to Abdullah Mullah al-Huwaysh (deputy prime minister and head of the Military Industrial Commission). Nonetheless, Iraq persisted in its attempts to purchase the high-grade aluminum tubes and a contract was still being negotiated as Coalition tanks rolled into Baghdad.

Mobile Death Factories

The ISG report dedicates an entire annex—20 pages of exhaustive analysis—to proving that the two suspected mobile bio-labs were not what Secretary of State Colin Powell claimed they were, before the U.N., in the run-up to war. But the report gives the discovery of Iraq's *actual* mobile bioweapons labs only a little over one page of attention.

After the 1995 defection of Saddam's son-in-law forced Iraq to admit to an extensive bioweapons program that it had been hiding, U.N. inspectors made an effort to eliminate it. But Saddam was not ready to give up all he had gained, and large portions of the bioweapons research program were continued in small mobile labs by a band of key scientists and technicians under the auspices of the Iraqi Intelligence Service. The ISG report says its investigators were unsure if any of this continuing bioweapons research was military-related. (No one ever bothered to ask the investigators if there was any *other* conceivable purpose for bioweapons.)

The ISG found evidence that at least five mobile bioweapons research labs were operating in Baghdad right up to the commencement of the Coalition invasion. At one site, which building residents claimed was a biological lab, investigators found chemicals, along with documents from lab employees asking for hazardous-duty pay for having to work with biological materials. Another lab, discovered in a Baghdad mosque, was filled with equipment belonging to a known bioweapons scientist. Still another clandestine lab was identified by the ISG team at the Baghdad Central Public Health Laboratory, which employees admitted was operated by the Intelligence Service for several years prior to 2003.

According to the ISG report, Samarra Drug Industries had tanks available for bio-agent production ranging from 100 to 10,000 liters that could have begun bioweapons production three to four weeks after the order was given. Just one of these 10,000-liter tanks, if filled with botulinum toxin, would be enough to wipe out the global population more than twice over.

And it could be worse: Even a thimbleful of smallpox germs would kill tens of millions. If smallpox were released by terrorists in the United States, where inoculations ceased in 1972, the result would be a disaster of almost unimaginable magnitude. With some estimates claiming that each infected person can infect between 10 and 17 others, the smallpox germ is the bioweapon of choice for terrorists. Given Saddam's close links to terror groups it would have been sheer folly to allow his regime to possess even the smallest capability to produce the germ.

The report states that the ISG found evidence that Iraq had in fact obtained smallpox cultures from the former Soviet Union in 1992. An Iraqi scientist also described for the ISG Iraq's efforts to develop smallpox for biological warfare by using eggs and viral cultures. ISG investigators visited two labs where they found equipment that appeared to be used for making animal vaccines, but "this dual-use equipment was assessed to be easily diverted to produce smallpox or other pathogenic viruses." The ISG also visited a location where animal pox vaccines were produced in tissue culture; its assessment was that this equipment could be used for the rapid production of large amounts of smallpox virus.

The ISG report states in bold font that investigators "uncovered no evidence to support smallpox R&D at ASVI [Al-Amiriyah Serum and Vaccine] Institute for possible use as an offensive BW agent." Since this was the only facility in Iraq previously known to be associated with smallpox, the ISG's declaration that no biowarfare research was being conducted there would seem to give the institute a clear bill of health. But the report also says that Dr. Rihab (a.k.a. Dr. Germ) made frequent visits to the institute to conduct unidentified biological-warfare research, and that the institute maintained a "small capability" for organic production; it needs to be stressed that when it comes to smallpox, you need only a very small amount to cause a catastrophic amount of damage.

A Tyrant's Designs

In summary, then, what the Iraqi Survey Group discovered was that Saddam was maintaining a biological-warfare research program right up to the Coalition invasion, and that he had the installed capability to produce bio-toxins. Would he have used them? An amazing conversation between Saddam and his inner circle was recorded in a captured but undated Iraqi document.

Saddam   I want to make sure that—close the door please (door slams)—the germ and chemical warheads, as well as the chemical and germ bombs, are available to [those concerned], so that in case we ordered an attack, they can do it without missing any of their targets?

Husayn Kamil   Sir, if you'll allow me. Some of the chemicals now are distributed, this is according to the last report from the Minister of Defense, which was submitted to you, Sir. Chemical warheads are stored and are ready at Air Bases, and they know how and when to deal with, as well as arm these heads. Also, some other artillery machines and rockets (missiles) are available from the army. While some of the empty "stuff" is available for us, our position is very good, and we don't have any operational problems. Moreover, in the past, many substantial items and material were imported; now, we were able to establish a local project, which was established to comply with daily production. Also, another bigger project will be finalized within a month, as well as a third project in the coming two to three months that will keep us on the safe side, in terms of supply. We, Sir, only deal in common materials like phosphorus, ethyl alcohol, and methyl (interrupted) . . .

Saddam   What is it doing with you, I need these germs to be fixed on the missiles, and tell him to hit, because starting the 15th, everyone should be ready for the action to happen at anytime, and I consider Riyadh as a target . . .

Husayn Kamil   (door slams) Sir, we have three types of germ weapons, but we have to decide which one we should use, some types stay capable for many years (interrupted).

Saddam   We want the long term, the many years kind. . . .

Husayn Kamil   . . . There has to be a decision about which method of attack we use; a missile, a fighter bomb, or a fighter plane.

Saddam   With them all, all the methods . . . I want as soon as possible, if we are not transferring the weapons, to issue a clear order to [those concerned] that the weapon should be in their hands as soon as possible. I might even give them a "non-return access." *[Translator Comment: to have access to the weapons; to take them with them and not to return them.]* I will give them an order stating that at "one moment," if I'm not there and you don't hear my voice, you will hear somebody else's voice, so you can receive the order from him, and then you can go attack your targets. I want the weapons to be distributed to targets; I want Riyadh and Jeddah, which are the biggest Saudi cities with all the decision makers, and the Saudi rulers live there. This is for the germ and chemical weapons. . . . Also, all the Israeli cities, all of them. Of course you should concentrate on Tel Aviv, since it is their center.

Husayn Kamil   Sir, the best way to transport this weapon and achieve the most harmful effects would come by using planes, like a crop plane; to scatter it. This is, Sir, a thousand times more harmful. This is according to the analyses of the technicians (interrupted) . . .

Saddam   May God help us do it . . . We will never lower our heads as long as we are alive, even if we have to destroy everybody.

And while biological weapons may have been the most dangerous near-term threat that Saddam could pose to the world, other WMD programs were also being fostered. As Oil for Food money began to fill his coffers, Saddam was restarting chemical-warfare, ballistic-missile, and even nuclear programs. After Desert Storm, Saddam encouraged Iraqi officials to, in his words, "preserve the nation's scientific brain trust essential for WMD." He told his close advisers that he wanted to keep Iraq's nuclear scientists fully employed, and this theme of preserving personnel resources persisted throughout the sanctions period. According to his science adviser, Ja'far Diya' Ja'far Hashim, "Saddam's primary concern was retaining cadres of skilled scientists to facilitate reconstitution of WMD programs after sanctions were lifted." Saddam instructed the general directors of Iraqi state companies to prevent key scientists from the pre-1991 WMD program from leaving the country. Saddam, as quoted by his presidential secretary, Abid Hamid Mahmud, also told scientists that they should "preserve plans in their minds" and "keep the brains of Iraq's scientists fresh."

Husayn Kamil—Saddam's son-in-law and minister of military industrialization—announced in a speech in 1995, to a large audience of WMD scientists at the Space Research Center in Baghdad, that WMD programs would be resumed and expanded as soon as U.N. inspectors left Iraq. Clearly, Saddam viewed inspectors and sanctions as little more than a temporary obstacle. In a written statement to the ISG, Saddam's presidential secretary stated that "if sanctions were lifted and there was no U.N. monitoring, then it was possible for Saddam to continue WMD activities and in my estimation it would have been done in total secrecy because he [Saddam] had learned from 1991."

How Imminent a Threat?

The question remains as to how long it would have taken Saddam to reconstitute WMD programs once he had escaped the sanctions regime. We have already seen the answer, in the case of bioweapons: a matter of weeks. For the rest of his programs, estimates vary. Tariq Aziz said recently that "Saddam would have restarted his WMD programs, beginning with the nuclear program, after sanctions." Aziz estimated that Iraq would have a full WMD capability two years after sanctions ended. Saddam's minister of military industrialization, Abdullah Mullah al-Huwaysh, told the ISG that Saddam would have reconstituted all of the proscribed programs within five years: This would have included having a sizeable nuclear inventory on hand for immediate use. Huwaysh also stated that in response to a Saddam inquiry regarding how long it would take to start mass production of chemical weapons, he told the dictator that mustard-gas production could start within six months, but Sarin and VX would take a bit longer. Other WMD scientists claimed they had the materials and equipment to start mustard production in days, though such a fast start could damage the production equipment. By 2002, Iraq was already purchasing the precursor chemicals for the production of Sarin.

The ISG report quotes one senior official as stating that by successfully targeting scientists from Russia, Belarus, Bulgaria, Yugoslavia, China, and several other countries, and coupling them with resident know-how, Saddam ensured that he could rebuild his entire WMD program within two years.

After 1991, Iraq's own resident WMD scientists were moved from government labs into universities: There they could carry out their work without fear of being targeted by Coalition aircraft or much bothered by U.N. inspectors. According to the ISG report, "Saddam used the Ministry of Higher Education and Scientific Research through its universities to maintain, develop, and acquire expertise, to advance or preserve existent research projects and developments, and to procure goods prohibited by U.N. sanctions." By 1997, the number of university instructors working on WMD-related projects increased from a handful to 3,300, while a further 700–800 were sent to WMD-related companies on a regular basis to help with technical problems.

As the billions in Oil for Food cash flowed in, Saddam "began investing his growing reserves of hard currency in his militaryindustrial complex, increasing access to dual-use items and materials, and creating numerous research and development programs." Between 1996 and 2002, the annual budget for the military-industrialization ministry—which was responsible for WMD development—increased over forty-fold; by the time the Coalition invaded, it had grown to 1 trillion Iraqi dinars. The military "technical research" projects at Iraqi universities had skyrocketed from about 40 projects in 1997 to 3,200; and the military-industrialization workforce had expanded by over 50 percent in just three years. Saddam's WMD program was ready to move into overdrive.

Financial salvation led Saddam to start thinking again about nuclear weapons. In 1999 he met with his senior nuclear scientists and offered to provide them with whatever they needed, and immediately thereafter new funds began to flow to the Iraqi Atomic Energy Commission (IAEC). In 2001, Saddam mandated a large budget increase for the IAEC and increased the salaries of nuclear scientists tenfold. He also directed the head of the IAEC to keep nuclear scientists together, and instituted new privileges for IAEC scientists, while also investing in numerous new projects. From 2001 onward, Saddam convened frequent meetings with the IAEC to highlight new achievements.

While money flowed back into the nuclear project, Saddam also maintained an extensive ballistic-missile program. He had previously told his ministers that he did not consider ballistic missiles to be WMD and that he would never accept missile-range restrictions. In 2002, Iraq began serial production of the Al Samoud II, a ballistic missile that violated U.N. range limits: Test firings reached 183 miles (294 km). By the time the Coalition invaded, 76 of these missiles had been produced and more were in the pipeline. Saddam also, in early 2002, directed the design and production of a missile with a range of 650 to 750 km, and told Huwaysh that he wanted it within six months. Huwaysh relates that when Saddam was informed that production would take longer, and that the twin Volga engines they could sneak through sanctions would reach only 550 km, he left the room "profoundly disappointed." The difference would keep Tel Aviv out of range. (These were not the only means Saddam pursued to strike at Israel: His al-Quds organization was building four UAVs—pilotless drones—that were to be turned over to Hamas for the express purpose of killing Israeli prime minister Ariel Sharon.)

What becomes clear, as example piles upon example in the ISG Report, is that this document that has been used by one side of the debate as proof that Saddam had no WMD capability actually says quite the opposite. The fact that no weapons stockpiles were found in Iraq does not mean that Iraq was not a threat. According to the report, Saddam could start producing deadly bioweapons within a week of deciding to do it; he retained the capability to produce smallpox; he had the capability to start producing chemical weapons such as mustard gas within days or at most weeks of deciding to do so; he was actively preparing to produce the nerve agents Sarin and VX; he was pouring cash into nuclear research; he was working on his ballistic-missile program even as the Coalition crossed the border into Iraq.

In short, the unholy trinity of the WMD world—bioweapons, chemical weapons, and nuclear weapons—were either readily available or in the process of being created, along with the missiles required to deliver them anywhere in the region, when Coalition armor rolled into Baghdad. Three years later, we should still be very glad it did.

John B. Judis and
Spencer Ackerman

➡ **NO**

The Selling of the Iraq War:
The First Casualty

Foreign policy is always difficult in a democracy. Democracy requires openness. Yet foreign policy requires a level of secrecy that frees it from oversight and exposes it to abuse. As a result, Republicans and Democrats have long held that the intelligence agencies—the most clandestine of foreign policy institutions—should be insulated from political interference in much the same way as the higher reaches of the judiciary. As the Tower Commission, established to investigate the Iran-Contra scandal, warned in November 1987, "The democratic processes . . . are subverted when intelligence is manipulated to affect decisions by elected officials and the public."

If anything, this principle has grown even more important since September 11, 2001. The Iraq war presented the United States with a new defense paradigm: preemptive war, waged in response to a prediction of a forthcoming attack against the United States or its allies. This kind of security policy requires the public to base its support or opposition on expert intelligence to which it has no direct access. It is up to the president and his administration—with a deep interest in a given policy outcome—nonetheless to portray the intelligence community's findings honestly. If an administration represents the intelligence unfairly, it effectively forecloses an informed choice about the most important question a nation faces: whether or not to go to war. That is exactly what the Bush administration did when it sought to convince the public and Congress that the United States should go to war with Iraq.

From late August 2002 to mid-March of [2003], the Bush administration made its case for war by focusing on the threat posed to the United States by Saddam Hussein's nuclear, chemical, and biological weapons and by his purported links to the Al Qaeda terrorist network. Officials conjured up images of Iraqi mushroom clouds over U.S. cities and of Saddam transferring to Osama bin Laden chemical and biological weapons that could be used to create new and more lethal September elevenths. In Nashville on August 26, 2002, Vice President Dick Cheney warned of a Saddam "armed with an arsenal of these weapons of terror" who could "directly threaten America's friends throughout the region and subject the United States or any other nation to nuclear blackmail." In Washington on September 26, Secretary of Defense Donald Rumsfeld claimed he had "bulletproof" evidence of ties between Saddam and Al Qaeda.

And, in Cincinnati on October 7, President George W. Bush warned, "The Iraqi dictator must not be permitted to threaten America and the world with horrible poisons and diseases and gases and atomic weapons." Citing Saddam's association with Al Qaeda, the president added that this "alliance with terrorists could allow the Iraqi regime to attack America without leaving any fingerprints."

Yet there was no consensus within the American intelligence community that Saddam represented such a grave and imminent threat. Rather, interviews with current and former intelligence officials and other experts reveal that the Bush administration culled from U.S. intelligence those assessments that supported its position and omitted those that did not. The administration ignored, and even suppressed, disagreement within the intelligence agencies and pressured the CIA to reaffirm its preferred version of the Iraqi threat. Similarly, it stonewalled, and sought to discredit, international weapons inspectors when their findings threatened to undermine the case for war.

Three months after the invasion, the United States may yet discover the chemical and biological weapons that various governments and the United Nations have long believed Iraq possessed. But it is unlikely to find, as the Bush administration had repeatedly predicted, a reconstituted nuclear weapons program or evidence of joint exercises with Al Qaeda—the two most compelling security arguments for war. Whatever is found, what matters as far as American democracy is concerned is whether the administration gave Americans an honest and accurate account of what it knew. The evidence to date is that it did not, and the cost to U.S. democracy could be felt for years to come.

The Battle over Intelligence

Fall 2001 Fall 2002

The Bush administration decided to go to war with Iraq in the late fall of 2001. At Camp David on the weekend after the September 11 attacks, Deputy Defense Secretary Paul Wolfowitz floated the idea that Iraq, with more than 20 years of inclusion on the State Department's terror-sponsor list, be held immediately accountable. In his memoir, speechwriter David Frum recounts that, in December, after the Afghanistan campaign against bin Laden and his Taliban sponsors, he was told to come up with a justification for war with Iraq to include in Bush's State of the Union address in January 2002. But, in selling the war to the American public during the next year, the Bush administration faced significant obstacles.

In the wake of September 11, 2001, many Americans had automatically associated Saddam's regime with Al Qaeda and enthusiastically backed an invasion. But, as the immediate horror of September 11 faded and the war in Afghanistan concluded successfully (and the economy turned downward), American enthusiasm diminished. By mid-August 2002, a Gallup poll showed support for war with Saddam at a post-September 11 low, with 53 percent in favor and 41 percent opposed—down from 61 percent to 31 percent just two months before. Elite opinion was also turning against war, not only among liberal Democrats but among former Republican officials, such as Brent Scowcroft and Lawrence Eagleburger. In Congress, even conservative

Republicans such as Senate Majority Leader Trent Lott and House Majority Leader Dick Armey began to express doubts that war was justified. Armey declared on August 8, 2002, "If we try to act against Saddam Hussein, as obnoxious as he is, without proper provocation, we will not have the support of other nation-states who might do so."

Unbeknownst to the public, the administration faced equally serious opposition within its own intelligence agencies. At the CIA, many analysts and officials were skeptical that Iraq posed an imminent threat. In particular, they rejected a connection between Saddam and Al Qaeda. According to a New York Times report in February 2002, the CIA found "no evidence that Iraq has engaged in terrorist operations against the United States in nearly a decade, and the agency is also convinced that President Saddam Hussein has not provided chemical or biological weapons to Al Qaeda or related terrorist groups." . . .

Had the administration accurately depicted the consensus within the intelligence community in 2002—that Iraq's ties with Al Qaeda were inconsequential; that its nuclear weapons program was minimal at best; and that its chemical and biological weapons programs, which had yielded significant stocks of dangerous weapons in the past, may or may not have been ongoing—it would have had a very difficult time convincing Congress and the American public to support a war to disarm Saddam. But the Bush administration painted a very different, and far more frightening, picture. Representative Rush Holt, a New Jersey Democrat who ultimately voted against the war, says of his discussions with constituents, "When someone spoke of the need to invade, [they] invariably brought up the example of what would happen if one of our cities was struck. They clearly were convinced by the administration that Saddam Hussein—either directly or through terrorist connections—could unleash massive destruction on an American city. And I presume that most of my colleagues heard the same thing back in their districts." One way the administration convinced the public was by badgering CIA Director Tenet into endorsing key elements of its case for war even when it required ignoring the classified findings of his and other intelligence agencies.

As a result of its failure to anticipate the September 11 attacks, the CIA, and Tenet in particular, were under almost continual attack in the fall of 2001. Congressional leaders, including Richard Shelby, the ranking Republican on the Senate Intelligence Committee, wanted Tenet to resign. But Bush kept Tenet in his job, and, within the administration, Tenet and the CIA came under an entirely different kind of pressure: Iraq hawks in the Pentagon and in the vice president's office, reinforced by members of the Pentagon's semi-official Defense Policy Board, mounted a year-long attempt to pressure the CIA to take a harder line against Iraq—whether on its ties with Al Qaeda or on the status of its nuclear program.

A particular bone of contention was the CIA's analysis of the ties between Saddam and Al Qaeda. In the immediate aftermath of September 11, former CIA Director James Woolsey, a member of the Defense Policy Board who backed an invasion of Iraq, put forth the theory—in this magazine and elsewhere—that Saddam was connected to the World Trade Center attacks. In

September 2001, the Bush administration flew Woolsey to London to gather evidence to back up his theory, which had the support of Wolfowitz and Richard Perle, then the Defense Policy Board chairman. While Wolfowitz and Perle had their own long-standing and complex reasons for wanting to go to war with Iraq, they and other administration officials believed that, if they could tie Saddam to Al Qaeda, they could justify the war to the American people. As a veteran aide to the Senate Intelligence Committee observes, "They knew that, if they could really show a link between Saddam Hussein and Al Qaeda, then their objective, . . . which was go in and get rid of Hussein, would have been a foregone conclusion."

But this theory immediately encountered resistance from the CIA and other intelligence agencies. Woolsey's main piece of evidence for a link between Saddam and Al Qaeda was a meeting that was supposed to have taken place in Prague in April 2001 between lead September 11 hijacker Mohamed Atta and an Iraqi intelligence official. But none of the intelligence agencies could place Atta in Prague on that date. (Indeed, receipts and other travel documents placed him in the United States.) An investigation by Czech officials dismissed the claim, which was based on a single unreliable witness. The CIA was also receiving other information that rebutted a link between Iraq and Al Qaeda. After top Al Qaeda leader Abu Zubaydah was captured in March 2002, he was debriefed by the CIA, and the results were widely circulated in the intelligence community. As The New York Times reported, Zubaydah told his captors that bin Laden himself rejected any alliance with Saddam. "I remember reading the Abu Zubaydah debriefing last year, while the administration was talking about all of these other reports [of a Saddam-Al Qaeda link], and thinking that they were only putting out what they wanted," a CIA official told the paper. Zubaydah's story, which intelligence analysts generally consider credible, has since been corroborated by additional high-ranking Al Qaeda terrorists now in U.S. custody, including Ramzi bin Al Shibh and September 11 architect Khalid Shaikh Mohammed.

Facing resistance from the CIA, administration officials began a campaign to pressure the agency to toe the line. Perle and other members of the Defense Policy Board, who acted as quasi-independent surrogates for Wolfowitz, Cheney, and other administration advocates for war in Iraq, harshly criticized the CIA in the press. The CIA's analysis of Iraq, Perle said, "isn't worth the paper it is written on." In the summer of 2002, Vice President Cheney made several visits to the CIA's Langley headquarters, which were understood within the agency as an attempt to pressure the low-level specialists interpreting the raw intelligence. "That would freak people out," says one former CIA official. "It is supposed to be an ivory tower. And that kind of pressure would be enormous on these young guys."

But the Pentagon found an even more effective way to pressure the agency. In October 2001, Wolfowitz, Rumsfeld, and Undersecretary of Defense for Policy Douglas Feith set up a special intelligence operation in the Pentagon to "think through how the various terrorist organizations relate to each other and . . . state sponsors," in Feith's description. Their approach echoed the "Team B" strategy that conservatives had used in the past: establishing a separate entity to offer alternative intelligence analyses to the CIA. Conservatives had done this in 1976, criticizing and intimidating the agency over its estimates of Soviet military strength, and again in 1998, arguing for the necessity of missile defense. (Wolfowitz had participated in both projects; the latter was run by Rumsfeld.) This time, the new entity—headed by Perle protégé Abram Shulsky—reassessed intelligence already collected by the CIA along with information from Iraqi defectors and, as Feith remarked coyly at a press conference earlier this month, "came up with some interesting observations about the linkages between Iraq and Al Qaeda." In August 2002, Feith brought the unit to Langley to brief the CIA about its findings. If the separate intelligence unit wasn't enough to challenge the CIA, Rumsfeld also began publicly discussing the creation of a new Pentagon position, an undersecretary for intelligence, who would rival the CIA director and diminish the authority of the agency.

In its classified reports, the CIA didn't diverge from its initial skepticism about the ties between Al Qaeda and Saddam. But, under pressure from his critics, Tenet began to make subtle concessions. In March 2002, Tenet told the Senate Armed Services Committee that the Iraqi regime "had contacts with Al Qaeda" but declined to elaborate. He would make similar ambiguous statements during the congressional debate over war with Iraq. . . .

By the fall of 2002, when public debate over the war really began, the administration had created consternation in the intelligence agencies. The press was filled for the next two months with quotes from CIA officials and analysts complaining of pressure from the administration to toe the line on Iraq. Says one former staff member of the Senate Intelligence Committee, "People [kept] telling you first that things weren't right, weird things going on, different people saying, 'There's so much pressure, you know, they keep telling us, go back and find the right answer,' things like that." For the most part, this pressure was not reflected in the CIA's classified reports, but it would become increasingly evident in the agency's declassified statements and in public statements by Tenet. The administration hadn't won an outright endorsement of its analysis of the Iraqi threat, but it had undermined and intimidated its potential critics in the intelligence community.

The Battle in Congress

Fall 2002

The administration used the anniversary of September 11, 2001, to launch its public campaign for a congressional resolution endorsing war, with or without U.N. support, against Saddam. . . .

In speeches and interviews, administration officials . . . warned of the connection between Saddam and Al Qaeda. On September 25, 2002, Rice insisted, "There clearly are contacts between Al Qaeda and Iraq. . . . There clearly is testimony that some of the contacts have been important contacts and that there's a relationship there." On the same day, President Bush warned of the danger that "Al Qaeda becomes an extension of Saddam's madness." Rice, like Rumsfeld—who the next day would call evidence of a Saddam-bin Laden link "bulletproof"—said she could not share the administration's evidence with the public without endangering intelligence sources. But Bob Graham, the Florida Democrat who chaired the Senate Intelligence Committee, disagreed. On September 27, Paul Anderson, a spokesman for Graham, told USA Today that the senator had seen nothing in the CIA's classified reports that established a link between Saddam and Al Qaeda.

The Senate Intelligence Committee, in fact, was the greatest congressional obstacle to the administration's push for war. Under the lead of Graham and Illinois Senator Richard Durbin, the committee enjoyed respect and deference in the Senate and the House, and its members could speak authoritatively, based on their access to classified information, about whether Iraq was developing nuclear weapons or had ties to Al Qaeda. And, in this case, the classified information available to the committee did not support the public pronouncements being made by the CIA.

In the late summer of 2002, Graham had requested from Tenet an analysis of the Iraqi threat. According to knowledgeable sources, he received a 25-page classified response reflecting the balanced view that had prevailed earlier among the intelligence agencies—noting, for example, that evidence of an Iraqi nuclear program or a link to Al Qaeda was inconclusive. Early that September, the committee also received the DIA's classified analysis, which reflected the same cautious assessments. But committee members became worried when, midway through the month, they received a new CIA analysis of the threat that highlighted the Bush administration's claims and consigned skepticism to footnotes. According to one congressional staffer who read the document, it highlighted "extensive Iraqi chem-bio programs and nuclear programs and links to terrorism" but then included a footnote that read, "This information comes from a source known to fabricate in the past." The staffer concluded that "they didn't do analysis. What they did was they just amassed everything they could that said anything bad about Iraq and put it into a document."

Graham and Durbin had been demanding for more than a month that the CIA produce an NIE on the Iraqi threat—a summary of the available intelligence, reflecting the judgment of the entire intelligence community—and toward the end of September, it was delivered. Like Tenet's earlier letter, the classified NIE was balanced in its assessments. Graham called on Tenet to produce a declassified version of the report that could guide members in voting on the resolution. Graham and Durbin both hoped the declassified report would rebut the kinds of overheated claims they were hearing from administration spokespeople. As Durbin tells tnr, "The most frustrating thing I find is when you have credible evidence on the intelligence committee that is directly contradictory to statements made by the administration."

On October 1, 2002, Tenet produced a declassified NIE. But Graham and Durbin were outraged to find that it omitted the qualifications and countervailing evidence that had characterized the classified version and played up the claims that strengthened the administration's case for war. . . .

Five of the nine Democrats on the Senate Intelligence Committee, including Graham and Durbin, ultimately voted against the resolution, but they were unable to convince other committee members or a majority in the Senate itself. This was at least in part because they were not allowed to divulge what they knew: While Graham and Durbin could complain that the adminis-tration's and Tenet's own statements contradicted the classified reports they had read, they could not say what was actually in those reports.

Bush, meanwhile, had no compunction about claiming that the "evi-dence indicates Iraq is reconstituting its nuclear weapons program." In the words of one former Intelligence Committee staffer, "He is the president of the United States. And, when the president of the United States says, 'My advisers and I have sat down, and we've read the intelligence, and we believe there is a tie between Iraq and Al Qaeda,' . . . you take it seriously. It carries a huge amount of weight." Public opinion bears the former staffer out. By November 2002, a Gallup poll showed 59 percent in favor of an invasion and only 35 percent against. In a December Los Angeles Times poll, Americans thought, by a 90 percent to 7 percent margin, that Saddam was "currently developing weapons of mass destruction." And, in an ABC/Washington Post poll, 81 percent thought Iraq posed a threat to the United States. The Bush administration had won the domestic debate over Iraq—and it had done so by withholding from the public details that would have undermined its case for war.

The Battle with the Inspectors

Winter–Spring 2003

. . . On February 5, Secretary of State Colin Powell took the administration's case to the Security Council. Powell's presentation was by far the most impressive the administration would make—according to U.S. News and World Report, he junked much of what the CIA had given him to read, call-ing it "bullshit"—but it was still based on a hyped and incomplete view of U.S. intelligence on Iraq. Much of what was new in Powell's speech was raw data that had come into the CIA's possession but had not yet undergone seri-ous analysis. In addition to rehashing the aluminum-tube claims, Powell charged, for instance, that Iraq was trying to obtain magnets for uranium enrichment. Powell also described a "potentially . . . sinister nexus between Iraq and the Al Qaeda terrorist network, a nexus that combines classic ter-rorist organizations and modern methods of murder." But Powell's evidence consisted of tenuous ties between Baghdad and an Al Qaeda leader, Abu Musab Al Zarqawi, who had allegedly received medical treatment in Baghdad and who, according to Powell, operated a training camp in Iraq specializing in poisons. Unfortunately for Powell's thesis, the camp was located in northern Iraq, an area controlled by the Kurds rather than Saddam and policed by U.S. and British warplanes. One Hill staffer familiar with the classified documents on Al Qaeda tells TNR, "So why would that be proof of some Iraqi government connection to Al Qaeda? [It] might as well be in Iran."

But, by the time Powell made his speech, the administration had stopped worrying about possible rebukes from U.S. intelligence agencies. On the con-trary, Tenet sat directly behind Powell as he gave his presentation. And, with the GOP takeover of the Senate, the Intelligence Committee had passed into the hands of a docile Republican chairman, Pat Roberts of Kansas. . . .

Aftermath

What we must not do in the face of a "mortal threat," Cheney instructed a Nashville gathering of the Veterans of Foreign Wars in August 2002, "is give in to wishful thinking or willful blindness." Cheney's admonition is resonant, but not for the reasons he intended. The Bush administration displayed an acute case of willful blindness in making its case for war. Much of its evidence for a reconstituted nuclear program, a thriving chemical-biological development program, and an active Iraqi link with Al Qaeda was based on what intelligence analysts call "rumint." Says one former official with the National Security Council, "It was a classic case of rumint, rumor-intelligence plugged into various speeches and accepted as gospel."

In some cases, the administration may have deliberately lied. If Bush didn't know the purported uranium deal between Iraq and Niger was a hoax, plenty of people in his administration did—including, possibly, Vice President Cheney, who would have seen the president's State of the Union address before it was delivered. Rice and Rumsfeld also must have known that the aluminum tubes that they presented as proof of Iraq's nuclear ambitions were discounted by prominent intelligence experts. And, while a few administration officials may have genuinely believed that there was a strong connection between Al Qaeda and Saddam Hussein, most probably knew they were constructing castles out of sand.

The Bush administration took office pledging to restore "honor and dignity" to the White House. And it's true: Bush has not gotten caught having sex with an intern or lying about it under oath. But he has engaged in a pattern of deception concerning the most fundamental decisions a government must make. The United States may have been justified in going to war in Iraq—there were, after all, other rationales for doing so—but it was not justified in doing so on the national security grounds that President Bush put forth throughout last fall and winter. He deceived Americans about what was known of the threat from Iraq and deprived Congress of its ability to make an informed decision about whether or not to take the country to war.

The most serious institutional casualty of the administration's campaign may have been the intelligence agencies, particularly the CIA. Some of the CIA's intelligence simply appears to have been defective, perhaps innocently so. Durbin says the CIA's classified reports contained extensive maps where chemical or biological weapons could be found. Since the war, these sites have not yielded evidence of any such weapons. But the administration also turned the agency—and Tenet in particular—into an advocate for the war with Iraq at a time when the CIA's own classified analyses contradicted the public statements of the agency and its director. Did Tenet really fact-check Bush's warning that Iraq could threaten the United States with UAVs? Did he really endorse Powell's musings on the links between Al Qaeda and Saddam? Or had Tenet and his agency by then lost any claim to the intellectual honesty upon which U.S. foreign policy critically depends—particularly in an era of preemptive war? . . .

It may well be that, in the not-too-distant future, preemptive military action will become necessary—perhaps against a North Korea genuinely bent on incinerating Seoul or a nuclear Pakistan that has fallen into the hands of radical Islamists. In such a case, we the people will look to our leaders for an honest assessment of the threat. But, next time, thanks to George W. Bush, we may not believe them until it is too late.

POSTSCRIPT

Was the War in Iraq Justified?

The controversy over possible ties between al Qaeda and Iraq is likely to continue until historians have an opportunity to examine all of the relevant intelligence information from the archives of the United States, Iraq, and the Czech Republic, and it may well persist even after such documents become available. For now, many of the relevant documents remain classified. It is notable, however, that with the substantial access the United States has gained to Iraqi documents and former Iraqi intelligence officials through its occupation of Iraq, there is as yet no new evidence that documents a relationship between Iraq and al Qaeda. Still, this is not definitive, as any such relationship might have included only a few key individuals on both sides, and might have involved relatively small amounts of money and limited but important exchanges of operational expertise and intelligence information.

For additional information on Iraq's WMD programs (or the lack thereof), see the report of the Iraq Survey Group, first posted on the CIA Web site, but now in a more accessible format at http://www.lib.umich.edu/govdocs/duelfer.html.

ISSUE 5

Should the United States Stay in Iraq?

YES: John McCain, from "Stay to Win" *Current History* (January 2006)

NO: William Odom, from "Withdraw Now," *Current History* (January 2006)

ISSUE SUMMARY

YES: John McCain, U.S. senator from Arizona and a veteran of the Vietnam War, argues that the withdrawal of U.S. troops from Iraq before stability is achieved there would lead to a bloody civil war, interference in Iraq by other states in the region, and a failed state that would become a haven for anti-American terrorists.

NO: William Odom, senior fellow at the Hudson Institute and former director of the National Security Agency, argues that all of the dire consequences predicted in the event of a U.S. withdrawal from Iraq—civil war, loss of American credibility, a haven for terrorists, and regional instability—have already taken place and will be made worse by a continuing U.S. military presence in Iraq.

T hrough much of 2006, even those American political leaders who opposed the decision to intervene in Iraq for the most part agreed that, having invaded Iraq, the United States could not withdraw its troops from that country without first establishing a stable and secure government to leave behind. This consensus began to break down, however, as sectarian violence in Iraq grew sharply and steadily in the months after the February 2006 bombing of an important Shiite mosque. As American public opinion, reacting to this violence and to continuing American casualties in Iraq, became more pessimistic on the prospects for success, members of both parties in Congress became more skeptical of the likelihood of success as well. The 2006 midterm elections, in which the Democratic party regained majority control of both the House and the Senate, were widely seen in part as a referendum on the war.

The midterm elections and the ongoing violence in Iraq—with Iraqi civilian casualties reaching over 3,000 killed per month and casualties among American soldiers edging up toward a total of 3,000 killed and over 20,000 wounded during the duration of the conflict—created considerable political momentum in the United States to consider alternatives to the current U.S. strategy in Iraq. By the end of 2006, various groups and individuals inside and outside of the Bush administration had proposed alternative strategies in a series of studies, reports, and leaks to the media. Most prominently, a bipartisan "Iraq Study Group" (ISG) created by the Congress in the spring of 2006 to assess U.S. strategy in Iraq, headed by former secretary of state James Baker and former chair of the House Committee on Foreign Affairs Lee Hamilton, concluded that the situation in Iraq was "grave and deteriorating" and urged that the United States shift its strategy to put more emphasis on training Iraqi security forces and less on direct U.S. military operations. The ISG did not rule out a short-term increase in U.S. troops in Iraq, but it suggested that the United States could begin reducing its troop deployments in Iraq substantially by the end of 2007.

Other options raised in late 2006 include the following. Several newspaper stories indicated that Vice President Cheney and his staff favored explicitly taking sides with Iraqi Shiites and Kurds and ending efforts to accommodate Iraqi Sunnis, an approach labeled the "80 percent Solution" because Shiites and Kurds comprise 80 percent of the Iraqi population and an even higher share of Iraqi oil reserves (for a newspaper op-ed proposing this strategy, see "Iraq Is Gone. Now What?" by Monica Duffy Toft, *The Washington Post*, November 13, 2006). This strategy risks alienating other Sunni countries in the region, including Saudi Arabia, and cementing the enmity of Iraqi Sunnis toward the United States.

A third possible strategy, which some have labeled "soft partition," would involve giving greater autonomy within a federal system to separate Shiite, Sunni, and Kurdish areas of Iraq, and establishing an agreement on the sharing of oil revenues among these regions (see Issue 6 on the possibility of partitioning Iraq).

A fourth strategy would be to seek a centrist coalition involving leaders from Iraq's three main ethnic groups and excluding leaders and factions that have resorted to wide-scale sectarian violence, such as the Shiite leader Moqtada Sadr and his "Mahdi army." This strategy would require that moderates in all factions risk the wrath of the extremist and violent groups within their own ethnic groups, and in particular, it would demand that Iraqi Prime Minister Nouri al-Maliki participate in the breakup of the Shiite coalition that put him in power.

Two final strategic options are those favored by William Odom and Senator McCain. Odom favors pulling U.S. troops out of Iraq, arguing that their continuing presence has already created the negative consequences that the critics of a pullout fear. Senator McCain urges keeping U.S. troops in Iraq to prevent even worse chaos from emerging, and in other venues he has argued for increasing the number of U.S. troops in Iraq to establish security and provide room for economic growth and political progress to take hold. As of late 2006, the White House was reported to be considering a short-term "surge" in the number of U.S. troops in Iraq, though it remains unclear whether this policy will actually be adopted and whether it would be linked to any of the other strategies outlined above.

YES ⤴

John McCain

Stay to Win

The news from Iraq is filled with numbers. The number of Iraqis streaming to the polls to determine their future democratically. A new constitution, enshrining fundamental rights, approved by a 4-to-1 margin, with two Sunni-dominated provinces dissenting. More than 2,000 Americans killed in action since the war began.

It is all being counted: the number of safe areas, the daily attacks, the Iraqi troop units trained, the billions spent per month. And yet, as has been so often the case in Iraq, these numbers cannot indicate where that country is heading, because the figures themselves point in different directions. There is, at the same time, both great difficulty and great hope. And just as Americans would be unwise to focus solely on the hopeful signs, so too would they be foolish merely to dwell on the difficulties.

I mention this not because I seek to whitewash the situation in Iraq. On the contrary, not all is well there. But as we look on events there, let us not forget that the Iraqi people are in the midst of something unprecedented in their history.

The world has witnessed Iraqis of all stripes exercising those very democratic habits that critics predicted could never take root in a country with little democratic tradition. On December 15, 2005, Iraqis braved death threats to elect their first free and independent parliament. Before that, they voted in January for an interim government. They put Saddam Hussein on trial and dictators throughout the world on notice. They produced a landmark constitution that, while not perfect, nevertheless upholds critical rights that go far beyond standards elsewhere in the region. And they adopted that constitution by free vote—the first time in history for an Arab country. Try as they might, the terrorists and the insurgents have proved unable to muster a veto against Iraqi democracy.

Despite the daily bombings and attacks, the terrorists have not achieved their goals. They have failed to incite a civil war, because Kurds and Shiites still have faith in the future and in American and Iraqi security efforts. The insurgents have not prevented Iraqis from joining the military and police, in spite of horrific attacks at recruiting centers. Oil exports continue, despite concerted efforts at sabotage. And the insurgents have not stopped the political process, even while they assassinate government officials and attack polling places.

Amid the debate about Iraq, the stakes for the United States, and current American policy, it is important not to forget just how far the Iraqi people have come. With US help, the dictator who ruled their lives is gone from power and the Iraqi people are establishing a true democracy. The Middle East will be forever changed by the choices American policy makers have made, and by the choices they will continue to make over the next months. They must get Iraq right.

Transcendent Stakes

The United States must get Iraq right because America's stake in that conflict is enormous. All Americans, whether or not they supported the US action to topple Hussein, must understand the profound implications of their country's presence there. Success or failure in Iraq is the transcendent issue for US foreign policy and national security, for now and years to come. And the stakes are higher than in the Vietnam War.

There is an understandable desire, nearly three years after the invasion, to seek a quick and easy end to the intervention in Iraq. We see this in the protests of antiwar activist Cindy Sheehan; we saw it recently in Senator John Kerry's call to withdraw troops whether or not the country is secured. But should America follow these calls, it would face consequences of the most serious nature. Because Iraqi forces are not yet capable of carrying out most security operations on their own, great bloodshed would occur if the main enforcer of government authority—coalition troops—drew down prematurely. If the United States were to leave, the most likely result would be full-scale civil war.

When America toppled Saddam Hussein, it incurred a moral duty not to abandon the Iraqi people to terrorists and killers. If the United States withdraws prematurely, risking all-out civil war, it will have done precisely that. I can hardly imagine that any US senator or any other American leader would want his nation to suffer that moral stain.

And yet the implications of premature withdrawal from Iraq are not moral alone; they directly involve America's national security. Instability in Iraq would invite further Syrian and Iranian interference, bolstering the influence of two terror-sponsoring states firmly opposed to US policy in the region. Iraq's neighbors—from Saudi Arabia to Israel to Turkey—would feel their own security eroding, and might be induced to act. This uncertain swirl of events would have a damaging impact on America's ability to promote positive change in the Middle East, to say the least.

Withdrawing before there is a stable and legitimate Iraqi authority would turn Iraq into a failed state in the heart of the Middle East. We have seen a failed state emerge after US disengagement before, and it cost Americans terribly. Before Al Qaeda's attacks on the United States on September 11, 2001, terrorists found sanctuary in Afghanistan to train and plan operations with impunity. We know that there are today in Iraq terrorists who are planning attacks against Americans. The United States cannot make this fatal mistake twice.

If America leaves Iraq prematurely, the jihadists will interpret the withdrawal as their great victory against a great power. Osama bin Laden and his followers believe that America is weak, unwilling to suffer casualties in battle. They drew that lesson from Lebanon in the 1980s and Somalia in the 1990s, when US troops hastily withdrew after being attacked. Today they have their sights set squarely on Iraq.

Zawahiri's Plan

A recently released letter from Ayman al-Zawahiri, bin Laden's lieutenant, to Abu Musab al-Zarqawi, the leading terrorist in Iraq, draws out the implications. The Zawahiri letter is predicated on the assumption that the United States will quit Iraq, and that Al Qaeda's real game begins as soon as the United States abandons the country. In his missive, Zawahiri lays out a four-stage plan—including the establishment of a caliphate in Iraq, the extension of a "jihad wave" to the secular countries neighboring Iraq, and renewed confrontation with Israel—none of which shall commence until the completion of stage one: *expel the Americans from Iraq*. Zawahiri observes that the collapse of American power in Vietnam—"and how they ran and left their agents"—suggests that "we must be ready starting now."

The United States cannot let them start, now or ever. America must stay in Iraq until the government there has a fully functioning security apparatus that can keep Zarqawi and his terrorists at bay, and ultimately defeat them. Some argue that it is America's very presence in Iraq that has created the insurgency; if America ends the occupation, it ends the insurgency. In fact, by ending military operations, the United States would likely empower the insurgency. Zarqawi and others fight not just against foreign forces but also against the Shiite Muslims, whom they believe to be infidels, and against all elements of the government. Sunni Muslim insurgents attack Kurds, Turkmens, Christians, and other Iraqis not simply to end the US occupation, but to recapture lost Sunni power. As the military analyst Frederick Kagan has written, these Sunnis are not yet persuaded that violence is counterproductive; on the contrary, they believe the insurgency might lead to an improvement in their political situation. There is no reason to think that an American drawdown would extinguish these motivations to fight.

Because it cannot pull out and simply hope for the best, because it cannot withdraw and manage things from afar, because morality and national security compel it, the United States has to see this mission through to completion. Calls for premature withdrawal of American forces represent, I believe, a major step on the road to disaster. Drawdowns must be based on conditions in Iraq, not arbitrary deadlines rooted in domestic American politics.

President Bush and his advisers understand this, and I praise their resolve. They know that the consequences of failure are unacceptable and that the benefits of success in Iraq remain profound. And yet at the same time there is an undeniable sense that things are slipping—more violence on the ground, declining domestic support for the war, growing incantations among Americans that there is no end in sight. To build on what has been accomplished, and to win the war in Iraq, the United States needs to make several significant policy changes.

A Counterinsurgency Strategy

The first is to adopt an effective military counterinsurgency strategy. For most of the occupation, US military strategy has been built around trying to secure the entirety of Iraq at the same time. With the Americans' current force structure and the power vacuum that persists in many areas of Iraq, that is not possible today. In their attempt to secure all of Iraq, coalition forces engage in search and destroy operations to root out insurgent strongholds, with the aim of killing as many insurgents as possible. But coalition forces cannot hold the ground indefinitely, and when they move on to fight other battles, the insurgent ranks replenish and the strongholds fill again. US troops must then reenter the same area and refight the same battle.

The example of Tal Afar, a city in northwestern Iraq not far from the Syrian border, is instructive. Coalition forces first fought in Tal Afar in September 2003, when the 101st Airborne Division took the city, then withdrew. Over the next year insurgents streamed back into the area. In September 2004 Stryker brigades and Iraqi security forces returned to Tal Afar, chasing out insurgents. They then left again, moving on to fight insurgents in other locations. Then in September 2005, the Third Armored Calvary Regiment swept into Tal Afar, killing rebels while others retreated into the countryside. Most US troops have already redeployed, and they may well be back again. The battles of Tal Afar, like those in other areas of Iraq, have become seasonal offensives, where success is measured most often by the number of insurgents captured and killed. But that is not success. And "sweeping and leaving" is not working.

Instead, coalition forces need to clear and stay. They can do this with a modified version of traditional counterinsurgency strategy. Andrew Krepinevich, Tom Donnelly, Gary Schmitt, and others have written about this idea. Whether called the "ink blot," "oil spot," or "safe haven" strategy, it draws on successful counterinsurgency efforts in the past. Rather than focusing on killing and capturing insurgents, this strategy emphasizes protecting the local population and creating secure areas where insurgents find it difficult to operate. US forces with Iraqi assistance would begin by clearing areas, with heavy force if necessary, to establish a zone as free of insurgents as possible. Security forces can then cordon off the zone and establish constant patrols, by American and Iraqi military and police, to protect the population from insurgents and common crime, and to arrest remaining insurgents as they are found.

In this newly secure environment, many of the tasks critical to winning in Iraq can take place—tasks that are not being carried out today. Massive reconstruction can go forward without fear of attack and sabotage. Political meetings and campaigning can take place in the open. Civil society can emerge. Intelligence improves, as it becomes increasingly safe for citizens to provide tips to the security forces, knowing that they can do so without being threatened. The coalition must then act on this intelligence, increasing the speed at which it is transmitted to operational teams. Past practice has shown that "actionable intelligence" has a short shelf life, and the lag involved in communicating it to security forces costs vital opportunities.

As these elements positively reinforce each other, the security forces then expand the territory under their control. Coalition and Iraqi forces have done this successfully in Falluja. They cleared the area of insurgents and held the city. Today Iraqi police and soldiers patrol the streets, with support from two US battalions. And when the Iraqi forces are at a level sufficient to take over the patrolling responsibilities on their own, American troops can hand over the duties. Falluja today is not perfect, but the aim is not perfection—it is an improvement over the insecurity that plagues Iraq today.

The Costs of Success

This kind of a counterinsurgency strategy has some costs. Securing ever increasing parts of Iraq and preventing the emergence of new terrorist safe havens will require more troops and money. It will take time, probably years, and mean more American casualties. Those are terrible prices to pay. But with the stakes so high, I believe Americans must choose the strategy with the best chance of success. The Pentagon seems to be coming around on this, and top commanders profess to employ a version already. If the United States is on its way to adopting a true counterinsurgency strategy, that is wonderful, but it has not been the case thus far. Soon after the recent operations in Tal Afar, most US troops were redeployed, leaving behind Iraqi units with Americans embedded. I hope this will be sufficient to establish security there, but it is also clear that there has been no spike in reconstruction activity in that city.

To enhance chances of success with this strategy, and enable coalition forces to hold as much territory as possible, America needs more troops in Iraq. For this reason, I believe that current ideas to effect a partial drawdown during 2006 are exactly wrong. While the United States and its partners are training Iraqi security forces at a furious pace, these Iraqis should supplement, not substitute for, the coalition forces on the ground. Instead of drawing down, the United States should be ramping up, with more civil-military soldiers, translators, and counterinsurgency operations teams. Decisions about troop levels should be tied to the success or failure of the mission in Iraq, not to the number of Iraqi troops trained and equipped. And while American policy makers seek higher troop levels for Iraq, they should at last face facts and increase the standing size of the US Army. It takes time to build a larger army, but had the United States done so even after its invasion of Iraq, its military would have more soldiers available for deployment now.

Knowing the enemy is the essential precondition to defeating him, and I believe US counterinsurgency strategy can do more to exploit divisions in the strands of the insurgency. Foreign jihadists, Baathist revanchists, and Sunni discontents do not necessarily share tactics or goals. Recent Sunni participation in the constitutional process—and especially the decision by Sunni parties to contest the December parliamentary elections—present opportunities to split Sunnis from those whose only goal is death, destruction, and chaos.

Building Support for Victory

Besides changing military strategy, US policy makers need to take several other steps to assure success in the war. To begin with, they need to start keeping senior officers in place. The Pentagon has adopted a policy of rotating generals in and out of Iraq almost as frequently as it rotates the troops. General David Petraeus, a fine officer who was the military's foremost expert in the training of Iraqi security forces, now uses his hard-earned experience and expertise at Fort Leavenworth. Others, including Generals James Conway, Ray Odierno, and Peter Chiarelli, have been transferred to Washington or elsewhere. This is deeply unwise. If these were the best men for the task, they should still be on the job. These generals and other senior officers build, in their time in Iraq, the on-the-ground and institutional knowledge necessary to approach this conflict with wisdom. They know, for example, the difference between a battle in Falluja and one in Tal Afar, or what kind of patrols are most effective in Shiite areas of Baghdad. These commanders—and their hard-won experience—need to stay in place.

Second, policy makers need to integrate counterinsurgency efforts at senior levels. While it is critical to focus American military efforts on insurgents, particularly against Sunni fighters using violence to improve their political position, the nonmilitary component is also essential. All Iraqis need to see a tangible improvement in their daily lives or support for the new government will slip. Sunnis need to feel that, should they abandon violence once and for all, there will be some role in the political process for them. The Iraqi people must feel invested in a newly free, newly powerful and prosperous country at peace.

There is a role for each element of the US government in this, whether it implies aid, trade, wells, schools, training, or anything else. US Ambassador Zalmay Khalilzad has done a fine job coordinating these efforts with the military campaign and the political process, but it needs to be done in Washington too. This should be the highest priority of President Bush's team, and must be managed by the most senior levels at the State Department, the Pentagon, the National Security Council, the US Agency for International Development, and any other agency that can contribute to the effort. To consign Iraq to the Pentagon to win or lose will simply not suffice.

In this regard, I am encouraged by Secretary of State Condoleezza Rice's recent testimony before the Senate Foreign Relations Committee, which laid out a more comprehensive, integrated political-military-economic strategy for Iraq. Implementing it is essential and will require a more formal interagency structure than we have seen to date.

Third, the United States needs to build loyalty in Iraq's armed forces. In building the armed forces at a rapid pace, US and Iraqi authorities have invited former militia members to join. In the short run, it is most practical to do what has been done thus far: swallow former militia units whole. In the long run, the focus must be on building diversified individual military units.

The lesson of Afghanistan is instructive. There, the United States insisted—over initial objections from the Afghan Ministry of Defense—that each new military unit be carefully calibrated to include Pashtuns, Tajiks, Uzbeks, and others. This diversification within units serves several important functions. Over time, it helps build loyalty to the central government. It makes it more difficult for militias to reconstitute, should any decide to oppose the government. And, more broadly, it helps build support for a unified nation. The multiethnic Afghan National Army has provided a powerful psychological boost in a deeply divided country. Simply seeing Pashtuns and Tajiks and Uzbeks, in uniform and working together, has had a great impact on Afghan public opinion and the way Afghans imagine their country.

In Iraq the policy has been to recruit former militia members as individuals, rather than as units, but the reality has fallen short. Building units in this way is more difficult and will require more time than accepting homogeneous Kurdish, Shiite, or Sunni units, for reasons of language, culture, and expediency. But that is precisely why it is so important to do. Standing up the Iraqi army is about more than generating manpower so that American troops can withdraw. The composition and character of the force that Americans leave behind will have social and political ramifications far beyond the military balance of power.

Fourth, policy makers should increase pressure on Syria. For too long, Syria has refused to crack down on Iraqi insurgents and foreign terrorists operating from its territory. President Bashar Assad said recently that his government distinguishes between those insurgents who attack Iraqis and those who attack American and British troops, suggesting they are "something different." This is the same mindset that has led Syria to defy the United Nations over the assassination of former Lebanese Prime Minister Rafik Hariri, give sanctuary to Palestinian terrorist organizations, and attempt to maintain some hold on Lebanon.

With the UN Security Council now engaged, the international community has an opportunity to apply real pressure on Syria to change its behavior on all these fronts. While multilateral sanctions keyed to Syrian cooperation with the Hariri investigation may be the starting point, that should not be the end. Any country that wishes to see the Iraqi people live in peace and freedom should join in pressuring Syria to stop Iraqi and foreign terrorists from using its soil.

The Other Battlefront

Finally, the United States needs to assure success in Iraq by winning the war on the home front. Even as the political-military strategy is being improved, the latest polls and protests suggest that the American public's support increasingly is at risk. If it disappears, the country will have lost this war as soundly as if its forces were defeated on the battlefield. A renewed effort at home starts with explaining precisely what is at stake in this war—not to alarm Americans, but so that they see the nature of this struggle for what it is. The president cannot do this alone. The media, so efficient in portraying the difficulties in Iraq, need to convey the consequences of success or failure there. Critics in the Democratic Party should outline precisely what they believe to be the stakes in this battle, if they are willing to suffer the consequences of withdrawal.

Another part of the effort includes avoiding rosy aspirations for near-term improvements in Iraq's politics or security situation, and more accurately portraying events on the ground, even if they are negative. The American people have heard many times that the violence in Iraq will subside soon—when there is a transitional government in place, when Hussein is captured, when there are elections, when there is a constitution, when there is an elected parliament. It would be better to describe the situation as it is—difficult right now, but not without progress and hope, and with a long, hard road ahead—and to announce that things have improved only when they in fact have.

Above all, winning the home front means reiterating the nation's commitment to victory and laying out a realistic game plan that will take America there. I believe that the vast majority of Americans, even those who did not support the initial invasion, wish to see their country prevail. They are prepared to pay the human and financial costs of this war if—but only if—they believe their government is on a measurable path to victory. That their government must give them. In this war as in all others, there are two fronts, the battlefield and the home front, and leaders must tend to both.

The Number That Counts

Despite bombs, daily attacks, and untold threats against the democratic process, Iraq has held free elections, with open campaigns and a truly free press. Iraq has ratified the most progressive constitution in the Arab world and instilled justice in a country that for so long lacked it. Iraq has put Hussein on trial and held his henchmen accountable for their murderous rule. In doing all these things and more, the Iraqi people have issued to their more peaceful, prosperous neighbors a profound challenge.

We have seen responses already in Lebanon's Cedar Revolution, Egypt's recent elections, and a proliferation of calls for democracy in the Arab world. As Iraq consolidates its democratic process, the challenge to its neighbors—and their necessary responses—will be starker still. The Iraqi people have shown their impulse toward democracy; they need security to hash out the many remaining differences that still divide them. They can get there, but they need America's support.

This much should be obvious: America, Iraq, and the world are better off with Hussein in prison rather than in power. Does anyone believe the stirrings of freedom in the region would exist if he still ruled with an iron fist? Does anyone believe the region would be better off if he were in power, using oil revenue to purchase political support? Does anyone believe meaningful sanctions would remain or that there would be any serious checks on his ambitions? The costs of this war have been high, especially for the more than 2,000 Americans, and their families, who have paid the ultimate price. But liberating Iraq was in America's strategic and moral interests, and Americans must honor their sacrifice by seeing this mission through to victory.

Victory will not come overnight. On the contrary, it will take more time, more commitment, and more support—and more brave Americans will lose their lives in the service of this great cause. And despite US cajoling, nagging, and pleading, few other countries around the world will share much of the burden. Iraq is for Americans to do, for them to win or lose, for them to suffer the consequences or share in the benefits. Progress in Iraq can be charted with all sorts of numbers. But in the end, there is only one United States of America, and it is to that nation that history will look for courage and commitment.

William Odom

 **NO**

Withdraw Now

Until Congressman John Murtha's call this fall for a pullout from Iraq, there was little serious public debate in the United States about whether it makes sense to continue a struggle that had been launched unwisely. Belatedly, that seems to be changing.

The Bush administration responded quickly to the Pennsylvania Democrat's challenge with a speech by the president at the US Naval Academy at the end of November, and with the release of a document entitled *A National Strategy for Victory in Iraq*. Neither the speech nor the strategy document indicated a significant change of course. Both appeared to suggest that President George W. Bush will continue to dig deeper into the hole he has created. The arguments trotted out for "staying the course" are the same ones we have long heard from the White House and the Defense Department.

A subtle reading of the administration's response might lead one to see it as the beginning of the end—a cover for a failed strategy by progressively redefining "victory" in Iraq to such a low standard that withdrawal seems acceptable. At this point, however, the former reading, suggesting intent to dig even deeper, seems the more plausible.

It never made sense to invade Iraq, and the longer US forces stay there, the greater the damage to America's interests. The war was and remains in the interest of Al Qaeda and Iran, both longtime enemies of Saddam Hussein. It has detracted from America's pursuit of Al Qaeda, and it has nearly destroyed the Atlantic alliance. From enjoying incredibly strong worldwide support in the fall of 2001, the United States has sunk to a new low in its standing in the world.

Darkness at the Tunnel's End

Supporters of the current policy offer a long list of justifications, most of which consist of dire predictions about what would transpire if the United States withdraws from Iraq. Yet most of these warnings—of civil conflict, lost US credibility, bolstered terrorists, hampered democracy, inadequate security, regional instability, and the like—already have come true. And others may come to pass no matter how long American forces remain in Iraq. I believe a much stronger case can be made that an early withdrawal will not make the situation all that much worse, and in some regards will improve it.

Reprinted from *Current History*, January 2006, pp. 3–7. Copyright © 2006 by Current History, Inc. Reprinted with permission.

Consider the danger of leaving a civil war in the aftermath of an American withdrawal. The Iraqis, in fact, are already fighting Iraqis. Insurgents have killed far more Iraqis than Americans. This is civil war. The United States created a civil war when it invaded; it cannot prevent a civil war by staying. As for American credibility: What will happen to it if the course the administration is pursuing proves a major strategic disaster? Would it not be better for America's long-term standing to withdraw earlier than later in this event?

Proponents of staying the course argue that withdrawal will embolden the insurgency and cripple the move toward democracy. There is no question the insurgents or other anti-American parties will take over the government once the United States leaves. But that will happen no matter how long the United States stays in Iraq. Any government capable of holding power there will be anti-American, because the Iraqi people are increasingly becoming anti-American.

The United States will not leave behind a liberal, constitutional democracy in Iraq no matter how President Bush's statements about progress in Iraq are increasingly resembling President Lyndon Johnson's assurances during the Vietnam War. Johnson's comments about the 1968 election are very similar to what Bush said in February 2005 after the election of a provisional parliament. Why should we expect an outcome in Iraq different from what occurred in Vietnam?

Leaving a pro-American liberal regime in place in Iraq is impossible. Postwar Germany and Japan are not models for Iraq. Each had mature—at least one generation old—constitutional orders by the end of the nineteenth century. Their states had both endured as constitutional orders until the 1930s. Thus General Lucius Clay in Germany and General Douglas MacArthur in Japan were merely reversing a decade and a half of totalitarianism—returning to nearly a century of liberal political change in Japan and a much longer period in Germany.

To impose a liberal constitutional order in Iraq would be to accomplish something that has never been done before. Of all the world's political cultures, an Arab-Muslim one may be the most resistant of any to such a change. The administration's supporters cite Turkey as an example of a constitutional order in an Islamic society. But Turkey (which has been known to backslide occasionally) has a decidedly anti-Arab culture.

A Terrorist Training Ground

It is also said that Iraq will become a haven for terrorists without a US military presence. But Iraq is already a training ground for terrorists—having become one since the United States invaded. The CIA has pointed out to the administration and Congress that Iraq is spawning so many terrorists that they are returning home to many other countries to further practice their skills there. The quicker a new dictator wins political power in Iraq and imposes order, the sooner the country will stop producing well-experienced terrorists.

Another argument made is that American training and support are essential to the creation of a viable Iraqi military. As President Bush puts it, "We will stand down as the Iraqis stand up." Yet the insurgents are fighting very effectively without US or European military advisers to train them. Why do the soldiers and police in the service of the present Iraqi government not do their duty as well? Because they are uncertain about committing their lives to this regime. They are being asked to take a political stand, just as the insurgents are. Political consolidation, not military-technical consolidation, is the challenge.

The issue, in other words, is not military training; it is institutional loyalty. The United States trained the Vietnamese military effectively. Its generals took power and proved to be lousy politicians and poor fighters in the final showdown. In many battles over a decade or more, South Vietnamese military units fought very well, defeating Vietcong and North Vietnamese Army units. But South Vietnam's political leaders lost the war.

Even if Washington were able to successfully train an Iraqi military and police force, the likely result, after all that, would be another military dictatorship. Experience around the world teaches us that military dictatorships arise when the military's institutional modernization gets ahead of political consolidation.

The Region at Risk

For those who worry about destabilizing the region, the sensible policy is not to stay the course in Iraq. It is rapid withdrawal, with Washington reestablishing strong relations with its allies in Europe, showing confidence in the UN Security Council, and trying to knit together a large coalition—including Europe's major states, Japan, South Korea, China, and India—to back a strategy for stabilizing the area from the eastern Mediterranean to Afghanistan and Pakistan. Until the United States withdraws from Iraq and admits its strategic error, no such coalition can be formed. Those who fear leaving a mess are actually helping make things worse while preventing a new strategic approach with some promise of success.

Iranian leaders see US policy in Iraq as being so much in Tehran's interests that they have been advising Iraqi Shiite leaders to do exactly what the Americans ask them to do. The December parliamentary elections have allowed the Shiites to take power legally. Once firmly in charge, they can settle scores with the Baathists and Sunnis. If US policy in Iraq begins to undercut Iran's interests, then Tehran can use its growing influence among Iraqi Shiites to stir up trouble, possibly committing Shiite militias to an insurgency against US forces.

The American invasion has vastly increased Iran's influence in Iraq, not sealed it out, and it is unlikely to shrink as the Shiite majority grasps the reins of government. Would it not be better to pull out now rather than continue America's present course of weakening the Sunnis and Baathists, opening the way for a Shiite dictatorship?

The civil conflict America leaves behind may well draw in Syria, Turkey, and Iran. But today each for or opposition to factions in the ongoing Iraqi civil war. The very act of invading Iraq almost ensured that violence would involve the larger region. And so it has and will continue, with or without US forces in Iraq.

Yet this does not mean the United States would leave the area. I believe that stabilizing the region from the eastern Mediterranean to Afghanistan is very much an American interest, one it shares with all its allies as well as with several other countries, especially China, Russia, and India.

The Global Balkans

Former national security adviser Zbigniew Brzezinski has called this region the "global Balkans," a name that recalls the role of the European Balkans during the two or three decades leading up to the outbreak of World War I. By themselves the Balkan countries were not that important. Yet several great powers, especially Russia and Austria, were jockeying for strategic advantage there as they anticipated the collapse of the Ottoman Empire and competition for control of the straits leading from the Black Sea into the Mediterranean. Britain and France wanted neither Russia nor Austria to dominate; Germany, although uninterested in the Balkans, was allied to Austria.

From a strategic viewpoint, the assassination of Archduke Ferdinand in Sarajevo in 1914 was unimportant, but it set in motion actions that soon brought all of the major powers in Europe to war. Four empires collapsed, and the doors were opened to the Communists in Russia and the Nazis in Germany as a result.

Brzezinski's point is that the Middle East and Southwest Asia have precisely that kind of potential for catalyzing wars among the major powers of the world today, although nothing in the region objectively merits such wars. (Middle East oil as a "strategic" factor is largely a red herring. Oil producers have always been willing to sell their oil, even to bitter enemies. The Soviet Union sold oil to the " imperialist" West during the height of the cold war.)

Brzezinski calls for the United States to lead the states of Europe plus Russia, Japan, and China in a cooperative approach to stabilizing this region so that it cannot spark conflicts among them. As he rightly argues, the task of stabilization is beyond the power of the United States alone. With allies, however, it can manage the challenge.

After Al Qaeda's attacks in the United States in September 2001, the European members of NATO invoked Article Five of the North Atlantic Treaty, meaning that they considered the attack on America as an attack on them all. Article Five had never been invoked before. Moreover, more than 90 countries worldwide joined one or more of five separate coalitions to support the US war against Al Qaeda. Seldom has the United States had so much international support. It was a most propitious time, therefore, for dealing with "the global Balkans" in precisely the way Brzezinski suggested.

Over the next year and a half, however, in the run-up to the invasion of Iraq, many neoconservatives, both inside and outside the administration, disparaged NATO and other US allies as unnecessary for "transforming the Middle East." Because the United States is a superpower, they insisted, it could handle this task alone. Accordingly, we witnessed Secretary of Defense Donald Rumsfeld's team and some officials in the State Department and the White House (especially in the vice president's office) gratuitously and repeatedly insult the Europeans, dismissing them as irrelevant. The climax of this sustained campaign to discard America's allies came in the UN Security Council struggle for a resolution to legitimize the invasion of Iraq in February–March 2003.

From that time on, we have seen most US allies stand aside and engage in schadenfreude over America's painful bog-down in Iraq. Winston Churchill's glib observation that "the only thing worse than having allies is having none" was once again vindicated.

The Wrong Strategy

Two areas of inquiry follow naturally from this background. First, how could the United States induce its allies to join its efforts in Iraq now? Why should they put troops in Iraq and suffer the pain with Americans? Could Washington seriously expect them to do so? Second, is remaining in Iraq the best strategy for a coalition of major states to stabilize the region? Would a large NATO coalition of forces plus some from India, Japan, and China enjoy more success?

On the first point, there is no chance that America's allies will join it in Iraq. How could the lead-convince their publics to support such a course of action? They could not, and their publics would not be wise to agree if their leaders pleaded for them to do so.

On the second point, Iraq is the worst place to fight a battle for regional stability. Whose interests were best served by the US invasion of Iraq in the first place? It turns out that Iran and Al Qaeda benefited the most, and that continues to be true every day US forces remain there. A serious review of America's regional interests is required. Until that is accomplished and new and compelling aims for managing the region are clarified, continuing the campaign in Iraq makes no sense.

Once these two realities are recognized, it becomes clear that US withdrawal from Iraq is the precondition to America's winning the support of allies and a few others for a joint approach to the region. Until that has been completed, they will not join such a coalition. And until that has happened, America's leaders cannot even think clearly about what constitutes US interests there, much less gain agreement about common interests for a coalition.

By contrast, any argument for "staying the course," or seeking more stability before the United States withdraws—or pointing out tragic consequences that withdrawal would cause—is bound to be wrong, or at least unpersuasive. Putting it bluntly, those who insist on staying in Iraq longer make the consequences of withdrawal more terrible and also make it harder to find an alternative strategy for achieving regional stability.

Once the invasion began in March 2003, all of the ensuing unhappy results became inevitable. The invasion of Iraq may well turn out to be the greatest strategic disaster in US history. And the longer America stays, the worse it will be. Until that is understood, the United States will make no progress with its allies or in devising a promising alternative strategy.

"Staying the course" may make a good sound bite, but it can be disastrous for strategy. Several of Hitler's generals told him that "staying the course" at Stalingrad in 1942 was a strategic mistake, that he should allow the Sixth Army to be withdrawn, saving it to fight defensive actions on reduced frontage against the growing Red Army. He refused, lost the Sixth Army entirely, and left his commanders with fewer forces to defend a wider front. Thus he made the subsequent Soviet offensives westward easier.

To argue, as some do, that the United States cannot leave Iraq because "we broke it and therefore we own it" is to reason precisely the way Hitler did with his commanders. Of course America broke it! But the Middle East is not a pottery store. It is the site of major military conflict with several different forces that the United States is galvanizing into an alliance against America. To hang on to an untenable position is the height of irresponsibility. Beware of anyone, including the president, who insists that this is the "responsible" or "patriotic" thing to do.

The Refuge of Scoundrels

Many US officers in Iraq, especially at company and field grade levels, know that while they are winning every tactical battle, they are losing strategically. And they are beginning to voice complaints about Americans at home bearing none of the pains of the war. One can only guess about the enlisted ranks, but those on a second tour—perhaps the majority today—are probably anxious for an early pullout. It is also noteworthy that US generals in Iraq are not bubbling over with optimistic reports the way they were during the first few years of the Vietnam War.

Their careful statements and caution probably reflect serious doubts that they do not, and should not, express publicly. The more important question is whether repressive and vindictive behavior by the secretary of defense and his deputy against the senior military—especially the Army leadership, which is the critical component in the war—has made it impossible for field commanders to make the political leaders see the facts.

Most officers and probably most troops do not believe that it is unpatriotic and a failure to support the troops to question the strategic wisdom of the war. They are angry at the deficiencies in matèriel support they get from the Department of Defense, and especially about the irresponsibly long deployments they must now endure because Rumsfeld and his staff have refused to enlarge the ground forces to provide shorter tours. In the meantime, they know that the defense budget lavishes funds on the maritime forces and programs like the Strategic Defense Initiative while the Pentagon refuses to increase dramatically the size of the Army.

One could justly anticipate that in conditions such as these, the opposition party—the Democrats today—would be advocating a pullout. Yet none were until Congressman Murtha surprised both the White House and his own party by putting things as plainly as I have. Although he has infuriated the administration and terrified some of his fellow Democrats, he seems to have catalyzed a political debate that is long overdue.

Why was it so late in coming? And why are so many Democrats still dodging and weaving on an issue of such dramatic importance for the country?

Why such an egregious evasion of political responsibility? I can only specu-late. The biggest reason is because Democrats were not willing to oppose the war during the 2004 presidential campaign. Former Vermont Governor Howard Dean alone took a clear and consistent stand on Iraq, and the rest of the Democratic Party trashed him for it. Most Democratic leaders in Congress voted for the war and let that vote shackle them later on. Now they are scared to death that the White House will smear them with lack of patriotism if they suggest pulling out.

Aid and Comfort

No one will be able to sustain a strong case for withdrawal in the short run without going back to the fundamental misjudgment of invading Iraq in the first place. Once the enormity of that error is grasped, the case for pulling out becomes easy to see.

The US invasion of Iraq mainly served the interests of three groups. It benefited Osama bin Laden's Al Qaeda, by making Iraq safe for Al Qaeda, by positioning US military personnel in places where jihadist operatives could kill them, by helping to radicalize youth throughout the Arab and Muslim world, by alienating America's most important and strongest allies—the Europeans—and by squandering US military resources that otherwise might be used to finish off Al Qaeda in Pakistan.

The invasion also benefited the Iranians, who had been invaded by Hussein's army and suffered massive casualties in an eight-year war with Iraq. And it benefited extremists in both Palestinian and Israeli political circles, who do not really want a peace settlement and who probably believe that bogging the United States down in a war in Iraq will give them the time and cover to wipe out the other side. The Iraq War was never in America's interest. It has not become so since the war began.

POSTSCRIPT

Should the United States Stay in Iraq?

It is tempting to draw analogies between U.S. involvement in Iraq and American intervention in and withdrawal from the Vietnam War a generation ago, and indeed Abramowitz explicitly uses this analogy at several points. This analogy is both instructive, because of clear parallels between the two conflicts, and potentially misleading, due to obvious differences. Among the parallels, U.S. efforts to set up an elected government that enjoys wide legitimacy have been hampered by anti-American nationalism, U.S. pressure on the Iraqi government to follow U.S. priorities risk resentment and even collapse of the government if it heeds U.S. wishes but alienates ordinary Iraqis, and Iraqi leaders, soldiers, and citizens have had strong incentives to ride free on U.S. efforts and let the United States do the heavy lifting as long as it is clear that the United States has no intention of withdrawing any time soon. (For an insightful overview of these dilemmas in the Vietnam War, see Leslie Gelb and Richard Betts, *The Irony of Vietnam: The System Worked.*) Among the obvious differences between Iraq and Vietnam, some are making it more difficult to either stay in or depart from Iraq, and others are making both options easier than they were in Vietnam. Ethnic differences among the Shiites, Sunnis, and Kurds in Iraq and the history of repression by the Sunnis against the other two groups create complications unlike any faced in Vietnam. The presence of large oil reserves and refining industries, largely in the Shiite south of Iraq and the Kurdish north, create greater potential for rapid economic development in Iraq than was the case in Vietnam, but these oil reserves are also a prize to be fought over and source of Iraqi suspicions that the United States is more concerned over oil than democracy in Iraq. The conflict in Iraq is more manageable than that in Vietnam in other ways, particularly the absence of a geographic safe haven for anti-American forces, the more limited extent of outside aid to these forces (North Vietnam received massive military aid from the Soviet Union and China), the relative ease of patrolling Iraq's desert borders (as compared to the dense jungles of Vietnam), and the much smaller number of U.S. forces deployed and casualties sustained (the United States had over half a million troops in Vietnam at the height of the war and ultimately lost over 60,000 American troops killed). The lower number of troops and casualties in Iraq, together with the absence of a military draft, have resulted in less active public opposition to a continued deployment.

For more on the strategic options discussed in the introduction to this issue, see the report of the Baker-Hamilton Iraq Study Group at http://www.usip.org/isg/iraq_study_group_report/report/1206/index.html. See also James Dobbins, "Iraq: Winning the Unwinnable War," *Foreign Affairs* (January/February 2005) and Joseph Biden and Leslie Gelb, "Unity Through Autonomy in Iraq," *The New York Times* (May 1, 2006).

ISSUE 6

Should the United States Foster a Partition of Iraq?

YES: **Timothy Noah,** from "Should We Partition Iraq?" *Slate* (April 27, 2004)

NO: **Rend al-Rahim,** from "Partition Is Not the Solution," *The Washington Post* (October 29, 2006)

ISSUE SUMMARY

YES: Timothy Noah, author of the "Chatterbox" column of the online magazine *Slate,* argues that a managed partition of Iraq might be preferable to the ongoing conflict in that country.

NO: Rend al-Rahim, director of the Iraq Freedom Foundation and former representative of the Interim Iraqi government to the United States, argues that any attempt to draw lines of partition through the mixed regions of Iraq would intensify sectarian violence, lead to intervention by Iraq's neighbors, and bring about a radicalized Sunni regime in the middle of Iraq and a fundamentalist Shiite regime under Iranian influence in the south of Iraq.

At the outbreak of World War I, what we now call Iraq was part of the Ottoman Empire. When this empire disintegrated as a result of the war, the League of Nations created a single Iraqi state from the three Ottoman provinces of Mosul in the predominantly Kurdish north, Baghdad in the Sunni middle region, and Basra in the Shiite south. (Sunnis and Shiites represent two different and often antagonistic branches of Islam.) Britain was given a mandate to oversee Iraq until its independence, and after a difficult period of rule marked by violent uprisings, Iraq became independent in 1932.

Subsequent developments, particularly the oppressive rule of Saddam Hussein, reinforced the ethno-religious differences among Iraqis. Saddam came from the Sunni city of Tikrit, and showed strong favoritism toward Baghdad and the surrounding Sunni areas in terms of both his appointments of top officials and his spending on public works. After his loss to the United States in the Persian Gulf War in 1991, Saddam brutally put down uprisings in both the Shiite south and the Kurdish north, slaughtering many citizens and even using chemical weapons. After years of struggle, the Kurdish region in the north became effectively independent of the rest of Iraq, fielding its own government under the protection of U.S. air forces, which maintained a "no-fly zone" above much of northern Iraq to keep out Saddam's air forces. Thus, when the United States overthrew Saddam Hussein in 2003, the Kurds welcomed the American forces as long as the United States was helping them maintain their independence, the Shiites for the most part tolerated the American occupation because they were likely to win any elections (about 60 percent of Iraqis are Shiites), and the Sunnis in the middle formed the core of the resistance to U.S. forces because they had lost their privileged position.

One element that complicates the ethno-religious tensions exacerbated by Saddam's rule is the fact that most of Iraq's oil reserves are in the Shiite south and the Kurdish north. It will be difficult to convince leaders in these regions to share their oil revenues with the Sunni groups around Baghdad who had recently been their oppressors. Incidents of violence have already broken out between Arabs and Kurds in the oil-rich cities over ownership of land and houses taken from Kurds and given to Arab settlers during Saddam's rule. A second complication is that Iraq's neighbors all have ties to some groups in Iraq and fears about others. Iran, which is predominantly Shiite, hopes for Shiites to come to power in Iraq and aspires to have influence over them, but would work hard to prevent Sunnis from returning to power. (Saddam launched an enormously bloody war against Iran in the 1980s.) Saudi Arabia, Syria, and Kuwait, all predominantly Sunni, worry about the prospect of Shiites coming to power in Iraq and building ties to Iran. Turkey and Iran both worry about continued Kurdish independence in Iraq because many Kurds in these two countries hope to join with Iraq's Kurds to form an independent Kurdistan.

The situation in Iraq after the 2003 invasion was ripe for a civil war fueled by historical grievances, contested economic resources, interference by neighboring countries, and fears of ethnic violence. In the view of many observers, by 2006 sectarian violence in Iraq constituted a civil war (defined as contestation over the governance of a country between armed groups that causes significant casualties). Violence escalated sharply after the bombing of the Samarra Askariya Shiite mosque in February 2006. This led to a series of violent attacks between Shiite and Sunni militants as a Shiite-dominated government, voted into power in January 2005 by the Shiites who constitute Iraq's largest ethnic block, attemped to exert control through army and police forces that many of Iraq's Sunnis view as little different from Shiite militias. By the fall of 2006, Iraqi casualties reached a rate of over 3,000 per month, and nearly two million Iraqis had fled the country.

Timothy Noah picked up on calls by a small but prominent set of military and foreign policy experts for a partition of Iraq. In this view, while partitions are often difficult, violent, and vulnerable to renewed conflict, a managed partition might be preferable to one that comes about as the result of civil war. Rend al-Rahim argues that a partition would only intensify and continue Iraq's civil war, and would lead to interference by Iraq's neighbors, who would try to assist their fellow Sunnis and Shiites. The result, she maintains, would be a radical Sunni regime in central Iraq that would harbor anti-Western terrorists and a fundamentalist Shiite regime in the South under Iranian domination.

YES ⤶

Timothy Noah

Should We Partition Iraq?

"Iraq is not salvageable as a unitary state." So writes Peter Galbraith, America's pre-eminent Kurdophile, in the May 13 New York Review of Books ("How To Get Out of Iraq"). Leslie Gelb, formerly an assistant secretary in Jimmy Carter's State Department and subsequently a diplomatic correspondent for the New York Times, made a similar point on the Times op-ed page in November. Ralph Peters, a retired Army lieutenant colonel who writes on military strategy, has been calling for the breakup of Iraq for nearly a year. Reluctantly, Chatterbox is starting to think Galbraith, Gelb, and Peters have a point.

"The Iraq we're trying to herd back together," Peters wrote in July 2003, "consists of three distinct nations caged under a single, bloodstained flag." Iraq was famously invented in 1921 by Winston Churchill, then the British colonial secretary tasked with carving up the recently defeated Ottoman Empire. Churchill's main concern was to consolidate areas containing, or suspected to contain, oil fields. He achieved that at the expense of long-term political stability. From the start, mistrust existed between the country's three predominant groups: the Shiite Arabs in the south, the Sunni Arabs in the middle, and the Kurds, who weren't Arabs at all, in the north. A succession of regimes managed to yoke these three groups together only through varying degrees of repression, with Saddam's the most repressive of all. Short of putting a tanned, rested, and ready Saddam back in charge—a possibility we can surely rule out—government by repression is no longer an option.

Peters and Gelb seem to believe that the Bush administration's attempt to maintain postwar Iraq under a centralized government was doomed from the start. Galbraith, a liberal Democrat who opposed Saddam's regime well before the GOP did, thinks a unified Iraq may once have been achievable. But the failure of the United States to maintain order after the fall of Baghdad—most especially, to stop the looting of all the country's major institutions save the oil ministry—caused Iraq's professional class, "the very people the US looks to in rebuilding the country," to lose "confidence in, and respect for, the US occupation authorities." Now, Galbraith says, Humpty Dumpty can't be put together gain.

How would partition work? Gelb and Galbraith propose a very loose federation on the model of the former Yugoslavia. (Gelb envisions something akin to Yugoslavia as ruled after World War II by Marshall Tito, a Communist leader who avoided Soviet control; Galbraith prefers the model of Yugoslavia after

Tito's death in 1980.) The obvious problem with this model is that the federation unraveled starting in the early 1990s, leading to bloody civil war. But Galbraith, who was ambassador to Croatia in the Clinton administration, maintains that Yugoslavia's breakup was not inevitable. If Slobodan Milosevic had been willing to settle for "a looser federation," Galbraith argues, "there is every reason to think that Yugoslavia—and not just Slovenia—would be joining the European Union this May." Gelb blames Europeans and Americans for taking too long to come to the aid of Bosnians and Croats but notes that the region is now relatively stable and that Kosovo will soon enjoy some form of autonomy.

The sharing of oil revenue would be the main function of the loose federation envisioned by Gelb, Galbraith, and Peters. Galbraith posits "a weak presidency rotating among the republics, with [further] responsibilities limited to foreign affairs, monetary policy, and some coordination of defense policy." Peters has a more radical proposal. By all means, he says, let's try the federal solution. But if the Sunnis, who are bitter about losing control over Iraq, persist in their violent rebellion against all proposed post-Saddam arrangements, Peters says we should dissolve the federation and create three "fully independent states." That, Peters notes, would "leave the Sunni Arabs to rot," since the Sunnis have no oil to speak of. In practice, Peters' plan to dissolve the federation altogether may well be what Gelb's and Galbraith's plans would lead to. "Loose federations rarely last," observes Joost Hiltermann, a human rights expert who has followed events in Iraq. (The organization he works for, International Crisis Group, has been urging Kurds to moderate their territorial demands, which would be advisable no matter what the larger outcome.)

Gelb and Galbraith both assume the Sunnis are probably ungovernable, at least for the near term. But partition, Galbraith argues, would at least limit the anarchy to "a finite area," thereby making the U.S. military's peacekeeping job easier to perform than it is now. Eventually, some sort of Sunni government would, one hopes, emerge, though given the region's propensity for thuggery (Saddam is a Sunni), it's hard to imagine that government would be a model of parliamentary democracy. Maybe the Peters threat to cut off oil revenues would help. The effectiveness of this threat can only be known down the road, when there is significant oil revenue to cut off.

Autonomy for the Shiite region is in many ways more problematic. The Shiites wouldn't starve, because they have oil. And there's no particular reason to think they don't know how to run a free and fair election. The worry is what that free and fair election would choose. In December, Gelb said it wasn't likely that the Shiites would preside over "a theocratic state." Taking into account subsequent events, Galbraith has to concede that the Shiites are, in fact, pretty likely to vote themselves a theocratic government. That would almost certainly mean the Shiites would impose restrictions on free speech and the rights of women that Westerners and more than a few Shiites would find repugnant. But Galbraith says that if we were able to remove ourselves relatively quickly, the Shiite government might be "less overtly anti-American."

Andrew Apostolou, director of research at the Foundation for the Defense of Democracies, a nonprofit group, is more hopeful that the Shiite theocrats can be defeated. "I don't believe that just because they're the loudest and the noisiest they're the most powerful," he told Chatterbox, citing an April 5 Guardian account of an election in Tar, a town of 15,000 people. Neither of the two Islamist candidates for 10 town council seats won. But Tar is hardly typical; it was the first town in Iraq to rise up against Saddam during the unsuccessful rebellion that followed the first Gulf war.

The third autonomous state created by the breakup of Iraq would be Iraqi Kurdistan. Autonomy is what Iraqi Kurds have long desired, and it's more or less what the No-Fly Zone created by the United States and Britain gave them after Gulf War I. The Kurds have already demonstrated that they can hold free elections and maintain a free press. An early March memo from the Coalition Provision Authority, unearthed last week by reporter Jason Vest, alludes vaguely to Kurdish corruption. (The Washington Post's "Reliable Source" columnist, Richard Leiby, says three sources told him the memo's author was former Pentagon aide Michael Rubin, though Rubin wouldn't confirm it.) The memo describes an evening with an Iraqi Kurd spent watching the Godfather trilogy and "discussing which Iraqi Kurdish politicians represented which character." But assuming that means the Kurdish leadership has a propensity for Chicago-style ward politics, its vices shouldn't cause much loss of sleep. In any event, Kurdish leaders would have a long way to go before they robbed Kurdistan of as much money as Rubin suggests the United Nations did under the Oil-for-Food program.

Just about everybody who's operating free of any bureaucratic imperatives (including Chatterbox) believes the Kurds should enjoy autonomy within whatever kind of Iraqi state emerges. God knows they've earned it. The awkward question, though, is how you grant autonomy to the Kurds while denying it to the Shiites and the Sunnis.

The probable answer is: You can't. But accepting a three-state solution, enclosed inside a loose federation or not, likely means giving up on certain aspirations. One aspiration is to make Iraq a democratic nation. More likely, it would be a two-thirds democratic federation or geographic region, with the possibility of a Sunni democracy down the road. Another aspiration is to establish the rule of law. In the short run, and perhaps even in the long, that would likely happen only in Iraqi Kurdistan. A third aspiration is to stop the killing. But that wouldn't happen in the Sunni territory, though it might happen later. A fourth and final aspiration is to avoid taking a country that was fascist, but not terribly theocratic, and allowing one-third of it to become a theocracy. This hope is not merely idealistic but also, conceivably, related to national security, insofar as the creation of any new Islamic theocracy provides a potential recruiting ground for al-Qaida. But Chatterbox doesn't have any great ideas about how to keep Iraqi Shiites from making that democratic choice. As Galbraith says, maybe they'll hate us less if we let them make that choice sooner rather than later.

What's most depressing about the Peters-Gelb-Galbraith scenario is that it would create three autonomous governments or independent states that represented only an incremental improvement on what was there before (except with regard to geopolitical stability). It would make us scratch our heads and wonder why we fought a war in Iraq. But that may be unavoidable, too.

Rend al-Rahim

→ NO

Partition Is Not the Solution . . .

Desperate to find solutions to the violence in Iraq and thus an exit strategy for the United States, an increasing number of lawmakers in Congress are considering Iraq's partition into Kurdish, Sunni and Shiite regions under the umbrella of a loose confederation. But partition is neither desirable nor feasible.

Neat partition lines are impossible because few regions in Iraq are ethnically or confessionally homogeneous. The governorates of Diyala, Mosul, Salahuddin, Hilla, Kirkuk and Basra are intermixed or have large minorities scattered throughout each province. In Baghdad, with probably a quarter of Iraq's population, the ethnic and sectarian groups are inextricably interwoven.

A plan to partition Iraq would plunge the country into total civil war far more widespread and bloody than the sectarian and factional violence we are witnessing now. The partition of India and Pakistan in 1947 resulted in 2 million dead and 11 million displaced. The death toll and refugee numbers from collective murder, reprisal killings and ethnic cleansing in Iraq would be comparable, dwarfing the casualties in Iraq today.

Nor would conflict end once areas had been purified at this horrific human cost. As in Kashmir, regions along the partition lines would continue to be contested for decades, leading to continued violence and warfare. The belt of towns surrounding Baghdad would be a war zone of competing territorial claims, as would the border regions skirting Kirkuk, Mosul and Diyala.

With the exception of the Kurdish regional government, the institutions of local governance, including regional councils, regional assemblies and the local police forces, are underdeveloped and fragmented, with little capacity to preserve the rule of law or deliver services. In such an environment, partition will inevitably lead to a meltdown of authority, and internecine fighting would intensify. We have had a harbinger of such warfare in the so-called stable areas in the south, where fighting has erupted in Basra, Diwaniyah and Amarah among the various Shiite factions; it has been contained only provisionally and with the greatest difficulty. With control of resources and absolute power as the beckoning prize, the factions would battle even more viciously for supremacy.

Iraq's neighbors would not stand by and passively witness the turmoil attending efforts at partition. There is too much at stake for all of them, and several are already meddling in Iraq's internal affairs. If Iraq is partitioned, Iran, Turkey, Syria and Saudi Arabia will intervene—either militarily and directly, as Turkey might do in Kurdistan and northern Iraq, or by increasing and expanding support to Iraqi factions, or both. In the case of Iran, a stepped-up nonmilitary Iranian presence and increased support for pro-Iranian groups are both feasible and likely options. Iraq would thus become the battleground of an undeclared war for control not only of Iraq but of the entire Middle East.

The most probable outcome of this violent competition for territory, resources and power would be a radical Sunni, Taliban-style regime in the west and in parts of central Iraq that would be a breeding ground for terrorism. In the south it is likely there would be a fundamentalist Shiite regime pliant to Iran's will. In both cases these would be authoritarian regimes hostile to pluralism and genuine democracy. Unchecked by a stunted and impotent national government, these governments would use their resources to promote their radical ideologies abroad, support like-minded movements in neighboring countries and destabilize the region. Meanwhile, Baghdad would remain a war-torn city with a fig-leaf government too feeble to hold itself together, let alone uphold the rule of law across the country.

These are hardly the outcomes for which the United States fought a war to remove Saddam Hussein from power and for which Iraqis and Americans continue to pay a price in precious lives and resources. Rather than seeking ways to weaken the national government, we should find ways to strengthen and empower it to do a better job, and seriously consider substantially increasing the number of Iraqi army troops and raising the number of U.S. forces at least temporarily.

At this stage, strengthening the national government and providing it with the tools and institutions to enforce the rule of law is far more likely to produce a stable country that can govern and defend itself and be a friend to the United States. This, rather than a misguided plan of partition, presents a viable exit strategy for the United States and a definition of success in Iraq.

We need to engage in new thinking and develop new strategies for Iraq, but above all, no matter how dire the situation, we must not grasp at options that look good in theory but would prove disastrous in practice.

POSTSCRIPT

Should the United States
Foster a Partition of Iraq?

Partitions have a mixed history as a solution to civil conflicts. Some partitions, such as that between the Greek and Turkish factions on Cyprus, have led to long-term peace and stability despite the fact that underlying tensions remain. Others, such as the division of Czechoslovakia into the Czech and Slovak republics, have been achieved peacefully. Some, like the political partition of Germany into East Germany and West Germany in the Cold War, have been reversed peacefully. Most partitions and re-unifications have taken place in the context of widespread violence, however, or have continued to be the source of sharp conflicts for decades, including the partitions of Korea and Vietnam into northern and southern regions, the breakup of Yugoslavia, the partition of India, Pakistan, and Bangladesh, and the partition of Israeli and Palestinian areas. Even those who advocate partition in Iraq do not expect that this could be accomplished easily or without violence—their main point is that partition may well be the outcome whether we encourage it or not.

For more on Iraq's history, see http://www.angelfire.com/nt/Gilgamesh/history.html. For competing arguments on the history of partitions, see Chaim Kaufmann, "When All Else Fails: Ethnic Population Transfers and Partitions in the Twentieth Century," *International Security* (Fall 1998), Rada Kumar, "The Troubled History of Partition," *Foreign Affairs* (January/February 1997), and Nicholas Sambanis, "Partition as a Solution to Ethnic War: An Empirical Critique of the Theoretical Literatures," *World Politics* (July 2000). Kaufmann argues partitions may be useful when other methods of conflict resolution have failed, while Kumar and Sambanis question the ability of partitions to contribute to long-term peace and stability.

Internet References . . .

The World Factbook

A first step toward better knowledge of the regional and bilateral policy concerns of the United States is to learn more about the other countries and political entities in the world. An excellent source, and one that is updated annually, is *The World Factbook*, which is a product of the Central Intelligence Agency. It can be bought from the commercial publishing house that prints it or it can be found at this site.

http://www.odci.gov/cia/publications/factbook/

International Information Programs

This Web site is operated by the U.S. Department of State's Office of International Information Programs. The site is divided into regional groups, among other things, and it gives a good array of the regional issues that are of current foreign policy concern.

http://usinfo.state.gov

Editor & Publisher

It is always good advice in diplomacy and other endeavors to try to see yourself as others see you. The publication *Editor & Publisher* has an excellent Web site to sample the foreign media newspapers, magazines, radio, television, and wire services. You can search by region, media types, and other categories.

http://www.editorandpublisher.com

Carnegie Endowment for International Peace

The Carnegie Endowment for International Peace is a good source for research, publications, and conferences regarding the relations among governments, business, international organizations, and civil society across different regions. It focuses on the economic, political, and technological forces driving global change.

http://www.carnegieendowment.org/

Brookings Institution

The Brookings Institution provides nonpartisan perspectives and expertise on issues facing the United States. It has focused on issues including improving the equity of the American democratic process, the performance of the economy, the health of society, the effectiveness of diplomacy and defense, the quality of public discourse, and the workings of institutions—public and private, domestic and international.

http://www.brookings.edu

The United States and the World: Regional and Bilateral Relations

*T*he debates in this section address some of the issues in American foreign policy that relate to various countries in different regions of the world. The range of issues include the difficulties of allying strategically with countries whose practices or policies otherwise run counter to U.S. ideals; determining how and when to act as a broker between groups engaged in ongoing regional struggles; managing relations with countries that have been hostile and could again become antagonistic toward the United States; and developing economic and political relations with countries with whom the United States shares common objectives in some areas and divergent objectives in others.

- Is Pakistan an Asset in the War on Terror?
- Should the United States Preemptively Attack Iranian Nuclear Facilities?
- Should the United States Send Peacekeeping Troops to Darfur?
- Is China's Rise Threatening to the United States?
- Should the United States Seek Negotiations and Engagement with North Korea?
- Is the U.S. Support for Israel a Key Factor in America's Difficulties in the Middle East?

ISSUE 7

Is Pakistan an Asset in the War on Terror?

YES: Teresita C. Schaffer, from "Strategic Trends in South Asia," Testimony Before the Subcommittee on Asia and the Pacific, House International Relations Committee (March 17, 2004)

NO: Sydney J. Freedberg Jr., from "The Hunt for Osama," *National Journal* (June 3, 2006)

ISSUE SUMMARY

YES: Teresita Schaffer, director of the South Asian Program at the Center for Strategic and International Studies, notes many problems in Pakistan's domestic and foreign policies, but holds out the hope that Pakistan is getting more serious about cracking down on terrorists in Pakistan and pursuing peace in its troubled relations with India.

NO: Sydney Freedberg, a journalist for *The National Journal,* notes that Osama bin Laden and other top al Qaeda and Taliban leaders are widely believed to be hiding in northern Pakistan, and he details the difficulties of getting the Pakistani government, and even more importantly the tribes in the relatively lawless northern regions of Pakistan, to cooperate in capturing bin Laden and closing down military operations by al Qaeda and the Taliban.

The United States and Pakistan have had a roller-coaster relationship for decades. The two countries have cycled between periods of cooperation and tension over a number of issues, including Pakistan's nuclear weapons programs, regional developments like the Soviet invasion and occupation of Afghanistan, Pakistan's alternation between relative democracy and military rule, the presence of terrorist groups in Pakistan, and Pakistan's relations with India over the disputed border region of Kashmir. (Kashmir is part of India, a largely Hindu country, but is predominantly Muslim like Pakistan, and many Kashmiris would prefer to be part of Pakistan.) In the 1970s, the United States limited its relations with Pakistan because of that country's active efforts to acquire nuclear weapons.

When the Soviet Union invaded Afghanistan in 1979, however, the United States developed a close relationship with Pakistan as both countries had an interest in providing arms and assistance to the Mujahideen warriors who were fighting against the Soviet occupation of Afghanistan and who used northern Pakistan as a safe haven and staging base. At the height of the Afghan conflict, over $500 million a year of U.S. military aid to the Afghan rebels passed through Pakistan, though some tensions remained as Pakistan's security services channeled much of this aid toward radical Islamic groups that were friendly to Pakistan.

Soon after the Soviet Union withdrew from Afghanistan in 1989, the United States abruptly re-imposed sanctions on Pakistan because of its nuclear weapons program. The United States even refused to deliver fighter aircraft for which Pakistan had already paid hundreds of millions of dollars. U.S. sanctions intensified after Pakistan tested its nuclear weapons for the first time in 1998 in response to a series of test nuclear explosions by India.

The relationship took another sharp turn after the 9/11 attacks, as Pakistan became critical to America's ability to remove the Taliban government of Afghanistan that had been providing a safe haven for Osama bin Laden and his al Qaeda terrorist organization. The United States ended its sanctions on Pakistan and provided renewed military and economic aid as Pakistan pledged to help in the war on terrorism. As Teresita Schaffer notes, the United States has kept up its close relationship with Pakistan since 9/11 even after it was revealed that Dr. Abdul Qadeer Khan, a top Pakistani nuclear scientist, had secretly provided assistance to the nuclear weapons programs of North Korea and other countries.

The renewed relationship has provided benefits to both sides since 9/11, but several underlying sources of tension remain in addition to Pakistan's nuclear weapons program. Several top level al Qaeda operatives have been captured in Pakistan and elsewhere with Pakistani assistance, yet northern Pakistan remains largely beyond the control of the Pakistani central government, and most intelligence analysts believe that numerous Taliban and al Qaeda operatives, perhaps including Osama bin Laden, are in this region. Pakistan has been reigning in militants who have been attacking Indian forces in Kashmir, but Pakistani President General Pervez Musharraf continues to do a delicate balancing act with militant Islamic groups in Pakistan, who are believed to have been behind several attempts to assassinate Musharraf. Musharraf's claim to a democratic mandate is also tenuous at best, as he took power in a bloodless military coup and has validated his rule with elections in which various restrictions made him the only practical candidate. Because the United States and Pakistan have profoundly different geopolitical positions, cultures, and histories, such domestic and international issues will likely continue to complicate U.S.-Pakistani relations.

YES ⤶

Strategic Trends in South Asia

Mr. Chairman, members of the committee,

I appear before you today at a time of great change in the South Asian region. Danger is now tempered by hope, driven in large measure by the recent moves by India and Pakistan to develop a peace process.

Mr. Chairman, in your letter of invitation, you asked me to speak about the strategic trends and challenges facing the region. The United States is dealing with four major issues in South Asia:

- Securing and strengthening peace. This is largely a function of the India-Pakistan relationship, which today is moving in the right direction. Discreet, imaginative, and persistent U.S. diplomacy needs to nurture this process.
- Controlling and, we hope, ending terrorism. In the South Asian context, and indeed in the world, this depends primarily on Pakistan. The U.S. government has placed great stress on Pakistan's cooperation in anti-terrorism policy. I believe it needs to pay more heed to Pakistan's need to develop stronger civilian institutions and a healthier political system, without which the anti-terrorism effort will fail.
- Preventing the spread of nuclear weapons and knowhow. The administration has accepted the Government of Pakistan's assurances that it will fully cooperate in closing down the nuclear black market. It has a credibility problem, however—and so does the United States.
- Developing a concept of regional security that fits the changing face of Asia. Here the U.S.-India relationship, and India's own development in the next decade, is key, and current U.S. policy is serving our needs well.

Let me discuss each of these issues in turn.

Securing Peace: A Hopeful Moment

India and Pakistan made a dramatic decision last January to re-start their peace process. I believe this created a significant opportunity. We may be witnessing a moment of strategic change.

Many peace overtures have been launched in the past decade, and several within the past few years. The factors that led earlier efforts to fail have not gone away. The India-Pakistan dispute is still a stubborn one, bound up

From Testimony Before the Subcommittee on Asia and the Pacific, House International Relations Committee by Teresita C. Schaffer, March 17, 2004.

112

with both nations' sense of identity, symbolized for both in different ways by the Kashmir issue. My recent discussions in India, in Pakistan, and on both sides of the dividing line in Kashmir lead me to be cautiously hopeful that this peace opening may be different.

In India, the government appears to have wide popular support for its decision to agree to talks with Pakistan. Though opinions vary, the predominant sentiment is guarded optimism. The Indian government has made considerable efforts to avoid scoring debating points in the media, even when deeply troubling issues came up, such as the revelations about the activities of Pakistan's nuclear scientist Abdul Qadeer Khan. Prime Minister Vajpayee has clearly concluded that having a peace process is good politics. His opponents in the Congress Party apparently feel the same way, since they have not criticized the peace moves even in the heat of the election campaign.

In Pakistan, even a frequent visitor like me was overwhelmed by the sense that the Pakistani government has made a far-reaching policy change, one that may turn out to be strategic. People representing many shades of opinion spoke consistently of the need for Pakistan to base its policy on "relentless realism." They welcomed incremental steps to improve India-Pakistan relations, including opening a bus route between the two sides of Kashmir and expanding India-Pakistan trade. These ideas may seem obvious, but in the past Pakistan has regarded incremental measures with suspicion, fearing that they would sideline its central concerns over Kashmir. Suspicion of India remains, and India's and Pakistan's ideas on how to address their major disputes are still far apart. What is new and encouraging, however, is this more practical, process-oriented approach to addressing them.

Perhaps most interestingly, I found people from many shades of political opinion on the Indian side of Kashmir uncharacteristically hopeful about the détente moves between India and Pakistan. In a place where cynicism is both common and understandable, separatist political parties spoke with hope about the potential for creating human links across the line if the bus service was established. They were more worried about the future of their talks with the Indian government, which they felt could only continue if the government was able to significantly reduce the human rights problems stemming from military operations in Kashmir.

On the Pakistan side of Kashmir, the mood of hope was weaker. This is not surprising: this is an area where creative thinking about Kashmir has been entirely absent for fifty-plus years. Even the modest economic progress one finds on the Indian side is lacking. But even there, it was clear that significant progress between India and Pakistan would be well received.

India and Pakistan have evidently both concluded that moving toward peace suits their interests. This creates today's positive mood. But progress depends on more than a good atmosphere. India and Pakistan will need to show great flexibility, imagination, and forbearance, and their determination will have to overcome periodic setbacks. Pakistan will need to continue preventing militants from crossing the Line of Control to feed the violent movement in Kashmir. As the security situation improves, Kashmiris will be looking for signs that the Indians are thinning out their security presence.

Some way will have to be found to connect Kashmiris themselves to the peace process, and to bring real change to their relationship with the Government of India. The governments' work is also vulnerable to the actions of spoilers, including hard-line militant groups who have used terrorism in the past.

I believe that the United States needs to help nurture the progress that has been made and encourage both parties to keep the process moving. In this election year I do not expect a major, high profile diplomatic initiative. But U.S. interests in the success of this enterprise are enormous, so our attention and our discreet, sophisticated support for India's and Pakistan's work must not flag.

Pakistan is the key to controlling terrorism:

The renewed U.S.-Pakistan relationship after September 11 was built on cooperation against terrorism, and on the understanding that this was a goal both countries needed to pursue for their own reasons. Pakistan's decision to end its support for the Taliban government in Afghanistan and to facilitate U.S. anti-terrorism operations in Afghanistan rested on this foundation. So did Pakistan's efforts to develop a decent relationship with the new Afghan government.

As you know, Mr. Chairman, the Pakistan government tried for at least the first two years after 9/11 to balance this objective against other long-standing Pakistani goals, including supporting militancy in Kashmir. It also tried to balance the U.S. interest in putting Al Qaeda out of business against the domestic pressures it faced from militant groups with historical ties to the Pakistani intelligence services. The result was a Pakistani policy beset by internal contradictions, and one that was not always in harmony with ours.

Compounding this problem was the weakness of the institutions representing the civilian side of the Pakistani state. The Pakistan Army has dominated politics there for years, but especially for the four-plus years since General Musharraf took power. The election of October 2002 brought in an elected civilian government. However, this government has remained weak in relation to Musharraf. The parliament took 15 months to reach agreement with Musharraf on the constitutional amendments he wanted to bring in by decree. Political parties remain weak, internally autocratic, and at logger-heads. I believe that this institutional disarray in Pakistan has left the government with no instruments to use in dealing with the militant movements other than the army itself, an army that remains ambivalent about ending the militants' lawless behavior.

In the past two months, following two well-publicized attempts on President Musharraf's life, there are indications that his government is making a new and more serious effort to cut back the role of the militants in Pakistan's political life. I hope this represents a strategic change. We will be better able to gauge that in the next few months. This would be the first step toward a far-reaching change in Pakistan's domestic political system that is essential, I believe, to ending the threat of terrorism in and from Pakistan.

But the change needs to go further. In the past four years, there has been much talk about the importance of restoring democracy in Pakistan. The big opportunity to do that was the election, but Pakistan missed that opportunity and, I would argue, the United States government did little to take advantage of it. Without a more balanced political scene in Pakistan, however, it is hard to see how the Pakistan government can get a handle on the terrorist "nests" that have moved into the ill-policed and shadowy parts of Pakistan's cities. And without healthy political institutions, it is hard to see how Pakistan's population will be able to give a government the legitimacy it needs to overcome the country's deep-seated problems.

At this point, it is hard to imagine a scenario in which the military would leave the center of Pakistan's political stage in the next five years. The United States needs a democracy policy, but one that recognizes the very difficult circumstances in which democracy needs to develop in Pakistan. The heart of such a policy, in my view, is support for strengthening Pakistan's institutions. At least half of the economic aid the U.S. has promised Pakistan should be specifically programmed for activities that will help Pakistanis rebuild the institutions on which decent government rests—both the political ones and the administrative machinery they need. The most urgent candidates for institutional rebuilding include the judiciary, the government's major administrative services, and the police. Restoring the vitality and credibility of the parliament is also essential, though countries with a parliamentary system may be better placed to provide this support than the U.S. Pakistan's civil society also needs support from its friends outside the country.

Many people have argued that our top priority in Pakistan should be educational reform, and specifically reform of the madrassahs. I agree that education is an urgent priority. However, I believe that strengthening institutions is a prerequisite for effective educational reform. At present, the education ministry is ill equipped to undertake the massive task of registering thousands of madrassahs, let alone imposing curriculum reform and monitoring the results.

The important point is that rebuilding institutions and educational reform are not alternatives to our anti-terrorism policy. They are requirements for it. Without more vigorous institutions, I do not believe Pakistan will be able to restore a healthy political and economic life, and without that transformation, I see no prospect of its sustaining an effective anti-terrorism policy.

Nuclear Proliferation

The recent peace moves between Pakistan and India offer the hope that these two nuclear-armed countries may ultimately eliminate the risk of nuclear war in the subcontinent. Recent developments make clear, however, that Pakistan has already contributed to the spread of nuclear weapons beyond this region, a grave setback for U.S. interests and for global security.

The administration has decided to accept the Pakistan government's explanation that its nuclear scientist, Dr. Abdul Qadeer Khan, engaged in a nuclear black market solely on his own, without government authorization. The administration is focusing its efforts on obtaining full Pakistani cooperation in rolling up the network for illicit sales and preventing future transfers.

Obviously, the transfers that have already taken place cannot be prevented, and closing down the "nuclear bazaar" is of enormous importance.

The U.S., as so often in the past, has a long list of important issues it is pursuing with Pakistan, and this is not the first time that an administration has found it necessary to make difficult choices among them. And this administration undoubtedly recalled, as it put together its response to Dr. Khan's activities, that punitive policies have a poor track record in bringing about major changes in Pakistan government policies, as witnessed by our inability to prevent Pakistan from developing nuclear weapons in the first place.

But by letting bygones be bygones, we risk creating once again the kind of awful misunderstanding that has gotten the U.S. in trouble in its relations with Pakistan in the past. The theory that Dr. Khan conducted all these nuclear transactions without the knowledge or authorization of anyone in the government or army is out of keeping with the way the Pakistan government normally works. How can we be sure that we are receiving full information on the operations of the nuclear black market? And how can we avoid having the Pakistan government conclude that the U.S. will overlook future actions that cross U.S. "red lines" in nuclear policy? A serious discussion of those issues, and of the policy options available to the United States, would get into intelligence issues that only the administration can address, and these would in any case not be suitable for discussion in this setting. But given the scale of Dr. Khan's activities, and the dangerous character of his customers, I believe that U.S. willingness to act in the event of future problems needs to be made both clear and credible.

A New Regional Security Paradigm

In the past, South Asia has been looked at as a set of problems and relationships separate from the two areas of major U.S. concern that flank the region, the Middle East and East Asia. I believe that the time has come to look at the region as part of a broader Asia/Middle East security continuum.

Looking at the Asian part of this picture, which is the concern of this subcommittee, consider the changes that have taken place in the past decade. China, already a major regional power from the security point of view, has become a global economic powerhouse, and its strength in both categories is likely to grow in the next decade provided its domestic stresses are skillfully managed. Japan has undergone an extended economic slump. This committee is well aware of the challenges U.S. policymakers face on the Korean peninsula. Indonesia's political fragility is well known. The rest of Southeast Asia has been through a decade of economic ups and downs.

These circumstances make it important for the United States to extend the network of strong friendships beyond the East Asian countries that have historically been the core of U.S. relations in Asia. The dramatic deepening of U.S. ties with India in this administration and the last one reflect in part our recognition that as Asia changes, we need to be involved in the entire region.

India has been one of the world's fastest growing countries in the past two decades. Its economic growth may exceed 7 percent this year. It has deepened its political, economic and security relations with the countries to its east. While Indian strategic thinkers still consider China to be India's principal strategic rival in the long term, both governments have decided to work toward a transformation of their bilateral relations. Evidence of this includes a more serious approach to their border dispute and a dramatic expansion of economic ties. Two-way trade is now estimated at $7 billion, nearly half India's two-way trade with the U.S. and four times its trade with Russia. India's world-class information technology companies are creating business connections in China that will surely be a force to be reckoned with in that global market.

India's economic expansion, together with the end of the Cold War and the linkages created by the Indian-American community, was the foundation for the expanded U.S.-Indian relations. However, in recent years, the most dynamic aspect of government-to-government relations has been in the security area. Increasingly, Indian and U.S. interests in Asian regional security are converging.

Current U.S. policy has responded effectively to these changing circumstances. Our dialogue with India has expanded beyond the traditional focus on South Asian problems. I believe this trend needs to be encouraged. The U.S. and India should be systematically comparing notes on trends in East Asia and the Middle East. And as the U.S. considers its security interests in Asia, it needs to get rid of the traditional "curry curtain" that has placed South and East Asia in separate mental categories. With much of the world's oil supply moving through the Indian Ocean, with India's increasing interest in the security of the area to its east, and with our own unique global role, we need to factor India explicitly into the way we look at Asia.

This subcommittee's responsibility for Asia and the Pacific gives it a unique role in maintaining the broad regional perspective today's world demands. I hope that you will continue to focus, as you are doing today, on the way the dangers and opportunities that confront the United States today in all of Asia.

Sydney J. Freedberg Jr.  **NO**

The Hunt for Osama

How Do We Find Osama bin Laden?

On September 10, 2001, most Americans could not have told you who he was, let alone where. On September 12, he was global enemy No. 1, a recognized world leader with regimented fighters, base camps, and a whole country as his sanctuary. That state of affairs lasted until late November. Then bin Laden eluded his pursuers at Tora Bora and vanished into the mountainous badlands of the Afghanistan-Pakistan frontier, resurfacing intermittently as a video image or a disembodied voice on tape.

In just three months, the man had moved from obscurity to infamy to myth. To this day, every syllable of his rare pronouncements is dissected and debated. The image of him in his cave has become an icon in everything from political cartoons to online ads, where you can punch the murderer of 3,000 Americans in the nose to win free video games.

The frustration about not getting bin Laden is palpable. Nearly five years after 9/11, neither the vaunted American military nor the clandestine CIA can get its hands on him. On talk radio and in Internet chat rooms, people ask why we can't just send in the Rangers, the 10th Mountain Division, the Marines, and the Green Berets and turn over every rock in Pakistan until we get him.

The answer, say soldiers, spies, and scholars alike, is that it would take limitless manpower to comb Pakistan's mountainous badlands and sprawling cities. Even smaller incursions could cause enough civilian casualties, and enough injury to Pakistani national pride, to topple Pakistani President Pervez Musharraf—leaving Islamabad's nuclear weapons loose, or worse, in the hands of fundamentalists in the volatile and heavily armed region where Iran, India, Afghanistan, and China converge. Even if U.S. forces were not overcommitted in Iraq, most experts agree, the only way to get bin Laden would still be by using the slow and steady squeeze, recruiting local informants one at a time until someone tips us off to where he's hiding.

The hunt for the real bin Laden is not simple, because the target is not simply bin Laden—and he is almost certainly not in any cave. "In the last videotape we've seen of him, his clothes are well pressed," said journalist Peter Bergen, one of the few Westerners to have interviewed bin Laden. "Caves don't have laundry facilities." Since that tape was shown, in October 2004,

From *National Journal*, vol. 38, issue 22, June 3, 2006, pp. 26–33. Copyright © 2006 by National Journal. All rights reserved. Reprinted with permission via Reprint Outsource Inc.

bin Laden has released only audio recordings: By now, the world's most recognizable fugitive could well have shaved his beard, gained some weight, traded his white robes for blue jeans, and moved to Laurel, Md., just as several of his 9/11 hijackers did. A single individual is almost impossible to find.

But the hunt for bin Laden, fortunately, is not a quest for a single individual. Those robes don't press themselves: Wherever bin Laden is, somebody nearby is doing his laundry. Someone is cooking his meals. Someone is buying his food. Someone is standing watch: "a minimum of one bodyguard who is charged with killing bin Laden in the event he's captured," Bergen speculates, and perhaps as many as the hundreds who guarded him in Afghanistan. If rumors of ill health are true—that he's receiving dialysis or was badly wounded at Tora Bora—a doctor is nearby. At least one car will be needed for emergencies, if not a whole convoy, which means maintenance and gas, which, like food and medicine, means raising money. And this entire infrastructure is just to keep bin Laden alive as the symbolic leader of radical Islam.

Someone in that infrastructure might one day slip, or talk too much, or be overheard. And then the trail can be picked up.

A Network of Vulnerabilities

If bin Laden wants to do anything besides exist—if, for example, he wants to release a tape—he needs not just a household but also a network. "They've got to have contact," said former CIA analyst Stanley Bedlington, "and this is a vulnerability." Bin Laden could record an audiotape by himself. But however the recording is made, he can't simply upload it over his high-speed modem, even if he has one, for fear of electronic eavesdropping. So that means at least one courier, and probably a chain of relays, including hired smugglers with no idea what they're carrying or for whom. The couriers have to get the physical tape from bin Laden's hideout to a town big enough to have either decent Internet access—which requires an additional Qaeda operative, this one Web-savvy enough to upload the recording—or a freelancer tied to sympathetic news outlets like Al Jazeera—which requires an operative with enough media savvy to contact a reporter and persuade him to pick up the tape from the "dead drop" where the last courier hid it.

If bin Laden wants to lend more than moral support to extremist groups around the globe, then the contacts, and the vulnerabilities, multiply exponentially. The courier network now has to move in both directions, bringing reports and requests in, as well as recordings and messages out. It also has to extend much farther, sharply increasing its exposure to surveillance. That's because to move missives and money across continents, an agent at some point has to get on an airplane, go online, or pick up the phone.

"We say they're anti-modern, but they love the tools of modernity and they're very good at using them," said Michael Scheuer, former head of the CIA's bin Laden unit and author of Imperial Hubris: Why the West Is Losing the War on Terror. And nowadays, he added, even small towns on the Pakistani frontier are "full of Internet cafés."

In Al Qaeda, however, it is only the low-level wannabes and fellow travelers who chatter casually on jihadi Web sites. Real field operatives use phones and e-mail more cautiously. Middle managers—men like 9/11 planner Khalid Shaikh Mohammed, captured in 2003, and computer engineer Muhammad Naeem Noor Khan, captured in 2004—seem to shuttle between major Pakistani cities, such as Karachi and Lahore, which have international airports and good communications, and the tribal badlands where bin Laden and his deputy Ayman al-Zawahiri are believed to be hiding. Those most-senior leaders themselves rely almost entirely on face-to-face meetings, having learned from leaks and from the mistakes of men like terrorist Abu Nidal and drug lord Pablo Escobar about America's ability to trace electronic communications.

"They're very careful about how they use the Internet and satellite phones," said retired Army Col. Patrick Lang, the former chief of human intelligence for the Defense Intelligence Agency. "If they weren't careful, we'd have got them by now." Eavesdropping might pick up lower-level operatives, but to reach the senior leaders, he said, "there's only one way to find them: start with an American who speaks some Islamic language, then recruit a 'daisy chain' of agents, one leading to another, until you get to someone who can tell you where these high-value targets are." It means befriending drug runners, ranting clerics, shady businessmen, and ordinary, innocent Muslims concerned about their radical relative's trip to Pakistan, until you find someone with the right contacts and the right human weakness to exploit.

"You have to start way out in the periphery," agreed Fred Burton, a former counter-terrorism agent for the State Department who worked with the Pakistanis to capture Ramzi Ahmed Yousef, plotter of the 1993 World Trade Center attack, in Islamabad two years later. The process is less James Bond than The Sopranos. "I've worked informants," Burton said. "They usually do this out of self-preservation. They're tired, they're fearful, they want out, and they realize they can't just walk away."

As U.S., Afghan, and Pakistani pressure mounts—more military sweeps, more air strikes, more money seized—life for bin Laden's network of subordinates becomes more intolerable, and snitching more attractive. "Eventually, something's got to give," Burton said. "It would probably happen very, very fast and be very, very violent."

Every explosion turns up the heat. Four strikes in the Pakistani border district of Waziristan this winter and spring—one by Pakistani troops and three attributed to U.S. missiles—reportedly killed three midranking Qaeda officers: a regional commander, a suspect in the 1998 African embassy bombings, and an aide to bin Laden deputy Zawahiri, although Zawahiri himself escaped.

"Violence is one of the greatest ways to collect intelligence," Scheuer said. Strikes panic survivors into fleeing or calling for help in ways that cameras and antennas can pick up. "I'm sorry to say this, but if you're not willing to inflict an enormous amount of collateral damage, you're going to lose," Scheuer added.

The danger, of course, is that dead bystanders can turn a military success into a political disaster. If Al Qaeda's dilemma is, lie low at the risk of irrelevance or take action at the risk of exposure, the American dilemma is, push so softly that nothing happens or push so hard that force drives neutral Muslims into the enemy camp. Nowhere is this balance more delicate than in Pakistan.

The Balancing Act

On January 13, 2006, one or more American missiles, probably launched from an unmanned Predator, exploded in the Pakistani border village of Damadola. Eighteen people died. At least two of the victims reportedly were Qaeda operatives, although the primary target, Zawahiri, escaped; more than a dozen civilians, including five children, were also killed. Thousands of Pakistanis took to the streets in protest. Even their own army's campaigns to clear out the border areas have met with bitter resistance from both armed tribesmen—hundreds have died in the fighting—and local politicians.

"The use of force will always backfire," said Akram Khan Durrani, the relatively moderate Islamist politician who was elected chief minister of Pakistan's Northwest Frontier Province in 2002 on a tide of anti-American fury after the fall of the Taliban. "If force worked, there would be complete peace in Iraq and Afghanistan."

Pakistan's central government publicly denounced the Damadola strike—though some sources suggest that it secretly gave its approval—and it has repeatedly refused to allow U.S. forces to pursue Taliban and Qaeda fighters across the porous Afghanistan-Pakistan border.

"'Collateral damage,' we can't afford that," said Jehangir Karamat, Pakistan's ambassador to Washington. "These are our people. This is our country. And which other country in this coalition has delivered as much as Pakistan has, and suffered as much as Pakistan?" he asked, citing the more than 600 Qaeda suspects captured and the more than 300 Pakistani soldiers killed in operations against Islamic militants since 9/11. Do not ask more of Pakistan than it can do, Karamat warned: "Our actions have to be very carefully calibrated. Otherwise, there can be a chaotic condition in Pakistan that doesn't serve anybody's interest."

Translation: Pakistan's president, Musharraf, has survived at least two assassination attempts since 9/11, midranking officers of his own military were involved, the Pakistani public detests his alliance with the United States, and one lucky bullet could put a new finger on the button of the Islamic world's only nuclear arsenal. "Everyone's worried about Iran; I think they should start worrying about Pakistan," said retired Lt. Col. Rick Francona, who was an Air Force intelligence officer. "Musharraf is really hanging by a thread."

And in Pakistan, all of the threads are dangerously intertwined: Pull too hard on Al Qaeda, and you may end up hanging Musharraf. For every Pakistani helping the United States, another is helping Al Qaeda; sometimes it's the same person. As U.S. spymasters recruit agent after agent into their "daisy chains," so does bin Laden—and he has a head start.

The secret to Al Qaeda's success is its ability to live off the social landscape. Why build $1 billion stealth bombers when you can hijack airliners with $1 box cutters? Why conquer Afghanistan when you can borrow it from the Taliban? Why risk your own operatives when you can outsource to sympathetic groups? Bin Laden can keep his own operation small and elusive by plugging in, selectively, to other, larger networks that can provide him with money, safe houses, recruits, and armed protection.

Pakistan offers not one but two host networks: the fiercely independent Pashtun tribes, which not only make up Afghanistan's largest ethnic group but also dominate the western provinces of Pakistan, and the well-organized militant Islamic groups that launch raids into Indian-controlled Kashmir in the east. And both tribesmen and militants have spent a generation working in close alliance with the same Pakistani security services that have been ordered to hunt down Al Qaeda.

"You can't extol jihadis as freedom fighters, as Musharraf did until [9/11], and then turn around and say, 'Just some of them are bad,'" said Husain Haqqani, a Pakistani politician and commentator who was arrested, harassed, and tortured by successive governments until coming to America, where he now heads the Center for International Relations at Boston University. "By using jihad as an instrument of policy in Kashmir and Afghanistan, Pakistan may think it has been using the jihadis, but the jihadis have been using Pakistan."

Pakistan's Western Front

After 9/11, the Pakistani army invaded Pakistan. In a series of "hammer and anvil" operations coordinated with U.S. forces on the Afghan side of the frontier, more than 70,000 Pakistani soldiers moved into Waziristan and other border districts—terrain so rugged and dangerous that even the British Empire gave up on permanent garrisons and largely let the obstreperous Pashtun tribes rule themselves.

"I could not imagine this number of troops marching up and down Waziristan," said Akbar Ahmed, who as a Pakistani government "political agent" on the frontier kept what he calls "the fiercest of the fierce" in line through the traditional British mixture of flattery, bribery, personal relationships (Ahmed's mother and wife are both descended from Pashtun royalty), and threats—but rarely bullets. Said Ahmed, now a professor at American University, "If I called in the army, if I called in the police, I had failed."

Most Pakistani troops are from the populous eastern province of Punjab, and they share neither language nor customs with the hill-country Pashtuns. "They're saying, 'These are foreign soldiers looking at our women, and this is unacceptable,'" Ahmed said. "Now troops are dying, tribesmen are dying, the tribal leadership has been marginalized, and into that vacuum has stepped—guess who!—the Taliban."

This April, the fugitive leader of the "Pakistani Taliban," Haji Omar (no relation to the Afghan Taliban leader, Mullah Omar), met a BBC reporter openly for an interview in Wana—not some lonely village, but Waziristan's summer capital. The guns-blazing approach has backfired disastrously, Ahmed said. "The British political agents would be revolving in their graves."

In truth, the British model has been disintegrating for decades. The Afghan-Pakistan border slashes the hill country in half, leaving (very roughly) 12 million Pashtuns as the dominant group in Afghanistan and another 28 million as an uneasy minority in more populous Pakistan. Any central government interference prompts longing glances across the easily crossed border, while Iranian, Russian, Chinese, and even Indian influence in Afghanistan threatens Pakistan's back door. So, after repeated defeats by much-larger India in the east, Pakistani generals sought "strategic depth" on their western frontier.

"People think Pakistan got involved in Afghanistan because the United States wanted to oppose the Soviets," Haqqani said. "It was the other way around. Pakistan tried very hard from the early 1970s to get the United States involved." It took the Soviet invasion in 1979 to trigger massive U.S. support, channeled through the CIA but mostly distributed to the holy warriors in the field by agents of Pakistan's Inter-Services Intelligence, the ISI.

"When we brought extremism into Afghanistan, both the United States and Pakistan acted together, because at that time the larger objective was to defeat the Soviet Union," said Ambassador Karamat, a former general himself. "That is when the seed was planted."

Tribal Loyalties

Twenty-five years of warfare in Afghanistan spilled ruinously across the border. More than 3 million Afghan refugees remain in northwest Pakistan today. Pakistani generals, Arab jihadis, and radical clerics gained power at the expense of traditional civilian and tribal authorities. And the locals developed a deep resentment of the United States, which pulled out as soon as Afghanistan's war with the Soviets was won, only to return, guns blazing, after 9/11.

"There was a growing realization among the Pashtuns that their sacrifices in the Afghan war—the war of the international community—brought [only] wrath for them," not the promised aid, said Durrani, the frontier province's chief minister. "The United States has always dishonored its words."

So the Pashtuns, as usual, found their own solution. Out of the refugee camps and the madrassah schools, many run by Islamic parties like Durrani's Jamiat Ulema Islam, arose the Taliban—"the students"—who sought to reunite Afghanistan with guns, tanks, and the Koran. At their back was the ISI with arms, money, and intelligence, still seeking a stable ally in its neighbor to the west. At the Taliban's side were Arab veterans of the 1980s jihad, exiled from their homelands as troublemakers and now settled along the frontier. Often, Durrani said, "the tribal people offered them the hands of their daughters and sisters in marriage."

Today, many Pashtuns feel that the Pakistani government has turned on them by supporting the United States against the Taliban and Al Qaeda—and they refuse to abandon the people who are their kinsmen by blood or by marriage. "The people who are getting killed in firefights with the Pakistani military, more often than not they're tribal people who're defending [their in-laws]," said Marvin Weinbaum of the Middle East Institute in Washington, who visited the region in 2005 as Durrani's guest.

Many observers say that more than tribal honor is protecting the extremists. For all the ferocity of the Pakistani military's assaults, "no high-value Taliban operatives have been wrapped up," said Christine Fair, an analyst with the U.S. Institute of Peace. Most arrests seem to be of unmarried foreigners who are neither Pashtuns nor Arabs, but rather Muslim Central Asians such as Chechens, Uighurs, and Uzbeks. There are reports of Pakistani frontier guards waving known Taliban across into Afghanistan, and even of ISI agents in Taliban camps. "American troops are dying in Afghanistan," Fair said, "not only because of Pakistani inaction but with Pakistani complicity."

Ambassador Karamat rejects such accusations. "The ISI does exactly what it is told," he said. "People say there are sympathizers within the military, but we have never tolerated subcultures. These are professional military organizations."

The hole in this argument is that Pakistan's president seized power in a military coup in October 1999. Just three months before, the civilian government had pulled back from a nuclear standoff with India and ordered Gen. Musharraf, as army commander, to retreat from border fighting with India along the Kargil Heights. And Pakistani troops were crossing the border in the first place to support Islamic militants in the disputed province of Kashmir.

Pakistan's Home-Front Problem

If the Pashtun borderlands are Pakistan's exposed back, Kashmir is its broken heart. Pakistan came into existence during a war with Hindu-dominated India over the majority-Muslim province. The two nations have fought three wars and countless skirmishes there since 1947. ISI aid for the Taliban in the west was a natural outgrowth of its long-standing support for Kashmiri militants waging a jihad in the east. After 9/11, Musharraf's government cracked down on its former allies on both fronts. But as recently as 2005, when an earthquake ravaged Kashmir, a banned group called Lashkar-e-Taiba—known for its fierce attacks on India—was in the forefront of providing relief.

"Why did they have the money?" asked the exile, Haqqani. "Why did they have the infrastructure? Why were they allowed to travel on military helicopters? It's a big difference from the way secular [aid groups] are treated." And Lashkar's front group, Jamaat-ud-Dawa, continues to operate legally and openly throughout Pakistan, while other, ostensibly banned organizations raise recruits and money more discreetly.

"All these organizations that have changed names are being watched," Karamat said. "Many of them have turned themselves into aid-giving agencies, especially during the earthquake, and they're doing a good job as far as social work is concerned. And with the relationship improving with India, I don't think these organizations will have a role in Kashmir. But if there is any evidence [of terrorist ties], there will certainly be a crackdown."

But the Pakistani government is drawing a distinction between Islamic groups that the Islamists themselves do not. "The jihadis operate throughout the country," Haqqani said, "and if an Al Qaeda figure shows up at the doorstep of a jihadi, they all help each other out."

Official leniency toward Kashmiri militant groups like Lashkar-e-Taiba, or toward the Taliban, gives them space to assist Al Qaeda in their turn. Pakistani police hauled one bin Laden aide, Abu Zubaydah, out of what was reportedly a Lashkar safe house in Faisalabad, a major Punjabi city far from the Afghan frontier. Ahmed Khalfan Ghailani, a Tanzanian tied to the 1998 bombings of U.S. embassies in Africa, was arrested after a shoot-out in Gujrat, another eastern city.

"I'm from Karachi," Haqqani said. "If I went to Gujrat, everyone would know [I'm] from outside. Ghailani was African!" He could never have made it to central Punjab without help. The highest-ranking Qaeda operative yet captured, 9/11 planner Khalid Shaikh Mohammed, was arrested in Rawalpindi, a town just outside the Pakistani capital that is home to army headquarters. He was caught after fleeing from what appeared to be his base of operations in Karachi—on the far side of Pakistan from the tribal borderlands, and yet the site of several key Qaeda arrests. "Track all the high-level arrests and put them on the map of Pakistan," Haqqani said. "Most have been arrested in Pakistan's major cities—not in the tribal areas—and in the homes of people associated with jihadi movements."

The Pakistani army and American air strikes are instruments too blunt to use in crowded cities. Even in the tribal badlands, "the offensives have declined because they've been a bust," said Bergen, yielding too few high-level captures to justify the soldiers and civilians killed. Seeking a compromise to get both Al Qaeda and the army out of the borderlands, the central government is now working with Durrani, the provincial chief minister, to revive the grand jirga, the traditional council of tribal leaders through which British and Pakistani civilian governments exercised their hands-off rule.

Some experts see this retreat as surrender. "Force is what matters in the Islamic world," Scheuer said. "Be brutal, or get out. We don't have to win their hearts and minds. What we want to do is kill bin Laden."

Others see the shift as wise strategy for a long war. "The cooperation of the Pakistani government at the lowest level is essential," said Robert Killebrew, a retired Special Forces colonel and a veteran of Vietnam. "If the captain at the [border] outpost is not willing to cooperate, you're not going to get anywhere. The way you do that is, you take time and you build trust," one contact at a time, until your daisy chain finally reaches someone who knows where bin Laden is hiding.

To make this work, Killebrew said, "the politics of Pakistan are key—and it's a miracle that Musharraf has managed to stay alive and in office this long. If you've got a fleeting shot at Osama bin Laden at the risk of embarrassing Musharraf, wait. We're going to get Osama bin Laden, and if we pass up a chance now, there will be another. It may take another five or 10 years. But, eventually, we'll get him."

A Terrorist's Trail

- To lead a multinational movement, bin Laden must have an infrastructure of contacts, one of which will one day betray him.

- Bin Laden's dilemma is between lying low at the risk of irrelevance and taking action at the risk of exposure.
- Most arrests of major Qaeda figures have been in Pakistan's cities, not in the tribal areas.

The Hunt for Osama

After 9/11, U.S. invasion forces and their Afghan auxiliaries drove many followers of Osama bin Laden across the border into Pakistan, a country that has become both ally and battleground in the war on terror. Pakistan's Inter-Services Intelligence agency has a 30-year history of supporting Islamic militants, both to the west in Afghanistan, where fiercely independent Pashtun tribes straddle the poorly defined frontier, and to the east in Kashmir, where India and Pakistan have fought three wars and countless skirmishes over the disputed province.

Since 9/11, however, President Pervez Musharraf has braved internal opposition, including at least two assassination attempts, in his efforts to root out Al Qaeda. Many suspects have been killed or captured in Pakistan's mountainous west, where sympathetic Pashtuns give shelter to the Taliban and Al Qaeda.

But it is in the cities of the populous east, where militant organizations are deeply buried in the Pakistani heartland, that the most-senior Qaeda operatives have been arrested, most famously 9/11 planner Khalid Shaikh Mohammed, captured in Rawalpindi.

POSTSCRIPT

Is Pakistan an Asset in the War on Terror?

It is quite possible that should Pakistani President Musharraf fall from power, his replacement would be a more difficult partner for the United States in the fight against terrorism. To the extent that Pakistan's elections have been open, conservative Islamist candidates have won many votes. Pakistan's poverty and low level of development remain endemic problems as well; Pakistan has a population of 134 million that is largely poor (annual GNP per capita is only $480) and illiterate (only 38 percent of the population can read).

The challenge of winning Pakistan's cooperation against al Qaeda and the Taliban became markedly more difficult after September 2006, when the Pakistani government negotiated an agreement with tribal leaders in the north of Pakistan that gave these leaders more autonomy. The Pakistani government committed in this agreement to end its series of military raids into the region, which had caused increasing casualties. Intelligence analysts and regional leaders, most notably Afghan President Hamid Karzai, publicly expressed concerns that this agreement would provide a safe haven for al Qaeda and Taliban forces to carry out attacks in Afghanistan and elsewhere, and indeed Taliban attacks in Afghanistan increased sharply through the fall of 2006.

For recent books on Pakistan, see Mary Anne Weaver, *In the Shadow of Jihad and Afghanistan;* Owen Bennett Jones, *Pakistan: Eye of the Storm;* and Stephen Philip Cohen, *The Idea of Pakistan.*

ISSUE 8

Should the United States Preemptively Attack Iranian Nuclear Facilities?

YES: Mario Loyola, from "Before They Go Nuclear: Iran and the Question of Preemption," *National Review* (August 28, 2006)

NO: Edward N. Luttwak, from "Three Reasons Not to Bomb Iran— Yet!" *Commentary* (May 2006)

ISSUE SUMMARY

YES: Mario Loyola, a former consultant to the Department of Defense, argues that the United States needs to publicly retain the option of a preemptive military strike against Iranian nuclear facilities to give leverage to U.S. diplomatic efforts to get Iran to end its nuclear weapons program.

NO: Edward N. Luttwak, a senior adviser at the Center for Strategic and International Studies, argues that the preemptive strikes on Iraq's nuclear facilities by the United States would alienate the Iranian public and lead Iran's government to retaliate against U.S. forces in Iraq and elsewhere in the Middle East.

$\mathbf{I}$n the four years since Iran was first reported in August of 2002 to be working to enrich uranium to the point that it could be used in nuclear weapons, Iran has successively broken out of a series of international safeguards and commitments on its nuclear programs. The International Atomic Energy Agency (IAEA), which provides nuclear technology to signatories of the Non-Proliferation Treaty (NPT) in exchange for these signatories' commitment to forego nuclear weapons and allow IAEA inspections, announced in June of 2003 that Iran was not meeting its NPT obligations. Iran promised in the fall of 2003 to suspend its uranium enrichment activities and allow snap inspections of its facilities, but by the summer of 2004 the IAEA once again reported that Iran was not meeting its commitments, and Iran retaliated by successively renewing its enrichment efforts through the course of 2005.

In January 2006, Iran escalated its confrontation with the international community by breaking the IAEA seals on its uranium enrichment facility at

Natanz. This led Germany, Britain, and France to break off nuclear talks with Iran and move toward supporting U.S. efforts to bring Iran's nuclear program before the UN Security Council, and in March the Council called on Iran to end its enrichment efforts within 30 days or face unspecified consequences. In response, Iranian President Mahmoud Ahmadinejad became even more defiant, announcing in April that Iran had succeeded in enriching uranium at its Natanz plant. The UN Security Council then approved a resolution on July 31 calling on Iran to end its enrichment and reprocessing activities by August 31 or face economic and diplomatic sanctions. Yet when the August 31 deadline passed without any concessions from Iran, the United States continued to find it difficult to convince other countries on the Security Council to actually implement substantial sanctions against Iran.

Despite pointed and public refusals by Bush administration officials to rule out the possibility of using force against Iran's nuclear facilities, U.S. policies toward Iran continued to be constrained through 2006 by a number of factors that made it difficult to make U.S. military threats credible or to win international support for strong sanctions. Other permanent members of the Security Council, most notably Russia, which has sold nuclear technology to Iran, remained reluctant to implement sanctions and could veto any effort to do so through the Security Council. As for military options, the use of force against Iranian facilities, as Edward Luttwak notes, could alienate the Iranian public, further incite Muslim opposition to the United States around the world, and lead Iran to retaliate by working to stimulate attacks on U.S. soldiers in Iraq by Shiite groups linked to Iran. On the other hand, as Mario Loyola notes, if the threat of U.S. military action against Iran is not credible, Iran may not have sufficient incentives to give up its nuclear weapons program. Even if other countries can be convinced to join and intensify the economic sanctions the United States has already imposed, it is unclear whether Iran would give up a weapons program that it has so publicly linked to its national security and international prestige.

YES ⬐

Mario Loyola

Before They Go Nuclear . . .

Conspicuously absent from the West's diplomatic strategy in the Iran nuclear crisis is any mention of preemption. Avoiding this now-vulgar term may help alleviate the administration's image problem, but the U.S. is starting to give the impression that it has given up on a vital element of its national defense. Iran has taken this as an invitation to speed up its nuclear program.

The Security Council debate before the Iraq War and the subsequent debate over pre-war intelligence are the key to understanding what has gone wrong. After David Kay famously reported in January 2004 that "we were almost all wrong" about WMD in Iraq, columnist George F. Will proclaimed the end of preemption: "The doctrine of preemptive war . . . presupposes a certain [amount of] certainty about what you're preempting."

This is incorrect. What argues for early preemption is the risk that self-defense may come too late if it waits too long. For preemption, the triggering threat is an unacceptable level of uncertainty. The reason we were considering preemption against Iraq was not that our intelligence misled us, but rather that Saddam Hussein never allowed for verification of Iraq's disarmament. Given the potential danger, what we needed was transparency.

But Security Council Resolution 1441, which sent the inspectors back into Iraq, never mentioned transparency or verification. Rather than placing the burden of proof squarely on Saddam, the resolution linked "serious consequences" to "further material breach," an issue on which the U.S. would naturally have to bear the burden of proof. So Secretary Colin Powell found himself back in the Security Council a few months later, presenting inferential intelligence assessments in support of specific claims about WMD, claims on which our case for war now suddenly depended. But this totally contradicted our strategic posture, which was that if we could not get clarity from Saddam, we would get it from Central Command: The burden of proof was on Saddam. Arguing about further material breach could only distract attention from what really mattered.

So long as the intelligence assessments could not confirm Iraq's disarmament, their particular conclusions were irrelevant. And the intelligence failure we have just wasted several years arguing about was just as irrelevant. Had the intelligence been perfectly truthful, the most it could have said was, "Mr. President, we don't know what's going on in Iraq. But it looks pretty bad." The decision facing the president would then have been exactly the same: Accept the unverified claims of a known liar, or remove the potential danger. And the potential danger was unacceptable—especially after 9/11 brought home just how dangerous the world had become.

By not first securing international acceptance of the general principles of the post-9/11 national-security strategy, we ended up arguing the case of Iraq on the basis of 20th-century norms that could not sustain the U.S. position. And when we went back to the Security Council in February 2003, we lost the case. All around the world, rogue states with lots of secrets to keep breathed a sigh of relief. The Security Council had refused to legitimize the enforcement of transparency through preemption—the only logical way to enforce it.

In an age of WMD, transparency is essential. The Europeans took the diplomatic lead on Iran's nuclear program because everything about it was so nebulous. Iran's "civilian" nuclear facilities are defended like strategic military targets, many of them buried thousands of feet underground, beyond the reach of bunker-busters. The program's justifications—energy insecurity and national scientific pride—were never very convincing; after the discovery of large, clandestine uranium-enrichment facilities, nobody at all believed them. The facilities themselves were arguably permitted under the nuclear-nonproliferation treaty, but building them secretly was not. There could be only one reason Iran would go to such lengths to keep an otherwise-legitimate program secret: It was trying to develop nuclear weapons, and it knew that the facilities would be military targets.

Led at first by France, Britain, and Germany, the West has maintained unity in its confrontation with Iran. The diplomatic strategy is based on an ordered progression—from referral by the IAEA, to a non-binding letter from the Security Council president, to a sanction-less Chapter VII resolution, to a resolution imposing economic sanctions. This approach has so far proven remarkably successful not only in isolating Iran from the rest of the international community, but also in isolating any support the Iranians may enjoy in the Council.

Unfortunately, the strategy also eliminates what little deterrence there may be against Iran's nuclear-weapons development. Several months ago, when asked whether the U.S. or Israel would use preemption if diplomacy failed (the question on everybody's mind), British foreign secretary Jack Straw reacted as if the question had been about space aliens: The use of force was "inconceivable," he said. And nothing we have said publicly (except the increasingly useless "all options remain on the table") has contradicted that assertion.

So at the very least, the Security Council progression appears to erect a series of stable and predictable hurdles between us and the legitimate use of force. Therefore, Iran can predict that an attack will not be triggered by the next several steps it takes in developing the WMD. The effect is naturally to make a negotiated settlement in the near term highly unattractive from Iran's point of view. As Kissinger taught, people who think they have time on their hands don't negotiate. Iran's bargaining position can only become stronger the further it proceeds.

And the further it proceeds, the more assertive and aggressive it becomes. Iranian special-operations forces are increasingly active in fomenting sectarian violence and attacks on coalition forces in Iraq. And Hezbollah's attack on Israel was widely understood as a shot across the bow in Iran's nuclear stand-off with the West.

At least instinctively, the administration recognizes the danger of dally-ing in the Security Council. It stayed on the sidelines until Iran was referred to the Council, but once the matter landed on U.N. ambassador John Bolton's desk, things in the Council have moved fast. At the end of July, the Council issued a draft resolution under Chapter VII demanding that Iran halt enrich-ment activities by the end of August, or face possible sanctions. The plan, then, is to impose sanctions in early September. But the sanctions will almost certainly be limited—and not aimed at oil. Their only lasting effect may be to push Iran out of the nonproliferation treaty altogether.

At that point, the U.S. will be able to claim that it gave diplomacy a chance. But absent an explicit threat to destroy Iran's nuclear facilities, diplo-macy never *had* a chance. At no point have we made Iran fear the conse-quences of proceeding. And we appear to have gotten this far in the Security Council only because of a tacit agreement that we would not resort to force without Council permission. The Chinese and Russians have made it clear that this is their understanding. Thus, once diplomacy fails, we are likely to have to invoke preemption in the teeth of even greater international opposition than if we had never gone to the Security Council in the first place.

This brings us to the most serious flaw in the current diplomatic strat-egy. Every time we take a major threat to the Security Council, we reinforce the perception that to use force preemptively, we need the Security Council's permission. But the Council cannot perform any such role, and it was never meant to. It was conceived only as the political committee of a standing mili-tary alliance, an alliance that did not survive the end of World War II long enough to sign the U.N. Charter as genuine allies. The reason the five perma-nent members of the Council are not allies is that their strategic interests are not in general alignment; it is therefore unrealistic to expect that they would reach agreement to authorize preemption against a threat to the peace.

In the current crisis, the Security Council has done nothing to prevent or remove the threat posed by Iran's nuclear program. Iran is now moving fast to produce as much lightly enriched uranium as it can. According to Valerie Lincy of the Wisconsin Project on Nuclear Arms Control, once Iran has a large-enough batch, it will be a short step to convert it to weapons grade. If Iran then expels the IAEA inspectors, no one knows how long it would take for them to produce enough for a nuclear device. We will from that point forward be living with an intolerable uncertainty. Under these circumstances, the U.S. should make clear that it will consider any further Iranian violation of the nonproliferation treaty an act of armed aggression within Article 51 of the U.N. Charter.

If we really want to give diplomacy a chance in Iran, we must put preemp-tion front and center. The Bush administration would do well to begin leaking feasibility plans for wide-ranging strikes against Iran's nuclear infrastructure. We should establish bright red lines, and stick to them.

The U.S. has no real problem with the prospect of a democratic, peaceful, and law-abiding Iran developing nuclear technology, because such an Iran would be able to give the West all the reassurance it needs. But this dictatorship does not represent the people of Iran and cannot be counted upon to act in their interest. Letting the mullahs have nukes will force the people of Iran, and the rest of the world, to live in a situation of terrifying uncertainty. It is reasonable to insist that if the Iranians want advanced nuclear technology, they need to get an advanced government first.

As things stand, we are in effect offering the mullahs in Tehran both nuclear weapons and regional hegemony. Before they cash in on the offer, we should take it off the table and offer them preemption instead. Let's see what flowers of peace Ahmadinejad can pluck from a nettle when he sets his mind to it.

Edward N. Luttwak

 **NO**

Three Reasons Not to
Bomb Iran—Yet

I know of no reputable expert in the United States or in Europe who trusts the constantly repeated promise of Iran's rulers that their nuclear program will be entirely peaceful and is meant only to produce electricity. The question is what to do about this. Faced with the alarming prospect of an Iran armed with nuclear weapons, some policy experts favor immediate preventive action, while others, of equal standing, invite us to accept what they consider to be inevitable in any case. The former call for the bombing of Iran's nuclear installations before they can produce actual weapons. The latter, to the contrary, urge a diplomatic understanding with Iran's rulers in order to attain a stable relationship of mutual deterrence.

Neither position seems adequately to recognize essential Iranian realities or American strategic priorities. To treat Iran as nothing more than a set of possible bombing targets cannot possibly be the right approach. Still more questionable is the illogical belief that a regime that feels free to attack American interests in spite of its present military inferiority would somehow become more restrained if it could rely on the protective shield of nuclear weapons.

In contemplating preventive action, the technical issue may be quickly disposed of. Some observers, noting that Iran's nuclear installations consist of hundreds of buildings at several different sites, including a number that are recessed in the ground with fortified roofs, have contended that even a prolonged air campaign might not succeed in destroying all of them. Others, drawing a simplistic analogy with Israel's aerial destruction of Iraq's Osiraq nuclear reactor in June 1981, speak as if it would be enough to drop sixteen unguided bombs on a single building to do the job. The fact is that the targets would not be buildings as such but rather processes, and, given the aiming information now available, they could indeed be interrupted in lasting ways by a single night of bombing. An air attack is not a demolition contract, and in this case it could succeed while inflicting relatively little physical damage and no offsite casualties, barring gross mechanical errors that occur only rarely in these days of routine precision.

The greater question, however, is neither military nor diplomatic but rather political and strategic: what, in the end, do we wish to see emerge in Iran? It is in light of that long-term consideration that we need to weigh both our actions and their timing, lest we hinder rather than accelerate the emergence of the future we hope for. We must start by considering the special character of American relations with the country and people of Iran.

II

The last time the United States seriously considered the use of force in Iran, much larger operations were envisaged than the bombing of a few uranium-enrichment installations. The year was 1978, and the mission was so demanding that a complete light-infantry division would have been needed just as an advance guard to screen the build-up of the main forces. The projected total number of troops in action—most of them from Iran's U.S.-equipped and U.S.-trained army—would easily have exceeded the maximum total fielded by the United States and its allies in Iraq since 2003. Their mission: to defend the country from a Soviet thrust to the Persian Gulf, in which motor-rifle divisions would descend from the Armenian and Azerbaijan Soviet Socialist Republics to link up with airborne divisions sent ahead to seize the oil ports.

That long-ago bit of contingency planning reflected sound intelligence on the contemporary transformation of the Soviet army from a ponderous battering ram to a fast-paced maneuver force. In the end, to be sure, it turned out that not Iran but neighboring Afghanistan was the Soviet target. But there is no question that, in facing the adventurism of an exceedingly well-armed Soviet Union in its final stage of militarist decline, the government of Iran could rely on the protection of its American alliance, an alliance in place ever since the Truman administration blocked Stalin's attempt to partition the country in 1946. From then on, and even in the perilous circumstances envisaged in 1978, the United States stood ready to risk the lives of American troops to defend Iran—it was that important in American strategy.

At stake in those decades was not just Iran's oil, although that counted for much more in 1946 than it does now: there was as yet no oil production to speak of in Saudi Arabia, Kuwait, or the United Arab Emirates, and Iraq was the only other oil exporter in the region. More significant than Iran's geology was, and is, its geography. During the cold war, its northern border on either side and across the waters of the Caspian Sea formed an essential segment of the Western perimeter of containment. Today, it is Iran's very long southern coastline that is of equal strategic importance, dominating as it does the entire Persian Gulf from its narrow southern entrance at the straits of Hormuz to the thin wedge of Iraqi territory at its head. All of the offshore oil- and gas-production platforms in the gulf, all the traffic of oil and gas tankers originating from the jetties of the Arabian peninsula and Iraq, are within easy reach of the Iranian coast.

Unchanging geographic realities thus favor a strategic alliance between the United States and Iran, with large benefits for each side. Only the strategic reach of the distant United States can secure Iran from the power of the Russians nearby—a power not in abeyance even now, as the recent nuclear diplomacy shows, and much more likely to revive in the future than to decline. Likewise, a friendly Iran can best keep troublemakers away from the oil installations on the

Arab side of the gulf, where there are only weak and corrupt desert dynasties to protect them.

III

The vehement rejection of the American alliance by the religious extremists in power ever since the fall of the Shah in 1979 therefore violates the natural order of things—damaging both sides, but Iran far more grievously. The cost to the people of Iran has been huge, starting with the 600,000 dead and the uncounted number of invalids from the 1980–88 war with Iraq, which American protection would certainly have averted, and continuing till now with the lost opportunities, disruptions, and inconveniences caused by the lack of normal diplomatic and commercial relations.

These impediments are so costly precisely because there is still so much interchange between the two sides, with Iranian-Americans traveling back and forth and not a few operating businesses in Iran while residing in the U.S., and vice-versa. Beyond that, millions of ordinary Iranians are keenly interested in all that is American, from youth fashions to democratic politics, and nothing can stop them from watching the Farsi-language television stations of Los Angeles; all attempts by Iran's rulers to prohibit the country's ubiquitous satellite antennas have failed.

That is part of a much wider loss of authority over Iranian society. The regime started off in 1979 with the immense prestige of Ayatollah Ruhollah Khomeini, initially the consensual leader of just about everyone in Iran: Westernizing liberals and traditionalist bazaar merchants, the modernizing middle classes and the urban poor, rural landlords angry at the Shah's land reforms and the peasant beneficiaries of those measures, old-line Tudeh Communists and anti-Communist radicals, and of course believing Muslims of every sort, from the moderately devout and quietist to the fanatical clerics of the more extreme theological schools.

Further fracturing the country's unity is the clerics' religious extremism. Their discriminatory practices arouse the resentment not only of such minor non-Islamic communities as the Bahais, Christians, Jews, and Zoroastrians, who conjointly amount to less than 1 percent of the population, but also of the Sunni Muslims who account for some 10 percent. In Tehran, home to more than a million of them, Sunnis are not allowed to have their own mosque, as they have in Rome, Tel Aviv, and Washington, D.C. The last sustained attempt to build a Sunni mosque was blocked by Mahmoud Ahmadinejad when he was mayor of Tehran.

Ahmadinejad's advent as president marks, indeed, a definite shift—from the institutionalized religious extremism in place since the fall of the Shah in 1979 to a more strident ultra-extremism. True, under Iran's theocratic constitution the elected president must obey the "Supreme Leader," a cleric of at least ayatollah rank, just as the elected Majlis parliament is subordinated to the unelected "Council of Guardians." Hence the views of the previous president, the elegant, learned, and mostly moderate Seyyed Muhammad Khatami, mattered not at all, as was soon discovered by the Western officials who wasted their time in negotiating with him. But Khatami was powerless because he was out of step with a regime that was responding to its ever increasing unpopularity by becoming ever more extreme. Ahmadinejad, by contrast, exemplifies that very trend.

Although the world now knows him for his persistent denial of the Holocaust and his rants against Israel and Zionism, at home Ahmadinejad's hostility is directed not against Iran's dwindling Jewish community but against the Sunnis. Lately, moreover, his ultra-extremism has antagonized even many of his fellow Shiites: he is an enthusiastic follower of both Ayatollah Muhammad Taqi Misbah Yazdi, for whom all current prohibitions are insufficient and who would impose an even stricter Islamic puritanism, and of a messianic, end-of-days cult centered on the Jamkaran mosque outside the theological capital of Qum. More traditional believers are alarmed by the hysterical supplications of the Jamkaran pilgrims for the return of Abul-Qassem Muhammad, the twelfth imam who occulted himself in the year 941 and is to return as the mahdi, or Shiite messiah. More urgently they fear that in trying to "force" the return of the mahdi, Ahmadinejad may deliberately try to provoke a catastrophic external attack on Iran that the mahdi himself would have to avert.

The shift from everyday extremism to a more active ultra-extremism is also manifest in the persecution of heterodox Shiites, both the Ahl-e-Haqq of western Iran and the far more numerous Sufi brotherhoods, who were previously left alone even by the rigorously fanatical Ayatollah Khomeini. Now, by contrast, Sufi gathering places are forcibly closed or attacked, and a major center in Qum was recently demolished, with hundreds of protesting Sufi dervishes arrested in the process.

Far more important than any of this is the antipathy of the regime for the Persian majority culture itself. Relentlessly favoring an essentially Arab Islamic culture instead, it condemns—though it has not been able to suppress— such cherished pre-Islamic customs as the fire-jumping ceremony that precedes the Nowruz celebrations of the Zoroastrian new year each spring. More generally, it elevates its narrow Islamism above the achievements and legacy of one of the world's major civilizations, whose millennial influence in everything from poetry and music to monumental architecture, from the higher crafts of carpets and miniatures to cuisine, continues to be felt in a vast area from the Balkans to Bengal right across central Asia.

The cultural dimension of their identity is especially significant for the Persians of the Iranian diaspora. This vast and growing group comprises a handful of political exiles and millions of ordinary people who could have prospered in Iran, and made Iran prosperous, but for their refusal to live under the rule of religious fanatics. Their cultural identity is what gives them a strong sense of cohesion quite independently of the Islam they were born into. While only a few have converted to Christianity, or are seriously engaged in the Zoroastrian revival that is promoted by some exiles, the majority have reacted to the extremism of Iran's present rulers by becoming, in effect, post-Islamic—that is, essentially secular but for a sentimental attachment to certain prayers and rituals.

In this, the exiles are presaging the future of Iran itself.

V

In contemplating American military action against Iran, it is important to recall these fundamental realities—now submerged but bound to reassert themselves as fundamentals always do. For the inhabitants of Iran are human beings like the rest of us, and extremist norms can be imposed on them only by brute force. A valid analogy is with the collapse of Communism in Eastern Europe and Russia and, in China, the retreat of Communism from the economic to the political realm alone. In each of these cases, even after all the depredations, massacres, destructions, and claimed transformations of decades of Communist rule, local cultures and historic identities reemerged largely intact and essentially unchanged—except for the principled rejection of Communist ideology.

It will be just the same in Iran when the fanatics who now oppress the non-fanatical majority lose power, as they inevitably will in time. Along with the reemergence of the country's suppressed Westernization that dates back to the 1920's, along with the restoration of its own beloved secular Persian culture, one can reasonably expect the United States to return to the scene as Iran's natural ally. But not everything will be as it was before, for the long and bitter years of religious oppression will have engendered widespread disaffiliation from politicized Islam, with some interest in its apolitical variants and perhaps some conversions to milder faiths, and certainly with an irresistible demand to strip the clerics of all political or judicial power.

That, as it happens, is one excellent reason not to move forthwith to bomb Iran's nuclear installations. For the long-term consequences of any American military action cannot be disregarded. Iranians are our once and future allies. Except for a narrow segment of extremists, they do not view themselves as enemies of the United States, but rather as the exact opposite: at a time when Americans are unpopular in all other Muslim countries, most Iranians become distinctly more friendly when they learn that a visitor is American. They must not be made to feel that they were attacked by the very country they most admire, where so many of their own relatives and friends have so greatly prospered, and with which they wish to restore the best of relations.

There is a second good reason not to act precipitously. In essence, we should not bomb Iran because the worst of its leaders positively want to be bombed—and are doing their level best to bring that about.

When a once broadly popular regime is reduced to the final extremity of relying on repression alone, when its leadership degenerates all the way down from an iconic Khomeini to a scruffy Ahmadinejad, it can only benefit from being engaged or threatened by the great powers of the world. The clerics' frantic extremism reflects a sense of insecurity that is fully justified, given the bitter hostility with which they are viewed by most of the population at large. In a transparent political maneuver, Ahmadinejad tries to elicit nationalist support at home by provoking hostile reactions abroad, through his calls for the destruction of Israel, his clumsy version of Holocaust denial that is plainly an embarrassment even to other extremists, and, above all, his repeated declarations that Iran is about to repudiate the Non-Proliferation Treaty it ratified in 1970.

There is a third reason, too. The effort to build nuclear weapons started more than three decades ago, yet the regime is still years away from producing a bomb.

VI

It was as far back as August 1974, when the overnight tripling of Iran's oil revenues seemed to offer boundless opportunities, that the Shah publicly announced his intention to fund the construction of 23 nuclear reactors with an electricity-producing capacity of 1,000 megawatts each—a huge total, enough to supply Iran's entire demand. His declared aim was to preserve the "noble" commodity of oil for the more valuable extraction of petrochemicals, instead of burning it as a furnace fuel.

That almost made economic sense at the time. Although many suspected— rightly—that the Shah's real aim was to acquire nuclear weapons (we now know that he was seeking to buy ballistic missiles as well), he did at least have a passingly plausible explanation. But that was before the immensity of Iran's natural-gas reserves became known. No such cover story can deceive anyone in 2006: with 812 trillion cubic feet of proven gas reserves (15 percent of the world's total), Iran can cheaply generate all the electricity it wants with gas turbines.

In 1975, the Shah contracted with the French for enriched uranium and with Germany's Kraftwerk Union consortium of Siemens and A.E.G. Telefunken, as well as with ThyssenKrupp, to build the first two pressurized light-water reactors and their generating units near Iran's major port city of Bushehr. Work progressed rapidly until July 1979, when, after an expenditure of some $2.5 billion, the Germans abandoned Bushehr because Iran's new revolutionary rulers refused to make an overdue progress payment of $450 million. It seems that Ayatollah Khomeini opposed nuclear devilry—and besides, anything done by the Shah was viewed with great suspicion.

At that point, one reactor (Bushehr I) was declared by the Germans to be 85-percent complete and the other (Bushehr II) 50-percent complete. Both were subsequently damaged during the war with Iraq that lasted until 1988, chiefly in air strikes flown by seconded French pilots. Siemens was asked to return to finish the work but, knowing that the German government would never allow the contract to proceed, refused.

Negotiations with the Russians began soon thereafter. But because of quarreling by different factions within Iran and protracted haggling with Minatom, the Soviet atomic-energy ministry, no agreement was reached until 1995, when Boris Yeltsin, by now the president of Russia, ignored American objections and approved the delivery of a VVER-1000 pressurized light-water reactor powered by slightly enriched uranium rods. Delivered as a single large module, the reactor was to be fitted into the Bushehr I building, which was to be quickly repaired, adapted, and completed by Iranian and Russian contractors.

But problems arose—more or less the same ones that might be encountered in remodeling a suburban kitchen, though on a somewhat larger scale. Today, some eleven years after the contract was signed, some 2,500 Russian technicians are still hard at work in famously hot Bushehr, and the reactor is still not quite ready. The United States, which originally opposed the Minatom contract, now accepts, presumably for good reason, that all is proceeding properly—the Russians alone are to process the uranium rods, and the level of Minatom's competence and efficiency has been adequately signaled by the pace of its performance so far.

Rather less is known about Iran's secret program to produce weapon-grade uranium by the centrifuge process, but there is no reason to believe that things are otherwise. What *is* known is that in 1995, the Pakistani thief and smuggler Abdul Qadeer Khan, who is regularly described as a scientist but who has never invented or developed anything at all, agreed to sell to Iran the complete centrifuge-technology package he had stolen from the European URENCO consortium. The package also included samples of Pakistani-made centrifuges, full-scale plans for a heavy-water and plutonium reactor and sepa-ration plant, and the drawings and calculations for a cannon-type uranium bomb that Pakistan had originally received from China.

Evidently not included in the package were the two first stages of the sep-aration process—the straightforward crushing and leaching needed to extract concentrated natural uranium or "yellow-cake" from uranium ore—and the less simple but not overly sophisticated chemical plant needed to convert yel-lowcake into the gas uranium hexafluoride, which is fed into centrifuges. But China made up for this lack in 1996, selling complete and detailed plans and blueprints to Iran after the United States successfully objected to the sale of the plant itself. It is now installed, big as life, near Isphahan, ready for use and evidently already tested. To judge by photographs, it could just as readily be incapacitated with fewer than twelve 1,000-pound bombs, though the target would have to be revisited periodically because chemical plants are easily repaired even after their seemingly spectacular destruction.

VII

But the core technology in the Khan package was that of the centrifuges them-selves. They were not the ultra-fast, carbon-fiber units that URENCO now uses but two early models: one built out of dense aluminum that is easier to manu-facture with the right machinery, and the other built out of a more efficient maraging steel but harder to manufacture. Both derive from a 1957 German design that was itself an improved version of the original aluminum centrifuges developed in the postwar Soviet Union by captured German scientists.

The fissile U-235 isotope of uranium that is needed for bombs is only 1.26-percent lighter than the mass of U-238 that comprises 99.3 percent of natural uranium. To extract it, only very fast centrifuges are of any use, turn-ing at the rate of at least 1,500 revolutions per second, a hundred times as fast as a domestic washing machine. Things that turn that fast easily break apart, and the detailed design is also far from simple: to reduce friction that would otherwise generate enough heat to melt the whole thing, the electri-cally powered rotor must spin in a vacuum, with a magnetic bearing. The Japanese, who are generally believed to be somewhat more advanced than the

Iranians in such matters, encountered considerable difficulties with their centrifuge plant.

Nor could Khan possibly sell enough centrifuges to Iran: to separate U-235 for a bomb in any reasonable amount of time, many centrifuges must be set to work at once. With the design now in Iran's possession, it would take at least 1,000 centrifuges working around the clock for at least a year to produce enough U-235 for a single cannon-type uranium bomb. Those 1,000 centrifuges must first be manufactured and then connected by piping into so-called "cascades"—and they must not break down, as poorly made centrifuges certainly will. (Of the 164 centrifuges that Iran already had in motion when the inspectors of the International Atomic Energy Agency [IAEA] shut down the cascade in November 2003, fully a third crashed when the electricity was turned off.) Nor is it easy to keep the cascade running correctly: because uranium hexafluoride becomes highly corrosive in contact with water vapor, it can easily perforate imperfect tubes—and any leaks will promptly damage more of the plant.

It is true that one potential obstacle to Iran's quest for U-235 did prove to be entirely insignificant. European firms, mostly German and Swiss, not only eagerly sold the high-strength aluminum, special maraging steel, electron-beam welders, balancing machines, vacuum pumps, machine tools, and highly specialized flow-forming machines for both aluminum and maraging steel centrifuges, but also trained Iranians in the use of all this equipment. Remarkably, or perhaps not, they were also willing to train Iranians in the processes specifically needed to manufacture centrifuges whose only possible purpose is to enrich uranium U-235. When the IAEA inspectors came around, they were able to read and photograph the labels on all the equipment, which neither the European manufacturers nor the Iranians had bothered to remove. It remains to be seen if any consequences will ensue.

Still, in spite of all the industrial assistance it received, it is not clear that the Iranian nuclear organization can manufacture centrifuge cascades of sufficient magnitude, efficiency, and reliability. There are many talented engineers among the Iranian exiles in the United States and elsewhere in the world, but perhaps not so many in Iran itself. Besides, demanding technological efforts require not just individual talents but well-organized laboratories and industrial facilities.

Organization is indeed Iran's weakest point, with weighty consequences: after a century of oil drilling, for example, the state oil company still cannot drill exploratory wells without foreign assistance. In another example, even though the U.S. embargo was imposed almost 25 years ago, local industry cannot reverse-engineer spare parts of adequate quality for U.S.-made aircraft, which must therefore remain grounded or fly at great peril—there have been many crashes. Similarly, after more than sixty years of experience with oil refining at Abadan, existing capacity still cannot be increased without the aid of foreign engineering contractors, while the building of new refineries with local talent alone is deemed quite impossible. Iran must import one third of the gasoline it consumes because it cannot be refined at home.

VIII

In sum, there is no need to bomb Iran's nuclear installations at this time. The regime certainly cannot produce nuclear weapons in less than three years, and may not be able to do so even then because of the many technical difficulties not yet overcome.

To this it might be objected that the nuclear program clearly has priority over everything else, and receives funding in huge amounts. That is true enough. Although there are no reliable expenditure numbers for Iran's nuclear program, there is no need of numbers to establish its sheer magnitude. When the secret installations and activities revealed in August 2002 are added to those already publicly known, the total is impressive. It includes the Saghand ore-processing plant and uranium mine, the Tehran nuclear research center with its (very old) U.S.-supplied 5-megawatt research reactor, the nuclear technology center at Isphahan with four small Chinese-supplied research reactors, the Isphahan zirconium-production plant, the Bonab atomic-energy research center, the Anarak nuclear-waste storage site near Yazd, the Ardekan nuclear fuel plant, the shuttered Lashkar Ab'ad laser isotope separation plant, the Parchim, Lavizan II, and Chalous development facilities that eluded inspection, the Yazd radiation processing center, and finally the four largest and most important installations: the Bushehr reactor, the Isphahan uranium-hexafluoride conversion plant, the heavy-water and plutonium reactor and separation plant at Arak near the Kara-Chai River, some 150 miles south of Tehran, and the huge Natanz centrifuge complex between Isphahan and Kashan (at $33°43'24.43''$ N, $51°43'37.55''$ E, in case any friendly pilot should ask).

The last-named facility contains more than two dozen separate buildings within a perimeter of 4.7 miles, but of greatest interest are the two huge underground hails of 250,000 square feet each. Built with walls six feet thick and supposedly protected by two concrete roofs with sand and rocks in between—impressive to contemplate even if no dice against today's penetrating munitions—these halls are large enough to hold as many centrifuges as the Iranians could possibly want to make any number of uranium bombs or for that matter to fuel many reactors, always assuming of course that they can successfully manufacture, assemble, and operate centrifuge cascades.

That they can indeed do so is what Iranian spokesmen themselves now claim, and none more emphatically than Ahmadinejad, who insists that his countrymen have already mastered all the required processes and techniques. But is he right? He does possess a Ph.D. in engineering—won, however, in a special program for Pasdaran veterans and in the field of urban traffic management rather than nuclear engineering. What undermines confidence in Ahmadinejad's opinion is his rather expansive way with the facts, including his repeated assertion that the centrifuge technology was developed by Iranians in Iran and is "the proud achievement of the Iranian nation"—somehow overlooking the 99.99 percent of it that was purchased from A.Q. Khan.

Ahmadinejad aside, even casual observers must wonder how the world knows so much, in such exceptional detail, about Iran's once secret nuclear program, certainly as compared with what it knows of North Korea's program or what it knew of Iraq's at any point in time. Moreover, only a fraction of what it knows about the installations and processes at Arak, Isphahan, Natanz, and all the other places was uncovered by the much-advertised inspections of the IAEA; the recent Nobel Peace Prize won by its director Mohamed ElBaradei must have been a reward for effort rather than achievement. Satellite photography, too, is only part of the explanation, because one needs to know exactly where to look before it can be useful.

The conclusion is inescapable that among the scientists, engineers, and managers engaged in Iran's nuclear program—most of whom no doubt hold the same opinion of their rulers as do almost all educated Iranians—there are some who feel and act upon a higher loyalty to humanity than to the nationalism that the regime has discredited. Iran's regime, extremist but not totalitarian, does not and cannot control the movement of people and communications in and out of the country as North Korea does almost completely, and as Iraq did in lesser degree.

IX

Because of the continuing flow of detailed and timely information out of Iran, it is possible both to overcome the regime's attempts at dispersion, camouflage, and deception and—if that should become necessary—to target air strikes accurately enough to delay Iran's manufacture of nuclear weapons very considerably. At the same time, there is no reason to attack prematurely, because there will be ample time to do so before it is too late—that is, before enough fissile material has been produced for one bomb.

And that brings us back to the beginning. What gives great significance to the factor of time is the advanced stage of the regime's degeneration. High oil prices and the handouts they fund now help to sustain the regime—but then it might last even without them, simply because of the power of any dictatorship undefeated in war. There is thus no indication that the regime will fall before it acquires nuclear weapons. Yet, because there is still time, it is not irresponsible to hope that it will.

By the same token, however, it is irresponsible to argue for coexistence with a future nuclear-armed Iran on the basis of a shared faith in mutual deterrence. How indeed could deterrence work against those who believe in the return of the twelfth imam and the end of life on earth, and who additionally believe that this redeemer may be forced to reveal himself by provoking a nuclear catastrophe?

But it is not necessary to raise such questions in order to reject coexistence with a nuclear Iran under its present leaders. As of now, in early 2006, with American and allied ground and air forces deployed on both sides of Iran in Afghanistan and Iraq, with powerful U.S. naval forces at sea to its south, with their own armed forces in shambles and no nuclear weapons, the rulers of Iran are openly financing, arming, training, and inciting anti-American terrorist organizations and militias at large. Under very thin cover, they are doing the same thing within neighboring Iraq, where they pursue a logic of their own by helping Sunni insurgents who kill Shiites, as well as rival Shiite militias that fight one another.

If this is what Iran's extremist rulers are doing now even without the shield of nuclear weapons to protect them, what would they do if they had it? Even more aggression is the only reasonable answer, beginning with the subversion of the Arabian oil dynasties, where very conveniently there are Shiite minorities to be mobilized.

These, then, are the clear boundaries of prudent action in response to Iran's vast, costly, and most dangerous nuclear program. No premature and therefore unnecessary attack is warranted while there is still time to wait in assured safety for a better solution. But also and equally, Iran under its present rulers cannot be allowed finally to acquire nuclear weapons—for these would not guarantee stability by mutual deterrence but would instead threaten us with uncontrollable perils.

POSTSCRIPT

Should the United States Preemptively Attack Iranian Nuclear Facilities?

Even though broad international sanctions against Iran have thus far not materialized, Iran's willingness to risk such sanctions over its nuclear program suggests that it is strongly committed to developing nuclear weapons. At a time when American troops have invaded and remain deployed in two of Iran's neighbors, Iraq and Afghanistan, Iranian leaders probably view nuclear weapons as the ultimate guarantor of the security of their regime. Indeed, it would be surprising if Iranian leaders did not draw the lesson from recent history that it has been much easier for the United States to take military action against states that lack nuclear weapons, like Iraq and Afghanistan, than against states that have them, such as North Korea.

In addition, Iranian leaders may view their pursuit of nuclear weapons as a means to bolster the domestic legitimacy of their rule at a time when many Iranians are becoming disillusioned with their country's limited economic growth, lack of democracy, international isolation, and restrictive religious regulations. Iran's leaders also appear to be confident that their power in the region is increasing not only as a result of their nascent nuclear program, but as a consequence of U.S. setbacks in Iraq and Israel's inability to defeat decisively the Iranian-backed Hezbollah militants in Lebanon who fired missiles into Israel during Israel's brief incursion into Lebanon in the summer of 2006.

Should Iran continue to pursue nuclear weapons, it may create incentives for other countries in the region, particularly the Sunni countries that have clashed with Iran in the past, to develop nuclear weapons as well.

For discussions of whether sanctions could induce Iran to end its nuclear weapons program, see George Perkovich and Silvia Manzanero, "Plan B: Using Sanctions to End Iran's Nuclear Program," *Arms Control Today* (vol. 34, issue 4, May 2004) and Kenneth Pollack, "Bringing Iran to the Table," *Current History* (November 2006, pp. 365–370). For an argument that Iran might forego nuclear weapons if the United States and others reassure Iran's government that they do not seek regime change in Iran, see Scott D. Sagan, *Foreign Affairs* (September/October 2006), pp. 45–59. For competing views on Iran's nuclear intentions, see Shahram Chubin and Robert Litwak, "Debating Iran's Nuclear Ambitions," *The Washington Quarterly* (Autumn 2003), pp. 99–114.

ISSUE 9

Should the United States Send Peacekeeping Troops to Darfur?

YES: Lawrence F. Kaplan, from "Crisis Intervention," *New Republic Online* (April 24, 2006)

NO: David Rieff, from "Moral Blindness," *New Republic* (June 5, 2006)

ISSUE SUMMARY

YES: Lawrence Kaplan, a senior editor at *The New Republic*, argues that the United Nations, the African Union, and NATO are unable or unwilling to intervene to stop genocide in Darfur, and that only a large intervention by U.S. military forces can do so.

NO: David Rieff, a contributing editor at *The New Republic*, argues that although some form of international intervention in Darfur might eventually be necessary, a unilateral U.S. intervention would further damage U.S. relations with the Muslim world and would end up either with the secession of Darfur under a U.S. or UN protectorate or a Iraq-style counterinsurgency against the government of Sudan and the Janjaweed fighters it sponsors.

The Darfur region of western Sudan has long had difficult relations with the rest of the country. After the British took control of Darfur in 1916 and incorporated it into Sudan, the region's economic development lagged behind that of the Sudanese regions around the Nile River valley and the capital of Khartoum, where the British focused their investments and where, more recently, the development of oil fields has bolstered the economy. This has contributed to resentment in the Darfur region toward the central government, and the area became embroiled in conflicts among Libya, Chad, and Sudan from the 1960s through the 1990s.

Tensions escalated in 2003 when rebel groups formed in Darfur and began attacking Sudanese government forces. A central complaint among these groups was that the Sudanese government was discriminating against the non-Arab tribes in Darfur (most of those living in Darfur are Muslim but not Arab). Sudanese government forces, stretched thin by deployments to conflicts in other regions of Sudan, fought back against the rebel forces by creating and equipping a militia, known as the "Janjaweed," from the Arab tribes of the north. These tribes, who are nomadic camel-herders, are culturally different from the farming peoples of Darfur. The Janjaweed, with the assistance of the Sudanese government, quickly went on the offensive through the Darfur region in 2004, using brutal tactics of rape and murder to clear entire villages of their inhabitants and destroying houses and livestock to prevent residents from returning. An estimated 400,000 have been killed in the conflict, which many observers have described as a "genocide," and by most accounts over 2 million residents of Darfur had become refugees by 2006.

Efforts by Chad and the African Union (AU) to establish and monitor a ceasefire in 2004 with 7,000 AU troops proved only partially successful. Similarly, U.S. Undersecretary of State Robert Zoellick negotiated an agreement between the government of Sudan and one of the main Darfuri rebel factions in May 2006 calling for the disarmament of both the Janjaweed militia and the rebel forces, but this accord has not been implemented. Fighting renewed in the summer of 2006, leading to proposals for deployment of a UN peacekeeping force of up to 20,000 soldiers to replace the small and ineffective AU force. The Sudanese government rejected calls for a UN force, but the UN Security Council approved a new peacekeeping force of 17,300 troops on August 31, 2006. The Sudanese government responded by renewing its offensive in Darfur and requesting that the AU force leave the region. In the face of the continued opposition of the Sudanese government, no UN force has been deployed to the region.

YES

Lawrence F. Kaplan

Crisis Intervention

Springtime has arrived on the nation's college campuses, but this year the students out marching in the streets are demanding a foreign intervention rather than protesting one. For months now they've been in full cry, and rightly so, over the international community's disinclination to halt the genocide in the Darfur region of western Sudan. Next Sunday, they and like-minded people around the United States will convene for a massive rally in the nation's capital.

But the marchers will have to contend with an unwelcome guest: the specter of Iraq.

Just as the shadow of Somalia loomed over policymakers a decade ago, generating excuses for inaction in Bosnia and Rwanda, the trauma of Iraq may now doom the rescue of Darfur. Even the most committed progressive activists seem confused about what exactly should be done next. "A CALL TO YOUR CONSCIENCE: SAVE DARFUR!," "TAKE ACTION NOW"—these are a few of the slogans that the Save Darfur Coalition suggests marchers affix to their placards at the April 30 rally. But it's purposefully unclear what the march organizers mean by "action" and on whose "conscience" they intend to call.

As their criticism of the particulars of the Iraq war has hardened into a broader indictment of U.S. foreign policy, the mostly progressive voices calling for action in Darfur have become caught in a bind of their own devising. Even as they demand intervention in Sudan, they excoriate Washington for employing U.S. military power without due respect to the opinion of the international community and against nations that pose no imminent threat to our own—which is to say, precisely the terms under which U.S. power would have to be employed in the name of saving Darfur.

Then again, the use of unilateral U.S. military power isn't the solution most Darfur activists have in mind. Even as western Sudan burns, Darfur advocates such as House Minority Leader Nancy Pelosi argue that the United States must employ its military power only on behalf of—and, more important, in concert with—international organizations such as the United Nations. The Save Darfur Coalition, a leading umbrella group for organizations bent on action, intends to save Darfur not by urging the Bush administration to launch air strikes against Sudan's murderous militias but by petitioning the White House to bolster funding for African Union peacekeepers and to lobby the United Nations.

But will the African Union put a halt to the killings in Darfur? Absolutely not. Its Arab members have stymied the force at every turn. Will the United Nations solve the crisis? That seems extremely unlikely as well. The organization amounts first and foremost to a collection of sovereign states, many of them adamantly opposed to violating Sudan's own sovereignty. Can NATO save the day? Not really, given the fears of entanglement expressed by its European members. As in Bosnia before it, the victims of Darfur can be saved by one thing and one thing alone: American power.

Unfortunately for the victims of Darfur, too many of their advocates have come to view that power as tainted, marred by self-interest and by its misapplication in Iraq. Hence, the contradiction at the heart of the Darfur debate, which pits the imperative to halt the persecution of innocents (Darfur activists have enshrined as their motto the biblical admonition not to "stand idly by the blood of thy neighbor") against a reflexive opposition to the only power that can actually do so.

With the latter sentiment in vogue as a result of the Iraq war, it is as if nothing has been learned and nothing remembered from the decade that went before. Never mind Bosnia. Never mind Kosovo. And, as long as Darfur activists like number two Senate Democrat Dick Durbin of Illinois cling to the mantra that the United States must be what he calls a "defensive nation," well, never mind Darfur either.

There are a few "progressive" Darfur activists who are willing to contemplate a military solution, but they face a thorny moral dilemma. The most vocal among them argue at once for Darfur's rescue and Iraq's abandonment, as if this counts as evidence of heightened moral awareness. But their willingness to exchange one moral catastrophe for another—a rapid withdrawal from Iraq, after all, would spark a humanitarian crisis and bloodbath of exactly the same magnitude that activists mean to halt in Darfur—is really proof of the reverse. Yet that doesn't seem to have occurred to those like *New York Times* columnist Nicholas Kristof, one of the most persistent advocates for launching an intervention in Darfur and also for winding down an intervention in Iraq.

Nor does the contradiction seem to have made an impression on organizations from Americans for Democratic Action to the National Council of Churches, which insist that we act in Darfur even as they insist that we evacuate Iraq without condition and regardless of consequence. In moral and humanitarian terms—that is, the very terms used to justify halting the slaughter in Darfur—their position is simply incoherent.

So, yes, march on Washington. Comfort your sensibilities. Testify to your virtue and good intentions. Offer assurance that your call to action is not a call for the unilateral or unprovoked exercise of American power. But don't pretend that Darfur will be saved by anything else.

David Rieff  **NO**

Moral Blindness: The Case Against Troops for Darfur

No issue in international politics commands a broader consensus than military intervention in Darfur. From the magazine *First Things* on the Catholic right to the Congressional Black Caucus, and from Senator Sam Brownback to the editors of this magazine, who recently declared with astonishing tone-deafness that The New Republic was making Darfur "a crusade"—a term that will undoubtedly play well in Jakarta, Islamabad, and Cairo, not to mention Khartoum—any American with a shred of human decency is presumed to support the deployment of forces in Darfur, and quickly. As [TNR]'s Richard Just has put it, "Darfur is an easy case. . . . Anyone who considers himself a liberal idealist should know where to stand on Darfur, and what must be done. The only people left on the outside of this coalition will be the most hard-hearted of the liberal realists; and I'm not sure those people deserve to be called liberals anyway."

Actually, I'm not sure Just gets to decide who is and who is not a liberal. But questions of anathematization aside, it is interesting that, in the matter of Darfur, liberal interventionists have been far keener on direct U.S. or [NATO] intervention than conservatives. Just, who is emblematic of the former camp, has written flatly that "the calculus is stark: Either we put Western troops on the ground in Darfur or we concede the likelihood that the genocide will run its gruesome course." By contrast, in *First Things*, Allen D. Hertzke wrote about a U.S. role in an intervention force with far less enthusiasm. He too insisted that, without U.S. involvement, there could be no improvement. But, where Just saw no option other than the dispatch of Western troops, Hertzke insisted that other "forceful and moral options" remained, including a "determined effort to expand and empower African Union forces, add U.S. logistical support, secure more aid, and massively increase diplomatic and economic pressure."

After having been proved so catastrophically wrong in Iraq, it did not seem unreasonable to hope that liberal idealists like those around [The New Republic] might now be prepared to think with less triumphalism and more sobriety about American military power. Crusades have a way of backfiring and—however good the intentions of those who call for them—causing harm in places where it is least expected. Yes, in the end, some form of international

First published in *The New Republic*, June 5, 2006 by David Rieff, permission of The Wylie Agency.

military deployment in Darfur may be necessary, both to protect Darfuri civilians from attacks by the government of Sudan and its *Janjaweed* surrogates and to enforce the recent Abuja peace agreement. But this does not mean that the deployment of American forces is the most desirable way to achieve this goal, let alone that such a military commitment is a moral imperative. To the contrary, there is a good case to be made that the United States is the *last* country that should be leading an international operation in Darfur.

To put the matter starkly, the United States no longer enjoys enough moral credibility in the world as a whole to intervene in Darfur in a way that would avoid deepening the civilizational crisis in which we find ourselves. Intervention would significantly exacerbate America's primary foreign policy challenge, a challenge far more significant in the long run than terrorism: that is, worldwide anti-Americanism. The reasons for this are straightforward and can be summed up by the words "the global war on terror" and by the names "Iraq," "Afghanistan," and "Israel-Palestine." Whether the United States is right or wrong—caught dead to rights or horribly misunderstood—is beside the point. The salient fact is that, in much of the world, the United States is viewed as a bully, an imperial aggressor, and a rogue state determined to apply one law to itself and another to everyone else. In the Islamic world, the situation is far worse. Again, rightly or wrongly, a strong majority of our planet's 1.5 billion Muslims believe that the United States is leading a new crusade against Islam. And it is in this explosive global context that advocates of an intervention in Darfur propose deploying our Armed Forces, as if rubbing salt on that global wound is somehow an insignificant or morally unworthy consideration.

Is it really necessary (after Abu Ghraib, and with Guantánamo still serving as a Jihadi recruiting poster) to explain how terribly dangerous a deployment of the U.S. Armed Forces is likely to be, particularly since, were it to occur, this occupation of Darfur—let's call things by their right names—would take place without even the fig leaf of a U.N. Security Council authorization? Do the interventionists truly believe that American power is so irresistible, and the United States so secure, that these questions need not be taken into account? On the evidence—or, more precisely, on the basis of the seeming indifference to the question—the answer would seem to be yes.

Obviously, the reason advocates of a U.S. military intervention in Darfur have not dwelt on these issues of global governance and of U.S. security is that they view them as insignificant when compared with the moral imperative of intervening in what Eric Reeves, the most eloquent and passionate proponent of intervention, has called the first genocide of the twentieth century. For Reeves, and for the many thousands of grassroots activists who have been instructed by him, the world that failed to prevent the slaughter of the Rwandan Tutsis must not fail the Darfuris. As Reeves has written, "Will the genocide be allowed to continue? Will international deference continue as the regime's *génocidaires* predictably and relentlessly assert the claim of 'national sovereignty?' How many must die before the world says, 'Enough?'"

Reeves's use of the term *génocidaires* reflects not only his moral commitment to stopping the killing in Darfur, but, more problematically, an analytical

framework that is not beyond challenge. Yes, in the United States, it is universally believed—so much so that the claim is even enshrined in a unanimous
congressional declaration—that a slow motion genocide has been taking place
in Darfur. But many reputable groups abroad, including the French section of
Doctors Without Borders, whose physicians have been on the ground in Darfur
for a very long time, reject claims like those made by Reeves. Does this matter,
since everyone agrees the government of Sudan has committed or abetted the
most terrible crimes in Darfur? On the most obvious level, the answer is no. The
Genocide Convention is itself a deeply flawed document, and the crimes of
the authorities in Khartoum have been unspeakable. But, on another level, the
recurrent use of the term "genocide" is a way of delegitimizing any questioning
of the intervene-now-no-matter-the-cost line. We failed to intervene in Rwanda,
and now we know we were wrong; Darfur is the Rwanda of today; hence the
only correct thing to do is intervene at once in Darfur. *Q.E.D.*

The problem with this—the eternal problem posed by the assertion of
this kind of Kantian categorical imperative in matters of war and peace—is the
problem of politics. Except for those who frankly favor the anti-government
insurgents in Darfur—and they are more to be found on the Christian right,
which has supported Minni Minnawi's Sudan Liberation Movement as it once
supported John Garang's insurgency in Southern Sudan—advocates of a U.S.
deployment have been maddeningly vague about what will transpire in Darfur
after foreign forces halt the killing.

To his credit, Reeves has written that any outside military force would
have to ensure that the rebel guerrillas do not take advantage of the foreign
presence to improve their position on the ground. But that is what an international deployment will almost inevitably do, which is why Minnawi and
others have been campaigning so hard for one. The deployment of foreign
troops, whose mission will be to protect Darfuri civilians, will allow the guerrillas to establish "facts on the ground" that will strengthen their claims for
secession. That is what makes the interventionists' claim that the intervention
will be purely "humanitarian"—that it will protect civilians being murdered,
raped, and displaced by the *Janjaweed* but do little or nothing else—so disingenuous. For it is virtually certain that this is not the way events will play out
if U.S. or [NATO] forces deploy. To the contrary, such a deployment can have
only one of two outcomes. The first will be the severing of Darfur from the
rest of Sudan and its transformation into some kind of international protectorate, à la Kosovo. But, at least in Kosovo, the protectorate was run by
Europeans—by neighbors. In Darfur, by contrast, it will be governed by Americans (who are already at war across the Islamic world) and possibly by [NATO]
(i.e., Africa's former colonial masters). Now there's a recipe for stability.

If anything, the second possibility is even worse. Assuming the intervention encounters resistance from the *Janjaweed* and the government of
Sudan (and perhaps Al Qaeda), the foreign intervenors will arrive at the conclusion that the only way to bring stability to Darfur is, well, regime change
in Khartoum: In other words, the problems of Darfur are, in fact, the product
of Al Bashir's dictatorship, and these problems can be meaningfully addressed
only by substituting a more democratic government. Such an intervention

may well end up being Iraq redux, and it is disingenuous to pretend otherwise. But, then, it was disingenuous to pretend that the United States could democratize Iraq at the point of a gun.

The idea that, after Bosnia, Rwanda, Kosovo, and Iraq, intelligent activists can still speak of humanitarian intervention as if it were an uncomplicated act of rescue without grave implications is a testimony to the refusal of the best and brightest among us to think seriously about politics.

Is this what the marriage of human rights and American exceptionalism has led us to? If so, God help us. My own view is that the main culprit here is human rightsism, a worldview that is based, as John Gray has put it, "on the moral intuitions of the liberal academy . . . a legalistic edifice from which politics has been excluded." Were politics present in their thinking, pro-Darfuri intervention activists would not use the reductionist dichotomy of victims and abusers that has been the staple myth of humanitarian intervention. The people being killed by the *Janjaweed* have political interests. So do the extended families of the *Janjaweed* themselves, who, lest we forget, are also Darfuris. To describe the former simply as victims deprives them of any agency. To describe the latter simply as killers precludes actually understanding the conflict as anything other than an eruption of human wickedness, rather like a volcano or an earthquake.

One debilitating defect of the liberal interventionism is that it ignores the political implications of what it calls for. Another is that, perhaps out of the honorable motives of despair and outrage, it champions the use of American hard power while acting as if American soft power, were it to be diligently and seriously applied, can never produce the intervention that might actually work—for example, one undertaken by African countries with, perhaps, the participation of forces from Islamic countries outside the region. Most gravely of all, liberal interventionism ignores the global political context in which it calls for the use of the U.S. military.

Leave aside Iraq—and the detestation with which the United States is now regarded—and focus on history. Reeves may sneer at the idea of national sovereignty and bemoan the African Union's insufficiently aggressive line toward the government of Sudan. The fact remains that the consensus in postcolonial Africa has been to maintain the national borders that existed at the time of independence, despite their obvious artificiality, because, in redrawing them, Africa might reap the whirlwind. But that is why there was so little sympathy in Africa for Katangese or Biafra secession; it is why most African leaders insist that the Eritrean secession remain an exception for the sake of continental stability. There is nothing stupid, venal, or contemptible about this. And, whatever Reeves may imagine, there are many thoughtful African leaders whose reluctance to confront Khartoum is based in large part on these considerations.

A sense of contemporary Africa should lead those concerned with the fate of Darfuris to emphasize an African—or, at the very most, a U.N.–response, rather than an U.S. or a [NATO] one. To their credit, the interventionists can put themselves in the place of the suffering peoples of Darfur. To their discredit, they cannot put themselves in the place of most people in the world who abhor U.S. military action. Again, the reigning global interpretation of

American power may be false, but it is also dominant. And unless, like the conservative writer Norman Podhoretz and his ilk, you believe the United States
should be harshly prosecuting what he has called "World War IV" against radical
Islam, you are obliged to acknowledge that an intervention, however good it may
be for the Darfuris, may be terrible for the rest of the world. If, on reflection,
Reeves and those who think like him believe that it is worth doing anyway, that is
a perfectly defensible position. What is indefensible is not seeing—or pretending
not to see—the problem.

POSTSCRIPT

Should the United States Send Peacekeeping Troops to Darfur?

$\mathbf{T}$he situation in Darfur remained unresolved through December 2006. At that time there was still no agreement to replace the AU peacekeeping force, whose mandate had been extended to the end of 2006, with a UN force. Meanwhile, violence in the region continued, contributing to an ongoing refugee problem and humanitarian crisis.

For analyses of the conflict in Darfur, see Gérard Prunier, *Darfur: The Ambiguous Genocide* (Cornell University Press, 2005); Julie Flint and Alex de Waal, *Darfur: A Short History of a Long War* (Zed Books, London, 2006); Doug Johnson, *The Root Causes of Sudan's Civil Wars*; Report of the International Commission of Inquiry on Darfur to the United Nations Secretary-General; and the overview of the conflict on Wikipedia at http://en.wikipedia.org/wiki/Darfur_conflict.

ISSUE 10

Is China's Rise Threatening to the United States?

YES: John J. Mearsheimer, from "China's Unpeaceful Rise," *Current History* (April 2006)

NO: Dennis J. Blasko, from "Rumsfeld's Take on the Chinese Military: A Dissenting View," *Current History* (September 2006)

ISSUE SUMMARY

YES: John J. Mearsheimer is the R. Wendell Harrison Distinguished Service Professor of Political Science and the codirector of the Program on International Security Policy at the University of Chicago. He argues that China's impressive economic growth will enable it to engage in an intense security competition with considerable potential for war.

NO: Dennis J. Blasko served as a military intelligence officer and foreign area officer specializing in China for the U.S. army and was army attaché in Beijing from 1992–1995 and in Hong Kong from 1995–1996. He argues the U.S. assessments of Chinese military modernization are biased to justify current U.S. policy and overstate the threat posed by China.

The relationship between the United States and China has been aptly described as one involving constructive ambiguity. The ambiguity derives from the multiple dimensions of American-Chinese interaction. At one level, the relationship involves two dominant powers with high levels of trade and monetary interdependence and increasing societal and cultural ties, who share common interests in a variety of issues ranging from fighting terrorism to maintaining stability in the global economy. On another level, it involves two dominant military and political powers with very different historical backgrounds who were key players occasionally on opposing sides of the bipolar world during the Cold War, the vestiges of which remain and are most visible in their ongoing discussions regarding the status of the people on the island of Taiwan and the divided Korean peninsula. On yet another level, it is the relationship between one country that defines itself in terms of liberal economic and political principles and another that has undergone a dramatically successful economic liberalization but continues to govern itself through a highly centralized political system and harshly repressed demonstrations in Tiananmen Square in 1989 and, more recently, in Hong Kong to counter societal movements toward democratization. It is also a relationship between a superpower with the most advanced military in the world and a growing regional power seeking to modernize its military capabilities, both of whom, despite their capabilities, are cognizant of their vulnerability in the current strategic environment. The ambiguity created by these and other dimensions of the American-Chinese relationship have been constructive to the extent that since the Sino-American rapprochement of 1971–1972, the two countries have managed tensions between themselves and developed a deeper and increasingly complex relationship.

Current dramatic events in the international arena have created new opportunities and risks for U.S.-Chinese relations. These events include the disintegration of the Soviet Union and the Warsaw Treaty Organization, the worldwide recognition of China as a major economic and political power as symbolized by its entry into the World Trade Organization and increasingly active roles in the United Nations the potential nuclear conflict between Pakistan and India, the importance of Pakistan in U.S. actions in Afghanistan and Iraq, the resurgence of U.S. involvement abroad in its fight against global terrorism, ongoing U.S. and regional concerns about North Korea, and increasing calls from the people of Taiwan for political independence. U.S. and Chinese responses to these events are likely to make the ambiguity in their relationship more difficult to maintain. Whether specificity in U.S.-Chinese relations will reveal a relationship that is more cooperative or competitive is a matter of debate.

John Mearsheimer argues that the nature of the international system drives states to compete in military and economic terms. As a consequence, China's economic rise is likely to drive it into an intense military competition with the United States and its neighbors. In contrast, Dennis Blasko argues that fears of China's economic and military development are overstated and do not conform to the known characteristics of the Chinese military, nor are they consistent with an objective assessment of recent Chinese behavior.

YES ↵   **John J. Mearsheimer**

China's Unpeaceful Rise

Can China rise peacefully? My answer is no. If China continues its impressive economic growth over the next few decades, the United States and China are likely to engage in an intense security competition with considerable potential for war. Most of China's neighbors—including India, Japan, Singapore, South Korea, Russia, and Vietnam—will join with the United States to contain Chinas power.

To predict the future in Asia, one needs a theory of international politics that explains how rising great powers are likely to act and how other states in the system will react to them. That theory must be logically sound and it must account for the past behavior of rising great powers.

My theory of international politics says that the mightiest states attempt to establish hegemony in their region of the world while making sure that no rival great power dominates another region. This theory, which helps explain US foreign policy since the country's founding, also has implications for future relations between China and the United States.

The Contest for Power

According to my understanding of international politics, survival is a state's most important goal, because a state cannot pursue any other goals if it does not survive. The basic structure of the international system forces states concerned about their security to compete with each other for power. The ultimate goal of every great power is to maximize its share of world power and eventually dominate the system.

The international system has three defining characteristics. First, the main actors are states that operate in anarchy, which simply means that there is no higher authority above them. Second, all great powers have some offensive military capability, which means that they have the wherewithal to hurt each other. Third, no state can know the intentions of other states with certainty, especially their future intentions. It is simply impossible, for example, to know what Germany or Japan's intentions will be toward their neighbors in 2025.

In a world where other states might have malign intentions as well as significant offensive capabilities, states tend to fear each other. That fear is compounded by the fact that in an anarchic system there is no night watchman for

From *The National Interest*, Fall 2005, pp. 81–87. Copyright © 2005 by National Interest. Reprinted by permission.

states to call if trouble comes knocking at their door. Therefore, states recognize that the best way to survive in such a system is to be as powerful as possible relative to potential rivals. The mightier a state is, the less likely it is that another state will attack it. No Americans, for example, worry that Canada or Mexico will attack the United States, because neither of those countries is powerful enough to contemplate a fight with Washington. But great powers do not merely strive to be the strongest great power, although that is a welcome outcome. Their ultimate aim is to be the hegemon—that is, the only great power in the system.

What exactly does it mean to be a hegemon in the modern world? It is almost impossible for any state to achieve global hegemony, because it is too hard to project and sustain power around the globe and onto the territory of distant great powers. The best outcome that a state can hope for is to be a regional hegemon, and thus dominate one's own geographical area. The United States has been a regional hegemon in the Western Hemisphere since the late 1800s. Although the United States is clearly the most powerful state on the planet today, it is not a global hegemon.

States that gain regional hegemony have a further aim: they seek to prevent great powers in other regions from duplicating their feat. Regional hegemons do not want peers. Instead, they want to keep other regions divided among several great powers, so that these states will compete with each other and be unable to focus on them. In sum, my theory says that the ideal situation for any great power is to be the only regional hegemon in the world.

The American Hegemon

A brief look at the history of American foreign policy illustrates the explanatory power of this theory. When the United States won its independence from Britain in 1783, it was a small and weak country comprised of 13 states strung along the Atlantic seaboard. The new country was surrounded by the British and Spanish empires and much of the territory between the Appalachian Mountains and the Mississippi River was controlled by hostile Native American tribes. It was a dangerous, threat-filled environment.

Over the course of the next 115 years, American policy makers of all stripes worked assiduously to turn the United States into a regional hegemon. They expanded America's boundaries from the Atlantic to the Pacific oceans as part of a policy commonly referred to as "Manifest Destiny." The United States fought wars against Mexico and various Native American tribes and took huge chunks of land from them. The nation became an expansionist power of the first order. As Senator Henry Cabot Lodge put it, the United States had a "record of conquest, colonization, and territorial expansion unequalled by any people in the nineteenth century."

American policy makers in that century were not just concerned with turning the United States into a powerful territorial state. They were also determined to push the European great powers out of the Western Hemisphere and make it clear to them that they were not welcome back. This policy, known as the Monroe Doctrine, was laid out for the first time in 1823 by President James Monroe in his annual message to Congress. By 1898, the last

European empire in the Americas had collapsed and the United States had become the first regional hegemon in modern history.

However, a great power's work is not done once it achieves regional hegemony. It then must make sure that no other great power follows suit and dominates its area of the world. During the twentieth century, there were four great powers that had the capability to make a run at regional hegemony: Imperial Germany (1900–1918). Imperial Japan (1931–1945), Nazi Germany (1933–1945), and the Soviet Union during the cold war (1945–1989). Not surprisingly, each tried to match what the United States had achieved in the Western Hemisphere in the nineteenth century.

How did the United States react? In each case, it played a key role in defeating and dismantling those aspiring hegemons. The United States entered World War I in April 1917 when Imperial Germany looked like it would win the war and rule Europe. American troops played a critical role in tipping the balance against the Kaiserreich, which collapsed in November 1918. In the early 1940s, President Franklin Delano Roosevelt went to great lengths to maneuver the United States into World War II to thwart Japan's ambitions in Asia and especially Germany's ambitions in Europe. During the war, the United States helped destroy both Axis powers. And after 1945, American policy makers made certain that Germany and Japan remained militarily weak. Finally, during the cold war, the United States steadfastly worked to prevent the Soviet Union from dominating Eurasia, and in the late 1980s helped relegate its empire to the scrap heap of history.

Shortly after the cold war ended, the first Bush administration's "Defense Guidance" of 1992, which was leaked to the press, boldly stated that the United States was now the most powerful state in the world by far and it planned to remain in that exalted position. In other words, the United States would not tolerate a peer competitor.

That same message was repeated in the famous "National Security Strategy" issued by the second Bush administration in October 2002. There was much criticism of this document, especially its claims about "preemptive war." But hardly a word of protest was raised about the assertion that the United States should check rising powers and maintain its commanding position in the global balance of power.

The bottom line is that the United States—for sound strategic reasons—worked hard for more than a century to gain hegemony in the Western Hemisphere. After achieving regional dominance, it has gone to great lengths to prevent other great powers from controlling either Asia or Europe.

What are the implications of America's past behavior for the rise of China? In short, how is China likely to behave as it grows more powerful? And how are the United States and the other states in Asia likely to react to a mighty China?

Predicting China's Future

China is likely to try to dominate Asia the way the United States dominates the Western Hemisphere. Specifically, China will seek to maximize the power gap between itself and its neighbors, especially Japan and Russia. China will want to make sure that it is so powerful that no state in Asia has the wherewithal to threaten it. It is unlikely that China will pursue military superiority so that it can go on a rampage and conquer other Asian countries, although that is always possible. Instead, it is more likely that China will want to dictate the boundaries of acceptable behavior to neighboring countries, much the way the United States makes it clear to other states in the Americas that it is the boss. Gaining regional hegemony, I might add, is probably the only way that China will get Taiwan back.

An increasingly powerful China is also likely to try to push the United States out of Asia, much the way the United States pushed the European great powers out of the Western Hemisphere. We should expect China to come up with its own version of the Monroe Doctrine, as Japan did in the 1930s.

These policy goals make good strategic sense for China. Beijing should want a militarily weak Japan and Russia as its neighbors, just as the United States prefers a militarily weak Canada and Mexico on its borders. What state in its right mind would want other powerful states located in its region? Most Chinese surely remember what happened in the past century when Japan was powerful and China was weak. In the anarchic world of international politics, it is better to be Godzilla than Bambi.

Furthermore, why would a powerful China accept US military forces operating in its backyard? American policy makers, after all, become apoplectic when other great powers send military forces into the Western Hemisphere. Those foreign forces are invariably seen as a potential threat to American security. The same logic should apply to China. Why would China feel safe with US forces deployed on its doorstep? Following the logic of the Monroe Doctrine, would not China's security be better served by pushing the American military out of Asia?

Why should we expect China to act any differently from how the United States did? Is Beijing more principled than Washington? More ethical? Less nationalistic? Less concerned about survival? China is none of these things, of course, which is why it is likely to imitate the United States and attempt to become a regional hegemon.

Trouble Ahead

It is clear from the historical record how American policy makers will react if China attempts to dominate Asia. The United States does not tolerate peer competitors. As it demonstrated in the twentieth century, it is determined to remain the world's only regional hegemon. Therefore, the United States can be expected to go to great lengths to contain China and ultimately weaken it to the point where it is no longer capable of ruling the roost in Asia. In essence, America is likely to behave toward China much the way it behaved toward the Soviet Union during the cold war.

China's neighbors are certain to fear its rise as well, and they too will do whatever they can to prevent the Chinese from achieving regional hegemony. Indeed, there is already substantial evidence that countries like India, Japan, and Russia, as well as smaller powers like Singapore, South Korea, and Vietnam, are worried about China's ascendancy and are looking for ways to contain it. In the end, they will join an American-led balancing coalition to check China's rise, much the way Britain, France, Germany, Italy, Japan, and even China joined forces with the United States to contain the Soviet Union during the cold war.

Finally, given Taiwan's strategic importance for controlling the sea lanes in East Asia, it is hard to imagine the United States, as well as Japan, allowing China to control that large island. In fact, Taiwan is likely to be an important player in the anti-China balancing coalition, which is certain to infuriate China and fuel the security competition between Beijing and Washington.

The picture I have painted of what is likely to happen if China continues its rise is not a pretty one. I actually find it categorically depressing and wish that I could tell a more optimistic story about the future. But the fact is that international politics is a nasty and dangerous business, and no amount of goodwill can ameliorate the intense security competition that sets in when an aspiring hegemon appears in Eurasia. That is the tragedy of great power politics.

Dennis J. Blasko

NO

Rumsfeld's Take on the Chinese Military: A Dissenting View

Every year since 1997, Congress has required the secretary of defense to report on China's military—its technological development, its strategy, and its operational concepts. The series of reports has evolved from short discussions of specific topics to, ostensibly, a comprehensive review of China's military power. This year's report, however, is not an impartial and complete assessment of China's military modernization so much as it is a political document attempting to justify established US policy. Indeed, the report fails to include a large body of open-source information that calls into question both the objectivity and thoroughness of its analysis.

To understand the "Annual Report to Congress: Military Power of the People's Republic of China 2006" prepared by the Office of the Secretary of Defense, readers must also understand how it fits into recent administration policy statements. Starting in June 2005, Defense Secretary Donald Rumsfeld asked the following three questions in a speech in Singapore: "Since no nation threatens China, one must wonder: Why this growing investment [in defense expenditures]? Why these continuing large and expanding arms purchases? Why these continuing robust deployments?"

A month later, the 2005 Pentagon report declared China to be facing a "strategic crossroads." In August, Secretary of State Condoleezza Rice observed in an interview with *The New York Times* that "finally, there's the question of Chinese military power; and yes, to many, including to me, it looks *outsized*. The Chinese military modernization looks outsized for its regional interests and so to comment on that is not to suggest that we believe China is becoming an adversary, but simply to say that that is something that has to be watched, and of course, that *the United States is going to continue to improve its own military capabilities* so that the balance in the Asian Pacific is maintained" (emphasis added).

In February 2006, the Pentagon's Quadrennial Defense Review (QDR) proclaimed that the choices China makes will be a key factor in "determining the international security environment of the 21st century" (the "strategic crossroads" theme again). It went on to note that, "of the major and emerging powers, China has the greatest potential to compete militarily with the United States and field disruptive military technologies that could over time offset traditional US

Reprinted from *Current History*, September 2006, pp. 263–29. Copyright © 2006 by Current History, Inc. Reprinted with permission.

military advantages absent US counterstrategies. . . . The outside world has little knowledge of Chinese motivations and decisionmaking or of key capabilities supporting its modernization. The United States encourages China to make its intentions clear and clarify its military plans." The QDR then describes the US "hedging strategy." This includes "further diversifying its basing structure," which has focused on air and naval deployments to Guam in the Pacific.

In light of these statements, it is no surprise that the executive summary of this year's annual report concludes by repeating Rumsfeld's three questions and states, "Absent greater transparency, international reactions to China's military growth will understandably hedge against these unknowns." A few pages later it expands on this thesis: "As President Bush declared in the 2006 National Security Strategy, the US 'seeks to encourage China to make the right strategic choices for its people, while we hedge against other possibilities.' This strategy is not unique to the United States; other regional actors, too, will naturally hedge against the unknown."

Ironically, a hedging strategy in Asia may be a prudent policy for the United States to pursue (though not necessarily based on the straw man of Chinese military expansion). Unfortunately, basing even a sound policy on faulty analysis undermines the confidence that the United States seeks to build among its own citizens and its friends throughout the world. In fact, the Pentagon's 2006 report provides little credible new information to support its suppositions about China's lack of transparency, undeclared motivations, or "military expansion."

The 2006 report begins with this dubious logic chain in the executive summary: People's Liberation Army "modernization" = "transformation" = "China's military buildup" = "China's military expansion." These terms are used interchangeably throughout the report with no attempt to distinguish what "modernization" or "transformation" is and what is "buildup" or "expansion." The report then makes a series of unsupported claims, distorts much of the information it presents, and omits aspects of China's military development that do not fit its "modernization = expansion" equation. When ambiguous evidence is encountered, the report assumes the direct interpretation even when other conclusions can be reasonably drawn. The Pentagon implies that *any* Chinese military modernization is unacceptable because it is equivalent to "military expansion."

The report presents only one conclusion ("modernization = expansion") and does not allow for the possibility of alternate analysis of the same information that might result in different policy options. This was the very shortcoming that the 9-11 Commission report pointed out as a principal cause of past intelligence failures, and rectifying it was one of the commission's primary recommendations.

Dubious Logic

The People's Liberation Army (PLA) modernization program has been under way for more than 25 years, with a significant increase in pace and scope since about 1999. Defending a country's sovereignty is a function of any government and the fact that a growing power like China wants to modernize its military is predictable. A primary tenet of PLA modernization is building a quantitatively smaller but technologically more advanced force than its personnel-heavy predecessor. At the same time, the PLA is transforming its force structure, doctrine, and military equipment to bring them into the twenty-first century. In this regard, the first two elements of the Pentagon report's equation are correct: the PLA's modernization is transformation.

"Modernization" by definition means that capabilities increase, often while numbers of personnel and equipment decrease because of technological advances. Fifteen years ago, the PLA had few or none of many modern military capabilities, such as advanced air defense systems, in-flight refueling, airborne warning and control, long-distance heavy-lift aircraft, fourth-generation fighters, and modern main battle tanks. As it has modernized, the PLA has gradually acquired many of these new systems, giving it a range of capabilities it simply did not have in the past. This has resulted in a "buildup," since zero plus anything is greater than zero.

But at the same time, as new weapons have entered the force, older weapons have been retired—some going to scrap, others going to the reserve force. Many weapon systems have been decommissioned without replacements as the PLA has downsized its force structure since 1997. For example, the Pentagon's 1998 report counted "approximately 70 submarines of all types"; in the 2006 report, the number of submarines is 55. While there are certainly some aspects of buildup in these developments, much of this is also an integral and expected part of modernization.

"Buildup" implies what existed before has increased in number. An example of China's buildup is found on page 5 of the report: "China has 400,000 ground force personnel deployed to the three military regions opposite Taiwan, an increase of 25,000 over the last year." The total number of 400,000 is, in fact, 25,000 more than the 375,000 cited in the 2005 Pentagon report, but no evidence is provided to justify any of these numbers to prove a "buildup." The day the report was issued, I asked the secretary of defense's office of public affairs how it arrived at these numbers. The response? "The report is as specific as the authors wish to be at this point."

The Chinese do not provide this level of detail, and the one reputable publication that does attempt to count numbers, *The Military Balance*, an annual publication of the International Institute for Strategic Studies (IISS), has exactly the same count for personnel in these regions from 2003 to 2006. There is no open-source information to account for an increase in major active-duty units in the Nanjing, Guangzhou, or Jinan military regions in the past year (and if classified data existed to support the claims made, it could be sanitized for inclusion in the report). If anything, personnel numbers have decreased as the PLA finished a 200,000-man reduction in 2005.

Forces that did not exist 15 years ago, particularly in the navy, air force, and strategic missile force, have indeed increased in number. For the most part, however, the ground forces have not undergone a buildup, though they are modernizing large quantities of equipment and modifying their force structure. (A few handfuls of new army missile, special operations, helicopter, and information warfare units are the exception to the general rule, but this growth has taken place over the past decade throughout the entire country, not only opposite Taiwan.)

"Military expansion," on the other hand, implies an intent to move into areas previously occupied (or unoccupied) by others, in addition to a "buildup" of forces. Here the Defense Department cites a lack of transparency about China's intentions as a reason to conclude that the PLA is expanding. In fact, however, a number of recent Chinese sources state that China's military modernization and economic development are not intended to challenge American interests.

While caution in assessing official government statements is sensible, it is inconsistent with the public record to imply that the Chinese government has not stated its intentions about military modernization and "expansion." For example, in September 2005, the English-language newspaper *People's Daily* editorialized that "China has no intention of challenging the United States' position in the world, including its position in East Asia. However, East Asia is the main stage for China, whose role as the country grows is bound to expand."

In all likelihood, senior Chinese officials have recently passed this same message to their American counterparts. One week after the Pentagon's 2006 report was released, PLA Air Force General Zheng Shenxia, commandant of the Academy of Military Science, told an international audience at a conference in Hangzhou that "China by no means seeks to replace America's position in the Asia-Pacific region." A public statement like this by a senior officer would have to be cleared by the Central Military Commission and would have to be consistent with messages already given to us officials privately.

This same idea, though couched in communist terminology, has been present in all of China's defense white papers as far back as 1998. "China does not seek hegemonism, nor does it seek military blocs or military expansion," the 1998 white paper stated. All white papers also specifically outline China's national security "goals and tasks." Unfortunately, even when the Chinese use terminology that Americans should understand (as in the *People's Daily* opinion), the Pentagon appears to dismiss it, treat it cynically, or question its meaning. Despite having conducted a series of high-level "defense consultative talks," the Defense Department does not appear to have resolved this issue of strategic intentions. Secretary Rumsfeld's "three whys" were answered implicitly by the 2006 Pentagon report equating "PLA modernization" with "military expansion."

Not all US military leaders have expressed the same sentiments reflected in Rumsfeld's questioning of Chinese intentions. In June 2005, General Peter Pace—now the chairman of the Joint Chiefs of Staff—remarked that "you judge military threat in two ways: one, capacity, and two, intent. There are lots of countries in the world that have the capacity to wage war. Very few have the intent to do so. And clearly we have a complex but good relationship with China. So there's absolutely no reason for us to believe there's any intent on their part."

PLA modernization includes transformation and it does have an important element of military buildup as many capabilities increase. But the evidence for "military expansion" is debatable at the very least and deserves a more complete and nuanced examination than the assertions in the Pentagon report provide.

Unsupported Claims

The Pentagon report's executive summary declares that "several aspects of China's military development have surprised US analysts, including the pace and scope of its strategic forces modernization." Yet the report provides no details about what in China's strategic modernization has surprised US analysts and seems unaware of the prediction made in the department's very first report to Congress in April 1997: "China probably will have the industrial capacity, though not necessarily the intent, to produce a large number, perhaps as many as a thousand, new missiles within the next decade. Most new missiles are likely to be short-range or medium-range, road-mobile, and fueled by solid propellants. All of them are expected to have greatly improved accuracy over current systems, and many will be armed with conventional warheads."

The numbers and types of missiles and their rate of growth described by the current report are completely consistent with the 1997 projection. (The 2006 report fails to mention, and does not try to resolve, discrepancies with the IISS estimate that the DF-31 intercontinental ballistic missile already is deployed or Taiwan's assertion that land attack cruise missiles have been deployed.) While numerous ballistic and cruise missile systems are reported "in development," if there is any surprise, it has been in the delay in many of them reaching operational capability (often previously predicted to be around 2005). This is not the implication of the executive summary's statement.

Another unsupported claim is found in the report's budget section. There the authors cite the Defense Intelligence Agency in estimating that China's total defense spending "will amount to between $70 billion and $105 billion in 2006—two to three times the announced budget." The report then lists several "funding streams" that could contribute to these numbers. However, the only specific examples the report gives are an undefined "small commission" that the PLA receives on an annual average of $600 million in foreign arms sales by China's defense industrial sector, and deliveries of an estimated $11 billion in foreign arms over six years. But this totals only about an additional $2 billion annually. No other estimates or factors are provided, yet they must somehow amount to roughly another $33 billion to $68 billion in 2006.

The report also does not mention or explain a discrepancy with its 2002 estimate that "China's defense spending may be some four times larger than its public announcement." That the estimated factor has actually been reduced over time (from four to two or three times the stated budget) has never been acknowledged by the Pentagon (or reported by the press). Nor does the Pentagon report refer to a 2005 RAND study, *Modernizing China's Military: Opportunities and Constraints,* which estimated that spending may be larger by a range of "1.4 to 1.7 times the official number" of China's announced defense budget for the year 2003. The RAND report provides figures for the extra-budgetary streams to account for its estimate. Ironically, this study, which the Pentagon apparently ignored in the preparation of its report, was paid for by the US Air Force. Shortly after the Pentagon report was released, the IISS estimated unofficial spending in a range from 1.7 (based on exchange rates) to 3.28 (based on purchasing power parity—which, the IISS advises, should be viewed with caution).

To the Pentagon's credit, in congressional testimony nearly a month after the release of the report, Assistant Secretary of Defense Peter Rodman noted these other budget estimates; nevertheless, the report itself does not contain this nuance. A fair rendering of the PLA budget debate requires a more complete examination than contained in this year's, or any previous, Pentagon report. Without more thorough information, it is no wonder that many press reports focus only on budget increases and the top-line guesstimate (over $100 billion) and fail to give any context to that figure. At the same time, the PLA constantly writes about the need to use available funds more efficiently to save money. Despite a decade of double-digit defense budget increases, the theme of saving money is a recurring topic of discussion. Even if actual funds available to the PLA were at the top of the estimate range, at its current size, it would still be a resource-constrained organization.

Distortions

The Defense Department report contains numerous instances that take ideas out of context or omit relevant information. Perhaps the most egregious example is the use of excerpts from an interview with PLA Lieutenant General Liu Yazhou to support, "in a more abstract form," the report's claim that, "as China's economy expands, so too will its interests and the perceived need to build a military capable of protecting them." The report quotes Liu as saying, "when a nation grows strong enough, it practices hegemony. The sole purpose of power is to pursue even greater power. . . . Geography is destiny. . . . [W]hen a country begins to rise, it should first set itself in an invincible position." This passage obviously is intended to imply that Liu is talking about China. However, the full text of these quotes (traced by Harvard's Iain Johnston to the January 2005 *Heartland Eurasian Review of Geopolitics*) reveals a very different context:

> The United States has been pursuing some kind of "New Empire" since the end of the cold war. This means that the US dominated the world with its political, military, cultural, and religious power. *When a nation grows strong enough, it practices hegemony. The sole purpose of power is to pursue even greater power.* . . . The Belgian prime minister Guy Verhofstadt recently referred to the US as a "very dangerous superpower." The world became dangerous because of the US threat. That leads up to the third meaning I wanted to discuss: geopolitics. *Geography is destiny.* That has been a constant truth since ancient times. Generally *when a powerful country begins to rise, it should first set itself in an invincible position.* (emphasis added)

Clearly, Liu is talking about the United States, not China. By referring to their "more abstract form," the Pentagon report misrepresents Liu's words to make them appear to support its argument.

THREATENING TAIWAN?

The 2006 defense department report on China's military claims that 400,000 ground troops are arrayed in the regions opposite Taiwan, an increase of 25,000 over the year before. The report provides no information about exactly what personnel are included in that number, with the implication being that all are combat troops. In fact, 400,000 probably *understates* the total number of ground force personnel in these regions. The International Institute for Strategic Studies (IISS) estimates that about 620,000 personnel are posted there. In addition to combat forces, a complete count would include most personnel in:

- headquarters and communications units for military regions, military districts, military subdistricts, and people's armed forces departments;
- logistics subdepartments, including hospitals and supply/repair depots;
- coastal and border defense units;
- garrison units not included in the categories above; and
- a variety of military schools with thousands of staff, faculty, and students.

The report notes that "200 tanks and 2,300 artillery pieces" have been added opposite Taiwan in the last year, but does not mention the new light amphibious tanks, main battle tanks, and artillery (which includes anti-aircraft artillery) that are replacing older weapons, mostly on a one-for-one basis (with many anti-aircraft guns going into the reserves). Indeed, there have been several new *reserve* anti-aircraft and artillery units formed in this area in the past year, but these units would not be among the "new" 25,000 troops mentioned in the Pentagon report. (If reserves were added into the mix, the number would be well over the 620,000 that the IISS cites.)

In short, the report fails to describe accurately the status of army (or reserve) forces opposite Taiwan. More to the point, assertions of a "buildup" in ground forces—that is, an expansion over previous years—remain unproved.

D. J. B.

Another distortion occurs regarding aircraft carrier developments. The report describes the status of the former Soviet carrier *Varyag* and presents four possibilities for its eventual use. The report notes that the ship was purchased "only 70 percent complete" and highlights "maintenance and repair on the hull and deck." What the report fails to mention is that the 70 percent does not include engines, rudders, or armament. The report also fails to provide any evidence that engines, rudders, or armament are being added to the vessel, presumably required for the ship to become operational—which is the outcome outlined in three of the four possible uses that the Pentagon believes China may have in mind regarding the ship's future. "Maintenance and repair on the hull and deck" would, however, be consistent with option four: a theme park casino.

Omissions

The report identifies the threat that international terrorism poses to China. However, the amount of antiterrorist training that the PLA, reserves, militia, People's Armed Police, and civilian police undertake is not examined except for passing mention in the context of special operations forces missions. Yet countering terrorism is a national interest shared by both the United States and China, and the Chinese government is expending a great deal of effort to deal with this potential threat. In a major change from previous policy, since 2003 the PLA has engaged in antiterrorist exercises with militaries from the Shanghai Cooperation Organization and Pakistan.

While Americans debate the status of their own border security, the Pentagon report might have included the fact that an unknown number of PLA troops and People's Armed Police undertake border defense responsibilities in conjunction with the civilian Ministry of Public Security. The Chinese have never quantified the number of troops dedicated to this task, but with some 14,000 miles of land borders with 14 countries, 200,000 or more personnel may be assigned this permanent mission. The report also does not explain the extent of ground force training in China's interior regions, nor does it mention the emphasis on air defense throughout China, not only opposite Taiwan and in the navy. Taking these roles into account may help to explain partially why China's military force appears "outsized" to some.

A text box in the report describes reserve and militia unit roles in information warfare, particularly in amphibious assault operations. To be sure, the militia especially has been reported to have established numerous high-technology information warfare units since 1998 and this mission certainly is among the tasks of the reserve forces. The report, however, fails to put this one mission into the context of other missions of the reserve force, which include local air defense, nuclear, biological, and chemical defense, rear-area security, traffic control, logistics support, and infrastructure repair after enemy strikes on mainland targets.

Another text box on "Legal Warfare" notes "Chinese military strategists are taking an increasing interest in international law as an instrument of policy in a conflict." Yet the report does not discuss the numerous Chinese military newspaper reports describing tactical "legal war" training on the "law of armed conflicts," the United Nations charter, treatment of prisoners of war, reporting of war crimes, and the handling of cultural artifacts and foreigners on the battlefield. While "legal war" techniques may be used strategically to justify China's position internationally, the concept also has important battlefield components that increase the possibility the PLA will behave as a professional military in future conflicts.

One omission reveals something about the bureaucracy involved in preparing these reports. China is said to be "considering committing troops to peacekeeping operations in Sudan." This was indeed true *in the summer of 2005*, when the first two Chinese peacekeepers deployed to the country. Over the remainder of 2005 and the first half of 2006, the number of Chinese peacekeepers grew to over 200 by the time the report was released (with more to follow).

NO / Dennis J. Blasko   **171**

Scant Credit

The 2006 report notes the possibility of "twin misperceptions"—first, that other countries might underestimate PLA capabilities and, second, that Chinese leaders might overestimate the proficiency of their own forces, either of which could lead to "miscalculation or crisis." These options are certainly possible, but it is also possible that other countries could overestimate PLA potentials. Furthermore, the Chinese military literature reveals many realistic leadership evaluations of PLA improvements and shortfalls in capabilities. Shortcomings frequently mentioned by the Chinese themselves include a shortage of properly trained commanders, staff, and technicians; a lack of joint operations capability; weaknesses in headquarters and night training; and inadequate training on new equipment entering the force. Although the Pentagon report does contain a few references to limitations in training, transportation capacities, and combat experience, these can easily be eclipsed by the emphasis on "military expansion."

The report uses half a sentence to credit China's defense white papers with "improvements in the quality of reporting," but then immediately notes a "selective approach to transparency restricted to secondary areas of military activity such as military exchanges, joint exercises, and confidence-building measures involving visits to previously secret facilities." The Pentagon report itself would have been more complete had it mentioned specifically, among other exchanges, that US observers were invited to and attended PLA exercises in Inner Mongolia in 2003 and 2005 (which included armored units and airborne drops); that US allies attended exercises and demonstrations of a light mechanized division in field training, a marine amphibious landing exercise, and special operations force capabilities in 2004; and that US officers and military academy cadets now routinely visit and attend courses at PLA academies. The Chinese press, once again, has reported on all of these events in some detail, yet there has been little, if any, official US reaction to any of these efforts at transparency. The report itself contains no information attributed to US participation in these activities.

A final irony is found in the report's reference to Zhanluexue (*The Science of Military Strategy*), which is said to give English-readers a "better understanding into official Chinese views of modern warfare." Then nothing more of it is mentioned. In fact, an entire chapter of that book discusses Chinese views of strategic deterrence and offers an alternate explanation for the same body of information available to the Pentagon report's authors. According to *The Science of Military Strategy*, "strategic deterrence is also a means for attaining the political objective. . . . Strategic deterrence is based on war fighting. . . . The more powerful the war fighting capability, the more effective the deterrence." To guarantee deterrence, China must build a capable force, demonstrate its determination to use that force if necessary, and ensure that potential opponents understand China's capability and determination.

Coupled with recent changes in China's policy that focus on preventing Taiwan's separation rather than forcing reunification, it can be argued that at its current stage of development, the PLA sees itself more as a deterrent force than a warfighting force. Following the outline in *The Science of Military Strategy*, China is building a capable force; it displays determination through military demonstrations, exercises, diplomacy, and propaganda; and it constantly checks to confirm that those it seeks to deter have received Beijing's messages.

The Pentagon report quotes intelligence community estimates that "China will take until the end of this decade or later for its military modernization program to produce a modern force capable of defeating a moderate-size enemy." Yet numerous Chinese writings set 2020 as the date for accomplishing its personnel improvement program and equipment modernization goals. In the meantime, China will also pursue a hedging strategy, focusing on deterrence, but preparing for the worst if deterrence fails.

Missing Evidence

Within the past year and a half, the Bush administration has unilaterally declared that no nation threatens China. It has pronounced China's military to be "outsized." It has implicitly suggested that China's military modernization amounts to expansion, and further emphasized its own hedging strategy in the region. Yet no one in the US government has explicitly stated what size force with what specific capabilities is appropriate for a permanent member of the UN Security Council sharing borders with 14 countries and becoming increasingly involved in international commerce and peacekeeping operations. Nor has the Bush administration defined what amount, if any, of Chinese military modernization is acceptable. Declared US policy, especially regarding technology transfer to China, can easily be interpreted to conclude that all Chinese military modernization is to be opposed.

If the US Congress seeks to acquire a full picture of the state of the Chinese military for the concerned American public, it should relieve the Defense Department of this annual requirement. It should give the intelligence community the task of providing a complete assessment of emerging PLA capabilities and intentions in the context of other aspects of PLA modernization and civil-military relations, as might be found in an unclassified National Intelligence Estimate.

It is unclear if such a comprehensive review would support existing US policy or if it would reveal a more complex situation than is portrayed by this year's Pentagon report, or both. But a fair presentation of all the evidence one way or the other is the least the US government can do. The answer that "the report is as specific as the authors wish to be at this point" is insufficient if a true debate is to take place on a topic of supreme importance to the United States, Asia, and the rest of the world.

POSTSCRIPT

Is China's Rise Threatening to the United States?

The answer to whether China's economic, political, and military rise is threatening to the United States depends on how their relationship is assessed. Unfortunately, the predictions of international relations theory regarding Sino-Americans are equally mixed; for example, Aaron Friedberg argues in support of John Mearsheimer that China's rise is threatening in "Ripe for Rivalry: Prospects for Peace in a Multipolar Asia," *International Security* (Winter 1993–1994). This perspective contends that the United States and China will remain competitors and that their competition is likely to get more intense as China continues to grow. *Foreign Policy* published a useful exchange between a realist policymaker, Zbigniew Brzezinski, and a realist academic, John Mearsheimer, about China and U.S.-Chinese relations. See "Clash of the Titans," *Foreign Policy* (January/February 2005).

In contrast, Andrew Nathan and Robert Ross support Dennis Blasko by arguing that China can be integrated peacefully and productivily into the international system in *The Great Wall and the Empty Fortress: China's Search for Security* (W. W. Norton, 1997). From this viewpoint, conflict is not inevitable, and continued interaction between the two countries may mitigate the potential threats each may perceive from the other. (For a review of Chinese foreign policy and international relations theory, see Thomas Robinson and David Shambaugh, eds. *Chinese Foreign Policy: Theory and Practice,* Oxford University Press, 1994.) Meanwhile, regional experts have argued that China, in particular, is undergoing dramatic changes and that its behavior must be understood in the context of evolving political, economic, and social processes taking place within the country. (See David Shambaugh, ed. *Power Shift: China and Asia's New Dynamics* (University of California Press, 2005).) This suggests that rather than trying to clarify the precise nature of Sino-American friendship, it may be constructive to recognize that this relationship is multifaceted and multidimensional, and that the resulting ambiguity may enable it to develop and provide mutual gains in some arenas, despite ongoing conflicts in others.

Information about contemporary U.S.-Chinese relations is available at the Department of State Web Bureau of East Asian and Specific Affairs at http://www.state.gov/p/eap/. The State Department also maintains a permanent electronic archive of information released prior to January 20, 2001, on U.S.-Chinese relations on the Web at http://www.state.gov/www/current/debate/china.html.

ISSUE 11

Should the United States Seek Negotiations and Engagement with North Korea?

YES: David C. Kang, from "The Debate over North Korea," *Political Science Quarterly* (vol. 119, no. 2, 2004)

NO: Victor D. Cha, from "The Debate over North Korea," *Political Science Quarterly* (vol. 119, no. 2, 2004)

ISSUE SUMMARY

YES: David C. Kang, associate professor of government at Dartmouth College, contends that the threat posed by North Korea is overblown because North Korea will continue to be deterred from acting aggressively and, consequently, that engagement offers the best strategy promoting economic, political, and military change.

NO: Victor D. Cha, associate professor of government and D.S. Song-Korea Foundation Chair in Asian Studies in the School of Foreign Service at Georgetown University and Asia director in the National Security Council of the U.S. government, argues that North Korea remains hostile and opportunistic. Engagement—if used at all—should be highly conditional, and the United States and its allies should remain prepared to isolate and contain North Korea if engagement fails.

The Korean Peninsula remains the most fortified and potentially the most militarily dangerous area in the world. The Democratic Peoples' Republic of Korea (DPRK, or North Korea) has a 1.1-million-man army facing opposing soldiers representing the United States and the Republic of Korea (ROK, or South Korea). These troops are separated by a narrow demilitarized zone (DMZ) that cuts across the country a very short distance north of the South Korean capital in Seoul. North Korea also produces and tests ballistic missiles, which it has supplied to Iran and Pakistan. Directed by a dictator, Kim Jong II, it is believed to possess stockpiles of biological and chemical weapons, and is known to possess the technology to produce nuclear weapons.

Politicians in the United States, South Korea, and other countries in the region have long debated how best to manage relations with North Korea, often evaluating the policy choices in partisan terms. In the 1990s, U.S. policy centered around the agreed framework under which the DPRK agreed to freeze and eventually dismantle its graphite-moderated nuclear reactors and related facilities at Yongbyon and Taechon, to reaffirm its member status in the Nuclear Non-Proliferation Regime, to comply with its International Atomic Energy Agency safeguards agreement, and to implement the North-South Denuclearization Agreement. In exchange, the United States agreed to lead an international consortium to oversee and finance the construction of two 1000-megawatt light water reactors, to compensate the DPRK for energy foregone by providing 500,000 metric tons of heavy fuel oil annually, and to take steps to reduce economic and financial restrictions on the DPRK. In parallel, South Korean President Kim Dae Jung instituted a "sunshine" policy of unconditional engagement with North Korea that included some personal family reunions, the exchange of food and other goods, and the building of a railroad and road system that could connect the North and South. When the George W. Bush administration entered office, it did not engage with North Korea. Instead, the president identified North Korea as a member of the "axis of evil" in his 2002 State of the Union Address.

In October 2002, despite the appearance of recently improved relations with the United States and Japan, North Korea announced the existence of a second secret nuclear program using highly enriched uranium and withdrew from the nuclear non-proliferation treaty. Thus, it acknowledged violating the nuclear non-proliferation treaty, the 1994 U.S.-DPRK Agreed Framework agreement, and the 1992 Korean De-Nuclearization Declaration.

The United States responded by demanding that North Korea comply with its nonproliferation agreements and suspended its shipments of heavy fuel oil under the terms of the Agreed Framework. The North Koreans responded by reactivating the Yongbyon nuclear facilities, dismantling the IAEA monitoring cameras, and expelling IAEA inspectors. In April and August 2003, the United States, North Korea, and China met in Beijing but made little progress in resolving their disputes. The North Korean delegation demanded bilateral negotiations with the United States and threatened to test nuclear weapons if the United States did not offer security assurances. The United States refused and demanded multilateral talks.

David Kang argues that provocative behavior by North Korea and the United States is making each state less secure and more suspicious, thereby making the crisis worse. He argues that engagement offers a way to diffuse the crisis and promote change in North Korea. In contrast, Victor Cha argues that North Korea blatantly violated its non-proliferation agreements and should not be trusted. Engagement should only be tried if the United States is willing to switch to strategies of isolation and containment if North Korea fails to carry out its promises.

YES ⤶

David C. Kang

Getting Back to "Start"

. . . [T]he nuclear revelations of October 2002 and the ensuing crisis intensified an already acute dilemma for both the United States and North Korea. For the United States, the focus on Iraq was now potentially diverted by an unwanted crisis over an "axis of evil" country in Northeast Asia. For North Korea, the slowly intensifying economic and diplomatic moves of the past few years were also potentially thwarted. For both sides, their worst suspicions were confirmed in the worst of ways. North Korea concluded that the United States had never had any intention of normalizing ties or concluding a peace treaty. The United States concluded that North Korea had never had any intention of abandoning its nuclear weapons program.

The North Korean regime is a brutal and morally reprehensible regime. It has enriched itself while allowing hundreds of thousands of its own citizens to die of starvation. That this regime is odious is not in question. Rather, the issue is: what tactics will best ameliorate the problems on the peninsula?

Many Western policy makers and analysts viewed the nuclear revelations with alarm and surprise. However, much of the Western hand-wringing has elements of Kabuki theater to it, and the accusations ring hollow. "Outrage and shock! at North Korean nuclear programs" is not so convincing in view of the fact that the Bush administration has been openly derisive of Kim Jong II, has been contemptuous of the Agreed Framework, and has known about North Korea's nuclear program since June 2001. An American intelligence official who attended White House meetings in 2002 said that "Bush and Cheney want this guy's head on a platter. Don't be distracted by all this talk about negotiations. . . . They have a plan, and they are going to get this guy after Iraq." A North Korea that feels threatened and perceives the U.S. administration to be actively attempting to increase pressure on it is unlikely to trust the United States.

Does North Korea have legitimate security concerns? If not, then their nuclear program is designed for blackmail or leverage. If the North does have legitimate security concerns, then it is not that surprising that such a program exists, given the open hostility toward the regime that the Bush administration has evidenced. However, despite the furor over the revelation, not much has changed on the peninsula. Deterrence is still robust. North Korea's basic strategy remains the same: simultaneously deter the United States and also

From *Political Science Quarterly*, vol. 119, no. 2, 2004, pp. 237–254. Copyright © 2004 by The Academy of Political Science. Reprinted by permission. References omitted.

find a way to fix the economy. The United States, for its part, faces the same choices it did a decade ago: negotiate, or hope that the North collapses without doing too much damage to the region.

Without movement toward resolving the security fears of the North, progress in resolving the nuclear weapons issue will be limited. It is unsurprising that the 1994 Agreed Framework fell apart, because it was a process by which both sides set out to slowly build a sense of trust and both sides began hedging their bets very early on in that process. Because neither the United States nor North Korea fulfilled many of the agreed-upon steps, even during the Clinton administration, the Framework was essentially dead long before the nuclear revelation of October 2002. Neither side acts in a vacuum; the United States and North Korea each react to the other's positions, and this interaction has led to a spiral of mistrust and misunderstanding. Threats and rhetoric from each side impact the other's perceptions and actions, and this interaction can be either a mutually reinforcing positive or a negative spiral.

The accepted wisdom in the United States is that North Korea abrogated the Framework by restarting its nuclear weapons program. The reality is more complicated, however. Both the Clinton and Bush administrations violated the letter and the spirit of the agreement. Admitting that the United States is hostile toward North Korea does not make one an apologist—the United States *is* hostile, and it is unconvincing to pretend that we are not. The Bush administration made clear from the beginning that it had serious doubts about the Agreed Framework and engagement with the North. This began with the inception of the Bush administration—South Korean President Kim Dae Jung's visit to Washington DC in March 2001 was widely viewed as a rebuke to his sunshine policy that engaged the North, with Bush voicing "skepticism" in regard to the policy. By the time of President Bush's now famous "axis of evil" speech, it had long been clear that the Bush administration did not trust the North. For the Framework to have had any hope of being even modestly successful, each side needed to have worked more genuinely toward building confidence in the other.

The 1994 Agreed Framework

The Agreed Framework of 1994 was not a formal treaty; rather, it was a set of guidelines designed to help two countries that were deeply mistrustful of each other find a way to cooperate. But both sides began backing out of the Agreed Framework well before the autumn of 2002. From its inception, the Bush administration made very clear how much it disdained the Framework, and the North had begun its nuclear program as far back as 1998. The core of the Framework was a series of steps that both sides would take that would ultimately lead to North Korea proving it had no nuclear weapons or nuclear weapons program and to the United States normalizing ties with the North and providing it with light-water nuclear reactors that could make energy but not weapons. Table 1 shows the key elements of the Framework.

Neither side fulfilled its obligations under the Framework. The key elements on the U.S. side were a formal statement of nonaggression (article 2.3.1),

Table 1

Key Conditions of the Agreed Framework

Agreed Framework Condition	Implemention and Discussion
The United States agrees to provide two light-water reactor (LWR) power plants by the year 2003 (article 1.2).	Four years behind schedule. There has been no delay in South Korean or Japanese provision of funds. The delay has been U.S. implementation and construction.
The United States agrees to provide formal assurances to the DPRK against the threat or use of nuclear weapons by the United States (article 2.3.1).	No. The United States maintains that military force is an option on the peninsula. The United States continues to target North Korea with nuclear weapons via the "Nuclear Posture Review."
The DPRK agrees to freeze its nuclear reactors and to dismantle them when the LWR project is completed (article 1.3).	Until December 2002.
The DPRK agrees to allow the International Atomic Energy Agency to monitor the freeze with full cooperation (article 1.3).	Until December 2002.
The United States and the DPRK agree to work toward full normalization of political and economic relations, reducing barriers of trade and investment, etc. (article 2.1).	Limited lowering of U.S. restrictions on trade, no other progress toward normalization or peace treaty. The United States continues to list North Korea as a terrorist state.
The United States and the DPRK will each open a liaison office in the each other's capital, aiming at upgrading bilateral relations to the ambassadorial level (articles 2.2, 2.3).	No.

Source: Compiled from KEDO, "Agreed Framework Between the United States of America and the Democratic People's Republic of Korea," Geneva, Switzerland, 21 October 1994.

provision of the light-water reactor (article 1.2), and progress toward normalization of ties (article 2.1). The reactor is now four years behind schedule. The United States also has not opened a liaison office in Pyongyang and has not provided formal written assurances against the use of nuclear weapons. The U.S. "Nuclear Posture Review" still targets North Korea with nuclear weapons. The North did freeze its reactors and allow IAEA monitoring, but in December 2002, it backed out of the agreement and expelled inspectors from North Korea.

It is possible to argue that the uranium enrichment plant is a more serious breach of the Framework than not providing a formal nonaggression pact or not providing a reactor. But this argument will be compelling only to domestic constituencies. Given U.S. reluctance to fulfill its side of the Framework, it was unlikely that the North would continue to honor its side of the agreement in the hope that at some point the Bush administration would begin to fulfill its side. The implicit U.S. policy has demanded that the North abandon its military programs, and only after it does so would the U.S. decide whether to be benevolent. As Wade Huntley and Timothy Savage write:

> The implicit signal sent to Pyongyang was that the Agreed Framework . . . was at its heart an effort to script the abdication of the DPRK regime.

Immediate reticence by the United States to implement certain specific steps toward normalization called for in the agreement, such as lifting economic sanctions, reinforced this perception. . . . [S]uch an underlying attitude could never be the basis for real improvement in relations.

The United States and North Korea are still technically at war—the 1953 armistice was never replaced with a peace treaty. The United States has been unwilling to discuss even a nonaggression pact, much less a peace treaty or normalization of ties. While the United States calls North Korea a terrorist nation and Donald Rumsfeld discusses the possibility of war, it is not surprising that North Korea feels threatened. For the past two years, U.S. policy toward the North has been consistently derisive and confrontational. Table 2 shows a selection of statements by U.S. and North Korean officials.

Table 2

Selected U.S.–North Korean Rhetoric over the Agreed Framework

Date	U.S. Statements	DPRK Statements
9 October 2000	"Neither government will have hostile intent towards the other." (Joint Communique)	
6 June 2001	"The U.S. seeks improved implementation [of the Agreed Framework], prompt inspections of past reprocessing . . . [and] a less threatening conventional military posture." (White House press release)	
11 June 2001		"Washington should implement the provisions of the D.P.R.K.–U.S. Agreed Framework and the D.P.R.K.–U.S. Joint Communique as agreed upon." (DPRK Foreign Ministry spokesman)
3 July 2001	"We need to see some progress in all areas . . . we don't feel any urgency to provide goodies to them . . ." (senior administration official, on the broadened demands to North Korea)	
29 January 2002	"States like these . . . constitute an axis of evil, arming to threaten the peace of the world." (George W. Bush, State of the Union speech)	
2 February 2002		"His [Bush's] remarks clearly show that the U.S.-proposed 'resumption of dialogue' with the DPRK is intended not for the improvement of the bilateral relations but for the realization of the U.S. aggressive military strategy. It is the steadfast stand and transparent will of the DPRK to counter force with force and confrontation with confrontation." (Korean Central News Agency)
1 June 2002	"We must take the battle to the enemy . . . and confront the worst threats before they emerge." (George W. Bush)	

(continued)

Table 2 (Continued)

Selected U.S.–North Korean Rhetoric over the Agreed Framework

Date	U.S. Statements	DPRK Statements
10 June 2002	"First, the North must get out of the proliferation business and eliminate long-range missiles that threaten other countries. . . . [T]he North needs to move toward a less threatening conventional military posture . . . and liv[e] up to its past pledges to implement basic confidence-building measures." (Secretary of State Colin Powell)	
29 August 2002	North Korea is "in stark violation of the Biological weapons convention. . . . [M]any doubt that North Korea ever intends to comply fully with its NPT obligations." (Undersecretary of State John Bolton)	
31 August 2002		"The D.P.R.K. clarified more than once that if the U.S. has a willingness to drop its hostile policy toward the D.P.R.K., it will have dialogue with the U.S. to clear the U.S. of its worries over its security." (North Korean Foreign Ministry spokesman)
20 October 2002		"If the United States is willing to drop its hostile policy towards us, we are prepared to deal with various security concerns through dialogue." (Kim Young Nam, Chair of the Supreme People's Assembly)
5 November 2002		"Everything will be negotiable, including inspections of the enrichment program. . . . [O]ur government will resolve all U.S. security concerns through the talks if your government has a will to end its hostile policy." (Han Song Ryol, DPRK ambassador to the UN)
29 December 2002	"We cannot suddenly say 'Gee, we're so scared. Let's have a negotiation because we want to appease your misbehavior.' This kind of action cannot be rewarded." (Secretary of State Colin Powell)	
5 January 2003	"We have no intention of sitting down and bargaining again." (State Department Spokesman Richard Boucher)	
9 January 2003	"We think that they [Russia] could be putting the screws to the North Koreans a little more firmly and at least beginning to raise the specter of economic sanctions." (senior U.S. official)	"[W]e have no intention to produce nuclear weapons. . . . After the appearance of the Bush Administration, the United States listed the DPRK as part of an 'axis of evil,' adopting it as a national policy to oppose its system, and singled it out as a target of pre-emptive nuclear attack. . . . [I]t also answered the DPRK's sincere proposal for conclusion of the DPRK–US non-aggression treaty with such threats as 'blockade' and 'military punishment'. . . ." (DPRK official announcement of withdrawal from the NPT)

Table 2 (Continued)

Selected U.S.–North Korean Rhetoric over the Agreed Framework

Date	U.S. Statements	DPRK Statements
23 January 2003	"First is regime change. It need not necessarily be military, but it could lead to that." (senior U.S. official)	

Sources: Jay Solomon, Peter Wonacott, and Chris Cooper, "North Asian Leaders Criticize Bush on North Korea," *Wall Street Journal,* 6 January 2003; Jay Solomon, Peter Wonacott, and Chris Cooper, "South Korea is Optimistic About End to Nuclear Crisis," *Wall Street Journal,* 4 January 2003; Michael Gordon, "Powell Says U.S. is Willing to Talk with North Korea," *New York Times,* 29 December 2002; "N. Korea pulls out of nuclear pact," MSNBC News Services, 10 January 2003; Leon Sigal, "North Korea is No Iraq: Pyongyang's Negotiating Strategy," Special Report, Nautilus Organization, 23 December 2002; Susan V. Lawrence, Murray Hiebert, Jay Solomon, and Kim Jung Min, "Time to Talk," *Far Eastern Economic Review,* 23 January 2003: 12–16.

The Bush administration began adding new conditions to the Agreed Framework early on in its tenure. On 6 June 2001, the White House included reduction of conventional forces in the requirements it wanted North Korea to fulfill, saying that "The U.S. seeks improved implementation [of the Agreed Framework], prompt inspections of past reprocessing . . . [and] a less threatening conventional military posture." On 11 June 2001, North Korea replied that "Washington should implement the provisions of the D.P.R.K.–U.S. Agreed Framework and the D.P.R.K.–U.S. Joint Communique as agreed upon." The Bush administration continued its stance. On 3 July 2001, a senior administration official said that "We need to see some progress in all areas . . . we don't feel any urgency to provide goodies to them."

In 2002, Secretary of State Powell added a reduction in the North's missile program to the list of conditions necessary for progress on the Framework. Missiles had originally been excluded from the Agreed Framework, and the Clinton administration had begun working out a separate agreement with the North about them. On 10 June 2002, Colin Powell said that "First, the North must get out of the proliferation business and eliminate long-range missiles that threaten other countries. . . . [T]he North needs to move toward a less threatening conventional military posture . . . and [toward] living up to its past pledges to implement basic confidence-building measures."

The North consistently maintained that it wanted the United States to lower the pressure. On 20 October 2002, Kim Yong Nam, Chair of the Supreme People's Assembly, said that "If the United States is willing to drop its hostile policy towards us, we are prepared to deal with various security concerns through dialogue." On 3 November 2002, Han Song Ryol, DPRK Ambassador to the UN, reiterated that "Everything will be negotiable, including inspections of the enrichment program. . . . [O]ur government will resolve all U.S. security concerns through the talks if your government has a will to end its hostile policy." As the crisis intensified, Colin Powell refused to consider dialogue with the North, remarking that "We cannot suddenly say 'Gee, we're so scared. Let's have a negotiation because we want to appease your misbehavior.' This kind of action cannot be rewarded."

As one North Korean diplomat noted: "The Agreed Framework made American generals confident that the DPRK had become defenseless; the only way to correct this misperception is to develop a credible deterrent against the United States." As of winter 2003, the situation was one of standoff. North Korean statements made clear their fear that the Bush administration would focus on pressuring North Korea once the situation in Iraq was stabilized. The 28 January 2003 statement of the Korean Anti-Nuke Peace Committee in Pyongyang concluded by saying that

> If the U.S. legally commits itself to non-aggression including the non-use of nuclear weapons against the DPRK through the non-aggression pact, the DPRK will be able to rid the U.S. of its security concerns. . . . Although the DPRK has left the NPT, its nuclear activity at present is limited to the peaceful purpose of power generation. . . . If the U.S. gives up its hostile policy toward the DPRK and refrains from posing a nuclear threat to it, it may prove that it does not manufacture nuclear weapons through a special verification between the DPRK and the U.S. . . . It is the consistent stand of the DPRK government to settle the nuclear issue on the Korean peninsula peacefully through fair negotiations for removing the concerns of both sides on an equal footing between the DPRK and the U.S.

Causes and Consequences of the October Revelation

Thus, the Agreed Framework of 1994 is dead. Both North Korea and the United States are now in essentially the same position they were in 1994—threatening war, moving toward confrontation. Given the levels of mistrust on both sides, this comes as no surprise. If North Korea feels threatened, threatening them is unlikely to make them feel less threatened. Gregory Clark pointed out that "Washington's excuse for ignoring the nonaggression treaty proposal has to be the ultimate in irrationality. It said it would not negotiate under duress. So duress consists of being asked to be nonaggressive?"

An intense security dilemma on the Korean peninsula is exacerbated by an almost complete lack of direct interaction between the two sides. Levels of mistrust are so high that both sides hedge their bets. The United States refused to provide formal written assurances of nonaggression to the North. The North thus retains its military and nuclear forces in order to deter the United States from acting too precipitously.

The consequences are fairly clear: the United States can continue a policy of pressure in the hope that the North will buckle and give in to U.S. pressure or collapse from internal weakness, or it can negotiate a bargain of normalization for nuclear weapons. Without resolving North Korea's security fears, the opportunity for any quick resolution of the confrontation on the peninsula will be limited. This is disappointing because North Korea, unlike Iraq, is actively seeking accommodation with the international community. Even while the Bush administration was increasing its pressure on the North, the North continued its voluntary moratorium on missile testing until 2003.

The North's tentative moves toward economic openness have also been sty-mied for the time being. In July 2002, North Korea introduced a free-market system, allowing prices to determine supply and demand for goods and ser-vices. In September 2002, it announced a special economic zone in Shinuiju. In the last six months of 2002, work was begun to clear a section of the demil-itarized zone to allow the reconnection of the railway between North and South Korea. To cap all of these developments, Kim Jong II finally admitted in September 2002, after three decades of denials, that the North kidnapped Japanese citizens in the 1970s.

If North Korea really wanted to develop nuclear weapons, it would have done so long ago. Even today, North Korea has still not tested a nuclear device, tested an intercontinental ballistic missile, or deployed a nuclear missile force. Even if North Korea develops and deploys nuclear weapons, it will not use them, because the U.S. deterrent is clear and overwhelming. The North wants a guarantee of security from the United States, and a policy of isolating it will not work. Isolation is better than pressure because pressure would only make it even more insecure. But even isolation is at best a holding measure. And the imposition of economic sanctions or economic engagement is equally unlikely to get North Korea to abandon its weapons program.

Above all, the North Korean regime wants better ties with the United States. The policy that follows from this is clear: the United States should begin negotiating a nonaggression pact with the North. It should let other countries, such as South Korea and Japan, pursue economic diplomacy if they wish. If the North allows UN nuclear inspectors back and dismantles its reac-tors, the United States could then move forward to actual engagement. But to dismiss the country's security fears is to miss the cause of its actions.

The Bush administration's reluctance to consider dialogue with the North is counterproductive. Even at the height of the Cold War, Ronald Reagan, despite calling the Soviet Union "the Evil Empire," met with Soviet leaders and held dialogue with them. The United States had ambassadorial relations with the Soviets, engaged in trade with the Soviets, and interacted regularly—precisely in order to moderate the situation and keep information moving between the two adversaries and to keep the situation from inadvert-ently escalating out of control. The United States was in far greater contact with the Soviet Union during the Cold War than it is with North Korea in 2004. By refusing to talk, the United States allows the situation to spiral out of control and harms its own ability to deal with the reality of the situation.

Does the October nuclear revelation provide any insight as to North Korea's foreign policy strategy? Essentially, no: North Korea has always sought to deter the United States and has viewed the United States as belligerent. Thus, the nuclear program is consistent with North Korea's attempts to pro-vide for its own security. It is also important to remember that a nuclear weap-ons program does not mean that North Korea is any more likely to engage in unprovoked military acts now than it was before. North Korea was deterred before the revelations, and it remains deterred after the revelations. The way to resolve the crisis is by addressing the security concerns of North Korea. If the United States genuinely has no intention of attacking North Korea or pressuring it for regime change, the administration should conclude a nonaggression pact. It is not that surprising that North Korea does not believe the Bush administration's occasional assurances about having no intention of using force when the administration refuses to formalize those assurances.

In terms of U.S. policy toward the North, the revelations are actually an opening. It is impossible to negotiate with a country over an issue whose existence they deny. In the case of the nuclear program, the United States has the opportunity to actually reach a conclusion to this problem. If the Bush administration were to handle negotiations adroitly, it could possibly finally resolve an issue that has plagued Northeast Asia for far too long.

Victor D. Cha   ➡ **NO**

Past the Point of No Return?

Many moderates argued, as David Kang has done, that this new nuclear confession reveals Pyongyang's true intentions. Although of concern, they argue, these actions represent North Korean leader Kim Jong II's perverse but typical way of creating a crisis to pull a reluctant Bush administration into serious dialogue. By "confessing" to the crime, in other words, Pyongyang is putting its chips on the table, ready to bargain away this clandestine program in exchange for aid and a U.S. pledge of nonaggression. Moderates would, therefore, advocate continued negotiations by the United States and its allies, providing incentives for the North to come clean on its uranium enrichment activities as well as to extend a more comprehensive nonproliferation arrangement to replace the Agreed Framework. In exchange for this, the allies would put forward a package of incentives including economic aid and normalization of political relations.

Before the world accepts this "cry for help" thesis, however, the North's confession must be seen for what it is—admission of a serious violation of a standing agreement that could, in effect, be North Korea's last gambit for peaceful engagement with the United States and its allies. North Korea's actions constitute a blatant breakout from the 1994 U.S.–DPRK Agreed Framework designed to ensure denuclearization of the North. Those who try to make a technical, legalistic argument to the contrary are patently wrong. Although the Agreed Framework dealt specifically with the plutonium-reprocessing facilities at Yongbyon, this document was cross-referenced with the 1991–1992 North–South Korea denuclearization declaration, which banned both North and South Korea from the uranium enrichment facilities now found to be covertly held in the North. Moreover, any legal gymnastics over this issue were rendered moot by North Korea's subsequent withdrawal from the nonproliferation treaty, the first in the NPT's history.

Moreover, the implications of this act extend beyond a mere violation of legal conventions. Arguably, all of the improvements in North–South relations, including the June 2000 summit, breakthroughs in Japan–North Korea relations in 2001, and the wave of engagement with the reclusive regime that spread across Europe, Australia, and Canada in 2000–2001, were made possible by what was perceived to be the North's good-faith intentions to comply with a major nonproliferation commitment with the United States in 1994. The subtext of this commitment was that the North was willing to trade in its

From *Political Science Quarterly,* vol. 119, no. 2, 2004, pp. 237–254. Copyright © 2004 by The Academy of Political Science. Reprinted by permission. References omitted.

rogue proliferation threat for a path of reform and peaceful integration into the world community. The subsequent diplomatic achievements by Pyongyang, therefore, would not have been possible without the Agreed Framework. And now the North has shown it all to be a lie.

Alternative Explanations for North Korean Misbehavior

Many of the justifications offered by either Pyongyang or mediating parties in Seoul (an irony in itself) for the HEU program and the restarting of the pluto-nium program at Yongbyon are, at best, suspect. North Korea claimed its actions were warranted as responses to American failure to keep to the timeta-ble of the Agreed Framework as well as to Washington's reneging on promises to normalize relations with the North. Moreover, they argued, the aggressive language of the United States and President Bush's "axis of evil" statements made these actions necessary. North Korean pursuit of the HEU program, however, as assistant secretary Kelly noted in the October 2002 meeting with Kang Sok Ju, predated the Bush administration's accession to office in 2001, and indeed, was well under way as Pyongyang was enjoying the benefits of Kim Dae Jung's sunshine policy from 1999 to 2002. There is no denying that the United States and the KEDO fell behind in the implementation of the Agreed Framework, in large part because the signing of the accord in October 1994 was followed by congressional elections that put in control Republicans with strong antipathy to Clinton (and by definition then, the Agreed Frame-work). The North Koreans were aware of this possibility and, therefore, sought during the negotiations a personal guarantee from President Clinton that the United States would do what it could to keep implementation on schedule. In other words, as far back as October 1994, Pyongyang was cognizant of such potential problems in implementation. To argue otherwise as justification for their illicit nuclear activities is a stretch. Moreover, although the Agreed Framework was not a legally binding document, arguably there is a distinc-tion between negligence in implementing a contract and completely breaking out of one. Washington could certainly be guilty of the former, but that does not warrant the other party's actions to do the latter.

Kim Jong Il's justification that he needs to wield the nuclear threat as a backstop for regime survival and deterrence against U.S. preemption also does not hold water. This is not because anyone should expect Kim to believe Bush's public assurances that he has no intention of attacking North Korea but because any logical reasoning shows that the North already possesses these deterrent capabilities. Its 11,000 artillery tubes along the DMZ hold Seoul hos-tage, and its Nodong ballistic missile deployments effectively hold Japan hos-tage. The warning time for a North Korean artillery shell landing in Seoul is measured in seconds (fifty-seven) and for a ballistic missile fired on the Japa-nese archipelago in minutes (ten). There is no conceivable defense against these threats, which would result in hundreds of thousands, if not millions, of casualties. As long as the United States values the welfare of these two key allies in Northeast Asia (as well as the 100,000-plus American service personnel and expatriate community), the North holds a credible deterrent against any hypothetical contemplation of American preemption.

Finally, the argument that with the latest crisis. North Korea is seeking direct negotiations with the United States rather than a bonafide nuclear weapons capability is both disturbing and logically inconsistent. North Korea seeks a nonaggression pact, these advocates argue, and a new relationship, by using the only leverage it can muster—its military threat. There are three glaring problems with this argument. First, the notion that North Korean proliferation is solely for bargaining purposes runs contrary to the history of why states proliferate. Crossing the nuclear threshold is a national decision of immense consequence and, as numerous studies have shown, is a step rarely taken deliberately for the purpose of negotiating away these capabilities. Second, even if one were to accept these as the true North Korean intentions, the moral hazard issues become obvious. Rather than moving Pyongyang in the direction of more-compliant behavior, indulging the North's brinkmanship is likely only to validate their perceived success of the strategy. Such coercive bargaining strategies in the past by the North might have been met with engagement by the United States, but in the aftermath of the October 2002 nuclear revelations, such behavior is more difficult to countenance. The difference, as I will explain below, largely stems from the gravity of North Korean misbehavior in 2002 and violation of the Agreed Framework.

Third, the "negotiation" thesis for North Korean proliferation, upon closer analysis, actually leads one to the *opposite* logical conclusion—in other words, a North Korean "breakout" strategy of amassing a midsized nuclear weapons arsenal. South Korean advocates of the negotiation thesis maintain that Pyongyang is aware of the antipathy felt by the Bush administration toward the Clinton-era agreements made with it. Therefore, Pyongyang seeks to leverage the proliferation threat to draw the Bush administration into bilateral negotiations, ostensibly to obtain a nonaggression pact, but in practice to obtain *any* agreement with this government. Ideally, this agreement would offer more benefits than the 1994 agreement, but even if this were not the case, the key point, according to these officials, is that the agreement would have the Bush administration's imprimateur rather than that of Clinton and therefore would be more credible in North Korean eyes.

Though plausible, such an argument, however, leads to a compelling counterintuitive conclusion. If North Korea wants a new and improved agreement and knows that this current administration is more "hard-line" than the previous one, then the logical plan of action would not be to negotiate away its potential nuclear capabilities (the modus operandi in 1994) but to *acquire* nuclear weapons and *then* confront the United States from a stronger position than they had in 1994. Indeed, North Korean actions in December 2002 appear to have been more than a bargaining ploy. If coercive bargaining had been the primary objective, then the North Koreans arguably would have needed to undertake only one of several steps to denude the 1994 agreement. On the contrary, their unsealing of buildings, disabling of monitoring cameras, expelling international inspectors, withdrawal from the NPT, restarting the reactor, and reprocessing represented a purposeful drive to develop weapons.

As one U.S. government official observed, "[W]e made a list of all the things the North Koreans might do to ratchet up a crisis for the purpose of negotiation. They went through that list pretty quickly."

What Follows Hawk Engagement?

There is no denying that Bush's "axis of evil" statements exacerbated a downward trend in U.S.–DPRK relations. But actions matter more than semantics. The problem is not what the United States, South Korea, or Japan may have done to irk the North. The problem is North Korea. What is most revealing about the North's actions is that hawkish skepticism vis-a-vis a real change in Kim Jong Il's underlying intentions, despite behavior and rhetoric to the contrary, remains justified.

This skepticism, as I have argued in *Foreign Affairs* (May/June 2002), is what informs the "hawk engagement" approach toward North Korea. Unlike South Korea's "sunshine policy" of unconditional engagement, this version of the strategy is laced with a great deal more pessimism, less trust, and a pragmatic calculation of the steps to follow in case the policy fails. In short, hawks might pursue engagement with North Korea for very different tactical reasons than might doves. Engagement is useful with rogues like North Korea because: first, "carrots" today can serve as "sticks" tomorrow (particularly with a target state that has very few); second, economic and food aid can start a slow process of separating the people of North Korea from its despotic regime; and third, engagement is the best practical way to build a coalition for punishment, demonstrating good-faith efforts at negotiating and thereby putting the ball in the North's court to maintain cooperation.

The 2002–2003 nuclear revelations confirm much of the skepticism that informs the hawk engagement approach. The premise of hawk engagement is that engagement should be pursued for the purpose of testing the North's intentions and genuine capacity to cooperate. If this diplomacy succeeds, then the sunshine policy advocates are correct about North Korea, and honest hawks (as opposed to ideological ones) would be compelled to continue on this path. But if engagement fails, then one has uncovered the North's true intentions and built the consensus for an alternate course of action. The nuclear violations, in this context, have created more transparency about the extent to which the North's reform efforts represent mere tactical changes or a true shift in strategy and preferences. As hawk engagement behevers had always expected, Kim Jong Il has now dropped the cooperation ball. What comes next? The first step is to rally a multilateral coalition for diplomatic pressure among the allies. The fall 2002 Asia Pacific Economic Cooperation (APEC) meetings in Mexico and the U.S.-Japan-Korea trilateral statement at these meetings were important first steps in this direction. Both Seoul and Tokyo decreed that any hopes Pyongyang might have for inter-Korean economic cooperation or a large normalization package of Japanese aid hinge on satisfactory resolution of the North's current violation. (People also have wrongfully discounted the significance of a similar statement made by APEC as a whole—the first of its kind from the multilateral institution to explicitly address a security problem.) A second important step was taken in November 2002, when the three allies, through KEDO, agreed to suspend further shipments of heavy fuel oil to North Korea that had been promised under the 1994 agreement until Pyongyang came back into compliance. A third step effectively "multilateralizing" the problem occurred in August 2003, when China hosted talks involving the United States, the DPRK, South Korea, Japan, China, and Russia. Although unsuccessful in resolving the crisis, these talks were critical to enlisting China and the region in a more proactive role in helping to solve the problem.

Pundits and critics have blasted the United States for its "no-talk, no-negotiation" position until North Korea rolls back its HEU program. Hawk engagement, in contrast, would posit that the Bush administration's relatively low-key response to North Korea's violation (especially when compared with its response to Iraq's), coupled with its withholding negotiations with Pyongyang until it first makes gestures to come back into compliance, is effectively an offer to the North of one last chance to get out of its own mess. In this sense, as Harry Rowen at Stanford University has observed, this *is* the negotiating position. Kim Jong Il needs to unilaterally and verifiably address international concerns by dismantling the HEU program and returning to the status quo ante. If he were to do this, then the possibility of new U.S.–DPRK negotiations involving quid pro quos of economic aid for nonproliferation would lie ahead.

Why Not Hawk Engagement Again?

Prominent figures in the United States, such as former President Carter, Ambassador Robert Gallucci, and others have argued for turning back the engagement clock and entering into new negotiations to gain access to the HEU program and to roll back the 1994 Agreement violations. In a related vein, other commentators and journalists have argued implicitly that the United States should pursue some form of hawk engagement in the aftermath of the HEU revelations to at least "test" whether North Korea is interested in giving up the program. Others have explicitly invoked the hawk engagement argument to criticize the Bush administration's nonengagement with North Korea.

I do not find engagement a feasible option after the HEU revelations for one very critical reason: the initial rationale for hawk engagement was based on some degree of uncertainty with regard to the target regime's intentions. As long as such uncertainty existed, as it did in 1994, and Pyongyang remained somewhat compliant thereafter with the standing agreements that were the fruits of engagement, it would have been difficult for hawks to advocate otherwise. Hence, even when the North Koreans test-fired a ballistic missile over Japan in 1998, conducted submarine incursions into the South, attacked South Korean naval vessels, and undertook other acts of malfeasance, I still believed that engagement, even for hawks, was the appropriate path. However, the current violations by the North are on a scale that removes any uncertainty in regard to its intentions. Its behavior does not represent minor deviations from the landmark agreement, but rather a wholesale and secretive breakout from it. Negotiating under these conditions, for hawks, would be tantamount to appeasement.

If the current impasse is resolved diplomatically, however, and the DPRK takes unilateral steps toward dismantlement of the facilities, then regional diplomatic pressures, allied entreaties, and public opinion would again compel hawks to pursue some form of engagement. Such engagement would not be informed by any newfound trust in North Korea or its intentions. Indeed, hawk engagement in such a scenario would be informed by infinitely more palpable skepticism and distrust than existed prior to the HEU revelations and would perhaps be characterized by an even shorter tolerance for additional misbehavior by the North before switching to an alternate, more coercive path.

Isolation and Containment

If the North Koreans do not take a cooperative path out of the current crisis, then from a hawk engagement perspective, there is no choice but isolation and containment. The strategy's general contours would be to rally interested regional powers to isolate and neglect the regime until it gave up its proliferation threat. Although this would be akin to a policy of benign neglect, it would not be benign. The United States and its allies would maintain vigilant containment of the regime's military threat and would intercept any vessels suspected of carrying nuclear- or missile-related materials in and out of the North. Secondary sanctions would also be levied against firms in Japan and other Asian countries involved in illicit North Korean drug trafficking in an effort to restrict the flow of remittances to the DPRK leadership. The United States and the ROK might also undertake a reorientation of their military posture on the peninsula, focusing more on long-range, deep-strike capabilities, and betting that the DPRK will respond by scaling back forward deployments in defense of Pyongyang.

This strategy of "malign neglect" would also entail more proactive humanitarian measures, including the continuation of food aid, designed to help and engage the North Korean people. The United States would urge China and other countries to allow the United Nations High Commissioner for Refugees to establish North Korean refugee processing camps in neighboring countries around the Peninsula, enabling a regularized procedure for dealing with population outflows from the decaying country. Potentially a more significant watershed in this regard would be passage of a bill clearing the way for the United States to accept any North Korean who meets the definition of "refugee" and desires safe haven in the United States. In this regard, the United States would lead by example in preparing to facilitate passage out of the darkness that is North Korea to those people who have the courage to vote with their feet. . . .

No doubt there are dangers associated with an isolation strategy, not least of which is North Korean retaliation. Pyongyang states clearly that they would consider isolation and sanctions by the United States an act of war. To support isolation, however, is not to crave war on the peninsula. Indeed after engagement has been proven to fail (as it has for hawk engagers after the HEU revelations), then isolation is the *least* likely strategy to provoke war, inasmuch as the remaining options (including preemptive military strikes) are all much more coercive.

There is no denying the gravity of the crisis in 2003–2004. For hawk engagement, the offer to Kim Jong Il to resolve concerns about his dangerous uranium enrichment and plutonium nuclear weapons programs if he wants to get back on the engagement path is, in effect, the last round of diplomacy. Not taking up this offer would mean a path of isolation and containment of the regime and an end to many positive gains Pyongyang has accumulated since the June 2000 inter-Korean summit. Given the high stakes involved, one hopes that Kim Jong Il makes the correct calculation. . . .

POSTSCRIPT

Should the United States Seek Negotiations and Engagement with North Korea?

While it is clear that North Korea poses a significant security to southeast Asia, policymakers and academics continue to disagree about how best to manage relations with the DPRK. An expanded discussion of the debate between Kang and Cha is available in their recent book, *Nuclear North Korea: A Debate on Engagement Strategies* (Columbia University Press, 2003). In addition, each has written additional books on North Korea including Victor Cha, *The US-Korea-Japan Security Triangle* (Columbia University Press, 2000). The Center for International Policy runs an Asia project that provides expert commentary on Korea and other related materials on its Web site at http://www.ciponline.org/asia/index.htm . The federal research division of the Library of Congress provides current information on North Korea on the Web at http://lcweb2.loc.gov/frd/cs/kptoc.html. The Department of State maintains current information about North Korea and U.S. foreign policy regarding South Korea on its Web site for the Bureau of East Asian and Pacific Affairs at http://www.state.gov/p/eap/ci/ks/ and North Korea at http://www.state.gov/p/eap/ci/kn/.

Debates about engagement versus containment in North Korea are very similar to long-standing debates in international relations about the use of incentives versus sanctions as tools of foreign policy. David Baldwin provides a useful analysis of these strategies in comparison to other tools of foreign policy in *Economic Statecraft* (Princeton University Press, 1985).

ISSUE 12

Is U.S. Support for Israel a Key Factor in America's Difficulties in the Middle East?

YES: John J. Mearsheimer and Stephen M. Walt, from "The Israel Lobby and U.S. Foreign Policy," *Middle East Policy* (Fall 2006)

NO: Josef Joffe, from "A World Without Israel," *Foreign Policy* (January/February 2005)

ISSUE SUMMARY

YES: Stephen Walt and John Mearsheimer, international relations scholars at Harvard University and the University of Chicago respectively, argue that the United States' unwavering support for Israel has undermined American interests in the Middle East. They assert that Israel is a strategic burden rather than an asset for the United States, and that the United States' policies toward Israel are largely driven by the political power of an "Israeli lobby" in the United States.

NO: Joseph Joffe, a leading German commentator on international affairs, maintains that if Israel had never existed, the United States would face many of the same problems it currently confronts in the Middle East. In his view, many of the challenges facing the United States are driven by problems within and between Arab states, rather than those between these states and Israel.

There is little doubt or debate that the United States has had close ties to Israel for many years. Israel has been the largest recipient of U.S. foreign aid for over two decades, the United States has vetoed many U.N. Security Council resolutions that were critical of Israeli policies, and the United States has supplied arms to Israel, including speeding up shipments of weapons and supplies during Israel's summer 2006 clash with Hezbollah fighters in southern Lebanon.

What has been subject to debate is whether U.S. support of Israel has been unconditional, and whether this support is consistent with American interests or is instead a consequence of interest-group politics. Advocates of close ties to Israel note that it is a democratic country in a region that has few democracies, and that it was a strategic ally against the Soviet Union during the cold war and an ally (and source of intelligence information) in the struggle against terrorism. Supporters of close ties also note that the U.S. public expresses highly favorable views of Israel in opinion polls, and that this, rather than the power of lobbying groups, is what shapes U.S. policies toward Israel. Indeed, even with broad public support, interest groups working for close relations with Israel are not always successful. These groups have lost several high-profile policy battles in Washington, including their failure to stop the sale of advanced radar aircraft to Saudi Arabia and their inability in the early 1990s to win continued U.S. support for loan guarantees for houses built in the settlements on territories Israel occupied after the 1967 war. Moreover, in this view many of the problems the United States faces in the Middle East are caused not by U.S. ties to Israel, but by poverty, inequality, and the lack of democracy within Arab regimes.

Critics of U.S. ties to Israel, including Stephen Walt and John Mearsheimer, argue that the United States has supported Israel too unconditionally, and that this has generated animosity in the Arab world and even contributed to terrorist attacks against the United States. In these authors' view, close U.S. ties to Israel are driven not by American strategic interests, but by a powerful lobbying coalition in the United States that insists on unwavering support for Israel even to the point of damaging American interests in the Middle East.

YES ↵

John J. Mearsheimer
and Stephen M. Walt

The Israel Lobby and U.S. Foreign Policy

U.S. foreign policy shapes events in every corner of the globe. Nowhere is this truer than in the Middle East, a region of recurring instability and enormous strategic importance. Most recently, the Bush administration's attempt to transform the region into a community of democracies has helped produce a resilient insurgency in Iraq, a sharp rise in world oil prices, terrorist bombings in Madrid, London and Amman, and open warfare in Gaza and Lebanon. With so much at stake for so many, all countries need to understand the forces that drive U.S. Middle East policy.

The U.S. national interest should be the primary object of American foreign policy. For the past several decades, however, and especially since the Six-Day War in 1967, a recurring feature—and arguably the central focus—of U.S. Middle East policy has been its relationship with Israel. The combination of unwavering U.S. support for Israel and the related effort to spread democracy throughout the region has inflamed Arab and Islamic opinion and jeopardized U.S. security.

This situation has no equal in American political history. Why has the United States adopted policies that jeopardized its own security in order to advance the interests of another state? One might assume that the bond between the two countries is based on shared strategic interests or compelling moral imperatives. As we show below, however, neither of those explanations can account for the remarkable level of material and diplomatic support that the United States provides to Israel.

Instead, the overall thrust of U.S. policy in the region is due primarily to U.S. domestic politics and especially to the activities of the "Israel lobby." Other special-interest groups have managed to skew U.S. foreign policy in directions they favored, but no lobby has managed to divert U.S. foreign policy as far from what the American national interest would otherwise suggest, while simultaneously convincing Americans that U.S. and Israeli interests are essentially identical.

In the pages that follow, we describe how the Israel lobby has accomplished this feat and how its activities have shaped America's actions in this critical region. Given the strategic importance of the Middle East and its

From *London Review of Books*, March 23, 2006, pp. 30–34, 62–63. Copyright © 2006 by Blackwell Publishing, Ltd. Reprinted by permission.

potential impact on others, both Americans and non-Americans need to understand and address the lobby's influence on U.S. policy.

Some readers will find this analysis disturbing, but most of the facts recounted here are not in serious dispute among scholars. Indeed, our account draws primarily on mainstream sources like *The New York Times, The Washington Post, Ha'aretz,* or *Forward.* It also relies on the work of Israeli scholars and journalists, who deserve great credit for shedding light on these issues. We also cite evidence provided by respected Israeli and international human-rights organizations. Similarly, our claims about the lobby's impact rely on testimony from the lobby's own members, as well as testimony from politicians who have worked with them. Readers may reject our conclusions, of course, but the evidence on which they rest is not controversial.

The Great Benefactor

Since the October War in 1973, Washington has provided Israel with a level of support dwarfing the amounts provided to any other state. It has been the largest annual recipient of direct U.S. economic and military assistance since 1976 and the largest total recipient since World War II. Total direct U.S. aid to Israel amounts to well over $140 billion in 2003 dollars. Israel receives about $3 billion in direct foreign assistance each year, which is roughly one-fifth of America's foreign-aid budget. In per capita terms, the United States gives each Israeli a direct subsidy worth about $500 per year. This largesse is especially striking when one realizes that Israel is now a wealthy industrial state with a per capita income roughly equal to that of South Korea or Spain.

Israel also gets other special deals from Washington. Other aid recipients get their money in quarterly installments, but Israel receives its entire appropriation at the beginning of each fiscal year and thus earns extra interest. Most recipients of American military assistance are required to spend all of it in the United States, but Israel can use roughly 25 percent of its aid allotment to subsidize its own defense industry. Israel is the only recipient that does not have to account for how the aid is spent, an exemption that makes it virtually impossible to prevent the money from being used for purposes the United States opposes, like building settlements in the West Bank.

Moreover, the United States has provided Israel with nearly $3 billion to develop weapons systems like the *Lavi* aircraft that the Pentagon did not want or need, while giving Israel access to top-drawer U.S. weaponry like Blackhawk helicopters and F-16 jets. Finally, the United States gives Israel access to intelligence that it denies its NATO allies and has turned a blind eye toward Israel's acquisition of nuclear weapons.

In addition, Washington provides Israel with consistent diplomatic support. Since 1982, the United States has vetoed 33 United Nations Security Council resolutions that were critical of Israel, a number greater than the combined total of vetoes cast by all the other Security Council members. It also blocks Arab states' efforts to put Israel's nuclear arsenal on the International Atomic Energy Agency's agenda.

The United States also comes to Israel's rescue in wartime and takes its side when negotiating peace. The Nixon administration resupplied Israel during the October War and protected Israel from the threat of Soviet intervention. Washington was deeply involved in the negotiations that ended that war as well as the lengthy "step-by-step" process that followed, just as it played a key role in the negotiations that preceded and followed the 1993 Oslo accords. There was occasional friction between U.S. and Israeli officials in both cases, but the United States coordinated its positions closely with Israel and consistently backed the Israeli approach to the negotiations. Indeed, one American participant at Camp David (2000) later said, "Far too often, we functioned . . . as Israel's lawyer."

As discussed below, Washington has given Israel wide latitude in dealing with the Occupied Territories (the West Bank and Gaza Strip), even when its actions were at odds with stated U.S. policy. Moreover, the Bush administration's ambitious strategy to transform the Middle East—beginning with the invasion of Iraq—was partly intended to improve Israel's strategic situation. The Bush administration also took Israel's side during the recent war in Lebanon and initially opposed calls for a ceasefire in order to give Israel more time to go after Hezbollah. Apart from wartime alliances, it is hard to think of another instance where one country has provided another with a similar level of material and diplomatic support for such an extended period. America's support for Israel is, in short, unique.

This extraordinary generosity might be understandable if Israel were a vital strategic asset or if there were a compelling moral case for sustained U.S. backing. But neither rationale is convincing.

A Strategic Liability

According to the website of the American-Israel Public Affairs Committee (AIPAC), "The United States and Israel have formed a unique partnership to meet the growing strategic threats in the Middle East. . . . This cooperative effort provides significant benefits for both the United States and Israel." This claim is an article of faith among Israel's supporters and is routinely invoked by Israeli politicians and pro-Israel Americans.

Israel may have been a strategic asset during the Cold War. By serving as America's proxy after the 1967 war, Israel helped contain Soviet expansion in the region and inflicted humiliating defeats on Soviet clients like Egypt and Syria. Israel occasionally helped protect other U.S. allies (like Jordan's King Hussein), and its military prowess forced Moscow to spend more in backing its losing clients. Israel also gave the United States useful intelligence about Soviet capabilities.

Israel's strategic value during this period should not be overstated, however. Backing Israel was not cheap, and it complicated America's relations with the Arab world. For example, the U.S. decision to give Israel $2.2 billion in emergency military aid during the October War triggered an Arab oil embargo and production decrease that inflicted considerable damage on Western economies. Moreover, Israel's military could not protect U.S. interests in the region.

For example, the United States could not rely on Israel when the Iranian Revolution in 1979 raised concerns about the security of Persian Gulf oil supplies. Washington had to create its own "Rapid Deployment Force" instead.

Even if Israel was a strategic asset during the Cold War, the first Gulf War (1990–91) revealed that Israel was becoming a strategic burden. The United States could not use Israeli bases during the war without rupturing the anti-Iraq coalition, and it had to divert resources (e.g., Patriot missile batteries) to keep Tel Aviv from doing anything that might fracture the alliance against Saddam. History repeated itself in 2003. Although Israel was eager for the United States to attack Saddam, President Bush could not ask it to help without triggering Arab opposition. So Israel stayed on the sidelines again.

Beginning in the 1990s, and especially after 9/11, U.S. support for Israel has been justified by the claim that both states are threatened by terrorist groups originating in the Arab or Muslim world, and by a set of "rogue states" that back these groups and seek WMD. For many, this rationale implies that Washington should give Israel a free hand in dealing with the Palestinians and with groups like Hezbollah, and not press Israel to make concessions until all Palestinian terrorists are imprisoned or dead. It also implies that the United States should go after countries like the Islamic Republic of Iran, Saddam Hussein's Iraq and Bashar al-Asad's Syria. Israel is thus seen as a crucial ally in the war on terror because its enemies are said to be America's enemies.

This new rationale seems persuasive, but Israel is, in fact, a liability in the war on terror and the broader effort to deal with rogue states.

To begin with, "terrorism" is a tactic employed by a wide array of political groups; it is not a single unified adversary. The terrorist organizations that threaten Israel (e.g., Hamas or Hezbollah) do not threaten the United States, except when it intervenes against them (as in Lebanon in 1982). Moreover, Palestinian terrorism is not random violence directed against Israel or "the West"; it is largely a response to Israel's prolonged campaign to colonize the West Bank and Gaza Strip.

More important, saying that Israel and the United States are united by a shared terrorist threat has the causal relationship backwards. Rather, the United States has a terrorism problem in good part because it is so closely allied with Israel, not the other way around. U.S. support for Israel is hardly the only source of anti-American terrorism, but it is an important one, and it makes winning the war on terror more difficult. There is no question, for example, that many al-Qaeda leaders, including Osama bin Laden, are motivated in part by Israel's presence in Jerusalem and the plight of the Palestinians. According to the U.S. 9/11 Commission, Bin Laden explicitly sought to punish the United States for its policies in the Middle East, including its support for Israel. He even tried to time the attacks to highlight this issue.

Equally important, unconditional U.S. support for Israel makes it easier for extremists like Bin Laden to rally popular support and to attract recruits. Public-opinion polls confirm that Arab populations are deeply hostile to American support for Israel, and the U.S. State Department's Advisory Group on Public Diplomacy for the Arab and Muslim World found that "citizens in these countries are genuinely distressed at the plight of the Palestinians and at the role they perceive the United States to be playing."

As for so-called rogue states in the Middle East, they are not a dire threat to vital U.S. interests, apart from the U.S. commitment to Israel itself. Although the United States does have important disagreements with these regimes, Washington would not be nearly as worried about Iran, Baathist Iraq or Syria were it not so closely tied to Israel. Even if these states acquire nuclear weapons—which is obviously not desirable—it would not be a strategic disaster for the United States. President Bush admitted as much, saying earlier this year that "the threat from Iran is, of course, their stated objective to destroy our strong ally Israel." Yet this danger is probably overstated in light of Israel's and America's own nuclear deterrents. Neither country could be blackmailed by a nuclear-armed rogue state, because the blackmailer could not carry out the threat without receiving overwhelming retaliation. The danger of a "nuclear handoff" to terrorists is equally remote. A rogue state could not be sure the transfer would be undetected or that it would not be blamed and punished afterwards.

Furthermore, the U.S. relationship with Israel makes it harder to deal effectively with these states. Israel's nuclear arsenal is one reason why some of its neighbors want nuclear weapons, and threatening these states with regime change merely increases that desire. Yet Israel is not much of an asset when the United States contemplates using force against these regimes, since it cannot participate in the fight.

In short, treating Israel as America's most important ally in the campaign against terrorism and assorted Middle East dictatorships both exaggerates Israel's ability to help on these issues and ignores the ways that Israel's policies make U.S. efforts more difficult.

Unquestioned support for Israel also weakens the U.S. position outside the Middle East. Foreign elites consistently view the United States as too supportive of Israel and think its tolerance of Israeli repression in the Occupied Territories is morally obtuse and a handicap in the war on terrorism. In April 2004, for example, 52 former British diplomats sent Prime Minister Tony Blair a letter saying that the Israel-Palestine conflict had "poisoned relations between the West and the Arab and Islamic worlds" and warning that the policies of Bush and then-Prime Minister Ariel Sharon were "one-sided and illegal." Unqualified U.S. support for Israel's recent assault on Lebanon has elicited similar criticism from many other countries as well.

A final reason to question Israel's strategic value is that it does not act like a loyal ally. Israeli officials frequently ignore U.S. requests and renege on promises made to top U.S. leaders (including past pledges to halt settlement construction and to refrain from "targeted assassinations" of Palestinian leaders). Moreover, Israel has provided sensitive U.S. military technology to potential U.S. rivals like China, in what the U.S. State Department inspector-general called "a systematic and growing pattern of unauthorized transfers." According to the U.S. General Accounting Office, Israel also "conducts the most aggressive espionage operations against the U.S. of any ally." In addition to the case of Jonathan Pollard, who gave Israel large quantities of classified material in the early 1980s, a new controversy erupted in 2004, when it was revealed that a key

Pentagon official (Larry Franklin) had passed classified information to an Israeli diplomat, allegedly aided by two AIPAC officials. Israel is hardly the only country that spies on the United States, but its willingness to spy on its principal patron casts further doubt on its strategic value. . . .

Conclusion

Can the lobby's power be curtailed? One would like to think so, given the Iraq debacle, the obvious need to rebuild America's image in the Arab and Islamic worlds, and the recent revelations about AIPAC officials passing U.S. government secrets to Israel. One might also think that Arafat's death and the election of the more moderate Mahmoud Abbas would have led Washington to press vigorously and evenhandedly for a peace agreement. In short, there are ample grounds for U.S. leaders to distance themselves from the lobby and adopt a Middle East policy more consistent with broader U.S. interests. In particular, using American power to achieve a just peace between Israel and the Palestinians would help advance the broader goals of fighting extremism and promoting democracy in the Middle East.

But that is not going to happen anytime soon. AIPAC and its allies (including Christian Zionists) have no serious opponents in the struggle for influence in Washington. Although a few countervailing forces do exist, they are either significantly weaker (in the case of pro-Arab or pro-Islamic groups) or not interested in broad foreign-policy questions (in the case of oil companies and weapons manufacturers). Organizations in the lobby know it has become more difficult to make Israel's case today, and they are responding by expanding their activities and staffs. Moreover, American politicians remain acutely sensitive to campaign contributions and other forms of political pressure, and major media outlets are likely to remain sympathetic to Israel no matter what it does.

This situation is dangerous for the United States because the lobby's influence causes trouble on several fronts. It increases the terrorist danger that all states face, including America's various allies. By preventing U.S. leaders from pressuring Israel to make peace, the lobby has also made it impossible to end the Israeli-Palestinian conflict. This situation gives extremists a powerful recruiting tool, increases the pool of potential terrorists and sympathizers, and contributes to Islamic radicalism around the world.

Furthermore, the lobby's campaign for regime change in Iran and Syria could lead the United States to attack those countries, with potentially disastrous effects. We do not need another Iraq. At a minimum, the lobby's hostility toward these countries makes it especially difficult for Washington to enlist them against al-Qaeda and the Iraqi insurgency, where their help is badly needed.

There is a moral dimension here as well. Thanks to the lobby, the United States has become the de facto enabler of Israeli expansion in the Occupied Territories, making it complicit in the crimes perpetrated against the Palestinians. This situation undercuts Washington's efforts to promote democracy abroad and makes it look hypocritical when it presses other states to respect human rights. U.S. efforts to limit nuclear proliferation appear equally hypocritical, given its willingness to accept Israel's nuclear arsenal, which encourages Iran and others to seek similar capabilities.

Moreover, the lobby's campaign to squelch debate about Israel is unhealthy for democracy. Silencing skeptics by organizing blacklists and boycotts—or by suggesting that critics are antisemites—violates the principle of open debate upon which democracy depends. The inability of the U.S. Congress to conduct a genuine debate on these vital issues paralyzes the entire process of democratic deliberation. Israel's backers should be free to make their case and to challenge those who disagree with them. But efforts to stifle debate by intimidation must be roundly condemned by those who believe in free speech and open discussion of important public issues.

Finally, the lobby's influence has been bad for Israel. Its ability to persuade Washington to support an expansionist agenda has discouraged Israel from seizing opportunities—including a peace treaty with Syria and a prompt and full implementation of the Oslo accords—that would have saved Israeli lives and shrunk the ranks of Palestinian extremists. Denying the Palestinians their legitimate political rights certainly has not made Israel more secure. The long campaign to kill or marginalize a generation of Palestinian leaders has empowered extremist groups like Hamas and reduced the number of Palestinian leaders who would be both willing to accept a fair settlement and able to make it work. This course raises the awful specter of Israel eventually occupying the pariah status once reserved for apartheid states like South Africa. Ironically, Israel itself would probably be better off if the lobby were less powerful and U.S. policy were more evenhanded.

Yet there is still a ray of hope. Although the lobby remains a powerful force, the adverse effects of its influence are increasingly difficult to hide. Powerful states can maintain flawed policies for quite some time, but reality cannot be ignored forever. What is needed, therefore, is a candid discussion of the lobby's influence and a more open debate about U.S. interests in this vital region. Israel's well-being is one of those interests, but its continued occupation of the West Bank and its broader regional agenda are not. Open debate will expose the limits of the strategic and moral case for one-sided U.S. support. It could also move the United States to a position more consistent with its own national interest, with the interests of the other states in the region, and with Israel's long-term interests as well.

Josef Joffe

NO

A World Without Israel

Since World War II, no state has suffered so cruel a reversal of fortunes as Israel. Admired all the way into the 1970s as the state of "those plucky Jews" who survived against all odds and made democracy and the desert bloom in a climate hostile to both liberty and greenery, Israel has become the target of creeping delegitimization. The denigration comes in two guises. The first, the soft version, blames Israel first and most for whatever ails the Middle East, and for having corrupted U.S. foreign policy. It is the standard fare of editorials around the world, not to mention the sheer venom oozing from the pages of the Arab-Islamic press. The more recent hard version zeroes in on Israel's very existence. According to this dispensation, it is Israel as such, and not its behavior, that lies at the root of troubles in the Middle East. Hence the "stato-cidal" conclusion that Israel's birth, midwifed by both the United States and the Soviet Union in 1948, was a grievous mistake, grandiose and worthy as it may have been at the time.

The soft version is familiar enough. One motif is the "wagging the dog" theory. Thus, in the United States, the "Jewish lobby" and a cabal of neoconservatives have bamboozled the Bush administration into a mindless pro-Israel policy inimical to the national interest. This view attributes, as has happened so often in history, too much clout to the Jews. And behind this charge lurks a more general one—that it is somehow antidemocratic for subnational groups to throw themselves into the hurly-burly of politics when it comes to foreign policy. But let us count the ways in which subnational entities battle over the national interest: unions and corporations clamor for tariffs and tax loopholes; nongovernmental organizations agitate for humanitarian intervention; and Cuban Americans keep us from smoking cheroots from the Vuelta Abajo. In previous years, Poles militated in favor of Solidarity, African Americans against Apartheid South Africa, and Latvians against the Soviet Union. In other words, the democratic melee has never stopped at the water's edge.

Another soft version is tile "root-cause" theory in its many variations. Because the "obstinate" and "recalcitrant" Israelis are the main culprits, they must be punished and pushed back for the sake of peace. "Put pressure on Israel"; "cut economic and military aid"; "serve them notice that we will not condone their brutalities"—these have been the boilerplate homilies, indeed the obsessions, of the chattering classes and the foreign-office establishment for decades. Yet, as Sigmund Freud reminded us, obsessions tend to spread. And so there are ever more creative addenda to the well-wrought root-cause theory. Anatol Lieven of the Carnegie Endowment for International Peace argues that what is happening between Israelis and Palestinians is a "tremendous obstacle to democratization because it inflames all the worst, most regressive aspects of Arab nationalism and Arab culture." In other words, the conflict drives the pathology, and not the other way around—which is like the street-fighter explaining to the police: "It all started when this guy hit back."

The problem with this root-cause argument is threefold: It blurs, if not reverses, cause and effect. It ignores a myriad of conflicts unrelated to Israel. And it absolves the Arabs of culpability, shifting the blame to you know whom. If one believes former U.N. weapons inspector Scott Ritter, the Arab-Islamic quest for weapons of mass destruction, and by extension the war against Iraq, are also Made in Israel. "[A]s long as Israel has nuclear weapons," Ritter opines, "it has chosen to take a path that is inherently confrontational. . . . Now the Arab countries, the Muslim world, is not about to sit back and let this happen, so they will seek their own deterrent. We saw this in Iraq, not only with a nuclear deterrent but also with a biological weapons deterrent . . . that the Iraqis were developing to offset the Israeli nuclear superiority."

This theory would be engaging if it did not collide with some inconvenient facts. Iraqis didn't use their weapons of mass destruction against the Israeli usurper but against fellow Muslims during the Iran-Iraq War, and against fellow Iraqis in the poison-gas attack against Kurds in Halabja in 1988—neither of whom were brandishing any nuclear weapons. As for the Iraqi nuclear program, we now have the "Duelfer Report," based on the debriefing of Iraqi regime loyalists, which concluded: "Iran was the preeminent motivator of this policy. All senior-level Iraqi officials considered Iran to be Iraq's principal enemy in the region. The wish to balance Israel and acquire status and influence in the Arab world were also considerations, but secondary."

Now to the hard version. Ever so subtly, a more baleful tone slips into this narrative: Israel is not merely an unruly neighbor but an unwelcome intruder. Still timidly uttered outside the Arab world, this version's proponents in the West bestride the stage as truth-sayers who dare to defy taboo. Thus, the British writer A.N. Wilson declares that he has reluctantly come to the conclusion that Israel, through its own actions, has proven it does not have the right to exist. And, following Sept. 11, 2001, Brazilian scholar Jose Arthur Giannotti said: "Let us agree that the history of the Middle East would be entirely different without the State of Israel, which opened a wound between Islam and the West. Can you get rid of Muslim terrorism without getting rid of this wound which is the source of the frustration of potential terrorists?"

The very idea of a Jewish state is an "anachronism," argues Tony Judt, a professor and director of the Remarque Institute at New York University. It resembles a "late-nineteenth-century separatist project" that has "no place" in this wondrous new world moving toward the teleological perfection of multi-ethnic and multicultural togetherness bound together by international law. The time has come to "think the unthinkable," hence, to ditch this Jewish state for a binational one, guaranteed, of course, by international force.

So let us assume that Israel is an anachronism and a historical mistake without which the Arab-Islamic world stretching from Algeria to Egypt, from Syria to Pakistan, would be a far happier place, above all because the original sin, the establishment of Israel, never would have been committed. Then let's move from the past to the present, pretending that we could wave a mighty magic wand, and "poof," Israel disappears from the map.

Civilization of Clashes

Let us start the what-if procession in 1948, when Israel was born in war. Would stillbirth have nipped the Palestinian problem in the bud? Not quite. Egypt, Transjordan (now Jordan), Syria, Iraq, and Lebanon marched on Haifa and Tel Aviv not to liberate Palestine, but to grab it. The invasion was a textbook competitive power play by neighboring states intent on acquiring territory for themselves. If they had been victorious, a Palestinian state would not have emerged, and there still would have been plenty of refugees. (Recall that half the population of Kuwait fled Iraqi dictator Saddam Hussein's "liberation" of that country in 1990.) Indeed, assuming that Palestinian nationalism had awakened when it did in the late 1960s and 1970s, the Palestinians might now be dispatching suicide bombers to Egypt, Syria, and elsewhere.

Let us imagine Israel had disappeared in 1967, instead of occupying the West Bank and the Gaza Strip, which were held, respectively, by Jordan's King Hussein and Egypt's President Gamal Abdel Nasser. Would they have relinquished their possessions to Palestinian leader Yasir Arafat and thrown in Haifa and Tel Aviv for good measure? Not likely. The two potentates, enemies in all but name, were united only by their common hatred and fear of Arafat, the founder of Fatah (the Palestine National Liberation Movement) and rightly suspected of plotting against Arab regimes. In short, the "root cause" of Palestinian statelessness would have persisted, even in Israel's absence.

Let us finally assume, through a thought experiment, that Israel goes "poof" today. How would this development affect the political pathologies of the Middle East? Only those who think the Palestinian issue is at the core of the Middle East conflict would lightly predict a happy career for this most dysfunctional region once Israel vanishes. For there is no such thing as "the" conflict. A quick count reveals five ways in which the region's fortunes would remain stunted—or worse:

States vs. States

Israel's elimination from the regional balance would hardly bolster intra-Arab amity. The retraction of the colonial powers, Britain and France, in the mid-20th century left behind a bunch of young Arab states seeking to redraw the map of the region. From the very beginning, Syria laid claim to Lebanon. In 1970, only the Israeli military deterred Damascus from invading Jordan under the pretext of supporting a Palestinian uprising. Throughout the 1950s and 1960s, Nasser's Egypt proclaimed itself the avatar of pan-Arabism, intervening in Yemen during the 1960s. Nasser's successor, President Anwar Sadat, was embroiled in on-and-off clashes with Libya throughout the late 1970s. Syria marched into Lebanon in 1976 and then effectively annexed the country 15 years later, and Iraq launched two wars against fellow Muslim states: Iran in 1980, Kuwait in 1990. The war against Iran was the longest conventional war of the 20th century. None of these conflicts is related to the Israeli-Palestinian one. Indeed, Israel's disappearance would only liberate military assets for use in such internal rivalries.

Believers vs. Believers

Those who think that the Middle East conflict is a "Muslim-Jewish thing" had better take a closer look at the score card: 14 years of sectarian bloodshed in Lebanon; Saddam's campaign of extinction against the Shia in the aftermath of the first Gulf War; Syria's massacre of 20,000 people in the Muslim Brotherhood stronghold of Hama in 1982; and terrorist violence against Egyptian Christians in the 1990s. Add to this tally intraconfessional oppression, such as in Saudi Arabia, where the fundamentalist Wahhabi sect wields the truncheon of state power to inflict its dour lifestyle on the less devout.

Ideologies vs. Ideologies

Zionism is not the only "ism" in the region, which is rife with competing ideologies. Even though the Baathist parties in Syria and Iraq sprang from the same fascist European roots, both have vied for precedence in the Middle East. Nasser wielded pan-Arabism-*cum*-socialism against the Arab nation-state. And both Baathists and Nasserites have opposed the monarchies, such as in Jordan. Khomeinist Iran and Wahhabite Saudi Arabia remain mortal enemies. What is the connection to the Arab-Israeli conflict? Nil, with the exception of Hamas, a terror army of the faithful once supported by Israel as a rival to the Palestine Liberation Organization and now responsible for many suicide bombings in Israel. But will Hamas disband once Israel is gone? Hardly. Hamas has bigger ambitions than eliminating the "Zionist entity." The organization seeks nothing less than a unified Arab state under a regime of God.

Reactionary Utopia vs. Modernity

A common enmity toward Israel is the only thing that prevents Arab modernizers and traditionalists from tearing their societies apart. Fundamentalists vie against secularists and reformist Muslims for the fusion of mosque and state under the green flag of the Prophet. And a barely concealed class struggle pits a minuscule bourgeoisie and millions of unemployed young men against the power structure, usually a form of statist cronyism that controls the means of production. Far from creating tensions, Israel actually contains the antagonisms in the world around it.

Regimes vs. Peoples

The existence of Israel cannot explain the breadth and depth of the Mukhabarat states (secret police states) throughout the Middle East. With the exceptions of Jordan, Morocco, and the Gulf sheikdoms, which gingerly practice an enlightened monarchism, all Arab countries (plus Iran and Pakistan) are but variations of despotism—from the dynastic dictatorship of Syria to the authoritarianism of

Egypt. Intranational strife in Algeria has killed nearly 100,000, with no letup in sight. Saddam's victims are said to number 300,000. After the Khomeinists took power in 1979, Iran was embroiled not only in the Iran-Iraq War but also in barely contained civil unrest into the 1980s. Pakistan is an explosion waiting to happen. Ruthless suppression is the price of stability in this region.

Again, it would take a florid imagination to surmise that factoring Israel out of the Middle East equation would produce liberal democracy in the region. It might be plausible to argue that the dialectic of enmity somehow favors dictatorship in "frontline states" such as Egypt and Syria—governments that invoke the proximity of the "Zionist threat" as a pretext to suppress dissent. But how then to explain the mayhem in faraway Algeria, the bizarre cult-of-personality regime in Libya, the pious kleptocracy of Saudi Arabia, the clerical despotism of Iran, or democracy's enduring failure to take root in Pakistan? Did Israel somehow cause the various putsches that produced the republic of fear in Iraq? If Jordan, the state sharing the longest border with Israel, can experiment with constitutional monarchy, why not Syria?

It won't do to lay the democracy and development deficits of the Arab world on the doorstep of the Jewish state. Israel is a pretext, not a cause, and therefore its dispatch will not heal the self-inflicted wounds of the Arab-Islamic world. Nor will the mild version of "statocide," a binational state, do the trick—not in view of the "civilization of clashes" (to borrow a term from British historian Niall Ferguson) that is the hallmark of Arab political culture. The mortal struggle between Israelis and Palestinians would simply shift from the outside to the inside.

My Enemy, Myself

Can anybody proclaim in good conscience that these dysfunctionalities of the Arab world would vanish along with Israel? Two U.N. "Arab Human Development Reports," written by Arab authors, say no. The calamities are home-made. Stagnation and hopelessness have three root causes. The first is lack of freedom. The United Nations cites the persistence of absolute autocracies, bogus elections, judiciaries beholden to executives, and constraints on civil society. Freedom of expression and association are also sharply limited. The second root cause is lack of knowledge: Sixty-five million adults are illiterate, and some 10 million children have no schooling at all. As such, the Arab world is dropping ever further behind in scientific research and the development of information technology. Third, female participation in political and economic life is the lowest in the world. Economic growth will continue to lag as long as the potential of half the population remains largely untapped.

Will all of this right itself when that Judeo-Western insult to Arab pride finally vanishes? Will the millions of unemployed and bored young men, cannon fodder for the terrorists, vanish as well—along with one-party rule, corruption, and closed economies? This notion makes sense only if one cherishes single-cause explanations or, worse, harbors a particular animus against the Jewish state and its refusal to behave like Sweden. (Come to think of it, Sweden would not be Sweden either if it lived in the Hobbesian world of the Middle East.)

Finally, the most popular what-if issue of them all: Would the Islamic world hate the United States less if Israel vanished? Like all what-if queries, this one, too, admits only suggestive evidence. To begin, the notion that 5 million Jews are solely responsible for the rage of 1 billion or so Muslims cannot carry the weight assigned to it. Second, Arab-Islamic hatreds of the United States preceded the conquest of the West Bank and Gaza. Recall the loathing left behind by the U.S.-managed coup that restored the shah's rule in Tehran in 1953, or the U.S. intervention in Lebanon in 1958. As soon as Britain and France left the Middle East, the United States became the dominant power and the No. 1 target. Another bit of suggestive evidence is that the fiercest (unofficial) anti-Americanism emanates from Washington's self-styled allies in the Arab Middle East, Egypt and Saudi Arabia. Is this situation because of Israel—or because it is so convenient for these regimes to "busy giddy minds with foreign quarrels" (as Shakespeare's Henry IV put it) to distract their populations from their dependence on the "Great Satan"?

Take the Cairo Declaration against "U.S. hegemony," endorsed by 400 delegates from across the Middle East and the West in December 2002. The lengthy indictment mentions Palestine only peripherally. The central condemnation, uttered in profuse variation, targets the United States for monopolizing power "within the framework of capitalist globalization," for reinstating "colonialism," and for blocking the "emergence of forces that would shift the balance of power toward multi-polarity." In short, Global America is responsible for all the afflictions of the Arab world, with Israel coming in a distant second.

This familiar tale has an ironic twist: One of the key signers is Nader Fergany, lead author of the 2002 U.N. Arab Human Development Report. So even those who confess to the internal failures of the Arab world end up blaming "the Other." Given the enormity of the indictment, ditching Israel will not absolve the United States. Iran's Khomeinists have it right, so to speak, when they denounce America as the "Great Satan" and Israel only as the "Little Satan," a handmaiden of U.S. power. What really riles America-haters in the Middle East is Washington's intrusion into their affairs, be it for reasons of oil, terrorism, or weapons of mass destruction. This fact is why Osama bin Laden, having attached himself to the Palestinian cause only as an afterthought, calls the Americans the new crusaders, and the Jews their imperialist stand-ins.

None of this is to argue in favor of Israel's continued occupation of the West Bank and Gaza, nor to excuse the cruel hardship it imposes on the Palestinians, which is pernicious, even for Israel's own soul. But as this analysis suggests, the real source of Arab angst is the West as a palpable symbol of misery and an irresistible target of what noted Middle East scholar Fouad Ajami has called "Arab rage." The puzzle is why so many Westerners, like those who signed the Cairo Declaration, believe otherwise.

Is this anti-Semitism, as so many Jews are quick to suspect? No, but denying Israel's legitimacy bears an uncanny resemblance to some central features of this darkest of creeds. Accordingly, the Jews are omnipotent, ubiquitous, and thus responsible for the evils of the world. Today, Israel finds itself in an analogous position, either as handmaiden or manipulator of U.S. might. The soft version sighs: "If only Israel were more reasonable. . . ." The semihard version demands that "the United States pull the rug out from under Israel" to impose the pliancy that comes from impotence. And the hard-hard version dreams about salvation springing from Israel's disappearance.

Why, sure—if it weren't for that old joke from Israel's War of Independence: While the bullets were whistling overhead and the two Jews in their foxhole were running out of rounds, one griped, "If the Brits had to give us a country not their own, why couldn't they have given us Switzerland?" Alas, Israel is just a strip of land in the world's most noxious neighborhood, and the cleanup hasn't even begun.

WANT TO KNOW MORE?

Tony Judt argues that Zionism is an anachronistic ideology and makes the case for Israel's becoming a binational state in "Israel: The Alternative" (*New York Review of Books,* Oct. 23, 2003). Bret Stephens maintains that binationalism is a recipe for civil war in "The Controversy of Israel" (*Jerusalem Post,* Oct. 31, 2003). In "Scurrying Towards Bethlehem" (*New Left Review,* July-August 2001), Perry Anderson doesn't quite want to abolish Israel, but he seeks to reduce it drastically by creating a Palestinian state that encompasses Gaza, the West Bank, the Galilee, and the coastline from Lebanon to Haifa.

Fouad Ajami examines the stalemate of secular political ideologies in the Middle East in his classic work, *The Arab Predicament: Arab Political Thought and Practice Since 1967* (New York: Cambridge University Press, 1992). Candid assessments of the developmental challenges confronting the Arab world can be found in the United Nations' "Arab Human Development Report 2002: Creating Opportunities for Future Generations" (New York: United Nations Development Programme, 2002) and "Arab Human Development Report 2003: Building a Knowledge Society" (New York: United Nations Development Programme, 2003). Bernard Lewis asks, "What Went Wrong?" (*Atlantic Monthly,* January 2002) in the Muslim world, and he concludes that the key problem may be a simple lack of freedom. In "Think Again: Middle East Democracy" (FOREIGN POLICY, November/December 2004), Marina Ottaway and Tom Carothers warn that failure to resolve the Arab-Israeli conflict prevents the United States from gaining credibility as an advocate of democracy in the region.

In "Think Again: Al Qaeda" (FOREIGN POLICY, May/June 2004), Jason Burke argues that although a resolution of the Israeli-Palestinian conflict would help alleviate political tensions in the region, it would not end the threat of militant Islam. Mark Strauss explores how anti-Israelism is, in part, the product of the backlash against globalization in "Antiglobalism's Jewish Problem" (FOREIGN POLICY, November/December 2003).

POSTSCRIPT

Is U.S. Support for Israel a Key Factor in America's Difficulties in the Middle East?

The critique of U.S. policies toward Israel by Professors Walt and Mearsheimer, originally published in the *London Review of Books* on March 23, 2006, provoked a fierce debate over U.S. politics and policies toward Israel. For a sampling of this debate, see the transcript of a panel organized by the *London Review of Books* at http://www.scribemedia.org/2006/10/10/transcript-israel-lobby/. The panel included Mearsheimer and several experts, policymakers, and commentators on the subject, including Shlomo Ben-Ami, Martin Indyk, Tony Judt, Rashid Khalidi, and Dennis Ross. For just a few of the many published responses to Walt and Mearsheimer, see Jeffrey Herf and Andrei Markovits, Letter to the London Review of Books (vol. 28, no. 7, April 6, 2006); Christopher Hitchens, "Overstating Jewish Power" (Slate.com, March 27, 2006); and Alan Dershowitz, "Debunking the Newest—and Oldest—Jewish Conspiracy: A Reply to the Mearsheimer-Walt 'Working Paper'" (Harvard Faculty Responses to KSG Working Papers, April 5, 2006). Professors Walt and Mearsheimer also responded to their critics in a symposium in *Foreign Policy* in July/August 2006, and in a letter on this symposium in this same journal in the September/October 2006 issue. These authors are at work on a more complete response to their critics that as of early 2007 was not yet in print.

Regarding the relationship between the Israeli-Palestinian conflict and anti-U.S. terrorism, most discussions of al Qaeda's goals note that al Qaeda statements criticize the United States for its support of Israel, but list this as only one of many of al Qaeda's disagreements with the United States. See, for example, Dan Byman, "Al-Qaeda as an Adversary: Do We Understand Our Enemy?" *World Politics* (October 2003). For an assessment of the wider challenges facing Arab countries in the Middle East, see the United Nations Arab Human Development Report 2003: *Building a Knowledge Society*.

Internet References . . .

The Department of Homeland Security

The Department of Homeland Security seeks to lead and coordinate a unified national effort to secure America; to prevent and deter terrorist attacks and protect against and respond to threats and hazards to the nation; and to ensure safe and secure borders, welcome lawful immigrants and visitors, and promote the free flow of commerce. This site provides extensive information about U.S. security policy.

http://www.dhs.gov/

The American Civil Liberties Union (ACLU)

The ACLU's stated objective is to conserve America's original civic values—the Constitution and the Bill of Rights. It does so by operating through the courts, through the legislatures and in local communities to defend and preserve the individual rights and liberties guaranteed to every person in this country by the Constitution and laws of the United States. Its Web site is a good first stop for information about issues that affect civil and political liberties.

http://www.aclu.org/

Democracy, Human Rights, and Labor

The Bureau of Democracy, Human Rights, and Labor (DRL) within the Department of State is the primary executive branch body responsible for human rights issues in American foreign policy.

http://www.state.gov/g/drl/

Gallup Poll News Service, Pew Research Center for the People and the Press, and PollingReport.Com

The Gallup Poll News Service, Pew Research Center for the People and the Press, and PollingReport.Com provide polling data and analyses of public opinion regarding a wide range of U.S. foreign and domestic policies.

http://gallup.com/

http://people-press.org/

http://pollingreport.com

American Foreign Policy: Domestic Politics and Institutions

*W*hile *American foreign policy has much to do with the world beyond the boundaries of the United States, domestic politics and internal decision-making processes significantly influence which policies the United States adopts. In addition, the institutions and policies put in place to address foreign policy issues can have profound effects on the domestic arena. Particularly in the post–9/11 strategic environment, foreign policy choices often involve a trade-off between the goal of stopping potential terrorists and undermining the freedoms of the citizens that such policies are seeking to protect.*

- Has the Department of Homeland Security Been a Success?

- Does Domestic Spying Help the United States?

- Is Loosening Immigration Regulations Good for the United States?

ISSUE 13

Has the Department of Homeland Security Been a Success?

YES: Tom Ridge, from Testimony Before the Senate Committee on Governmental Affairs (September 13, 2004)

NO: Michael Crowley, from "Playing Defense: Bush's Disastrous Homeland Security Department," *The New Republic* (March 15, 2004)

ISSUE SUMMARY

YES: Tom Ridge, former secretary of homeland security, argues that the new department has made great progress in bringing together federal, state, and local security agencies and improving the coordination and information exchange among them to prevent terrorist attacks.

NO: Michael Crowley, senior editor of *The New Republic,* argues that the Department of Homeland Security is disorganized and underfunded and has not set the right priorities for best preventing new terrorist attacks.

After investigations of the 9/11 attacks uncovered evidence that U.S. intelligence and law enforcement agencies had failed to share information that might have helped prevent the attacks from succeeding, Congress and the Bush administration created the Department of Homeland Security (DHS) to better coordinate federal, state, and local anti-terror efforts. Organizing the new department presented the daunting organizational challenge of merging 22 different agencies with 170,000 employees, including the Coast Guard, the Secret Service, the Federal Emergency Management Agency, the Customs Service, the Border Patrol, and the Immigration and Naturalization Service. President Bush appointed Pennsylvania Governor Tom Ridge to be the first secretary of homeland security.

To the American public, the DHS is best known for its color-coded warning system, which raises and publicizes the level of alert in accordance with the intelligence information on terrorist threats that DHS receives. This warning system remains a work in progress—it remains unclear exactly what law enforcement and preparedness activities should be raised where and at whose expense at different levels of alert. Also, while repeated alerts thus far have thankfully not been followed by any actual attacks on U.S. territory (and going on alert may have helped prevent such attacks), this raises the danger that law enforcement agencies and the public will take fewer precautions with each new alert.

For security experts, however, more critical to the progress of DHS than its public alert system is the less visible success or failure of DHS in its efforts to integrate and coordinate threat information and response options among federal, state, and local law enforcement, intelligence, and military agencies. Here, it is more difficult for outsiders to assess DHS's progress. In even the best case scenario, bringing together 22 agencies with different missions and priorities, and getting them to share information that they ordinarily work hard to keep secret, is a difficult task. Secretary Ridge points to improved border controls and progress on technological links allowing federal, state, and local agencies to communicate with one another, but Crowley highlights continuing difficulties in even the high-priority task of merging the federal government's 12 separate terrorist watch lists. Crowley also points to the possibility that DHS's efforts to integrate threat information may be superceded by those of the existing Terrorist Threat Integration Center housed at the CIA's headquarters, and he notes that DHS has had difficulty attracting and keeping highly qualified people and winning bureaucratic turf struggles with the CIA, the FBI, and the Department of Defense. Many of these problems are to some extent the predictable growing pains of a new agency charged with merging organizations and integrating powerful departments outside of its budgetary control, though Crowley argues that even in view of these expected difficulties, DHS could have performed much better in its formative first two years, which will shape DHS's path for many years to come.

YES

Tom Ridge

Testimony Before the Senate Committee on Governmental Affairs

...I am pleased to have this opportunity to update the Committee on the Department's activities and improvements to our nation's homeland security posture, and to discuss important new initiatives undertaken by President Bush to enhance our intelligence capabilities and strengthen our ability to fight the war on terror.

This is particularly timely in the wake of the thoughtful and thorough recommendations made by the Commission on the Terrorist Attacks on the United States.

As the Commission recognized, in the aftermath of September 11th, it was clear that the nation had no centralized effort to defend the country against terrorism, no single agency dedicated to homeland security. As all of you know, these tragic attacks required a swift and drastic change to our understanding of what it mean to secure America.

With your help, the Department of Homeland Security was established to bring together all of our scattered entities and capabilities under one central authority to better coordinate and direct our homeland security efforts.

In the span of our eighteen month existence, we have made tremendous progress. I want to thank the Commission and Congress for recognizing the tremendous strides we have already made.

From our borders to our "hometowns," from our coastline to the skies, we are safer, more secure and better prepared today than ever before.

Yet, we must not rest on past accomplishments; we must look toward the future and guard vigilantly against complacency. Nowhere is this more important than with our intelligence operations. Every day, terrorists are hard at work to discover a vulnerability, to uncover a gap in our substantial network of layered security.

Every day, hundreds of pieces of intelligence come to us, some the public is aware of, such as the recent Al-Zawahiri tape and information gleaned from the tragedy at the school in Beslan, and much that the public never hears about. We must be even more determined and more diligent in our efforts to detect and defeat their plans for terror.

From Testimony before the Senate Committee on Governmental Affairs by Tom Ridge, September 13, 2004.

That is why improved coordination and cooperation across all segments of the intelligence community has been an absolute imperative of the homeland security mission . . . and one which the President has fully embraced and addressed with recent reform initiatives.

Since the inception of the Department of Homeland Security, we have improved intelligence capabilities and information sharing with our partners in the federal government as well as state, local, tribal and private sector partners on the front lines of homeland security across America.

The President has already undertaken a number of important initiatives that reform our intelligence collection and analysis. Last month, he issued a series of executive orders implementing some of these reforms.

The President established the National Counterterrorism Center, which will build on the important work already underway at the Terrorist Threat Integration Center, or TTIC. TTIC, itself, was an initiative of this administration that recognized the need for a centralized approach to terrorist threat assessments for the nation. This new Center—the NCTC—will become our Nation's shared knowledge bank for intelligence information on known or suspected terrorists.

It will centralize our intelligence efforts, and help to ensure that all elements of our government receive the source information they need to combat terrorist threats.

It will provide a better unity of effort within the Intelligence Community, and improve our linkage with law enforcement. By enhancing the flow of critical information, we greatly enhance our ability do our job—protecting Americans and securing the homeland.

The President has also directed that additional actions be taken to improve the sharing of terrorism information among agencies and that needed improvements be made in our information technology architecture. And last week, the President announced yet another important step in his reform agenda. In a meeting with senior Congressional leadership, he conveyed his proposal for the creation of a National Intelligence Director.

The creation of both the National Intelligence Director, and the new Counterterrorism Center, were recommendations made by the 9/11 Commission and endorsed by the President. They are critical building blocks to enhancing our nation's intelligence system.

Under the President's plan, the National Intelligence Director would be given full budgetary authority over the National Foreign Intelligence Program appropriation.

The Director will also be given responsibility for integrating foreign and domestic intelligence, and will be provided with the management tools necessary to effectively oversee the intelligence community.

The Director will report to the President, and serve as the head of the U.S. Intelligence Community. He will be assisted in his work by a cabinet-level Joint Intelligence Community Council. The JICC is critical to ensuring solid advice to the National Intelligence Director, as well as the opportunity for Departments to shape intelligence priorities together. The new Director provides centralized leadership for our national intelligence efforts, and will ensure a joint, unified effort to protect our national security.

The Department of Homeland Security will play an important role within this new structure, and will directly benefit from this centralized leadership and the enhanced flow of information it will provide. The Department of Homeland Security's Office of Information Analysis will participate in the new Counterterrorism center.

As a member of the intelligence community, we will have full access to a central repository of intelligence information. DHS and other members of the Intelligence Community will now go to one place that will formulate an integrated approach to consolidated threat assessments and related intelligence and planning support.

This centralization is critical to our efforts. DHS analysts will have access to the work of other government intelligence analysts, and vice versa. This new, integrated structure will create a more open flow of information, leaving us better informed regarding terrorist threats, and better able to address vulnerabilities and secure our nation.

Just as important, we can effectively and efficiently channel that information to those who need it by using new communication tools such as the Homeland Security Information Network.

This network is a real-time, Internet-based collaboration system that allows multiple jurisdictions, disciplines and emergency operation centers to receive and share the same intelligence and the same tactical information. This year we have expanded this information network to include senior decision-makers, such as governors and homeland security advisors in all 50 states, territories and major urban areas.

It was an ambitious goal, but one which we met ahead of schedule. And we are still working—namely to provide increased security clearances and secret level connectivity not only at the state level but also for private sector leaders and critical infrastructure owners and operators.

In order to increase compatibility and reduce duplication, we are working to integrate this information network with similar efforts of our partners in the federal government, including the Law Enforcement Online and Regional Information Sharing System.

And all of our federal partners—as well as many others—participate in the Department's new Homeland Security Operations Center. This 24 hour nerve center synthesizes information from a variety of sources and then distributes information, bulletins, and security recommendations as necessary to all levels of government.

Our progress in intelligence and information sharing demonstrates the links we have made between prevention and protection.

By establishing a comprehensive strategy combining vulnerability and threat assessment with infrastructure protection, we are taking steps daily to protect the public and mitigate the potential for attack.

We have significantly bolstered our nation's security by implementing a layered system of protections along our borders and at our ports of entry, on our roadways, railways, and waterways, and even far from our borders and shores.

I am confident that we are more secure today than we were on or before September 11th, 2001.

I would like to note that September is National Preparedness Month. This month, 82 organizations and all 56 states and territories are combining efforts to encourage millions more people to be prepared and get involved in the common effort for the common good.

Unfortunately, we've seen in the past few weeks just how important preparedness can be. The people of Florida have been hit with two hurricanes—and the damage has been considerable—but the long lines to purchase plywood and other supplies are indicators that citizens know how to be ready.

And the Federal Emergency Management Agency knows how to be ready as well. They have helped thousands of Floridians recover from Charley and Frances by strategically pre-positioning disaster supplies so they could reach affected areas faster.

Along with local authorities in Florida—and volunteers from around the country—they have done a remarkable job—and the people of Florida are grateful for their efforts. The spirit embodied by FEMA workers is not unusual to the men and women of the Department of Homeland Security. We work together with countless partners every day to ensure that our country is protected.

I've focused today on the President's actions to strengthen and unify our intelligence efforts. However, there is a whole breadth of issues that are covered by the findings and recommendations of the Commission—which are both indicative of, yet also insufficient to capture, the full scope of this Department and our mission.

We have pulled together 22 agencies and 180,000 employees into a unified Department whose mission is to secure the homeland.

We are operating as a single unit—one team, one fight. Yet long term integration takes time—and we are daily challenged to ensure strong internal organization, as we continue to build bridges with all of our partners.

As we continue to evolve into a more agile agency, we look forward to continuing our close working relationship with Congress. I appreciate—and value—the mechanism for Congressional oversight laid out in the Constitution.

This Committee faces the important work of building upon the President's initiatives to strengthen and improve our intelligence capabilities. I commend your efforts in this area—and in examining and assessing the important work of the September 11th Commission. We, at DHS, look forward to working with this Committee, and with the Congress as a whole, in this important endeavor.

After all, working together is the only way we can accomplish our goals—and no doubt, those goals are the same—preserve our freedoms, protect America and secure our homeland.

I've said it many times, but it is no less true in this chamber—homeland security is about the integration of a nation.

It's about the integration of our national efforts, not one department or one organization, but everyone tasked with our nation's protection. Indeed, everyone must be pledged to freedom's cause, because everyone is its beneficiary and, thus, everyone its ultimate protector.

In the end, we are all united in our determination to defeat our terrorist enemies and secure our nation for this and future generations. . . .

Michael Crowley NO

Playing Defense: Bush's Disastrous Homeland Security Department

Last December, I called the Department of Homeland Security's (DHS) main line. "Thank you for your interest in the Department of Homeland Security," a recorded voice responded. "Due to the high level of interest in the department all lines are currently busy. . . . We encourage you to call back soon." A beep was followed by a click. It was a good thing I wasn't calling to report an anthrax attack. . . .

Unanswered phones are a small but telling example of how DHS is faring one year after the department opened its doors last March. Far from being greater than the sum of its parts, DHS is a bureaucratic Frankenstein, with clumsily stitched-together limbs and an inadequate, misfiring brain. No one says merging 170,000 employees from 22 different agencies should have been easy. But, even allowing for inevitable transition problems, DHS has been a disaster: underfunded, undermanned, disorganized, and unforgivably slow-moving.

And, yet, George W. Bush can't stop praising it. . . . In a September 11 anniversary address at Quantico, Virginia, Bush mentioned DHS no less than twelve times, saying, "Secretary [Tom] Ridge and his team have done a fine job in getting the difficult work of organizing the department [sic]." And, at an event celebrating the department's one-year anniversary this week, Bush declared that the department had "accomplished an historic task," and that Ridge has done a "fantastic job" of making the United States safer.

That's nonsense. DHS has failed to address some of our most serious vulnerabilities, from centralizing intelligence to protecting critical infrastructure to organizing against bioterror. Many a policy wonk who has evaluated the department has come away despondent. Zoe Lofgren, a senior Democrat on two House committees that oversee DHS, puts it this way: "We are arguably in worse shape than we were before [the creation of the department]. . . . If the American people knew how little has been done, they would be outraged."

⋅⟨◉⟩⋅

If the September 11 attacks provided one essential lesson about the federal bureaucracy, it is that rival agencies need to better share intelligence so they can "connect the dots" and more quickly track down suspected terrorists. Improving intelligence coordination was a fundamental rationale for creating DHS, and so the bill establishing the department also gave birth to a brand new government office, the directorate of Information Analysis and Infrastructure Protection (IAIP). IAIP was designed to receive vast amounts of both raw and analyzed data from intelligence agencies like the CIA and FBI, allowing DHS analysts to search for patterns that individual agencies might have missed. Bush called this one of DHS's "primary tasks": "to review intelligence and law enforcement information from all agencies of government and produce a single daily picture of threats against our homeland."

But, even before DHS opened its doors, Bush dramatically undermined the IAIP—and, by extension, the entire department. Without consulting Congress— or telling the IAIP's planning staff—he announced the creation of the Terrorist Threat Integration Center (TTIC), a quasi-independent agency that would assume most of the intelligence powers originally intended for the new department. Now TTIC, and not DHS, would become the clearinghouse of anti-terror intelligence. The decision not only eliminated the chief rationale for IAIP's existence; it exacerbated a problem the new agency had been created to improve. That is, rather than cutting through bureaucratic turf battles, TTIC may have complicated them further. Staffed by officials from a variety of existing intelligence agencies, TTIC is housed in the CIA's offices in Langley, Virginia, and its director reports to CIA Director George Tenet. Explained a former administration anti-terror official, "Tenet said the CIA is not going to give up its responsibility on threat-reporting and threat analysis. He put a mark in the sand and said, 'No way am I going to give this up to a new organization [DHS] . . .'".

But TTIC has only further confused the interagency intelligence picture, according to a recent report on homeland security information-sharing by the Markle Foundation. "TTIC's creation has caused confusion among state and local entities, and within the federal government itself, about the respective roles of the TTIC and DHS," explained the report, which was overseen by former Aetna executive Zoe Baird and former Netscape CEO James Barksdale. "This confusion needs to be resolved." Even the agency's deputy director, Russell Travers, conceded as much in testimony to the 9/11 Commission in January: "There is a degree of ambiguity between our mission and some other analytic organizations within the government." Internally, TTIC analysts— who tend to be junior and inexperienced—still need permission from intelligence agencies before sharing their data with other parts of the government. The Markle report says that approach "further locks the government into a system that has proven unsuccessful for the sharing of information in the past." Perhaps worst of all, there's no requirement that other intelligence agencies share with TTIC at all. "The original idea [behind DHS] was that a fusion center doesn't allow anyone to make decisions about what flows into it. The analysts are there to look and decide," says a Senate Democratic aide. So much for that idea.

Then again, it's not clear why anyone would trust DHS with something as important as raw intelligence. Consider the story of Paul Redmond, IAIP's first director. Although most of IAIP's intelligence-analysis duties have been given to TTIC, it is still responsible for finding and fixing vulnerabilities in the nation's infrastructure. However, when Redmond appeared before a House subcommittee last June, it was clear that IAIP couldn't handle even this task. Redmond reported that, three months after DHS had begun operations, IAIP had filled just one-quarter of its analyst slots, "because we do not have the [office] space for them." Committee members of both parties were appalled. "Why should I feel comfortable today, Mister Redmond?" asked Republican Representative Chris Shays. "Why should I feel that we made a good decision [about creating IAIP]? . . . Do you feel that, given the incredible importance of your office, that that's a pretty surprising statement to make before this committee?" Apparently, Redmond's performance didn't go over well with the Bush administration, either. Soon after, he quietly announced his resignation for "health reasons."

Redmond was only running IAIP to begin with because the best man for the job had been passed over. That man was John Gannon, formerly a top official at the CIA. Gannon had run IAIP's transition team and was expected to become its director. "If there was anyone in government qualified to do that job, he was the guy," says a person familiar with the IAIP. But the administration didn't turn to Gannon—some suspect because he was a Clinton appointee. Unfortunately, the Pentagon official who was the administration's first choice to fill the position said no. So did the next candidate. And the next. In all, more than 15 people turned down entreaties that they apply for the job, according to *The Washington Post*. "When [the administration] finally realized there was nobody but Gannon to offer the job [to, Gannon] was so pissed off he went elsewhere," says Rand Beers, a former administration counterterrorism official now advising John Kerry. (Gannon is now staff director of the House Homeland Security Committee.)

The story illustrates the trouble the administration has had bringing top-flight talent to DHS. "They definitely were not attracting the superstars," says a former administration national security official. "I often felt like I was dealing with the B team or even the C team. You can chalk that up to growing pains, . . . [but] it doesn't leave you that comforted." For instance, although several agents from an existing FBI critical infrastructure protection office were expected to make the leap to DHS, virtually none were willing to do so. "A lot of agents said, 'Why would I go *there*?'" reports one former administration official. "[I]ntelligence professionals have been much more willing to go to the CIA or Departments of Justice, Defense, or State," reported the Gilmore Commission, a group of homeland security experts assembled by Congress and charged with periodically reviewing U.S. defenses against terrorism. . . .

Meanwhile, DHS's leadership has already suffered a slew of defections. Within six months, several key officials who helped launch the new department were gone—including Ridge's chief of staff, Bruce Lawlor, and deputy secretary, Gordon England, both of whom left on rocky terms. The department's chief financial officer, Bruce Carnes, also departed in December. Such defections have further stalled the department's progress. "A lot of time has been lost because the department's management hasn't been tip-top," says a Senate Democratic aide.

And, in case you were wondering, the search for someone to run IAIP settled on a former Marine Corps general named Frank Libutti. But Libutti, while an experienced soldier, lacks any intelligence background. And his pile-driving, military style isn't winning many converts. . . .

❦

It's not just the department's weak leadership that's causing problems. DHS has also been hamstrung by the forced assimilation of rival agencies. "[M]any of the agencies and employees subsumed by the integration continue to have no identity with or 'buy-in' to their parent organization," the Gilmore Commission warns. Nowhere is this more true than in DHS's new Border and Transportation Security (BTS) directorate, which combined the Immigration and Naturalization Service (INS) with the old Customs Service. The basic idea made sense: INS and Customs had lots of overlapping duties. And, for years, INS had been a reform-resistant organizational disaster. But combining the two has pleased neither agency. Customs officials complain they were forced to incorporate many of the INS's worst management elements into their relatively efficient culture, especially at the Immigrations and Customs Enforcement agency (ICE), which is BTS's investigative arm. "The INS has not been abolished," says a mid-level ICE worker in a Northeastern city. "It's alive and well, and running ICE." Customs had a good computer system but was forced to inherit INS's notoriously "horrible" one, this worker complains. He adds that the INS-based system in his office is so baffling that he needs a new staffer "basically full-time to operate [it]." Some Customs officials have even had to revert to pen and paper for record-keeping.

Of course, former INS workers see it differently. "Basically, [Customs officials] are saying, . . . '[N]ow you live in our house and you're going to play by our rules,'" says Michael Knowles, a union representative for former INS workers at the American Federation of Government Employees. . . .

The squabbling has fostered resentment toward the Bush administration. "Some of the people up there writing the law didn't have any clue what was happening on the ground," the ICE worker fumes. "They pushed these agencies together so fast that there was very little opportunity for these guys to figure out how to make things work." And it may be affecting job performance. In a November letter to the Senate Judiciary Committee, Allen Martin, an ICE official who is head of the Customs Investigators Association, warned that "[m]orale in the field is at an all-time low. There is a real lack of identity, mission focus, and direction."

In some cases, however, dueling government agencies were never merged in the first place—even though Bush had explained that "ending duplication and overlap" would save money and coordinate anti-terror efforts. Take the array of offices within DHS that manage grants and training for local first responders.

The White House had initially intended to combine programs run by the Federal Emergency Management Agency and the Department of Justice's Office of Domestic Preparedness (ODP). But, after protests from both agencies—and members of Congress who have come to love ODP as a useful pork-delivery mechanism—they were kept separate. (Instead of being merged into DHS's Emergency Response and Preparedness directorate, ODP was nonsensically stashed in the department's border-security division.) "The current structure suffers from a duplication of preparedness efforts and a lack of coordination among relevant entities," the Gilmore Commission found—another way of saying, "What a mess." "They have created a completely illogical system," says Seth Jones of the RAND Corporation, who helped to write the Gilmore report. "The point is that not all the decisions about how to build the department were done logically. There are some pretty clear structural issues."

Poor planning has led to confusion throughout DHS. "There are some people over there who still don't know what's going on," says a state homeland security policy expert. "It's not that they're not smart. They literally don't know where they fit in." One official I spoke to recently wasn't sure of the current name of her office. Bio-expert Tara O'Toole says such disorder has very real consequences. "I don't know who's in charge of biodefense for the United States. And, given that I do this all the time," she says, "that's very alarming to me."

⋅⟨◉⟩⋅

B-grade talent and organizational confusion would be less of a problem if the department were showing better results. But, so far, there's been little progress. In many areas it seems that, in the race against the terrorists, DHS is wearing boots of lead.

Take the department's failure to create a consolidated terrorist "watch list." When it was discovered that the CIA had been watching two of the eventual September 11 hijackers as early as 2000 but never notified other agencies that might have stopped their entry into the United States, no task became more urgent than combining the government's twelve separate rosters of suspected terrorists. Outside experts, including the Markle task force, said that merging the watch lists could take as little as six to twelve months. The task initially fell to DHS, which claimed last year to be making progress. "I think we're fairly close to finalizing the consolidation itself," Ridge told a Senate committee last April. Five months later, a DHS press release assured that all federal agents would soon be working "off the same unified, comprehensive set of anti-terrorist information." Six months later, the lists are still not merged—and responsibility for the job has been transferred from Ridge's hapless department to the FBI.

Indeed, information-sharing among government agencies remains hamstrung. Unifying computers and sharing data is inherently complex, and the Bush administration has given DHS few resources for such a massive task. Insufficient funding for new employees at DHS—whose leadership the White House has kept skeletal for fear of growing the bureaucracy—has left the department's information-technology (I.T.) offices badly undermanned, slowing the process of interfacing government computers. For instance, in the office of Chief Information Officer Steve Cooper, "[I]f two people go out to lunch, there's no one to answer the phones," says James Carafano, a homeland security specialist at the Heritage Foundation. Nor does Cooper seem to have the kind of decisive authority his job requires. Last year, for instance, the department issued a $500 million I.T. purchase agreement that he tried, unsuccessfully, to block. "What's the point of having a CIO if he is not given budget control over the department's I.T.?" asked one private sector tech CEO at a House hearing last fall. Adding to the indignity, when a House subcommittee recently ranked the cybersecurity of various federal departments and agencies, DHS finished with the lowest score and a failing grade.

More serious is the flow of information between DHS and state and local governments. In an address last week commemorating the department's one-year anniversary, Ridge bragged that DHS has "created a powerful and constant two-way flow of information." But the Markle Foundation saw things differently. "The sharing of terrorist related information between relevant agencies at different levels of government has only been marginally improved in the last year" and is "ad hoc and sporadic at best," the report found. Last week, Ridge unveiled a new high-tech system that will connect DHS with state and local agencies and ameliorate the communication problem. But, from Ridge's description, it sounds mainly like he has discovered WiFi. "We'll be able to send photos and maps, even streaming video," Ridge bragged. "We'll even be able to access data at the scene of a crime . . . through wireless laptops." Alas, it's not clear that the system Ridge so breathlessly described is a solution. The real problems with info-sharing involve a lack of guidelines for classifying data, deciding who gets to see it, and teaching local officials proper analytical skills. The new system is "a step in the right direction," Carafano allows. "But there's a long way to go."

DHS is also having trouble holding its own against other government agencies, falling prey to the very sort of bureaucratic sumo wrestling it was supposed to supercede. For instance, last May Ridge signed an agreement with Attorney General John Ashcroft ceding most control over terrorism-financing investigations to the Department of Justice, even though former Customs officials, now at ICE, had traditionally had that job and wanted to keep it. ICE workers were dismayed at Ridge's decision, and, according to one department official, felt his inexperienced staff had been outmaneuvered by wilier FBI and Justice Department officials.

The Department of Defense (DOD) has also toyed with DHS. The Pentagon has reportedly been territorial about encroachments onto its own homeland defense functions, willing to share only unglamorous duties it never wanted in the first place—such as anti-drug-trafficking responsibilities. The Pentagon is "punting stuff they don't really want" to the new department, says a DHS official. Otherwise, says a congressional aide, "DOD just ignores them." A lack of respect for DHS's authority may help explain the delay in efforts like unifying terrorist watch lists. "Ridge can't bang heads outside the department," says Rob Atkinson, vice president of the Progressive Policy Institute.

But that wouldn't explain the department's failure to begin securing the nation's infrastructure. Assessing the nation's thousands of vulnerable industrial sites, railways, electric grids, and so on is supposed to be central to the DHS mission. But 30 months after September 11, almost nothing has been done. Last year, an impatient Congress asked DHS to produce a plan for its nationwide risk assessment—not the actual assessment, just a plan for devising it—by December 15, 2003. The deadline came and went. Two days later, the White House quietly issued a directive giving DHS an entire year to develop a "plan" explaining its "strategy" for how to examine infrastructure. An actual infrastructure analysis, one DHS official told Congress last fall, could take five years. No one says it is easy to inventory the vulnerabilities of all 50 states. But DHS looks curiously slow when you consider that, by last summer, a George Mason University graduate student had used publicly available data to map every commercial and industrial sector in the country, complete with their fiber-optic network connections. And, as DHS struggles with devising an infrastructure-assessment plan, it is doing nothing to oversee critical facilities, like the hundreds of chemical plants nationwide—most of which still have little or no security.

⋞◈⋟

It's tempting to blame Tom Ridge for his department's shortfalls. Certainly, he has been a flawed spokesman. At a town-hall meeting in a Washington, D.C., suburb this week, Ridge admitted that most Americans still don't know what to do in the event of an attack. "A massive public education campaign needs to take place before an incident occurs," Ridge said—a strange assertion from someone who has had two years to conduct one (remember, Ridge was director of the White House Office of Homeland Security before he became DHS secretary last January). Then again, Ridge's prior communication efforts have left something to be desired. Everyone seems to hate his department's color-coded alert system, which Congress is determined to revamp. When the department's public-information website, Ready.gov, was unveiled a year ago, it was filled with useless and even misleading information (among other things, it vastly overstated the destructive power of a dirty bomb). And then, of course, there was Ridge's advice about buying duct tape last February, which touched off a semi-panicked rush to hardware stores and made Ridge a laughingstock on late-night television. (DHS's press office did not respond to my request to interview Ridge and other officials.)

Of course, Tom Ridge can only be as effective as the White House makes him. And, so far, Bush hasn't given Ridge the money or authority to match his "urgent and overriding mission." One indicator is the department's frugal budget. Last month, the White House unveiled a $40 billion budget for DHS, which it touted as a 10 percent spending increase from the previous year. But that figure is hardly as generous as it seems. More than half the new spending will go to tax incentives for pharmaceutical companies to develop new vaccines. In other words, there's very little new money for beefing up the department's shoddy management. Indeed, Bush's budget *cuts* several vital DHS projects, such as funding for local first responders, border patrol, and federal air marshals.

Homeland security experts say this parsimony reflects a lack of White House commitment to the new department. "The reality of Washington is that, if you have a new organization and there's not leadership from the top saying, 'You need to take on this role, and you have my authority behind you,' it's just not going to happen," says one person who helped produce the Markle report. "I think what is lacking now, for whatever reason, is White House muscle and leadership. There's just been no sustained attention." Adds a person who worked on the Gilmore Commission report: "Unless the president says, 'OK, Mister Secretary of Defense, Mister CIA Director, Mister Attorney General: You all get your little shits together, or you're gonna be on the street,' [DHS] is going to be marginalized."

Ultimately, perhaps we shouldn't be surprised. The president, after all, never wanted this department in the first place. The original idea came from Joe Lieberman—and Bush only embraced it when it looked like Lieberman's plan might pass without his support. But Bush certainly does like using DHS as a rhetorical weapon. His 2002 battle with Senate Democrats over union provisions in the DHS bill—during which he said the bill's opponents were "more interested in special interests in Washington and not interested in the security of the American people"—helped Republicans win back the Senate that November. No doubt Bush will be telling voters this fall that it was he who championed the department, implying that a Democrat couldn't be trusted to run it.

Bush may have inadvertently revealed his real motives a day after calling for the new department in June of 2002. Sitting in the Cabinet Room of the White House, flanked by his GOP allies, Bush declared that the new department would "enable all of us to tell the American people that we're doing everything in our power to protect the homeland." In the case of the Department of Homeland Security, Bush seems to prefer the telling to the doing.

POSTSCRIPT

Has the Department of Homeland Security Been a Success?

The DHS suffered an important setback when President Bush's nominee to succeed Tom Ridge, New York Police Commissioner Bernard Kerik, had to withdraw his nomination after news accounts revealed numerous improprieties in Kerik's professional and personal life. The new nominee to be DHS Secretary, Michael Chertoff, a primary author of the U.S.A. Patriot act, is widely regarded as a brilliant prosecutor and has the bureaucratic experience in Washington that Kerik lacked. Chertoff lacks operational experience in the agencies that comprise DHS, however, and in comparison to Ridge he does not enter office with a high political profile or with the strong public and Congressional momentum that Ridge had from the creation of DHS. This does not mean that Chertoff cannot rise to the task of standing up to powerful departments and interest groups, but it does make these challenges even more difficult than they were for Secretary Ridge. Two early tests for Chertoff are whether he can be more successful than Ridge at improving screening of air cargo, only 5 percent of which is currently screened because of the airlines' reluctance to take on the added expense involved, and in improving the security of chemical plants and storage facilities, which are vulnerable to attacks that could cause tens of thousands of casualties but which have successfully lobbied against tougher regulation.

For more on the issue of homeland security, see the DHS Web site at www.dhs.gov. For a critique of DHS, see Stephen Flynn, *America the Vulnerable: How Our Government Is Failing to Protect Us from Terrorism*. Other relevant sources include Graham Allison, *Nuclear Terrorism: The Ultimate Preventable Catastrophe*, which focuses on the problem of nuclear weapons that might be stolen by or sold to terrorists; Richard A. Clarke, *Against All Enemies: Inside America's War on Terror*, which details efforts in the Clinton administration and George W. Bush's first administration in fighting terrorism from the perspective of a top national security council staff person on terrorism issues; and the *9/11 Commission Report*.

ISSUE 14

Does Domestic Spying Help the United States?

YES: Charles Krauthammer, from "How Do You Think We Catch the Bad Guys?" *Time* (January 9, 2006)

NO: Bob Barr, from "Presidential Snooping Damages the Nation," *Time* (January 9, 2006)

ISSUE SUMMARY

YES: Charles Krauthammer, *Washington Post* opinion columnist, argues that domestic spying and tough interrogation techniques are an important part of the United States' counterterrorism policy and that their use helps to explain why the terrorists have not successfully hit the United States since 9/11/2001.

NO: Bob Barr, member of the House of Representatives from Georgia from 1995–2003, argues that President Bush's directive for the National Security Agency to spy on domestic citizens represents an abuse of presidential power and is contrary to the express and implied requirements of federal law as specified by the Fourth Amendment freedoms of the Constitution.

The president and the U.S. Congress acted quickly in the aftermath of the terrorist attacks on 9/11/2001 to reinforce national security. An article in the *New York Times* in December of 2005 made it known that part of these efforts included an executive order from President Bush authorizing the National Security Agency (NSA) to monitor certain phone calls made by U.S. citizens without the court oversight specified in the 1978 Foreign Intelligence Surveillance Act (FISA).

Supporters of what has become known as "warrantless wiretapping" argue that the oversight specified in FISA did not give the president sufficient speed and agility to respond to a potential terrorist threat. They further argue that the Congressional Joint Authorization for the Use of Military Force of September 18, 2001 and Article Two of the U.S. Constitution both give President Bush the necessary authority to authorize the NSA surveillance program.

Critics contend that the president's assertion of inherent powers under Article Two of the Constitution is suspect, but more importantly, that warrantless wiretapping violates the Fourth Amendment right of U.S. citizens to be secure against unreasonable searches and seizures. Consequently, it is a direct violation of personal liberties and freedoms. Furthermore, the president's actions represented an excessive assertion of Executive authority, which undermines the separation of powers. Specifically, they maintain that Congressional Joint Authorization for the Use of Military Force did not authorize the warrantless domestic wiretapping of U.S. citizens. In addition, prior to the public release of the program's existence, the president had failed to notify congressional intelligence committees of this program as required by the National Security Act of 1947.

In response to the critics, supporters have argued that the publication and release of classified information about the program was, itself, likely illegal and that the leaking of this information may have undermined the program's effectiveness and put the American people at risk.

Charles Krauthammer argues in favor of the NSA surveillance programs, asserting that the enhanced security they have provided—as indicated by the lack of additional terrorist attacks within the United States since 9/11—justifies concerns about "civil liberties, violating the constitution, [and] jeopardizing the very idea of freedom." In contrast, Bob Barr argues this action represents a "breathtaking assertion of presidential power" and a challenge to personal freedoms that could escalate to the surveillance of "every aspect of our lives."

YES

Charles Krauthammer

How Do You Think We Catch the Bad Guys?

Recent revelations about the actions of the Bush Administration in the war on terror have given it the image of a cross between Big Brother and Torquemada. Most recently comes the story of the National Security Agency (NSA) intercepting and monitoring communications from overseas to al-Qaeda operatives in the U.S. This followed reports of "black sites" in Eastern Europe and elsewhere, where high-level al-Qaeda operatives were kept incommunicado and under stress in conditions well below even Motel 6 standards. Which followed reports of various "coercive interrogation" techniques (most notoriously, water boarding, or mock drowning) used to get information out of the likes of Khalid Sheikh Mohammed, architect of the 9/11 attacks.

This has all been variously portrayed as trampling on civil liberties, violating the Constitution, jeopardizing the very idea of freedom and otherwise destroying all that is sacred in America. Well, that's one way to look at it. But there's another way to look at it—as a triumph of counterterrorism, the beginning of the answer to the question that for the past four-plus years has been on everyone's mind but that no one could figure out: Why haven't we been hit again?

On Sept. 12, 2001, there wasn't a person in Washington who did not think that it was only a matter of days or weeks or at most months before the jihadists would strike again. It has been more than four years. Al-Qaeda knows its inability to repeat 9/11 is a blow to its prestige and pretensions of leading a global jihad. Anyone can put a bomb in a Bali discothèque. But in more than four years, al-Qaeda has not been able to do anything in America even on the scale of Madrid or London.

Why? It turns out there were people who knew the answer but couldn't say, lest they blow the secret programs that were behind our current interval of safety. But now that the programs are blown, the Administration should stop being defensive about its secret prisons and intercepted communications. It should step forward and say, "O.K. You got us. We didn't want to talk about this stuff openly, but now you know. We have not been hit again because we've been capturing high-level operatives and getting them to talk in secret prisons, where they're incommunicado and disoriented and desperate. We've been using interrogation techniques that will probably be outlawed by John McCain but have got us important information.

"How do you think we caught Jose Padilla, who was sent to the U.S. to explode a dirty bomb and spread radiation throughout an American city? He was sent by a couple of captured al-Qaeda big shots, Abu Zubaydah and Khalid Sheik Mohammed, whom we interrogated using techniques that Senators have ostentatiously decried and that sparked the McCain amendment. You connect the dots. And then there were the two attacks thwarted by the NSA eavesdropping: a plot to bring down the Brooklyn Bridge and a plot to bomb pubs and train stations in Britain. Historians will have to tell you about the other plots that were stopped. But the former NSA director already said that 'this program has been successful in detecting and preventing attacks inside the United States.'"

So now we know. What we already knew, to explain the absence of a second 9/11, was the offense part, not the defense. We knew about the war in Afghanistan, which had scattered al-Qaeda and degraded its capacities. We knew about the war in Iraq, which has become a magnet worldwide for jihadists, diverting energy to that front from the American front. But the defensive part, gathering critical preventive intelligence through all kinds of techniques—savory, unsavory, high tech and clandestine—had not been known.

Now we know. In this light, let's have the debate. Have we gone too far? Do we want to back off? It is interesting that the Democrats, who have been braying about presidential arrogance, law breaking and even possible impeachment over the NSA spying, dare not suggest that the program be abolished.

Why? Because, according to a Rasmussen poll, 64% of Americans, a free and very sensible people, support eavesdropping on calls between suspected terrorists abroad and people in the U.S. Because even Democrats know that the once clandestine activities they denounce so floridly are the once obscure answer to the question everyone has been asking: How did Bush keep us safe?

Bob Barr

NO

Presidential Snooping Damages the Nation

Back in the 1930s, when confronted with clear evidence he had violated the law, Georgia's then agriculture commissioner and gubernatorial candidate Eugene Talmadge popped his bright red suspenders and dared those accusing him of corruption to do something about it, declaring, "Sure, I stole, but I stole for you." He was elected Governor in 1932. Accused of breaking the law in the current debate over electronic spying, President George W. Bush has, in his own way, dared the American people to do something about it. For the sake of our Constitution, I hope they will.

Let's focus briefly on what the President has done here. Exactly like Nixon before him, Bush has ordered the National Security Agency (NSA) to conduct electronic snooping on communications of various people, including U.S. citizens. That action is unequivocally contrary to the express and implied requirements of federal law that such surveillance of U.S. persons inside the U.S. (regardless of whether their communications are going abroad) must be preceded by a court order. General Michael Hayden, a former director of the NSA and now second in command at the new Directorate of National Intelligence, testified to precisely that point at a congressional hearing in April 2000. In response, the President and his defenders have fallen back on the same rationale used by Nixon, saying essentially, "I am the Commander in Chief; I am responsible for the security of this country; the people expect me to do this; and I am going to do it." But the Supreme Court slapped Nixon's hands when he made the same point in 1972. And it slapped Bush's hands when, after 9/11, he asserted authority to indefinitely detain those he unilaterally deemed "enemy combatants"—without any court access.

Bush's advocates also argue that the congressional resolution authorizing military force in Afghanistan and elsewhere—to bring to justice those responsible for the 9/11 attacks—authorized those no-warrant wiretaps. But there is absolutely nothing in the clear language of that resolution or in its legislative history suggesting that it was intended to override specific federal laws governing electronic surveillance. If Bush succeeds in establishing this as a precedent, he will have accomplished a breathtaking expansion of unilateral Executive power that could be easily applied to virtually any other area of domestic activity as long as a link to national security is asserted.

Finally, presidential defenders have argued that efficiency demands bypassing the courts. There again, the clear language of the law does them in. Even pre–Patriot Act law provided a very robust mechanism through which a President, facing what he believes is such an emergency that the short time needed to secure court approval for a wiretap would obviate the need for one, can order a tap without prior court approval as long as he eventually gets an O.K. within three days. If that degree of flexibility does not suit a President, it is hard to imagine what provision would. And if the President thought the law governing eavesdropping was misguided or impractical, he should have proposed amendments.

The Supreme Court has unanimously rejected the assertion that a President may conduct electronic surveillance without judicial approval for national security, noting in 1972 that our "Fourth Amendment freedoms cannot properly be guaranteed if domestic security surveillances may be conducted solely within the discretion of the Executive Branch." Rather than abiding such a clear missive, the Administration instead is taking the road mapped out nearly two centuries ago by Andrew Jackson, who, in response to a Supreme Court decision he didn't like, ignored it and is said to have declared, "The Supreme Court has made its decision. Now let them enforce it."

Alleged associates of al-Qaeda are today's targets of that breathtaking assertion of presidential power. Tomorrow, it may be your phone calls or e-mails that will be swept up into our electronic infrastructure and secretly kept in a growing file attached to your name. Then everyone you contact could become a suspect, a link in an ever lengthening chain that would ensnare us all in the files of the largest database ever created through unlimited electronic spying that touches every aspect of our lives.

POSTSCRIPT

Does Domestic Spying Help the United States?

The presidential authorization of NSA to conduct domestic surveillance has raised important constitutional issues regarding the second and fourth amendments and the balance of Congressional and Executive authority. It has also brought attention to the issue of national secrecy and the release or publication of classified information, and it has highlighted the tension between fighting the war on terror versus maintaining the personal and political freedoms that Americans hold dear.

The issues involved are summarized well in the Testimony of Anthony Clark Arend, before the Privacy and Civil Liberties Oversight Board (December 5, 2006) and Elizabeth Bazan and Jennifer Elsea, "Presidential Authority to Conduct Warrantless Electronic Surveillance to Gather Foreign Intelligence Information," Congressional Research Service, January 5, 2006, (http://thewall.civiblog. org/rsf/CRS_Jan_5_2006_Bazan_Elsea.html). For a review of the broader issues of balancing civil liberties and security in democratic societies, see Richard Matthew and George Shambaugh, "From National Security to Individual Liberties: The Pendulum of Democratic Responses to Terrorism," *Analyses of Social Issues and Public Policy* vol. 5, no. 1 (2005), pp. 223–233 (http://www.asap-spssi.org/ abstracts/0501matthew2.htm).

ISSUE 15

Is Loosening Immigration Regulations Good for the United States?

YES: George W. Bush, from "Letting the People Who Contribute to Society Stay," *Vital Speeches of the Day* (May 15, 2006)

NO: Mark Krikorian, from "Not So Realistic: Why Some Would-be Immigration Reformers Don't Have the Answer," *National Review* (September 12, 2005)

ISSUE SUMMARY

YES: George W. Bush, president of the United States, argues that the United States can both be a law-abiding country with secure borders and a nation that upholds its tradition of welcoming immigrants.

NO: Mark Krikorian, executive director of the Center for Immigration Studies and a visiting fellow at the Nixon Center, argues that immigration reforms promoting guest workers or amnesty are unrealistic and prone to fraud and paralysis.

The United States of America—along with Canada, Latin America, Australia, and New Zealand—is one of the most multinational societies. Over time, about half of all of the world's immigrants have settled in the United States. Attracted by hopes of democracy, economic opportunity, and the possibility of social mobility through education and hard work, people from Europe, Africa, Asia and the Americas have come to United States. Despite often facing difficulties in adjustment, many stay, raise families, and become part of the cultural fabric of the United States. Over time, the United States has benefitted enormously from the labor, intellect, and entrepreneurship that immigrants have brought with them. Despite these benefits, once groups get settled, new immigrants are often viewed as interlopers competing for social services and threatening jobs by displacing them.

Those who want to restrict immigration argue that legal immigration undermines American jobs by providing a source of cheaper labor, and illegal immigration imposes large costs of public services. The majority of illegal immigrants in the United States are located in the Southwest, with approximately

234

43 percent believed to reside in California alone. To discourage illegal immigration and reduce its social costs, Californian voters enacted Proposition 187 in November 1994, which cut off undocumented aliens from medical and other public services, including education for their children. When he entered office, President George W. Bush took a more moderate view of immigration and promoted the use of temporary worker visas and other strategies for reducing the flow of illegal immigrants while enabling foreigners to work in the United States. This position was supported by large companies, such as Wal-Mart, who argued that immigrants helped address a shortage of low-wage workers.

Since the September 11 attacks, immigration policy has increasingly been embedded within debates about U.S. national security and counterterrorism policy. Those in favor of tighter restrictions argue that at least 15 of the 19 September 11 hijackers should have been denied visas based on the immigration laws of the time. Strategies to keep would-be terrorists out include the creation of a database to track all foreign students called the Student and Exchange Visitor Information System (Sevis) and a U.S. Visitor and Immigration Status Indication Technology System (US Visit) to monitor immigrants. Republican members of the House of Representatives, including Duncan Hunter of California and James Sensenbrenner of Wisconsin, have linked their support for the president's antiterrorism policy to more restrictive immigration reforms—especially tougher standards by the states to issue drivers licenses, tighter rules to grant political asylum, and the completion of the fence on California's border.

Supporters of immigration argue that increased restrictions on immigration since September 11 are already imposing costs on certain sectors of the U.S. economy, especially in higher education and the engineering and high-technology industries. In the long run, denying access to these sectors by the best and the brightest minds from around the world will decrease America's economic competitiveness and reduce its security. Many immigrants into the United States are highly skilled individuals seeking additional training or job opportunities. Once trained, many of these people remain in the United States, enhancing its companies and the strength of its economy. Others return home, taking with them an understanding of U.S. culture and society. During the Cold War, the U.S. Information Agency attracted foreigners seeking university training as a means of exposing future leaders to American culture and ideas. This practice had a profound effect on the economic and political policies pursued throughout Latin America and Asia. Today this practice is restricted to younger students from the Middle East. Beyond imposing financial costs on U.S. universities, restricting access to others seeking an American education undermines the opportunity to expose future foreign leaders to American culture and ideals.

President Bush argues that a temporary worker program would meet the needs of our economy, provide honest immigrants with a way to provide for their families while respecting the law, and promote the American tradition of the melting pot, while maintaining security. In contrast, Mark Krikorian argues that the proposals currently being considered are administratively unrealistic and impractical and, consequently, are likely to generate more rather than less fraud and abuse.

YES ⬋

George W. Bush

Letting the People Who Contribute to Society Stay

Good evening. I've asked for a few minutes of your time to discuss a matter of national importance—the reform of America's immigration system.

The issue of immigration stirs intense emotions, and in recent weeks, Americans have seen those emotions on display. On the streets of major cities, crowds have rallied in support of those in our country illegally. At our southern border, others have organized to stop illegal immigrants from coming in. Across the country, Americans are trying to reconcile these contrasting images. And in Washington, the debate over immigration reform has reached a time of decision. Tonight, I will make it clear where I stand, and where I want to lead our country on this vital issue.

We must begin by recognizing the problems with our immigration system. For decades, the United States has not been in complete control of its borders. As a result, many who want to work in our economy have been able to sneak across our border, and millions have stayed.

Once here, illegal immigrants live in the shadows of our society. Many use forged documents to get jobs, and that makes it difficult for employers to verify that the workers they hire are legal. Illegal immigration puts pressure on public schools and hospitals, it strains state and local budgets, and brings crime to our communities. These are real problems. Yet we must remember that the vast majority of illegal immigrants are decent people who work hard, support their families, practice their faith, and lead responsible lives. They are a part of American life, but they are beyond the reach and protection of American law.

We're a nation of laws, and we must enforce our laws. We're also a nation of immigrants, and we must uphold that tradition, which has strengthened our country in so many ways. These are not contradictory goals. America can be a lawful society and a welcoming society at the same time. We will fix the problems created by illegal immigration, and we will deliver a system that is secure, orderly, and fair. So I support comprehensive immigration reform that will accomplish five clear objectives.

First, the United States must secure its borders. This is a basic responsibility of a sovereign nation. It is also an urgent requirement of our national security. Our objective is straightforward: The border should be open to trade

From *Vital Speeches of the Day*, May 15, 2006. Copyright © 2006 by George W. Bush.

and lawful immigration, and shut to illegal immigrants, as well as criminals, drug dealers, and terrorists.

I was a governor of a state that has a 1,200-mile border with Mexico. So I know how difficult it is to enforce the border, and how important it is. Since I became President, we've increased funding for border security by 66 percent, and expanded the Border Patrol from about 9,000 to 12,000 agents. The men and women of our Border Patrol are doing a fine job in difficult circumstances, and over the past five years, they have apprehended and sent home about six million people entering America illegally.

Despite this progress, we do not yet have full control of the border, and I am determined to change that. Tonight I'm calling on Congress to provide funding for dramatic improvements in manpower and technology at the border. By the end of 2008, we'll increase the number of Border Patrol officers by an additional 6,000. When these new agents are deployed, we'll have more than doubled the size of the Border Patrol during my presidency.

At the same time, we're launching the most technologically advanced border security initiative in American history. We will construct high-tech fences in urban corridors, and build new patrol roads and barriers in rural areas. We'll employ motion sensors, infrared cameras, and unmanned aerial vehicles to prevent illegal crossings. America has the best technology in the world, and we will ensure that the Border Patrol has the technology they need to do their job and secure our border.

Training thousands of new Border Patrol agents and bringing the most advanced technology to the border will take time. Yet the need to secure our border is urgent. So I'm announcing several immediate steps to strengthen border enforcement during this period of transition:

One way to help during this transition is to use the National Guard. So, in coordination with governors, up to 6,000 Guard members will be deployed to our southern border. The Border Patrol will remain in the lead. The Guard will assist the Border Patrol by operating surveillance systems, analyzing intelligence, installing fences and vehicle barriers, building patrol roads, and providing training. Guard units will not be involved in direct law enforcement activities—that duty will be done by the Border Patrol. This initial commitment of Guard members would last for a period of one year. After that, the number of Guard forces will be reduced as new Border Patrol agents and new technologies come online. It is important for Americans to know that we have enough Guard forces to win the war on terror, to respond to natural disasters, and to help secure our border.

The United States is not going to militarize the southern border. Mexico is our neighbor, and our friend. We will continue to work cooperatively to improve security on both sides of the border, to confront common problems like drug trafficking and crime, and to reduce illegal immigration.

Another way to help during this period of transition is through state and local law enforcement in our border communities. So we'll increase federal funding for state and local authorities assisting the Border Patrol on targeted enforcement missions. We will give state and local authorities the specialized training they need to help federal officers apprehend and detain illegal immigrants. State and local law enforcement officials are an important part of our border security and they need to be a part of our strategy to secure our borders.

The steps I've outlined will improve our ability to catch people entering our country illegally. At the same time, we must ensure that every illegal immigrant we catch crossing our southern border is returned home. More than 85 percent of the illegal immigrants we catch crossing the southern border are Mexicans, and most are sent back home within 24 hours. But when we catch illegal immigrants from other country [sic] it is not as easy to send them home. For many years, the government did not have enough space in our detention facilities to hold them while the legal process unfolded. So most were released back into our society and asked to return for a court date. When the date arrived, the vast majority did not show up. This practice, called "catch and release," is unacceptable, and we will end it.

We're taking several important steps to meet this goal. We've expanded the number of beds in our detention facilities, and we will continue to add more. We've expedited the legal process to cut the average deportation time. And we're making it clear to foreign governments that they must accept back their citizens who violate our immigration laws. As a result of these actions, we've ended "catch and release" for illegal immigrants from some countries. And I will ask Congress for additional funding and legal authority, so we can end "catch and release" at the southern border once and for all. When people know that they'll be caught and sent home if they enter our country illegally, they will be less likely to try to sneak in.

Second, to secure our border, we must create a temporary worker program. The reality is that there are many people on the other side of our border who will do anything to come to America to work and build a better life. They walk across miles of desert in the summer heat, or hide in the back of 18-wheelers to reach our country. This creates enormous pressure on our border that walls and patrols alone will not stop. To secure the border effectively, we must reduce the numbers of people trying to sneak across.

Therefore, I support a temporary worker program that would create a legal path for foreign workers to enter our country in an orderly way, for a limited period of time. This program would match willing foreign workers with willing American employers for jobs Americans are not doing. Every worker who applies for the program would be required to pass criminal background checks. And temporary workers must return to their home country at the conclusion of their stay.

A temporary worker program would meet the needs of our economy, and it would give honest immigrants a way to provide for their families while respecting the law. A temporary worker program would reduce the appeal of human smugglers, and make it less likely that people would risk their lives to cross the border. It would ease the financial burden on state and local governments, by replacing illegal workers with lawful taxpayers. And above all, a temporary worker program would add to our security by making certain we know who is in our country and why they are here.

Third, we need to hold employers to account for the workers they hire. It is against the law to hire someone who is in this country illegally. Yet businesses often cannot verify the legal status of their employees because of the widespread problem of document fraud. Therefore, comprehensive immigration reform must include a better system for verifying documents and work eligibility. A key part of that system should be a new identification card for every legal foreign worker. This card should use biometric technology, such as digital fingerprints, to make it tamper-proof. A tamper-proof card would help us enforce the law, and leave employers with no excuse for violating it. And by making it harder for illegal immigrants to find work in our country, we would discourage people from crossing the border illegally in the first place.

Fourth, we must face the reality that millions of illegal immigrants are here already. They should not be given an automatic path to citizenship. This is amnesty, and I oppose it. Amnesty would be unfair to those who are here lawfully, and it would invite further waves of illegal immigration.

Some in this country argue that the solution is to deport every illegal immigrant, and that any proposal short of this amounts to amnesty. I disagree. It is neither wise, nor realistic to round up millions of people, many with deep roots in the United States, and send them across the border. There is a rational middle ground between granting an automatic path to citizenship for every illegal immigrant, and a program of mass deportation. That middle ground recognizes there are differences between an illegal immigrant who crossed the border recently, and someone who has worked here for many years, and has a home, a family, and an otherwise clean record.

I believe that illegal immigrants who have roots in our country and want to stay should have to pay a meaningful penalty for breaking the law, to pay their taxes, to learn English, and to work in a job for a number of years. People who meet these conditions should be able to apply for citizenship, but approval would not be automatic, and they will have to wait in line behind those who played by the rules and followed the law. What I've just described is not amnesty, it is a way for those who have broken the law to pay their debt to society, and demonstrate the character that makes a good citizen.

Fifth, we must honor the great American tradition of the melting pot, which has made us one nation out of many peoples. The success of our country depends upon helping newcomers assimilate into our society, and embrace our common identity as Americans. Americans are bound together by our shared ideals, an appreciation of our history, respect for the flag we fly, and an ability to speak and write the English language. English is also the key to unlocking the opportunity of America. English allows newcomers to go from picking crops to opening a grocery, from cleaning offices to running offices, from a life of low-paying jobs to a diploma, a career, and a home of their own. When immigrants assimilate and advance in our society, they realize their dreams, they renew our spirit, and they add to the unity of America.

Tonight, I want to speak directly to members of the House and the Senate: An immigration reform bill needs to be comprehensive, because all elements of this problem must be addressed together, or none of them will be solved at all. The House has passed an immigration bill. The Senate should act by the end of this month so we can work out the differences between the two bills, and Congress can pass a comprehensive bill for me to sign into law.

America needs to conduct this debate on immigration in a reasoned and respectful tone. Feelings run deep on this issue, and as we work it out, all of us need to keep some things in mind. We cannot build a unified country by inciting people to anger, or playing on anyone's fears, or exploiting the issue of immigration for political gain. We must always remember that real lives will be affected by our debates and decisions, and that every human being has dignity and value no matter what their citizenship papers say.

I know many of you listening tonight have a parent or a grandparent who came here from another country with dreams of a better life. You know what freedom meant to them, and you know that America is a more hopeful country because of their hard work and sacrifice. As President, I've had the opportunity to meet people of many backgrounds, and hear what America means to them. On a visit to Bethesda Naval Hospital, Laura and I met a wounded Marine named Guadalupe Denogean. Master Gunnery Sergeant Denogean came to the United States from Mexico when he was a boy. He spent his summers picking crops with his family, and then he volunteered for the United States Marine Corps as soon as he was able. During the liberation of Iraq, Master Gunnery Sergeant Denogean was seriously injured. And when asked if he had any requests, he made two: a promotion for the corporal who helped rescue him, and the chance to become an American citizen. And when this brave Marine raised his right hand, and swore an oath to become a citizen of the country he had defended for more than 26 years, I was honored to stand at his side.

We will always be proud to welcome people like Guadalupe Denogean as fellow Americans. Our new immigrants are just what they've always been—people willing to risk everything for the dream of freedom. And America remains what she has always been: the great hope on the horizon, an open door to the future, a blessed and promised land. We honor the heritage of all who come here, no matter where they come from, because we trust in our country's genius for making us all Americans—one nation under God.

Thank you, and good night.

Not So Realistic

The Senate is again considering various proposals to address our massive illegal-alien problem, and the competing bills have one thing in common: They claim to offer "realistic" solutions to the supposedly unrealistic desire to enforce the law. Writer Tamar Jacoby, perhaps the most energetic salesman of the McCain-Kennedy amnesty bill, used some form of "realistic" ten times in her testimony at a July Senate hearing. Senators Kennedy, Cornyn, Brownback, and Feingold all touted the realism of their preferred solutions at the same hearing, and the *New York Times* and *Washington Post* have done the same in numerous editorials.

The problem, of course, is that no one has checked whether our very real immigration bureaucracy is capable of implementing *any* of these proposals. And this is no trivial concern: The success of any proposal depends on registering and screening millions and millions of illegal aliens within a short period of time—a daunting task.

It is therefore necessary to look first at the administrative mandates of the two most popular immigration bills. The McCain-Kennedy bill would offer amnesty to the approximately 11 million illegal aliens in the United States, by re-labeling them "temporary" workers, and after six years, it would grant them permanent residence. The Department of Homeland Security would have to determine that the person was, in fact, an illegal alien on the date of the bill's introduction; that he hadn't left the United States in the meantime; that he was employed in the United States at the time of the bill's introduction—"full time, part time, seasonally, or self-employed"; that he has remained so employed, which he can prove with records from the government, employers, labor unions, banks, remittances, or "sworn affidavits from nonrelatives who have direct knowledge of the alien's work"; that he, if not employed, was a full-time student; that he has "not ordered, incited, assisted, or otherwise participated in the persecution of any person on account of race, religion, nationality, membership in a particular social group, or political opinion"; and that he is not a security threat, a criminal, a polygamist, or a child abductor. This required background check is to be conducted "as expeditiously as possible"—for potentially 11 million people.

Now consider the better of the two major bills before the Senate, the Cornyn-Kyl bill, which has stronger enforcement provisions and isn't quite an

From *The National Review*, September 12, 2005, pp. 38–39. Copyright © 2005 by National Review, Inc, 215 Lexington Avenue, New York, NY 10016. Reprinted by permission.

amnesty. (It instead requires illegals to return home and sign up for its version of a "temporary" worker program from abroad, and there is no permanent-residence offer.)

A central component of the bill is "Deferred Mandatory Departure," which would give illegals who register with the government five years to get their affairs in order and leave, something you might call an "exit amnesty." The bill instructs the immigration service to determine many of the same things that McCain-Kennedy requires, including "the alien's physical and mental health, criminal history and gang membership, immigration history, involvement with groups or individuals that have engaged in terrorism, geno-cide, persecution, or who seek the overthrow of the United States government, voter registration history, claims to United States citizenship, and tax his-tory." And the Cornyn-Kyl bill has even more specific deadlines: All applica-tions are to be processed within one year of its enactment, and at that time the Department of Homeland Security also must have ready a new document for applicants that would be machine-readable, tamper-resistant, and have a biometric-identification component.

The point is not that these requirements are inappropriate; if you're going to be registering illegal aliens, you'd certainly want to know about their health status and involvement with terrorism. But the most pressing question remains: Is it achievable? What would happen, in the real world, if one of these "realistic" solutions were to become law?

Two words: "fraud" and "paralysis."

Will We Ever Learn?

We've attempted much smaller programs like this in the past, and the story has been the same each time: The lack of administrative capacity, combined with intense political pressure, causes the immigration service to drop every-thing else to meet impossible deadlines—and ineligible applicants get through anyway.

The closest parallel is the administration of the 1986 Immigration Reform and Control Act by the old Immigration and Naturalization Service. Some 3 million illegal aliens (out of 5 million total) applied for amnesty, and 90 per-cent were approved. Fraud was omnipresent, especially in the farm-worker portion, where applicants presented fake proof of employment—sometimes as flimsy as a handwritten note on a scrap of paper—and gave ludicrous stories, like, "I've picked watermelons from trees," or "harvested purple cotton."

A report from the inspector general's office of the Department of Justice noted years later that "given the crush of applications under the program and the relative fewer investigative resources, INS approved applications absent explicit proof that they were in fact fraudulent." Two of the fraudulent appli-cations that were approved were from Egyptian brothers in New York: Mahmud and Mohammed Abouhalima, who went on to participate in the first World Trade Center bombing.

We've seen paralysis before, too. On several occasions during the past decade Congress briefly opened a window for illegal aliens to apply for green

NO / Mark Krikorian   243

cards without first returning home (by getting married to a citizen or legal resident, for instance, or by being sponsored by an employer). Hundreds of thousands applied under the program, and INS had to scramble to redirect resources. As a result, the backlog of unresolved cases ballooned to around 6 million in 2003, and wait times at some immigration offices were two years or more—even for relatively straightforward matters.

Unrealistic mandates like these are largely to blame for the backlog of immigration applications, which is now "only" 4.5 million. Since it can't work through these anytime soon, the immigration service often issues work permits and travel documents to many green-card applicants right when they submit their forms, knowing that it will be years before anyone actually reads the application. This is the present situation at the agency that is supposed to carry out extensive, complicated new responsibilities under the proposed immigration bills.

So, if an immigration package anything like McCain-Kennedy or Cornyn-Kyl were to pass, the following would almost assuredly occur: Immigration offices would be deluged by millions of applications that would need to be approved under a tight deadline; harried DHS employees would be forced to put aside their other duties to meet the onslaught; candidates for citizenship—foreign spouses of Americans, refugees, skilled workers sponsored by employers—would effectively be pushed to the back of the line; political pressure would force DHS to cut corners in adjudicating the applications; and huge numbers of ineligible applicants would be approved (in addition to the huge numbers of eligible applicants).

The workload created by any such program would be larger than the annual number of visas currently issued worldwide by the State Department (approximately 5 million), and many times larger than the annual number of green cards issued by DHS (around 1 million). Delays, mistakes, and fraud may not be what the supporters of the immigration bills have in mind, but they are nonetheless the guaranteed outcome. None of this is to pin blame on the bureaucrats charged with implementing congressional mandates. Rather, the proposals themselves are the problem, measures animated by an almost utopian spirit, one that seeks to solve an enormous and long-brewing problem with one swift masterstroke.

Things don't work that way in the real world. Instead, the illegal population needs to be decreased via muscular, across-the-board immigration enforcement over a long term. Rather than wait for a magic solution, we can implement an attrition strategy right now, using available resources. We could, for instance, immediately reject fake Social Security numbers submitted by employers on behalf of new employees (the government currently looks the other way). Or the Treasury Department could instruct banks that the Mexican government's illegal-alien ID card is no longer a valid form of identification. Or a small portion of enforcement resources could be devoted to random raids at day-labor gathering spots. This has an added advantage: As more resources become available—be they monetary or technological—they could easily bolster the attrition approach, as opposed to current proposals, which from the get-go require vast and untested programs.

An attrition strategy would adopt the conservative goal of shrinking the illegal-alien population over time by making it unappealing to be an illegal alien in the first place. As a result, fewer people would come here illegally, and those already here would be more inclined to deport themselves. Over the space of several years, what is now a crisis could be reduced to a manageable nuisance.

Now that's realistic.

POSTSCRIPT

Is Loosening Immigration Regulations Good for the United States?

Within the United States, political debate over immigration reform has often taken place within Congress. Even today, leading members of Congress tend to take a more restrictive stance on immigration than President George W. Bush. James Gimpel and James Edwards provide a good overview of the politics of immigration reform before September 11, 2001. See James G. Gimpel and James R. Edwards, *The Congressional Politics of Immigration Reform* (Allyn and Bacon, 1999), Michael Fix and Jeffrey Passel, "Immigration Debate: Myths About Immigrants," *Foreign Policy* (Summer 1994), James C. Clad, "Immigration Debate: Slowing The Wave," *Foreign Policy* (Summer 1994), and David Techenor, *Dividing Lines: The Politics of Immigration Control in America* (Princeton, 2002). For additional arguments regarding the costs of denying foreign students access to American universities, see Sylvia H. Kless, "We Threaten National Security by Discouraging the Best and Brightest Students From Abroad," *The American Chronicle of Higher Education* (October 8, 2002).

The United States Citizenship and Immigration Services provides online information regarding immigration into this country. See http://uscis.gov/graphics/index.htm. The Center for Immigration Studies provides research and policy analysis of the negative economic, social, demographic, fiscal, and other impacts of immigration on the United States. See http://www.cis.org/.

Internet References . . .

The Council of Economic Advisors and The National Economic Council

The U.S. government has an array of Web sites from which you can gain information about the state of the U.S. economy. Two of the best Web sites are for the Council of Economic Advisors and the National Economic Council. The Council of Economic Advisors is staffed by economists and is responsible for advising the president of the United States on the state of the U.S. economy. Among other material, they generate the annual *Economic Report to the President.* The National Economic Council is staffed by economic and political policy experts. It is responsible for coordinating policy making for domestic and international economic issues, coordinating economic policy advice for the president, ensuring that policy decisions and programs are consistent with the president's economic goals, and monitoring implementation of the president's economic policy agenda.

http://www.whitehouse.gov/cea/

http://www.whitehouse.gov/nec/

World Trade Organization

The World Trade Organization (WTO) is perhaps the most important organization involved in economic globalization. Established by a recent revision of the General Agreement on Tariffs and Trade, the WTO deals with the global rules of trade, services, and a variety of other forms of economic interchange among countries. This site provides extensive information about the organization and international trade today.

http://www.wto.org

Centre for Economic and Social Studies on the Environment

The Centre for Economic and Social Studies on the Environment (CESSE), located in Brussels, Belgium, was created following the 1972 Stockholm conference, which was the first UN conference on the environment. The CESSE conducts multidisciplinary research on the qualitative and quantitative evaluation of economic-environmental interactions. It organizes itself around the goal of "sustainable development," the standard that is at the heart of the global warming conference in Kyoto. Commentary at this site is available in English and French.

http://www.ulb.ac.be/ceese/

U.S. International Economic and Environmental Issues

*M*any *observers believe that the growth of international interdependence among countries was one of the major developments in the latter half of the twentieth century and that this trend will not only continue but strengthen in the twenty-first century. The debates in this unit address several issues involving the global economy, energy, and the Earth's environment that present a challenge to American foreign policymakers.*

- Is Economic Globalization Good for the United States?

- Is Outsourcing Good for the United States?

- Should the United States Fight Climate Change?

- Is It Realistic for the United States to Move toward Greater Energy Interdependence?

ISSUE 16

Is Economic Globalization Good for the United States?

YES: Murray Weidenbaum, from "Globalization Is Not a Dirty Word," *Vital Speeches of the Day* (March 1, 2001)

NO: Robert Kuttner, from "Globalism Bites Back," *The American Prospect* (March/April 1998)

ISSUE SUMMARY

YES: Murray Weidenbaum, the Mallinckrodt Distinguished University Professor of Economics at Washington University in St. Louis, Missouri, asserts that opposition to economic globalization is based largely on 10 dangerous myths.

NO: Robert Kuttner, founder and coeditor of *The American Prospect,* argues that calls for virtually unchecked globalism are naive, and he points out a number of problems that the trend toward globalism has revealed.

One of the important political and economic changes during the twentieth century was the rapid growth of economic globalization (or interdependence) among countries. The impact of international economics on domestic societies has expanded rapidly as world industrial and financial structures have become increasingly intertwined.

This intermeshing of the global economy has numerous and often profound impacts on the lives of everyday people. For example, exports create jobs. The United States is the world's largest exporter, providing other countries with $958.5 billion worth of U.S. goods and services in 1999. Creating these exports required employing some 16 million Americans. However, while exports create jobs, other jobs are lost to imports. The textiles, clothes, toys, electronics, and many other items that Americans buy were once produced extensively in the United States by American workers. Now most of these items are produced overseas by workers whose wages are substantially lower.

Foreign trade also supplies a great deal of the petroleum and other imported resources to fuel cars, homes, and industries. Inexpensive imports into industrialized countries from less economically developed countries also help to keep inflation down and the standard of living up. The cost of some, perhaps most, imported items would be higher if they were made in the United States by American workers earning American wages.

In addition to trade, the trend toward globalization includes factors such as the growth of multinational corporations (MNCs), the flow of international investment capital, and the increased importance of international exchange rates. Americans have over $4 trillion invested in other countries; foreign nationals and companies have over $5 trillion invested in the United States.

The issue here is whether this economic globalization and integration is a positive or negative trend for Americans. For about 60 years, the United States has been at the center of the drive to open international commerce. The push to reduce trade barriers that occurred during and after World War II was designed to prevent a recurrence of the global economic collapse of the 1930s and the war of the 1940s. Policymakers believed that protectionism caused the Great Depression, that the ensuing human desperation had provided fertile ground for the rise of dictators who blamed scapegoats for what had occurred and who promised national salvation, and that these fascist dictators set off World War II. In sum, policymakers thought that protectionism caused economic depression, which caused dictators, which caused war. Free trade, by contrast, would promote prosperity, democracy, and peace.

Based on these political and economic theories, American policymakers took the lead in establishing a new international economic system. As the world's dominant superpower, the United States played the leading role in establishing the International Monetary Fund (IMF), the World Bank, and the General Agreement on Tariffs and Trade (GATT). The latest GATT revision talks were completed and signed by 124 countries (including the United States) in April 1994. Among the outcomes was the establishment of a new coordinating body, the World Trade Organization (WTO).

Recently, the idea that globalization is either inevitable or necessarily beneficial has come under increasing scrutiny and been met with increasing resistance. Some analysts question how widely the benefits are distributed in a society. One complaint is that globalization is used by corporations to abandon American workers by moving operations to less developed countries where the MNCs exploit cheap labor. Besides the negative economic impact on the workers who lose their jobs, the so-called export of jobs raises another issue. That is, what is the morality of buying products manufactured by MNCs in countries where businesses are free to pay workers almost nothing, give them no benefits, and perhaps even use child labor? Is there a benefit if MNCs avoid environmental laws by moving to a country with less strict requirements? If global warming is really a threat, does it make any difference whether the industrial emissions come from the United States or Zimbabwe?

The validity of these and numerous other points are contested in the following selections. In the first, Murray Weidenbaum seeks to dispel what he feels are 10 myths about globalization and to show that the trend has been beneficial to most Americans. In the second, Robert Kuttner contends that what he considers unchecked globalism contains negative aspects that will eventually lead to a strong and destructive reaction of economic nationalism.

YES ↵

Murray Weidenbaum

Globalization Is Not a Dirty Word

Delivered to the Economic Club of Detroit, Detroit, Michigan, January 22, 2001

Today I want to deal with a perplexing conundrum facing the United States: this is a time when the American business system is producing unparalleled levels of prosperity, yet private enterprise is under increasing attack. The critics are an unusual alliance of unions, environmentalists, and human rights groups and they are focusing on the overseas activities of business. In many circles, globalization has become a dirty word.

How can we respond in a constructive way? In my interaction with these interest groups, I find that very often their views arise from basic misunderstandings of the real world of competitive enterprise. I have identified ten myths about the global economy—dangerous myths—which need to be dispelled. Here they are:

1. Globalization costs jobs.
2. The United States is an island of free trade in a world of protectionism.
3. Americans are hurt by imports.
4. U.S. companies are running away, especially to low-cost areas overseas.
5. American companies doing business overseas take advantage of local people, especially in poor countries. They also pollute their environments.
6. The trade deficit is hurting our economy and we should eliminate it.
7. It's not fair to run such large trade deficits with China or Japan.
8. Sanctions work. So do export controls.
9. Trade agreements should be used to raise environmental and labor standards around the world.
10. America's manufacturing base is eroding in the face of unfair global competition.

That's an impressive array of frequently heard charges and they are polluting our political environment. Worse yet, these widely held myths fly in the face of the facts. I'd like to take up each of them and knock them down.

From *Vital Speeches of the Day*, March 1, 2001. Copyright © 2001 by City News Publishing Co. Reprinted by permission.

1. Globalization Costs Jobs

This is a time when the American job miracle is the envy of the rest of the world, so it is hard to take that charge seriously. Yet some people do fall for it. The facts are clear: U.S. employment is at a record high and unemployment is at a 30 year low. Moreover, the United States created more than 20 million new jobs between 1993 and 2000, far more than Western Europe and Japan combined. Contrary to a widely held view, most of those new jobs pay well, often better than the average for existing jobs.

Of course, in the best of times, some people lose their jobs or their businesses fail, and that happens today. However, most researchers who have studied this question conclude that, in the typical case, technological progress, not international trade, is the main reason for making old jobs obsolete. Of course, at the same time far more new jobs are created to take their place.

2. The United States Is an Island of Free Trade in a World of Protectionism

Do other nations erect trade barriers? Of course they do—although the trend has been to cut back these obstacles to commerce. But our hands are not as clean as we like to think. There is no shortage of restrictions on importers trying to ship their products into this country. These exceptions to free trade come in all shapes, sizes, and varieties. They are imposed by federal, state, and local governments. U.S. import barriers include the following and more:

- Buy-American laws give preference in government procurement to domestic producers. Many states and localities show similar favoritism. . . . [T]he Jones Act prohibits foreign ships from engaging in waterborne commerce between U.S. ports;
- many statutes limit the import of specific agricultural and manufactured products, ranging from sugar to pillowcases;
- we impose selective high tariffs on specific items, notably textiles; and many state and local regulatory barriers, such as building codes, are aimed at protecting domestic producers.

It's strange that consumer groups and consumer activists are mute on this subject. After all, it is the American consumer who has to pay higher prices as a result of all of this special interest legislation. But these barriers to trade ultimately are disappointing. Nations open to trade grow faster than those that are closed.

3. Americans Are Hurt by Imports

The myth that imports are bad will be quickly recognized by students of economics as the mercantilist approach discredited by Adam Smith over two centuries ago. The fact is that we benefit from imports in many ways. Consumers get access to a wider array of goods and services. Domestic companies obtain lower cost components and thus are more competitive. We get access to vital metals and minerals that are just not found in the United States. Also, imports prod our own producers to improve productivity and invest in developing new technology.

I'll present a painful example. By the way, I have never bought a foreign car. But we all know how the quality of our domestic autos has improved because of foreign competition. More recently, we had a striking example of the broader benefits to imports. In 1997–98 the expanded flow of lower-cost products from Asia kept inflation low here at a time when otherwise the Fed could have been raising interest rates to fight inflation. The result would have been a weaker economy. Moreover, in a full employment economy, imports enable the American people to enjoy a higher living standard than would be possible if sales were limited to domestic production.

In our interconnected economy, the fact is that the jobs "lost" from imports are quickly replaced by jobs elsewhere in the economy—either in export industries or in companies selling domestically. The facts are fascinating: the sharp run-up in U.S. imports in recent years paralleled the rapid growth in total U.S. employment. Both trends, of course, reflected the underlying health of our business economy.

The special importance of imports was recently highlighted by the director of the Washington State Council on International Trade: "The people who benefit most critically are families at the lower end of the wage scale who have school-age children and those elderly who must live frugally." She goes on to conclude: "It is a cruel deception that an open system of free trade is not good for working people."

4. U.S. Companies Are Running Away Especially to Low Cost Areas Overseas

Right off the bat, the critics have the direction wrong. The flow of money to buy and operate factories and other businesses is overwhelmingly into the United States. We haven't had a net outflow of investment since the 1960s. That's the flip side of our trade deficit. Financing large trade deficits means that far more investment capital comes into this country than is leaving.

But let us examine the overseas investments by American companies. The largest proportion goes not to poor countries, but to the most developed nations, those with high labor costs and also high environmental standards. The primary motive is to gain access to markets. That's not too surprising when we consider that the people in the most industrially advanced nations are the best customers for sophisticated American products. By the way, only one-third of the exports by the foreign branches of U.S. companies goes to the United States. About 70 percent goes to other markets, primarily to the industrialized nations.

Turning to American investments in Mexico, China, and other developing countries, the result often is to enhance U.S. domestic competitiveness and job opportunities. This is so because many of these overseas factories provide low-cost components and material to U.S.-based producers who are thus able to improve their international competitiveness.

In some cases, notably the pharmaceutical industry, the overseas investments are made in countries with more enlightened regulatory regimes, such as the Netherlands. "More enlightened" is not a euphemism for lower standards. The Dutch maintain a strong but more modern regulatory system than we do.

5. American Companies Doing Business Overseas Take Advantage of Local People and Pollute Their Environments

There are always exceptions. But by and large, American-owned and managed factories in foreign countries are top-of-the-line in terms of both better working conditions and higher environmental standards than locally-owned firms. This is why so many developing countries compete enthusiastically for the overseas location of U.S. business activities—and why so many local workers seek jobs at the American factories. After all, American companies manufacturing overseas frequently follow the same high operating standards that they do here at home.

I serve on a panel of Americans who investigate the conditions in some factories in China. I wish the critics could see for themselves the differences between the factories that produce for an American company under its worldwide standards and those that are not subject to our truly enlightened sense of social responsibility.

I'll give you a very personal example of the second category of facilities. While making an inspection tour, I tore my pants on an unguarded piece of equipment in one of those poorly-lit factories. An inch closer and that protruding part would have dug into my thigh. I also had to leave the factory floor every hour or so to breathe some fresh air. When I said that, in contrast, the American-owned factories were top-of-the-line, that wasn't poetry.

Yes, foreign investment is essential to the economic development of poor countries. By definition, they lack the capability to finance growth. The critics do those poor countries no favor when they try to discourage American firms from investing there. The critics forget that, during much of the nineteenth century, European investors financed many of our canals, railroads, steel mills, and other essentials for becoming an industrialized nation. It is sad to think where the United States would be today if Europe in the nineteenth century had had an array of powerful interest groups that were so suspicious of economic progress.

6. The Trade Deficit Is Hurting Our Economy and We Should Eliminate It

Yes, the U.S. trade deficit is at a record high. But it is part of a "virtuous circle" in our economy. The trade deficit mainly reflects the widespread prosperity in the United States, which is substantially greater than in most of the countries we trade with. After all, a strong economy, such as ours, operating so close to full employment and full capacity depends on a substantial amount of imports to satisfy our demands for goods and services. Our exports are lower primarily because the demand for imports by other nations is much weaker.

The acid test is that our trade deficit quickly declines in the years when our economy slows down and that deficit rises again when the economy perks up. Serious studies show that, if the United States had deliberately tried to curb the trade deficit in the 1990s, the result would have been a weak economy with high inflation and fewer jobs. The trade deficit is a byproduct of economic performance. It should not become a goal of economic policy.

There is a constructive way of reducing the trade deficit. To most economists, the persistence of our trade imbalance (and especially of the related and more comprehensive current account deficit) is due to the fact that we do not generate enough domestic saving to finance domestic investment. The gap between such saving and investment is equal to the current account deficit.

Nobel laureate Milton Friedman summed up this point very clearly: "The remarkable performance of the United States economy in the past few years would have been impossible without the inflow of foreign capital, which is a mirror image of large balance of payments deficits."

The positive solution is clear: increase the amount that Americans save. Easier said than done, of course. The shift from budget deficits (dissaving) to budget surpluses (government saving) helps. A further shift to a tax system that does not hit saving as hard as ours does would also help. The United States taxes saving more heavily than any other advanced industrialized nation. Replacing the income tax with a consumption tax, even a progressive one, would surely be in order—but that deserves to be the subject of another talk.

7. It's Not Fair to Run Such Large Trade Deficits With China or Japan

Putting the scary rhetoric aside, there really is no good reason for any two countries to have balanced trade between them. We don't have to search for sinister causes for our trade deficits with China or Japan. Bilateral trade imbalances exist for many benign reasons, such as differences in per capita incomes and in the relative size of the two economies. One of the best kept secrets of international trade is that the average Japanese buys more U.S. goods than the average American buys Japanese goods. Yes, Japan's per capita imports from the United States are larger than our per capita imports from Japan ($539 versus $432 in 1996). We have a large trade deficit with them because we have more "capita" (population).

8. Sanctions Work, So Do Export Controls

It is ironic that so many people who worry about the trade deficit simultaneously support sanctions and export controls. There is practically no evidence that unilateral sanctions are effective in getting other nations to change their policies or actions. Those restrictions on trade do, however, have an impact: they backfire. U.S. business, labor, and agriculture are harmed. We lose an overseas market for what is merely a symbolic gesture. Sanctions often are evaded. Shipping goods through third countries can disguise the ultimate recipient in the nation on which the sanctions are imposed. On balance, these sanctions reduced American exports in 1995 by an estimated $15–20 billion.

As for export controls, where American producers do not have a monopoly on a particular technology—which is frequent—producers in other nations can deliver the same technology or product without the handicap imposed on U.S. companies. A recent report at the Center for the Study of American Business showed that many business executives believe that sanctions and export controls are major obstacles to the expansion of U.S. foreign trade.

9. Trade Agreements Should Be Used to Raise Environmental and Labor Standards Around the World

At first blush, this sounds like such a nice and high-minded way of doing good. But, as a practical matter, it is counterproductive to try to impose such costly social regulations on developing countries as a requirement for doing business with them. The acid test is that most developing nations oppose these trade restrictions. They see them for what they really are—a disguised form of protectionism designed to keep their relatively low-priced goods out of the markets of the more advanced, developed nations. All that feeds the developing nations' sense of cynicism toward us.

In the case of labor standards, there is an existing organization, the International Labor Organization [ILO], which has been set up to deal specifically with these matters. Of all the international organizations, the ILO is unique in having equal representation from business, labor, and government. The United States and most other nations *are* members. The ILO is where issues of labor standards should be handled. To be taken more seriously, the United States should support the ILO more vigorously than it has.

As for environmental matters, we saw at the unsuccessful meetings on climate change at the Hague [recently] how difficult it is to get broad international agreement on environmental issues even in sympathetic meetings of an international environmental agency. To attempt to tie such controversial environmental matters to trade agreements arouses my suspicions about the intent of the sponsors. It is hard to avoid jumping to the conclusion that the basic motivation is to prevent progress on the trade front.

I still recall the sign carried by one of the protesters in Seattle, "Food is for people, not for export." Frankly, it's hard to deal with such an irrational position. After all, if the United States did not export a major part of its abundant farm output, millions of people overseas would be starving or malnourished. Also, thousands of our farmers would go broke.

The most effective way to help developing countries improve their working conditions and environmental protection is to trade with and invest in them. As for the charge that companies invest in poor, developing nations in order to minimize their environmental costs, studies of the issue show that environmental factors are not important influences in business location decisions. As I pointed out earlier, most U.S. overseas direct investment goes to developed nations with high labor costs and also high environmental standards.

10. America's Manufacturing Base Is Eroding in the Face of Unfair Global Competition

Unfortunately, some of our fellow citizens seem to feel that the only fair form of foreign competition is the kind that does not succeed in landing any of their goods on our shores. But to get to the heart of the issue, there is no factual basis for the charge that our manufacturing base is eroding—or even stagnant. The official statistics are reporting record highs in output year after year. Total industrial production in the United States today is 45 percent higher than in 1992—that's not in dollars, but in terms of real output.

Of course, not all industries or companies go up—or down—in unison. Some specific industries, especially low-tech, have had to cut back. But simultaneously, other industries, mainly high-tech, have been expanding rapidly. Such changes are natural and to be expected in an open, dynamic economy. By the way, the United States regularly runs a trade surplus in high-tech products.

It's important to understand the process at work here. Technological progress generates improved industrial productivity. In the United States, that means to some degree fewer blue-collar jobs and more white-collar jobs. That is hardly a recent development. The shift from physical labor to knowledge workers has been the trend since the beginning of the 20th century. On balance, as I noted earlier, total U.S. employment is at an all-time high.

If you have any doubt about the importance of rising productivity to our society, just consider where we would be if over the past century agriculture had not enjoyed rising productivity (that is, more output per worker/hour). Most of us would still be farmers.

It is vital that we correct the erroneous views of the anti-globalists. Contrary to their claims, our open economy has raised living standards and helped to contain inflation. International commerce is more important to our economy today than at any time in the past. By dollar value and volume, the United States is the world's largest trading nation. We are the largest importer, exporter, foreign investor, and host to foreign investment. Trying to stop the global economy is futile and contrary to America's self-interest.

Nevertheless, we must recognize that globalization, like any other major change, generates costs as well as benefits. It is essential to address these consequences. Otherwise, we will not be able to maintain a national consensus that responds to the challenges of the world marketplace by focusing on opening markets instead of closing them. The challenge to all of us is to urge courses of action that help those who are hurt without doing far more harm to the much larger number who benefit from the international marketplace.

We need to focus more attention on those who don't share the benefits of the rapid pace of economic change. Both private and public efforts should be increased to provide more effective adjustment assistance to those who lose their jobs. The focus of adjustment policy should not be on providing relief from economic change, but on positive approaches that help more of our people participate in economic prosperity.

As you may know, I recently chaired a bipartisan commission established by Congress to deal with the trade deficit. Our commission included leaders of business and labor, former senior government officials, and academics. We could not agree on all the issues that we dealt with. But we were unanimous in concluding that the most fundamental part of an effective long-run trade adjustment policy is to do a much better job of educating and training. More Americans should be given the opportunity to become productive and highwage members of the nation's workforce.

No, I'm not building up to a plea to donate to the college of your choice, although that's a pretty good idea.

Even though I teach at major research universities—and strongly believe in their vital mission—let me make a plea for greater attention to our junior colleges. They are an overlooked part of the educational system. Junior colleges have a key role to play. Many of these community oriented institutions of learning are now organized to specially meet the needs of displaced workers, including those who need to brush up on their basic language and math skills. In some cases, these community colleges help people launch new businesses, especially in areas where traditional manufacturing is declining. A better trained and more productive workforce is the key to our long-term international competitiveness. That is the most effective way of resisting the calls for economic isolationism.

Let me leave you with a final thought. The most powerful benefit of the global economy is not economic at all, even though it involves important economic and business activities. By enabling more people to use modern technology to communicate across traditional national boundaries, the international marketplace makes possible more than an accelerated flow of data. The worldwide marketplace encourages a far greater exchange of the most powerful of all factors of production-new ideas. That process enriches and empowers the individual in ways never before possible.

As an educator, I take this as a challenge to educate the anti-globalists to the great harm that would result from a turn to economic isolationism. For the twenty-first century, the global flow of information is the endless frontier.

Robert Kuttner  **NO**

Globalism Bites Back

The Asian financial crisis is a practical rebuttal to the naive internationalism that is America's foreign economic policy. Naive globalism includes these precepts:

- The freest possible movement of goods and services maximizes economic efficiency, hence human well-being. If free competition is good nationally, it is even better globally.
- With a few basic ground rules, such as respect for private property and equal access to markets, liberal capitalism is essentially self-regulating.
- At bottom, there is one true form of capitalism. It entails a relatively minimal role for the state. In principle, the size of the public sector and the level of taxation and public services are matters for national choice. The burden of proof, however, is always on government intervention, since taxation restricts individual choice and depresses incentives, while regulation distorts market prices.
- Above all, markets should be transparent and porous, and prices should be set by private supply and demand. Investors anywhere should be free to buy shares of institutions—or entire institutions— anywhere in the globe. They should be free to invest or speculate in currencies, and withdraw their investment at their pleasure.

All of this supposedly maximizes material well-being, of rich countries and of poor ones. People who resist this model are said to be economic nationalists, protectionists, and Luddites [opponents of technological change]. But there are several problems with this narrative.

꧁꧂

First is the ancient issue of political democracy itself. As sages since Aristotle have observed, man is a political animal. Either societies are tolerably self-governing, or they are dictatorships. A democratic society, of course, requires a polity. And for better or worse, the locus of the polity is the nation-state. There is no global state, hence no global polity and no global citizenship. I am a voting citizen of the United States of America, not of the Republic of Nafta

[A play on NAFTA, the North American Free Trade Agreement among Canada, Mexico and the United States].

Simple globalism removes from the compass of democratic deliberation key questions of self-governance. Several Asian nations are now, in effect, wards of the International Monetary Fund. More subtly, the pressures of laissez-faire globalism remove from national deliberation key questions of political economy that have no scientifically "correct" answer—what should be social, what should be private? Regional development policies, social safety net policies, cultural policies, industrial policies, and more have all been challenged as counter to the rules of GATT [General Agreement on Tariffs and Trade] or NAFTA or the WTO [World Trade Organization].

Naive globalism creates a bias against the mixed economy. If you believe that laissez-faire is really optimal, this is a constructive bias. But the entire history of capitalism is littered with counter-examples. Market economies have unfortunate tendencies to financial panics that spill over into purchasing-power collapses and serious (and avoidable) depressions. Unregulated capitalism yields monopolies, gouges consumers, fails to invest adequately in public goods, and produces socially intolerable distributions of income and wealth.

Simple globalism undermines the project of the mixed economy in several distinct respects. It punishes nations that elect policies of high wages and generous social benefits. It pulls capital into corners of the globe where there is less regulation, which in turn makes it harder for the advanced nations to police their capital markets and social standards.

Globalism also tips the domestic political balance—in favor of the forces that want more globalism. Capital is of course mobile, and labor, except for immigration, is not. Investors, who are free to move money to locations of cheap wages and scant regulation, gain power at the expense of citizens whose incomes are mainly based on wages and salaries. That tilt, in turn, engenders more deregulation and more globalism. The global money market, not the democratic electorate, becomes the arbiter of what policies are "sound." In this climate, a [U.S.] Democratic president or [British] Labour prime minister can snub the unions, but he'd better not offend Wall Street or the City of London. So even the nominally left party begins behaving like the right party— which then alienates the natural base of the party that is the supposed champion of the mixed economy.

There is an emergent set of global regulatory authorities, but they are stunningly undemocratic. In the nineteenth century, the so-called "money issue" dominated American politics: Would credit be cheap, so businesses could expand and farmers finance their crops—or would it be dear, to the benefit of creditors and the constraint of the young nation's economic potential? The Populists wanted an "elastic currency," freed from the tyranny of gold. In the epic compromise of 1913, the elastic currency was created—but entrusted to the nation's bankers, via the Federal Reserve.

If the Federal Reserve operates domestically at one remove from democratic accountability, the IMF and the World Bank operate at two removes. The World Trade Organization . . . adjudicates fair play for investors, but not workers or citizens. Even worse, the WTO lacks the evolved rules of evidence, due process, public hearings, and the strictures against conflict of interest that characterize courts in mature democracies. If the WTO arbitrarily rules against a U.S. company, as it did recently in the case of Kodak's complaint against Japan's closed market, the only appeal is to diplomatic pressure, and the State Department has bigger fish to fry.

As Jeff Gerth reported in the *New York Times* ["Where Business Rules," January 9, 1998], all over the world, quasi-official standard-setting authorities dominated by business are laying down the rules of global commerce. So the century-old project of making raw capitalism socially bearable is undermined in countless ways by naive globalism. Domestically, there are regulatory agencies, political constituencies, and a legacy of democratic deliberation and case law. These are neatly swept away in the name of free trade. The global market trumps the mixed economy.

Regional free trade areas like NAFTA . . . unite labor markets as well as product markets, even if they don't intend to. The European Union, at least, seeks to be an emergent polity, cognizant of a "democratic deficit" in which industry and finance currently have too much influence at the expense of citizenship. There is no such recognition in NAFTA, and, . . . [there] are plenty of unintended consequences.

⋅⟨⊙⟩⋅

Globalism particularly intensifies the aspect of capitalism that is most vulnerable to herd instincts and damaging irrationalities—financial markets. As George Soros, who knows the hazards well enough to have made billions from them, recently wrote, "Financial markets are inherently unstable, and international financial markets are especially so."

In Asia today, the irrationality of financial markets is on parade. Asia is not Mexico. The nations that got into trouble, for the most part, have policies that orthodox economists prize: high savings rates, balanced budgets, disciplined and efficient labor forces, and high rates of productivity growth. As in other newly industrializing countries before them (the United States, Germany, France, Brazil, Japan), East Asian development has been partly state-led. But until the crisis hit, the IMF [International Monetary Fund] was lauding most of these countries.

What happened . . . was a largely financial panic based on worries by foreign investors that exchange rates would decline, and the value of their investments along with them. Thanks to the IMF's own "stabilization" policies, these fears became self-fulfilling prophecies. It is ironic in the extreme that an institution that was created precisely to counter the tyranny and irrationality of speculative private capital flows became their battering ram—as well as an agent of gratuitous austerity. . . .

A related irony is that East Asia thrived on a variant model of capitalist development that largely (and prudently) eschewed the lure of foreign capital, precisely in order to retain control. If you borrow money in another currency, or rely on foreign investors who have no long-term commitment to your economy, you are at their mercy. This was Mexico's fate. As MIT economist . . . Alice Amsden, a Korea expert, has observed, it was only after Korea acceded to international pressure to open its domestic capital markets that its currency came under pressure. Its "fundamentals" were, and are, sound.

The hypocrisy of the U.S. government and the IMF is breathtaking. When every major money-center bank was technically insolvent in the early 1980s because of bad bets on Third World loans, the Federal Reserve did not close them down. It allowed them to cook their books until the bad debts could be retired. And when the U.S. got in hock to foreign investors because of accumulated trade imbalances, the authorities worked to rig the value of the dollar, so that foreigners would keep buying our bonds. Nobody demanded that enterprises be closed down wholesale. Indeed, the entire history of our own Great Depression was one of containing the damage and figuring out ways to keep enterprises open. We should treat Asia as well as we treat ourselves.

⋅✿⋅

The real issues, it seems to me, are these: What are the proper terms of engagement between a national, democratic polity and a global economy? As international institutions necessarily replace national ones, to whom are these institutions democratically accountable, and what substantive policies should they pursue?

The social bargain of the 1940s respected recent history. The statesmen of that era created an international financial system that allowed member states to build mixed economies and avoid panics and depressions. Trade was promoted, but not as an end in itself. Speculation and the freedom of private capital movement were subordinated to the general good, and not seen as the essence of liberty. . . .

[T]he new generation of global governing bodies needs to be rendered democratically accountable. These institutions need to pay attention to the fates of ordinary people, not just to investors. Their stewards need to read some history. . . .

The members of Congress who voted down fast-track authority last fall were damned as archaic nativists—a weird left-right coalition. There were indeed a few jingoists, but for the most part the opponents were [House Democratic Leader Richard] Gephardt Democrats who rightly insist on different terms of engagement before we continue to globalize. If laissez-faire at least produced reliable prosperity, it would be harder to challenge. But it produces terrible financial instability, as well as hardship.

There are cheap versions of this counter-narrative; it is easy to throw raw meat to an electorate that has suddenly suffered undeserved hardship at the hands of foreign forces. But if you want to see real economic nationalism—the ugly kind that leads to Caesarism and war—watch what happens in the IMF's wake. The naive internationalists, like their ancestors early in this century, are playing with real fire. Our challenge is nothing less than to rebuild the mixed economy for which earlier liberals struggled so nobly, and to defend it against the predations of facile globalism.

POSTSCRIPT

Is Economic Globalization Good for the United States?

There can be no doubt that the global economy and the level of interdependence have grown rapidly since World War II. In many ways, globalization has been extraordinarily beneficial—it has promoted economic and political liberalization, accelerated economic development, and brought people from around the world together in new and remarkable ways. For an optimistic assessment of globalization, see Thomas Freedman, *The Lexus and the Olive Tree* (Douglas and McIntyre, Ltd, 2001).

Despite its touted benefits, globalization affects different countries and different groups of people within them differently. Some benefit more than others and some are more vulnerable to the changes it generates. As a result, globalization and its effects are contentious. To learn more about the pros and cons of globalization, read Frank Lechner and John Boli, eds., *The Globalization Reader* (Blackwell Press, 2004).

One of the most remarkable shifts in political momentum in recent years has been the marked increase in the resistance to globalization. Meetings of international financial organizations such as the IMF and the WTO used to pass unnoticed by nearly everyone except financiers, scholars, and government officials. Now they often occasion mass protests, such as the riots that broke out in Seattle, Washington, in 1999 at a meeting of the WTO. For more on this and other political areas of policy dispute in the United States, see Edward S. Cohen, *The Politics of Globalization in the United States* (Georgetown University Press, 2001).

One of the oddities about globalization, economic and otherwise, is that it has created a common cause between people of marked conservative views and those of marked liberal views. More than anything, conservatives worry that their respective countries are losing control of their economies and, thus, a degree of their independence. Echoing this view, archconservative 2000 presidential candidate Patrick Buchanan warned that unchecked globalism threatens to turn the United States into a "North American province of what some call The New World Order."

The attacks of September 11, 2001 highlighted the dark side of globalization by demonstrating how the modern transportation, communication and financial systems that enrich the global economy also empower those who would use these systems as weapons against us. Critics of globalization—including Benjamin Barber, Thomas Homer-Dixon, Samuel Huntington, and Robert Kaplan—emphasize the inability of governments to provide security to their people and territory. For more on this, see Richard Matthew and George Shambaugh, "Sex, Drugs, and Heavy Metal: Transnational Threats and

National Vulnerabilities," *Security Dialogue* (June 1998) and Moises Naim, "Five Wars of Globalization," *Foreign Policy* (January/February 2003). Even if the threats of terrorism and overt violence can be managed, the increasing dependence of the United States on foreign sources of energy to fuel its cars and foreign financing to finance its expanding national deficits increase its dependence on others and make it vulnerable to changes in those countries politics and policies.

People of a liberal viewpoint share the conservatives' negative views of globalization but for different reasons. This perspective is less concerned with sovereignty and security and more concerned with workers and countries being exploited and the environment being damaged by MNCs that shift their operations to other countries to find cheap labor and to escape environmental regulations. Referring to the anti-WTO protests in 1999, AFL-CIO president John J. Sweeney told reporters, "Seattle was just the beginning. If globalization brings more inequality, then it will generate a violent reaction that will make Seattle look tame." For a critique of U.S. globalization policy, read Jagdish N. Bhagwati, *The Wind of the Hundred Days* (MIT Press, 2001).

For all these objections, the thrust among governments is to continue to promote expanded globalism. "Turning away from trade would keep part of our global community forever on the bottom. That is not the right response," President Bill Clinton warned just before leaving office. Soon after taking office, President George W. Bush made much the same point, saying, "Those who protest free trade are no friends of the poor. Those who protest free trade seek to deny them their best hope for escaping poverty."

For now, the upsurge of feelings against globalism have pressed policy-makers and analysts to consider what reforms are necessary to continue globalization while instituting reforms that will help quiet the opposition. For one such view, see Dani Rodrik, *The New Global Economy and Developing Countries: Making Openness Work* (Overseas Development Council, 1999), in which Rodrik argues, "Globalization can succeed and be sustained only if appropriate domestic policy measures are undertaken to cushion the impact on groups that are adversely affected and, even more important, to equip all sectors of society to take advantage of the benefits of globalization rather than be undermined by it."

ISSUE 17

Is Outsourcing Good
for the United States?

YES: **Edward Luce and Khozem Merchant**, from "The Logic is Inescapable," *The Financial Times* (January 28, 2004)

NO: **Ronil Hira**, from Testimony Before the Committee on Small Business, U.S. House of Representatives (June 18, 2003)

ISSUE SUMMARY

YES: Edward Luce and Khozem Merchant argue that cost savings, labor flexibility, and the rising productivity of largely non-unionized youthful labor forces in India and elsewhere make offshore outsourcing beneficial to both U.S. firms, who can use their savings to retain higher skilled workers, and U.S. consumers, who benefit from access to low-cost, high-quality goods and services.

NO: Ronil Hira, who is the chair of the R&D Policy Committee for the Institute of Electrical and Electronics Engineers of the United States of America, argues that global outsourcing is leading to a loss of high-value/high-wage jobs in the natural sciences and engineering, which, in turn, undercuts U.S. innovation and leadership in the science, technology, and service sectors, attracts bright young people to countries other than the United States, and increases U.S. reliance on others for critical military and national security technologies.

Building on David Ricardo's classic concept of comparative advantage, companies today are increasingly taking advantage of low cost communications, transportation, and data transfer technologies to specialize on their core products or services and rely on outside contractors to provide a wide range of other functions traditionally carried out internally. While much outsourcing is done locally, political debates tend to focus on offshore outsourcing or "offshoring," which involves outsourcing to a third party that is based in a foreign country. Offshore outsourcing became prevalent in basic manufacturing in the 1960s and 1970s as companies took advantage of lower cost labor in developing countries. In the 1980s, offshore outsourcing extended to the information technology sector with a growing use of foreign workers in Central Europe and South Asia for technical writing and software development.

Current trends include the growing use of overseas locations for customer call centers and other service oriented activities, and the rise of business process outsourcing (BPO) where complete business functions within a company (such as the payroll or employee benefits) are provided by external contractors. With the rise of BPO, outsourcing is increasingly viewed by companies as a strategic choice rather than simply a means of decreasing production costs. By allowing basic functions to be managed externally, BPO enables companies to focus their internal resources on increasing their competitiveness and maximizing their comparative advantage.

Outsourcing tends to be provided by large and generally multinational companies and consulting firms. As outsourcing develops, more and more companies are becoming enterprise service providers (ESP) meaning that they are capable of providing multiple services and business functions to their clients. Offshore outsourcing tends to be concentrated in certain countries depending on the type of services provided. For example, China and Mexico provide a substantial amount of outsourcing in manufacturing, India and Ireland provide outsourcing in information technology and call centers, and Malaysia provides call centers and financial processing.

The shift in offshore outsourcing from manufacturing to high-wage, high-value sector jobs has renewed a political debate about its impact jobs in the United States. Some argue, for example, that the location of high-wage, high-value jobs matters. High-wage, high-value jobs often generate positive spillover effects. In the short term, high-wage jobs generate high levels of consumption and high levels of tax revenue. In the long term, high-value jobs attract highly skilled people who are likely to be innovative and produce new products and improvements in existing technology and manufacturing processes. Furthermore, successful high-wage, high-value companies are likely to attract other high-wage, high-value companies that can benefit from the infrastructure and highly educated workforce that is in place. (This process is called conglomeration economics.) Indiana, Michigan, Ohio, and Ontario are notorious for offering companies large tax incentives and other benefits to attract them to their state or province. This competition is often very beneficial to the companies as each state—or country—"races to the bottom" by competing to offer each of the companies the sweetest deal possible.

On the other hand, others argue that the most significant impact of offshore outsourcing is its effect on the decline in U.S. jobs. This process began with a decline in manufacturing and so-called blue collar jobs, and is now extending to high technology and service sectors and other so-called white collar jobs. The number of U.S. jobs in certain sectors like textiles and basic manufacturing has been declining since the 1960s due to general structural changes in the world economy rather than outsourcing per se. Despite this, the public's focus on offshore outsourcing has made this issue politically sensitive with politicians in both political parties promising to stop the outflow of American jobs. Even those, like Edward Luce and Khozem Merchant, who argue in favor of the benefits of outsourcing recognize that companies must be sensitive to a potential backlash. At the same time, critics of outsourcing, like Ronil Hira, argue that political action is necessary to forestall its negative consequences.

YES ↩

Edward Luce and
Khozem Merchant

'The Logic Is Inescapable': Why India Believes Commercial Imperatives Will Help It Beat the Offshore Backlash

When chief executives from India's booming software and services industry gather for an international conference next week they will celebrate another year in which thousands of jobs have flooded into the country, part of a tide of outsourcing of employment to India by western companies. But chatter at the event organised by Nasscom, the trade body of India's software and services companies, may be about threats as much as about celebration. After so much success in persuading western companies to transfer jobs offshore, India is alive to the danger of a backlash.

Last week the US Senate passed an amendment that would prevent private companies from using offshore workers in order to compete successfully against government workers on some contracts opened up to competition. The amendment was in fact more modest than it initially appeared, since it applied only to the US Treasury and the Department of Transportation. Yet the bill has triggered a furore in India, which sees the measure as a harbinger of other such measures and evidence that it is the principal target of a protest against outsourcing. Indian politicians have proclaimed the legislation as an example of US double standards on free trade and Arun Shourie, India's minister for information technology, even suggested that the move would endanger the revival of the Doha round of world trade talks that broke down in Cancun last year but has recently been resuscitated.

India's acute sensitivity to rising protectionist sentiment in the west cannot be written off as paranoia. Hardly a day goes by without one of the Democratic US presidential candidates pledging to "keep American jobs in America" (see below). In the UK, where there is a greater focus on the "offshoring" of call centre and back office work than on software contracts, trade unions that oppose offshoring are garnering strong sympathy in some quarters and have called for boycotts of companies that move jobs out of Britain. Could India's booming service sector be falling prey to rising western fears that jobs will disappear? The risk cannot be dismissed. But much of it is overstated. There are three reasons to believe that US and UK private companies, which generate almost all of India's outsourcing business, will locate an increasing share of their operations in India and other developing countries in the coming years. First is the size of the cost savings that offshoring has generated for the companies that have already moved a significant chunk of their operations to India. This applies both to India's mainstream software development sector, which is principally located in Bangalore, Hyderabad, Mumbai and New Delhi, and to its call centre industry. A recent report by the McKinsey Global Institute estimates that of every Dollars 1 that is "offshored" the company gains 58 cents in net cost reduction "even as they gain a better (or identical) level of service." In other words, companies that have so far failed to shift operations to India—whether it is software development, IT systems integration, customer support, back office work, or personnel management—will be at a large and growing competitive disadvantage. "Assuming you have done your management research properly, the logic of offshoring to India is inescapable," says the New Delhi head of a large US company, which has 23,000 employees in India. "There is almost literally no limit to the supply of qualified graduates in the labour market." India has the youngest demographic profile of any big country in the world, including China. More than half its 1.05bn population is under the age of 25 and its labour force is projected to continue expanding until at least 2020. This, combined with the country's growing investment in higher education, particularly engineering and communications, means that the supply of qualified English-speaking labour will continue to outstrip demand and help keep a lid on wage inflation. "We were able to employ 800 fully qualified people in six months at cost savings of 40 to 50 per cent," says R.K. Rangan, the Mumbai manager of Prudential, the UK insurer, which runs a call centre. "It would have been hard—if not impossible—to ramp up at that rate in the UK."

Second, the process is still in its infancy. Although India's business process outsourcing sector has grown by almost 60 per cent a year since 2000, it still employs only 245,000 people. India's more established software development sector still employs fewer than 1m people, although it too is growing at about 30 per cent a year. Recent surveys of US corporate investment plans indicate that further potential is likely to be realised quite rapidly. Marc Hebert, head of **Sierra Atlantic**, a US software consultancy firm with almost 500 employees in Hyderabad, says it is now routine for start-up software companies in the US to outsource up to 80 per cent of their development work to India and China. More significantly, **Sierra Atlantic** found that a majority of venture capitalists in Silicon Valley now make it a requirement that start-up companies subcontract some software development to India or China. The implications for larger and more established US software companies—many of which currently subcontract little or no work to India—are profound. Most could be forced for competitive reasons to emulate the practices of start-ups in Silicon Valley. "We expect to see a rapid catch-up, with India's compound growth at about 50 per cent a year over the next five years," says Mr. Hebert. Furthermore, barely any of India's future growth is expected to come from western government outsourcing, which is where any backlash against the offshore shift seems most likely to manifest itself. Just 2 per cent of India's estimated Dollars 15bn (Pounds 8.2bn, Euros 12bn) of outsourcing earnings in

2003 were generated by the US public sector. Trade unions in the US and the UK are talking about boycotting private companies such as American Express and Lloyds TSB that offshore jobs to India. But Indian executives believe this threat is overplayed. "The threat is mostly symbolic at the moment," says Kiran Karnik, head of Nasscom, the Indian trade body. "We would say we are concerned rather than alarmed." Third, in contrast to conventional wisdom in the US and the UK, India's service sector productivity is improving rapidly and in some cases matches or outstrips western levels. Western executives say India has attained a level of experience that enables them to "re-engineer" work processes much more rapidly than they would in their domestic operations.

The combination of low wages and the relative flexibility of an almost wholly nonunionised and youthful labour force enables investors to undertake tasks that were previously ignored. For example, wage costs amount to about 30 per cent of a typical call centre in India, compared with 70 per cent in the US or the UK. This gives an Indian call centre the latitude to add extra functions and continue operations round the clock. "Companies are now using offshoring to drive revenue growth (in addition to cost savings)," says Diana Farrell, director of McKinsey Global Institute in San Francisco. "One airline was able to chase delinquent bills that it could not afford to chase before, because it lacked staff or took too much time." The head of the India offshore units of one US investment bank, which has relocated equity research work from the US to Mumbai, says the logic of shifting highly skilled jobs to India is also compelling. "In reality the wage differential (after factoring in other costs) of a guy who works at a commoditised call centre in India and an equivalent centre in the US is slim," he says. "But the economies of scale for higher value-added work like equity research are much smaller for you to break even—say, 25 employees in equity research as against 500 seats in a call centre." That logic could equally apply to professions such as chartered accountancy, legal services, medical consultations and publishing. Indeed, it is the potential of outsourcing to create large-scale migration of jobs, rather than its relatively modest results to date, that has so unnerved public opinion in the west. "Look at your average call centre worker in Liverpool," says Omkar Goswami, chief economist of the Confederation of Indian Industry. "He watched his father lose his old economy shipbuilding job in the 1980s but he found employment in the newly emerging service sector. Now even that job is under threat and he is wondering what on earth will replace it." In fact, as western businesses are increasingly pointing out, the gains to the US and UK consumer—and therefore to the domestic job markets—can be considerable, whether it is in the cost savings that are used to upgrade the skills of the labour force or in the greater exports that will go to a wealthier Indian market. But it is hard to illustrate the argument to those facing imminent redundancy. "It is easy to identify a particular job that has been lost, far more difficult to point to the new jobs that have been indirectly created," says one US executive. Mr Karnik says: "Instead of pointing out the logic of Ricardian economics (the original theory of comparative advantage) we express great sympathy with individuals whose jobs are going. But the ultimate point is that the western consumer is benefiting from lower costs and your company can now afford to retrain you for higher-skilled work." evertheless, India's outsourcing industry does face a number of potential constraints to growth. One is the fact that some proactive western outsourcers are starting to bump up against their country risk limits. India and Pakistan's recent rapprochement may be encouraging. But many investors recall that less than two years ago the nuclear-armed neighbours almost went to war.

Some Indian "third-party" outsourcers, which provide an alternative for western companies that do not want to set up their own site in India, are establishing subsidiaries in the Philippines and elsewhere in order to reassure investors. Another concern, especially in the US, is data privacy and the physical security of work sites, although so far no investor has complained of leakage of customer information by Indian employees, and most software and call centre work is carried out through dedicated telecommunications facilities rather than over the internet. Nasscom says it is working with the IT Association of America, its counterpart, to develop acceptable common standards both for consumers' digital privacy—a particular concern among insurers—and to build firewalls against other security breaches, including terrorism. Ultimately, though, these are secondary areas of friction that few believe have the potential to check India's galloping growth of offshore contracts. The most dramatic scenario so far projects that the US will lose 3.3m jobs by 2015, up from 473,000 so far, according to a widely cited study by Forrester. But this is small fry by the standards of the 1980s, when the US lost millions of manufacturing jobs to east Asia and Mexico. Against this are the gains in productivity and competitiveness to the US private sector and the jobs that will be directly and indirectly created as a result. "There is far too much emotion in this debate," says Ms Farrell. "There is a view—an incorrect view—that every job gained in India is a job lost in the United States. If enough people start thinking this way, we could be in for a whole lot of bad regulations in the US."

HEAT UNDER US WHITE COLLARS

Charles Schumer, the Democratic senator from New York, admits his record on free trade has been "mixed." But his anger over the disappearance of US high-technology jobs to India and China, he says, has caused him to reconsider some "fundamental assumptions" about whether open trade can ever make sense in a world of free capital flows, high-speed communications and an educated global population. "It doesn't fit the free trade model when these high-end jobs migrate overseas," he said at a Brookings Institution forum this month. "We've bet the ranch for a long time (that) the highest value-added jobs will stay here because we're the best educated." Since the rise of east Asian economies in the 1980s, the US has largely reconciled itself to the loss of low-skilled manufacturing jobs. More than 2.5m have disappeared during the tenure of President George W. Bush with few signs of a protectionist backlash. But the gradual move overseas of higher-end technology and white-collar jobs has touched a raw nerve. Paul Craig Roberts, an economist who has warned that outsourcing poses a serious threat to the US economy, says that when he talks to high school and college students "they spend a great deal of time searching for an occupation that can't be wiped out underneath them." Political debate over the issue has escalated sharply. John Kerry, one of the Democratic presidential frontrunners, has called for curbs on outsourcing of government contracts and a "right to know" law that would force all call centres to disclose their location. John Edwards, another leading candidate, says the outsourcing of jobs is part of "an extraordinary sea change" in the economy that is devastating middle-class America. Government proposals to counter outsourcing have taken several forms, according to a study by the National Foundation for American Policy, which opposes outsourcing. At the state level, several states have barred offshore companies from doing government contract work. New Jersey, for example, reworked a call centre contract—at a cost of about Dollars 900,000 (Pounds 490,000, Euros 710,000)—to require that a dozen of the jobs remain in the state rather than going to India. And in Indiana last year the governor cancelled a Dollars 15m contract with Tata, an Indian company, even though its bid was Dollars 8m less than that of the nearest US competitor. Several other states are considering legislation that would restrict foreign-based call centres or ban the outsourcing of government jobs. The federal government has so far done little. Several bills have been introduced in Congress that would restrict companies from bringing cheaper foreign workers to the US to do jobs previously done by Americans. And the omnibus 2004 spending bill soon to be signed by Mr. Bush contains an amendment that would prevent private companies that take over some government contracts in the federal transport and Treasury departments from moving that work offshore. Tita Freeman, a representative of the Business Roundtable of US chief executives, says that, while its impact would be limited, the amendment is "isolationist in nature" and would discourage job creation. US high-technology companies, which believe that outsourcing will be crucial to their future competitiveness, have been acutely attuned to the legislative threats, however, and are ready to fight back. The chief executives of Hewlett-Packard, Dell, International Business Machines and other companies warned this month that restrictions on outsourcing would imperil one of the most productive sectors of the US economy. "There is no job that is America's God-given right any more," said Carly Fiorina, HP's chief executive. "We have to compete for jobs." —Edward Alden

Ronil Hira

➡ **NO**

Global Outsourcing of Engineering Jobs: Recent Trends and Possible Implications

1. Introductory Remarks

Let me begin by thanking Chairman Manzullo and other distinguished Members of the House Committee on Small Business for inviting IEEE-USA to testify on the subject of the global outsourcing of white-collar jobs—an increasingly controversial issue with serious implications for individual Americans and the future economic and technological competitiveness of the United States. . . .

I am testifying here on behalf of the more than 235,000 U.S. members of the Institute of Electrical and Electronics Engineers. . . . The Institute of Electrical and Electronics Engineers is a transnational technical and professional society made up of more than 382,000 individual members in 150 countries. The IEEE's primary purposes are to advance the theory and practice of electrical, electronics, computer and software engineering; improve the careers of our members and increase their ability to innovate and create wealth for the benefit of the societies in which they live and work. IEEE-USA was established in 1973—in the midst of an earlier economic downturn—to promote the professional careers and technology policy interests of IEEE's U.S. members.

Nearly 70% of IEEE-USA's members work for private businesses, primarily in the aerospace and defense, bio-medical technology, computers and communications, electrical and electronics equipment manufacturing and electric power industries. Approximately 1/3 of our industry members work for firms with 500 or fewer employees. Ten percent of our members work for Federal, state and local governments. Another ten percent teach at American schools of engineering or work at non-profit research organizations. Most of the rest are self-employed and work as consultants to businesses and government.

2. Global Outsourcing—Recent Trends and Future Projections

Pete Engardio and his colleagues at *Business Week* have assembled a comprehensive and very compelling description of the global outsourcing phenomenon. The graphics, statistical tables and sidebars in their February 3, 2003 article entitled "Is Your Job Next" explain related trends and their implications for white collar workers, including U.S. engineers and scientists, in startling detail.

The article provides an alarming picture of the kinds and numbers of white-collar jobs that major American companies are shifting to overseas locations, mostly in developing economies in the Far East, Latin America and Eastern Europe. The article also makes it very clear that the most important economic and strategic driver behind global outsourcing is the ready availability of substantial numbers of skilled professionals in other countries who are willing and able to work for much less than their counterparts in the United States.

The following tables describe global outsourcing of white collar jobs in more detail. To illustrate the trend , the first table identifies several major U.S. based employers who are currently outsourcing important scientific and engineering work to lower cost, offshore locations.

Table 1

Major U.S. Exporters of Science and Engineering Jobs

Company	Numbers of workers and country	Types of work
Accenture	5,000 to the Philippines by 2004	Accounting and software
General Electric	20,000 to India and China in 2003	Aircraft and Medical R&D
Intel	3,000 to India by 2006	Chip design, tech support
Microsoft	500 to India and China in 2003	Software design, IT support
Oracle	4,000 in India	Software design and support
Phillips	700 in China	Consumer electronics R&D

Source: Business Week

The second table compares recent increases in the numbers of natural science and engineering degrees awarded in countries to which white-collar jobs are being outsourced with similar statistics for the United States.

Table 2

Science and Engineering Degree Production in Selected Countries

Country	BA and BS degrees		MA, MS and PhD degrees	
	1989	1999	1989	1999
China	127,000	322,000	19,000	41,000
India	165,000	251,000	64,000	63,000
Philippines	40,000	66,000	255	937
Mexico	32,000	57,000	340	63,000
United States	196,000	220,000	61,000	77,000

Source: National Science Foundation

The third table describes the cost of engineering talent in the United States and four other countries based on the concept of purchasing power parity.

Table 3

Annual Salary Requirements for an Engineer in Selected Countries

Country	Purchasing power parity	Annual salary
United States	1.0	$70,000
Hungary	0.367	$25,690
China	0.216	$15,120
Russia	0.206	$14,420
India	0.194	$13,580

Source: Ron Hira, Columbia University

The fourth table includes estimates of the numbers and kinds of white-collar jobs likely to be outsourced in the years immediately ahead.

Table 4

Projected Numbers of US Jobs to be Moved Offshore*

Profession	By 2005	By 2010	By 2015
Architecture	32,000	83,000	184,000
Business Operations	61,000	162,000	348,000
Computer Science	109,000	277,000	473,000
Law	14,000	35,000	75,000
Life Sciences	3,700	14,000	37,000
Management	37,000	118,000	288,000

* To low wage countries such as China, India, Mexico and the Philippines
Source: Forrester Research Inc.

3. Global Outsourcing of Jobs Exacerbates U.S. Engineering Unemployment

Unemployment among America's engineers has spiked sharply upward from 2.0% in 2001 to 4.2% in 2002 to more than 6.0% in the first quarter of 2003.

The unemployment problem is even worse for all electrical, electronics, computer and software engineers. According to the Bureau of Labor Statistics at the U.S. Department of Labor, unemployment among electrical and electronics engineers reached 7.0% in the first quarter of 2003. 6.5% of all computer hardware engineers and 7.5% of computer software engineers were also unemployed during the same period. These are *unprecedented* levels for each occupation.

IEEE-USA is concerned that these increases in engineering unemployment may not be a short term, cyclical phenomenon that will correct itself when the economy begins its long anticipated upturn. Instead, current engineering unemployment is the result of much more fundamental structural changes in the U.S. economy that could have very serious, long-term affects—not only on the future viability of engineering as a high-wage/high value added career—but on the nation's economic and technological competitiveness and the continuing ability of small businesses to be a major driver of innovation and job creation in the United States.

The current economic and employment problems we face are complex and interrelated. There are no easy answers or silver bullets in terms of public policy recommendations. But we do think that the continuing movement of manufacturing facilities and blue-collar jobs, and the growing willingness of major employers to move essential service functions and white collar jobs of all kinds to lower cost, offshore locations is a major contributing factor to our current unemployment crisis.

4. Global Outsourcing Has Economic, Technological and Security Implications

Traditionally, the United States has been a leader in technological innovation—a major contributor to improvements in productivity, economic growth and personal well-being that took place during the 1990's. Engineers and scientists at colleges and universities, at businesses of all sizes and at public and private research organizations have long been prime movers in the conversion of scientific discoveries into useful products and services and in technological innovation. A nation's ability to innovate is at the core of its economic and technological strength. Location matters when it comes to the innovation process because it generates enormous local spillover benefits and feeds on itself. An obvious example is Silicon Valley.

Global outsourcing of high wage/high value added engineering jobs threatens this leadership on a number of fronts.

- The movement of more and more manufacturing and related service functions to offshore locations means that many technological improvements in manufacturing processes that are discovered and perfected as goods are produced will be developed in other countries.
- The outsourcing of information technology applications development and delivery outside of the United States will reduce opportunities for continuing domestic innovations in software, data communications and data security applications.
- The downward pressure on job opportunities, wages and working conditions that will occur as more and more scientific and engineering jobs are shifted to lower cost offshore locations is likely to reduce the willingness of America's best and brightest young people to pursue careers in science and engineering.
- Personal economic and national security will be subject to increasing risk as responsibility for more and more private, proprietary and mission critical military and national security data is transferred to other countries.

5. Global Outsourcing Has Costs As Well As Benefits

Global outsourcing is often justified as absolutely critical to the preservation and enhancement of corporate viability and the quality of life in the United States in an increasingly competitive, technology-driven global economy. While there are benefits to global outsourcing, proponents often fail to address the related costs. There are serious, long-term consequences for many Americans, their communities and the nation as a whole. Such adverse consequences may include:

- Loss of employment and income for more and more American professional workers if outsourcing continues to exert downward pressure on job opportunities, wages and other forms of compensation.
- Loss of payroll and income taxes at the national, state and local levels at a time when demands on pay as you go social insurance programs, such as Social Security and Medicare, and the need for improvements in our communications, educational, health care and transportation infrastructures are beginning to accelerate.
- Loss of employer contributions to government sponsored unemployment insurance and workmen's compensation programs that will be needed to help sustain the increasing numbers of displaced workers whose jobs have been moved offshore.
- Loss of national economic and technological competitiveness and increasing dependence on foreign sources of supply for consumer products, military hardware and defense systems as well as the technical talent needed to design, produce and maintain them.
- Further imbalances in international trade and the US balance of payments as America is forced to buy more products and outsourced services than its sells to its major trading partners.

6. Public Policy Alternatives

As I said at the outset of my testimony, the causes of current economic and related employment problems are complex and appropriate policy options for addressing them will require some creativity. We do know that offshore outsourcing is accelerating and policymakers can mitigate some of its negative impacts.

Before we can deal effectively with complex economic problems, we must first learn more about their causes and effects. Reliable statistical information about the current magnitude of global outsourcing and its effects on national and international labor markets is sorely lacking. One policy recommendation, therefore, is to pool the resources of interested parties—educators, employers, government agencies, labor unions and professional societies—to identify the kinds and possible sources of statistical information needed to "get our arms around" the global outsourcing phenomenon.

The current non-immigrant system that brings in temporary foreign workers with H-1B (specialty occupations) and L-1 (intra-company transfers) visas has *accelerated* movement of work offshore as temporary workers in management positions outsource work to overseas colleagues, and as temporary workers who have returned home use their knowledge and connections in the U.S. market to competitively bid for outsourced work. A policy shift away from reliance on guest workers and towards permanent immigration would help minimize this problem.

Increasing reliance on high tech temporary workers has had other negative impacts apart from increased unemployment. Charges of abuse and exploitation of temporary workers are on the rise. Similarly, there are frequent reports of displaced American engineers and IT workers being forced to train their L-1 visa replacements as a condition of their severance package. The H-1B and L-1 visa programs should be reformed to limit these abuses and bring the programs back in line with Congress' original intent. Much engineering and information technology work needs to be done onsite in the U.S., and American workers should have preference over foreign guest workers.

Additionally, Congress should monitor current World Trade Organization (WTO) General Agreement on Trade in Services' (GATS) mode 4, movement of natural persons, negotiations. Many countries have pushed the U.S. to make it even easier to misuse the H-1B and L-1 visas.

Another possible policy option is to identify appropriate tax and other financial incentives needed to encourage employers to create and retain more high wage/high value added manufacturing and service sector jobs by establishing and maintaining more high end research, design, development and manufacturing facilities in the United States.

Current offshore outsourcing has affected U.S. workers more than larger U.S. companies, so another appropriate policy response is to provide assistance to employed, underemployed and dislocated workers in the form of tax incentives to help pay for lifelong learning (continuing education and training), including tax credits for employers that offer training or retraining in high demand technical, management and marketing skills; tax-favored savings accounts to help pay for job and career-related education and training expenses incurred by individual taxpayers; and possibly even relocation accounts to help workers move from low growth to high growth labor markets.

And finally, related to national security considerations, Congress may wish to increase enforcement of "deemed export laws" to reduce the likelihood that mission critical and other sensitive technologies will be transferred overseas through global outsourcing of scientific and engineering jobs.

POSTSCRIPT

Is Outsourcing Good for the United States?

The assessment of outsourcing is largely a function of perspective on what one defines as individual and social welfare. From a classic economic liberal viewpoint, maximizing consumption by granting consumers greater access to a wider range of better quality, more efficiently produced, and less expensive goods is best for the individual and for society as a whole. Outsourcing enables companies to focus their people and resources on maximizing their comparative advantage rather than using them to provide other services that offshore workers can better supply to the company or its clients. Thus, outsourcing helps increase the competitiveness and productivity of American companies while providing consumers with better and cheaper goods and services.

On the other hand, from a political economy perspective, offshore outsourcing promotes the movement of increasingly productive and high paying jobs around the globe. While the shift in the location of jobs around the world is inconsequential in purely economic terms, the costs of job losses are highly concentrated while the benefits of increased efficiency associated with the redistribution of jobs are highly diffuse. As a consequence, those who lose their jobs are more likely to be vocal and mobilize politically than those who benefit from access to cheaper goods. The political mobilization of those who lose their jobs is likely to increase as outsourcing continues its migration from manufacturing to higher wage jobs. This makes offshore outsourcing a politically sensitive topic.

Furthermore, although offshore outsourcing may benefit consumers by increasing efficiency and lowering costs, it entails economic and political costs. While the principle of comparative advantage suggests that each country should produce what it produces best, those that produce high-value goods and high-wage jobs will benefit over time substantially more than those who do not. As political scientists argue, it is more beneficial to have local factories producing computer chips than potato chips—the former is much more likely to generate high incomes and revenues and generate higher value-added production. From this viewpoint, creating and maintaining a competitive advantage in highly valued goods by keeping high-value and high-wage jobs at home is more important than promoting efficiency and increasing consumption.

Daniel Drezner provides a useful discussion of the political debates over outsourcing through an article in *Foreign Affairs* (May/June 2004) and his blog, which also provides useful links. See http://www.foreignaffairs.org/20040501faessay 83301/daniel-w-drezner/the-outsourcing-bogeyman.html and http://www.danieldrezner. com/blog .

ISSUE 18

Should the United States Fight Climate Change?

YES: **William J. Clinton**, "Global Climate Change: Building a Future for Our Grandchildren," *Vital Speeches of the Day* (December 8, 2005)

NO: **Jason Lee Steorts**, "Scare of the Century: The Alarms and Assertions about Global Warming Have Gone Reprehensibly Too Far," *National Review* (June 5, 2005)

ISSUE SUMMARY

YES: William J. Clinton, former president of the United States, contends that global warming is real, that environmentally sound practices are economically feasible on personal and national levels.

NO: Jason Lee Steorts, deputy managing editor of *National Review,* argues data on global warming is not consistent and the fears of global warming are being fanned by politicians, the media, and some scientists.

In a very short time, technology has brought some amazing things. But these advances have had by-products. A great deal of prosperity has come about through industrialization, electrification, the burgeoning of private and commercial vehicles, and a host of other inventions and improvements that consume massive amounts of fossil fuel (mostly coal, petroleum, and natural gas). The burning of fossil fuels sends carbon dioxide (CO_2) into the atmosphere. The discharge of CO_2 from burning wood, animals exhaling, and some other sources is nearly as old as Earth itself, but the twentieth century's advances have rapidly increased the level of discharge. Since 1950 alone, global CO_2 emissions have increased 278 percent, with more than 26 billion tons of CO_2 now being discharged annually. There are now almost 850 billion tons of CO_2 in the atmosphere.

Many analysts believe that as a result of this buildup of CO_2, we are experiencing a gradual pattern of global warming. The reason, according to these scientists, is the *greenhouse effect.* As CO_2 accumulates in the upper atmosphere, it creates a blanket effect, trapping heat and preventing the nightly cooling of the Earth. Other gases, especially methane and chlorofluorocarbons (CFCs, such as freon), also contribute to the thermal blanket.

Many scientists and others believe that global warming is evident in changing climatological data. It is estimated that in the last century the Earth's average temperature rose about 1.1 degrees Fahrenheit. In fact, of the 10 warmest years since global record keeping began in 1856, 9 of those years occurred in the 19 years between 1980 and 1998.

Not everyone believes that global warming caused by a CO_2 buildup is occurring or worries about it. Some scientists do not believe that future temperature increases will be significant, either because they will not occur or because offsetting factors, such as increased cloudiness, will ease the effect. Others believe that recent temperature increases reflect natural trends in the Earth's warming and cooling process.

Whatever the reality may be, the 1990s saw efforts to constrain and cut back CO_2 emissions. The Earth Summit held in Rio de Janeiro in 1992 was the first of these efforts. At Rio, most of the economically developed countries (EDCs) signed the Global Warming Convention and agreed to voluntarily stabilize emissions at their 1990 levels by the year 2000. They also resolved to reconvene in 1997 to review progress under the agreement. However, five years later many of the EDCs, including the United States, had made no progress toward meeting the goals set in 1992.

The 1997 meeting was held in Kyoto, Japan. The negotiations were too complex to detail here. The more important point for this debate is the treaty's provisions. They are: (1) The EDCs must reduce CO_2 and other greenhouse gas emissions by 6 to 8 percent below their respective 1990 levels by 2012. The U.S. cut will be 7 percent; Europe's will be 8 percent; Japan's, 6 percent. (2) EDCs can trade emissions quotas among themselves. (3) No sanctions for failure to meet standards were set. The parties to the treaty will meet in the future to establish sanctions. (4) The less developed countries (LDCs), including China and India, are exempt from binding standards but may opt to adopt voluntary goals. (5) The treaty will go into effect when ratified by at least 55 countries representing at least 55 percent of the world's emissions of greenhouse gases.

In October 2004, Russia joined over 80 countries—including all members of the European Union, Japan, and Canada among a total of 18 industrialized countries—in ratifying the Kyoto protocol. Consequently, the treaty went into effect for those who ratified it in February 2005. President George W. Bush has opposed the Kyoto Treaty and rejected domestic regulatory limits on the emission of greenhouse gasses.

The debate over global warming has intensified in the past several years as an increasing number of scientific reports documenting global warming have been published. Great Britain and other governments have produced their own studies and called for extensive environmentally focused policy changes. Public awareness has also increased with the airing of former vice president Al Gore's movie, *An Inconvenient Truth*. Former President Clinton argues that concerns about global warming are real and that they can be addressed effectively without the economic costs suggested by those who oppose policies focused on environmental sustainability. In contrast, Jason Lee Steorts argues that the costs of pursuing environmentally sustainable policies are extraordinarily high, and are unnecessary because the fear of global warming is a matter of excessive hype over an ambiguous natural phenomenon.

YES ⤶   **William J. Clinton**

Global Climate Change

T hank you very much. Thank you Mr. Mayor. I'm very grateful to the City of Montreal; to the Sierra Club of Canada and my long-time friend, Elizabeth May, for inviting me here to speak today. And the Government of Canada for hosting this historic meeting on climate change.

I seem to walk into trouble every time I come to Quebec to give a speech. The last time I was here, Mr. Mayor, you remember I was here to talk about federalism right before the referendum. So, I want to try to talk about an issue that is full of controversy, but of profound importance to the future of our children and grandchildren in a way that I hope will permit all who care about this issue without regard to what specific approaches they favour to think about the facts.

I just got back from a week long trip in which I went all the way from the northernmost part of the inhabited world—I went to St. Petersburg, the largest most northernmost city on the globe—then to Kiev, Ukraine to do some of my AIDS work. And then I flew to Sri Lanka and Indonesia, where the summer is beginning, working on the Tsunami relief recovery for the United Nations. And I came back to Munich and London.

And when I was just wandering around the world, I read the following headlines: that scientists had dug more deeply than ever before into the Antarctic core and now could measure greenhouse gases—both methane and carbon dioxide—over the last 650,000 years. And the levels were markedly higher than at any point over the last 650,000 years. Now keep in mind the last ice age only receded 15,000 years ago, which enabled people to move up out of East Africa, across the world and to establish civilizations in every continent. That was when I was in Kiev I read that.

Then, I flew to Sri Lanka in the scorching heat of the early summer, and I read that 95 per cent of the glaciers in the Himalayas are melting, leading to a tripling of mudslides and other disasters from overflowing mountain lakes.

And then, as I flew back North, I read that the countries of the North Atlantic are at risk at getting markedly colder in the years ahead because of global warming, because more fresh water is flowing into the oceans and it's messing up the current rotation, and may block normal temperature changes and aggravate the winters in the North Atlantic. Those were just three little articles in six days.

From *Vital Speeches of the Day*, December 8, 2005.

At our Global Initiative, which the Mayor mentioned, in New York around the opening of the UN, we were told that insurance losses from severe weather events in the last 10 years were triple those of any previous decade in history. And I know that if the climate warms for the next 50 years at the rate of the last 10, rising sea levels in the North Atlantic will claim at least 50 feet of Manhatten Island. It might good for the value of the real estate that is left there, but it will be a very bad thing indeed. It will be a harbinger of changing of agricultural production patterns, millions of food refugees created throughout the world, intense disruptions.

There was an article the other day, Mr. Mayor, about the prospect that the North Pole might melt enough now in the summer time for people to have a sea route right across the top of the earth, and that won't raise the water level because the North Pole is all ice anyway. But it's hard to believe that the North Pole could melt without significant run off of the Ice Cap on Greenland. And if that were to happen the environmental consequences would be calamitous, indeed.

So, there is no longer any serious doubt that climate change is real, accelerating and caused by human activities. We are uncertain about how deep and the time of arrival of the consequences. But, we are quite clear that they will not be good. So, what should we do about it? Well, when I was President, I did what I could do in an atmosphere that was, to put it mildly, hostile. We took a lot of executive actions to green the White House and the executive branch of government. We applied higher efficiency standards to appliances in the United States. I sought and lost a carbon tax, and then sought and lost a 25-percent tax credit for the production or purchase of clean energy products.

But, we were active in a partnership for a new generation of vehicles with our auto manufacturers, and in the development of the Kyoto climate change accord, which in the end actually got Vice-President Gore personally involved with. It was not a perfect agreement, and there were criticisms of it at the time. The two most important of which were, first, that Kyoto would hurt the economies of the developed nations by chaining them to greenhouse gas reductions that were not achievable, and certain to lead to top down bureaucratic solutions that would wreck economic growth. The second was that Kyoto did not include developing nations which were already large greenhouse gas emitters in which given present rates of growth would become larger than even the United States, the worst offender, in the next few decades.

The second criticism was fair; the first one was just flat wrong. It was factually wrong. And we know from every passing year, we get more and more objective data that if we had a serious disciplined effort to apply on a large scale existing clean energy and energy-conservation technologies, we could meet and surpass the Kyoto targets easily in a way that would strengthen, not weaken our economies. That's the main point I came here to make.

The main point I want to make to the developed countries is that I believe if you look all around the world . . . what was the big issue in Germany in the last election? Do we have enough flexibility in the labour markets to generate enough new jobs? How can we preserve a sense of social justice? Decent pay, decent benefits, a secure retirement, a strong middle class, and still reach out to the developing world on honourable trade terms. How can we possibly do that when we can't create new jobs?

But, if you look at the United States where we did have a couple million new jobs last year, but in the 90s, we averaged nearly three million new jobs a year, every year, partly because information technology was a source of new jobs for us. It was eight per cent of our job base, but 30 per cent of our job growth. It rifled through the whole economy. If the developed world wants to do the right thing by the developing world, and share the benefits of the future, it will require far more than reducing agricultural subsidies. It will require genuinely more open markets, a serious attempt at investment, a whole different way of thinking about this, and we will never have the political consensus to do it unless the wealthier countries can create substantial numbers of new jobs at home every year. We have not found in this decade, the answer to that.

In the United States, our unemployment rate is still quite low, but partly because we have had two per cent of the work force stop looking for jobs. That is, in our country, unemployment is a function of work force participation. So, if you're not looking for a job—even though you could work—you're not counted as unemployment. If work force participation rates were the same as they were a decade ago, the unemployment rate would be about a percent-and-a-half higher.

Every country has got this challenge. How are we going to meet it? By a serious commitment to a clean energy future, that's how. We can create jobs out of wind energy, out of solar energy, out of bio-fuels, out of hybrid engines, out of a systematic determination to change the lighting patterns, the insulation patterns, the efficiency standards of all buildings and all appliances. We could make, in America, there is no telling how many jobs we could create if we'd just made a decision that in the rebuilding of New Orleans, it could become America's first "green" city. We would restore all the wetlands, and every building would have solar cells.

Now, I say this because I think this has bearing on how we break the log jam here. You've just got to decide if you believe this or not, and if you can think you can convince anybody else of it. But, there are lots of hopeful signs here that if we decided to maximize clean energy development, maximize energy conservation technologies, maximize appropriate research, and have the best and most efficient use of old energy sources of oil and coal. If we did all of that, could we find common ground to do something before climate change makes it too late to have meetings like this? We'll have a meeting like this in 40 years on a raft somewhere if we come to Canada to meet—unless we do something.

Well, there's (sic) a lot of hopeful signs. As the Mayor said, you've got over 190 mayors committed actually to meet the Kyoto accords. Think about this: if a mayor commits to meet the Kyoto accords, what's the difference in that and a country committing? A country commits to an abstract goal. If a mayor—an executive officer—makes a commitment, the mayor, he or she has decided already you're thinking: "how in the world am I going to do this?" And, before long, you put out a list of the 20 things you're going to do. And then you go and do it. Once you moved from the abstract to the particular, you drastically increase the level of support for whatever it is you're doing, and you occupy people in doing something they can see as positive, and good for the economy.

I take it no one in Denmark is embarrassed that they generate 20 per cent of their electricity from wind. That no one in The Philippines is ashamed that they generate 27 per cent of their electricity from geothermal. That Germany is proud to generate over 16,000 megawatts of electricity from wind. That Japan is glad that they have overtaken the United States, as has Germany, in the generation of electricity from solar cells. I think that the million (sic) people in the developing world—largely in Latin America, but other places as well—who have solar cells unconnected to central power stations on their homes, that generate enough electricity to turn on the lights and cook the food, for a monthly payment that is more or less equal to a month's supply of candles, are proud that they have that.

So, what I'd like to say is, if there is a way to bring the countries of the world together, maybe it's around treating this agenda the way you would if you were the mayor of a large city: "Here's what I am going to do!" And always know that if you aggregated these up that would actually produce the results we are trying to achieve. And it's not just the mayors in the United States. We have 11 states comprising one-third of our automobile usage who have promised to cut their carbon emissions by a third. We have other states who have promised to cut emissions from power plants.

We have an enormous number of private companies now getting into this. General Electric's Chairman Jeffrey Immelt has said that climate change technologies are going to be at the centre of his company's profit strategy in the next decade. I just built this massive presidential library and it has 308 solar cells on it. I cut my greenhouse emissions by 34 per cent. It will take me a year-and-a-half to pay for the cost of those solar cells, after which, for the remaining life of that building—conservatively another 98½ years—I get a third of my electricity for free and I will reduce my damage to my children and grandchildren's future by one third. We can all do this.

Here's the point I'm trying . . . let me just say this. We just had a major television squib on our network news last week in America showing this new solar company out in California actually spraying nano-solar technology on thin sheets of aluminium, which may revolutionize the economics all over again. But, I want to make this one simple point. I hear people all the time when I say this—this is almost 2006—look at me in a slightly patronizing tone and say: "Oh, there he goes again. He's been saying this stuff for 30 years, and everybody knows this can only be a small part of the answer. Everybody knows solar and wind could never be anything as much as oil and coal and nuclear and all that. Everybody knows that." Well, that's just not true.

If you look at the geothermal capacity of Japan alone, they could produce over half their electricity with geothermal. If you look at wind, the difference in wind and solar, and traditional energy sources is, wind and solar are more like blackberries, cell phones and flat-screen televisions—the more you use the cheaper it gets. Wind is going up to 30 per cent a year utilization—that means it doubles every two-and-a-half years. Every time it doubles, the price drops 20 per cent. If you want the price to drop faster, increase the capacity faster.

Last year, solar cell usage—had been going up 30 per cent per year—last year, it increased 57 per cent in one year. Every time the capacity doubles, the price drops 20 per cent. America spends roughly $180-billion (US) a year on gasoline—varies depending on the price. If we spent half of that for seven years building wind mills, then we generate more electricity from wind than any other source. It's just not true you can't take any of this to scale. It's just that we are sort of rooted in old patterns of organization and financing.

But, to make the main point, we know the capacity is there. In our country, 20 per cent of all electricity is consumed by lighting. If every home replaced every incandescent light bulb with a compact fluorescent one, which costs three times as much, lasts 10 times as long, emits one third as much greenhouse gases, every purchaser of a light bulb would save 25 to 40 per cent, no matter how many bulbs they purchased, just as long they were being used. And we would cut the greenhouse gas emissions attributable to lighting in America by 50 per cent. We could create a lot of jobs transferring the production of light bulbs from incandescent to compact fluorescent—with another new technology just over the horizon I might add.

So, I just don't believe all of this stuff about how: "well, all these things are nice to talk about, but we can't really get there." We're still wasting . . . most electric power plants waste 60 per cent of the base heat of the fuel going into them, whatever it is. You know, I saw Amery Lovens the other day at my Global Initiative—and a lot of you know him—but he's been out there saying this stuff for 30 years, and people have laughed at him for 90 per cent of his adult life. And no one's laughing anymore because we now know that conservation is good economics. Conservation creates energy just as much as alternative sources do.

After the Gulf Coast was destroyed by Katrina, I was down in a little town in Alabama talking to a bunch of shrimpers. They were African-Americans, European-Americans and Vietnamese-Americans. You know what they wanted to know? Could I get them a bio-fuel plant. Because diesel was three dollars-a-gallon, and we can make bio-fuels for a buck-and-a-half now—and we just about got it done, parenthetically.

The reason I'm saying this is not to say that these agreement don't matter. They do matter, a lot. I like the Kyoto agreement; I helped to write it, and I signed it. But, it did have the flaw of not having everybody in the world signing onto the market mechanism. And now that's largely cured; China, India, Brazil, a lot of countries are interested in participating in this. You can see the emergence of a carbon market. But, one of our states, New Mexico, has already signed on to the climate change exchange in the United States. So, there is going to be a major carbon market.

And I think it's important that we find—if we can get it—a multilateral way of going forward. If we all work together, it's hard to see how we can fail. And if we don't, it's hard to see how we can succeed. My country has four per cent of the world's population, 20 per cent of the world's GDP, and we did have, when I left office, 25 per cent of the greenhouse gases. It may be down to 23½ or 24 percent now, just because of the rapid growth in China and India.

But, the point is we've all got to find a way to do this together. And I think that if you ask yourself: why did 190 mayors agree to do this . . . who weren't all left-of-centre. Some of them were conservatives. One of the mayors in America that signed onto this Kyoto thing came from a small farming community in Nebraska, and he bragged about the fact that he was a conservative Republican who had voted for the President twice and strongly supported him. But he said: "You know, I'm a farmer, and they told me that we had to go fight terrorists on the principle of precaution." There is no place in the world where it's more important to apply the principle of precaution than in the area of climate change.

There are two big obstacles to agreement, it seems to me. One is the general observation made—more eloquently than I can make it—hundreds of years ago by Machiavelli:

There is nothing so difficult in human affairs than to change the established order of things because those who will be hurt by the change are quite certain of their loss, while those who will benefit are uncertain of their gain.

We are trying to create an enormous new world here. And that's why the more concrete examples we have of success, the more important it is. Even though it may not be as satisfying as having everyone say: "Ok, we're going to get to this level of reductions, by this date."

Second problem is the old energy economy is well-organized, well-financed and well-connected politically. The new economy is, by and large, entrepreneurial, creative, still-undercapitalized, and the markets are not all that well-organized. Now, our Congress—and I appreciate that they adopted a new solar credit in 2005, which I thought was a good thing—but I tried for years to get a 25 per cent credit for the production or purchase of clean and alternative energy technologies, and I couldn't pass it. So, we're moving that way.

But, we have got to get people to think about how to jump start this. So, when British Petroleum adopts their new slogan, Beyond Petroleum—insofar as it is reflected in real actions—that's good. When Royal Dutch Shell finances wind mills, that's good. I think every oil country in the world ought to take some of the benefits of that 65-dollar oil, and become energy countries—not just oil countries. Why shouldn't the oil countries of the world finance the development of solar and wind power? You could do it all over the Middle East. You could start at the Equator and work out. It would be a way of generating jobs, reducing poverty, increasing development and avoiding future impacts of climate change.

So, when we did discuss at my Global Initiative, the biggest dollar commitment we had—this is very interesting—was from a large European insurance company, Swiss Re, who committed $300-million to clean energy projects in Europe over the next few years. Why did they do that? Because they're going to go broke if global warming keeps running up the numbers of intense weather events. You can't figure out how to insure or reinsure against an unpredictable and ever-expanding number of risks. And the leader is a wise and thoughtful man, so that's how they made their commitment.

So, my plea is that we get more coiporations, cities, other local governments and NGOs involved in this; that we try to go forward multi-laterally;

that we not give up on market mechanisms. This carbon market is going to take off, as long as we don't walk away from it. It's going to be an enormously successful thing and incredibly important in trying to help us deal with this, and moving big dollars around and getting big projects done.

And finally, that if we can't agree on targets, that we do what we would do if we were all mayors: we would change the terms of the game. You don't want to agree on a target, here's a hundred projects we can do. They will produce the results that the target seeks to achieve. They will be pro-free market. They will create jobs. They won't put anybody out of work. They'll give us an enormous new set of opportunities. And if all of our oil companies want to embrace them, then they can finance them, and diversify their operations, and create jobs, and make more money. And we could do the same thing in research, whether it is clean coal or hydrogen research.

I think it's important to point out—before I give up the podium here— that in a certain way, all energy is solar energy. We should never forget that in our solar system, over 98 per cent of the mass is still up there in the sun, and all the rest of us—all the people wandering around and all the planets that share the solar system with us—are one-and-a-half per cent of the mass. That we are all kept alive every day by about a billionth of that mass that escapes and comes down to Earth. A lot of which is refracted from the clouds and back into space. We are living here in literally a biological miracle. And oil and coal and oil shale—all that stuff—were just solar energy longer ago. And so, if some how we can one day figure out how to create energy the way you do when hydrogen compresses together and releases three-tenths of a per cent of its mass to do all the good that it has done, that would be wonderful.

In the meanwhile, I think it's crazy for us to play games with our children's future by not agreeing to do what manifestly we know will drastically enhance the economy as well as protect the environment. And give us a chance to share this planet together.

So I say again, if we can't agree on targets, my advice is let's all pretend that we had a job and had to do something, instead of just talking about it. Let's all pretend we had a job and had to do something! And see if we can get agreements on actions, projects: how much are we going to increase wind energy? How much are we going to increase solar energy? How much are we going to increase the efficiency of our buildings, our electricity generation, our appliances? How quick are we going to convert to new lighting? How many vehicles are we going to produce that are hybrid vehicles? And by the way, Detroit needs to stop producing hybrid vehicles that just have bigger engines and don't get any more fuel mileage. How are we going to do that? And how quickly can we do that?

Who can refuse to have that discussion? That is a discussion that will generate millions and millions of jobs in the developed world and the developing world alike. That is a discussion that just might give us a chance to give our grandchildren the same set of opportunities that most of us took for granted. You know we have a heavy obligation because we now know since the dawn of the Industrial Revolution, very few people knew that we would come to this day. But we know, we know what's happening to the climate. We have a highly predictable set of consequences if we continue to pour greenhouse gases into the atmosphere. And we know we have an alternative that will lead us to even greater prosperity.

So, again, my plea is for us all to get together, let's try to go forward together. And if you can't agree on a target, agree on a set of projects so everybody has something to do when they get up in the morning. This is a terrible thing to paralyze ourselves, and give people an excuse, and let anybody off the hook from doing something. Let's find a way to walk away from here and walk into the future together, so that we all have something that will give our grandchildren this planet in a more prosperous and more humane way.

Thank you very much and God bless you all.

Jason Lee Steorts   **NO**

Scare of the Century

But what, oh what, would the earth do without *Time* magazine?

"Suddenly and unexpectedly," *Time* announced in a recent issue, "the crisis is upon us." Haven't noticed the crisis? You must not be looking very hard. "The climate is crashing, and global warming [what else?] is to blame." *Time* accordingly devoted a special report to saving Mother Gaia. The report is half anti-Republican polemic, half catalogue of global warming's supposed ills—and none receives greater emphasis than the melting of polar ice. We see a photograph of a polar bear, standing all by his lonesome at the water's edge, and are told that the poor fellow might drown because "polar ice caps are melting faster than ever." Later, we learn that "the journal *Science* published a study suggesting that by the end of the century, the world could be locked in to an eventual rise in sea levels of as much as 20 ft."

Science magazine has itself been prone to hysteria. The issue that *Time* mentions contains no fewer than eight studies and articles about the ice caps, and begins with a news story warning that "startling amounts of ice slipping into the sea have taken glaciologists by surprise; now they fear that this century's greenhouse emissions could be committing the world to a catastrophic sea-level rise." The policy implications of such reportage are clear, but in case you missed them, *Time* connects the dots: "Curbing global warming may be an order of magnitude harder than, say, eradicating smallpox or putting a man on the moon. But is it moral not to try?"

The answer is, yes, it may indeed be moral not to try. What is not moral is to distort the truth for political ends—which is precisely what has been done with the ice-caps story. Here's what you haven't read.

The world has two major ice sheets, one covering most of Greenland and the other covering most of Antarctica. While melting sea ice has captured its share of attention, it's the land sheets that matter. Sea ice is already in the water, so its melting doesn't raise ocean levels. But if land ice melts, the sea gets higher. *Time* wants you to be very worried about this: "By some estimates, the entire Greenland ice sheet would be enough to raise global sea levels 23 ft., swallowing up large parts of coastal Florida and most of Bangladesh. The Antarctic holds enough ice to raise sea levels more than 215 ft." Farewell, Dhaka, we shall miss thee.

From *The National Review*, June 5, 2006, pp. 35–38. Copyright © 2006 by National Review, Inc, 215 Lexington Avenue, New York, NY 10016. Reprinted by permission.

Or not. Those numbers sound impressive, but the chances of the ice caps' fully melting are about as high as the chances of *Time*'s giving you an honest story on global warming. The truth is that there's no solid evidence supporting the conclusion that we've locked the ice caps in to a melting trend. Let's look at Antarctica and Greenland in turn.

About Antarctica, University of Virginia climate scientist Patrick J. Michaels is direct: "What has happened is that Antarctica has been gaining ice." He explains that there has been a cooling trend over most of Antarctica for decades. At the same time, one tiny portion of the continent—the Antarctic Peninsula—has been warming, and its ice has been melting. The peninsula constitutes only about 2 percent of Antarctica's total area, but almost every study of melting Antarctic ice you've heard of focuses on it.

So what about the rest of the continent? In 2002, *Nature* published a study by Peter Doran that looked at Antarctic temperature trends from 1966 to 2000. What it found was that about two-thirds of Antarctica got colder over that period. At the same time, Antarctica has gotten snowier, and as the snow has accumulated the ice sheet has grown. Snowfall is probably rising because water temperatures around Antarctica have gotten slightly—repeat, slightly—warmer. As a result, there is more surface evaporation, making for higher humidity and more precipitation. Higher humidity also means more clouds, which might explain the cooler weather.

How much ice has Antarctica gained? In a 2005 study published in *Science*, Curt Davis used satellite measurements to calculate changes in the ice sheet's elevation, and found that it gained 45 billion tons of ice per year between 1992 and 2003. Far from flooding the coasts, that's enough to lower sea levels by roughly 0.12 millimeters annually.

This doesn't mean the trend of increasing Antarctic ice will continue forever. *Science* captured headlines in March when it published a study by Isabella Velicogna arguing that, between 2002 and 2005, Antarctica has been losing ice mass. Velicogna used a pair of satellites to measure the gravitational pull exerted by the Antarctic ice sheet, which in turn allowed her to calculate its mass. Her data suggest that, over the past three years, the sheet has lost about 152 cubic kilometers of ice per year. That would be the equivalent of about 0.4 millimeters of annual sea-level rise.

But three years do not a trend make. To begin with, such a short sampling period is a blip in the slow rhythms of climate change. Moreover, 2002—the year in which the study began—was a high-water mark for Antarctic ice, so it's not too surprising to see some decline since then. Alarmism over Velicogna's study is on the order of going to the beach at high tide, drawing a line at the water's edge, and fretting a few hours later that the oceans are drying up.

And Greenland? Various studies show that warmer temperatures are causing the ice sheet there to lose mass at the margins. But, as in Antarctica, higher sea temperatures are also causing greater snowfall and building up ice in the interior. As Richard Lindzen of MIT observes, "If you're just going to look at what's falling off the sides and ignore what's collecting on top, that's not exactly kosher." The question is whether the net change is positive or negative.

Earlier this year, Eric Rignot and Pannir Kanagaratnam published a study in *Science* that used satellite measurements to calculate ice loss around Greenland's coasts. They also used models to determine how much ice was vanishing from surface melt, and how much was accumulating from greater snowfall. Adding it all up, they got a decade of deficits: 91 cubic kilometers of ice lost in 1996, rising to 224 cubic kilometers in 2005. That translates to a sea-level rise of 0.23 millimeters in 1996 and 0.57 millimeters in 2005.

But, as the web publication CO2 Science has pointed out, their model-based estimate of the ice gain in Greenland's interior was implausibly small. In fact, *Science* had earlier published a study by Ola Johannessen that used satellite measurements to determine how much the ice sheet was growing. Johannessen found that, between 1992 and 2003, it was gaining on average 5.4 centimeters of elevation per year.

That may not sound like a lot, but it adds up. Michaels, the University of Virginia professor, calculates that it amounts to about 74 cubic kilometers of ice per year. Rignot and Kanagaratnam could have subtracted that number from their estimate of coastal ice loss, which would have given them a negative total only for the past five years: 17 cubic kilometers lost in 2000, rising to 92 cubic kilometers in 2005. That would be equivalent to only 0.04 millimeters of sea-level rise in 2000 and 0.23 millimeters in 2005.

Add all the numbers from Greenland and Antarctica up, and you get a rather piddling total. In 2005, Jay Zwally of NASA published a study in the *Journal of Glaciology* that looked at the ice-mass changes for both Greenland and Antarctica from 1992 to 2002. He concluded that the total ice loss was equivalent to a sea-level rise of just 0.05 millimeters per year. At that rate, it would take the oceans a millennium to gain 5 centimeters, and a full 20,000 years to rise by a meter. To the hills, anyone?

A Longstanding Pattern

Granted, the Zwally study doesn't include the last three years—years in which, according to some measurements, Antarctica has switched from gaining ice to losing it, and Greenland's rate of loss has accelerated. But you don't need to invoke man-made global warming to explain what's going on.

Consider Greenland again. Yes, temperatures there are warmer than they were a decade ago. But many climate scientists think this is the result of a phenomenon called the Atlantic Multidecadal Oscillation (AMO)—a pattern of slow, repeating changes in the ocean's surface temperatures. The AMO affects both the Atlantic tropics and the regions farther north. When the AMO is in its positive phase, temperatures rise in both places—which should cause more Caribbean hurricanes, and increase the speed at which Greenland's glaciers discharge into the sea. This appears to be just what is happening. "The AMO changed from negative to positive in 1995," Michaels wrote on Tech Central Station. "Since then hurricanes have become very active and glacier output has been accelerating." Is this man's fault? Models suggest that the AMO has been going on for at least 1,400 years. Maybe things would have turned out differently had Charlemagne signed the Kyoto Protocol, but the odds are against it.

In fact, we have temperature records indicating that Greenland was as warm as it is today during the first half of the 20th century. From 1920 to 1930, Greenland saw significant warming, and temperatures stayed high through the '40s. A team of scientists led by Petr Chylek looked at Greenland's temperature record in a study forthcoming from *Geophysical Research Letters.* They write that the increase in Greenland's temperature between 1920 and 1930 was "of a similar magnitude" to the increase between 1995 and 2005. But the earlier warming happened faster: "The rate of warming in 1920–1930 was about 50% higher." 2003 was a hot year, but "the years 2004 and 2005 were closer to normal[,] being well below temperatures reached in [the] 1930s and 1940s." Moreover, "although . . . 1995–2005 was relatively warm, almost all decades within 1915 to 1965 were even warmer."

If today's temperatures are causing Greenland's coastal ice to slide into the sea, it must have been positively galloping there 80 years ago. That's significant, because the warming period in the early 20th century took place well before fossil-fuel burning could have triggered global warming. So we can't say with any confidence that what we're seeing in Greenland today is our fault. Chylek's team concludes its study with the observation, "We find no evidence to support the claims that the Greenland ice sheet is melting due to increased temperature caused by increased atmospheric concentration of carbon dioxide."

As with Greenland, so with the world. There is no consensus that human activity is the main cause of climate change. Reluctant though one is to question *Time*'s authority in matters scientific, it's simply wrong when it declares: "In the past five years or so, the serious debate has quietly ended. Global warming, even most skeptics have concluded, is the real deal, and human activity has been causing it."

What we know is that the global average temperature has risen by about 1 degree Celsius or less since the late 1800s. We also know that industrial activity has raised atmospheric carbon-dioxide concentrations, and that this increase should make things warmer. But there is wide disagreement about the extent to which carbon-dioxide emissions are responsible for the warming we've seen so far, and how much warming they will cause in the future.

Fred Singer of George Mason University points out that "we have historic [temperature] records in Europe going back a thousand years. It was much warmer then than today. The Arctic was much warmer a thousand years ago than it is today. Polar bears survived. The ice caps survived." And data from ice cores suggest that previous interglacial periods were warmer than the one we're going through now.

Moreover, the models scientists use to predict the effects of carbon-dioxide emissions are biased to overpredict global warming. They assume that atmospheric concentrations of CO_2 will increase by about 1 percent a year. In fact, this is more than twice the observed rate. In the last ten years, the average increase was 0.49 percent; in the decade before that, it was 0.42 percent; and in the decade before that, it was 0.43 percent. But scientists keep feeding the models 1 percent. That's more than a 100 percent margin of error. Three cheers for precision.

It's not surprising, then, that actual warming in recent years has been lower than the models say it should have been. By creating a false sense of alarm, the models make the ice-cap debate much shriller than it should be. For example, the authors of the *Science* study that *Time* refers to were able to predict a sea-level rise of several meters only because they took as Gospel the 1 percent–per–year CO2 increase. That gave them a tripling of atmospheric CO2 by 2100 and a quadrupling by 2130. But as Michaels points out, observed data suggest this quadrupling won't happen till 2269. "By then," he writes, "energy-production technology will probably have turned over two or three times and this will never have become an issue."

The Worse the Better

Why are scientists using the wrong numbers? Richard Lindzen of MIT thinks that, while most scientists were originally agnostic on the question whether human activity was causing global warming, "environmentalists and the media would exaggerate." That eventually built up a public concern, and politicians responded by throwing research dollars at scientists. If global warming turned out not to be a problem, those dollars would go away. Better to keep us worried: "You've developed a scientific community that will do whatever it needs to do to make sure the answer isn't obtained. Why should taxpayers pay for people not to find an answer?"

Lindzen doesn't mean that there is a conspiracy among scientists, but rather that the funding process gives an incentive toward pessimism. If you have doubts about this, consider how frequently climate scientists tell us that things are worse than we thought. If a scientific study isn't biased in such a way as to look for an alarming outcome, the odds that its findings will be better than expected are equal to the odds that they will be worse than expected. In other words, it's a coin toss; an unbiased research process should produce better-than-expected results and worse-than-expected results in roughly equal proportion. Michaels got interested in this notion. He looked at a single day last December when 15 findings on global warming were released to the press. Fourteen fell into the worse-than-expected category. But if none of the studies that produced the findings was biased, the odds of getting a 14-to-1 ratio are less than 1 in 2,000.

Of course, even if man-made global warming is the primary cause of the mild temperature and sea-level rises being observed, this doesn't settle the question of what to do about it. The environmental lobby's answer is: Ratify the Kyoto Protocol. *Time* isn't even subtle about it, calling George W. Bush's environmental record "dismal" and specifically citing his abandonment of Kyoto. But he abandoned it for good reason. The U.S. Energy Information Administration estimates that the treaty would cost the American economy $300 billion to $400 billion a year. Any decision about whether to pay such a price should be based on cost-benefit analysis. What, then, is the benefit?

In a word, nothing. Kyoto wouldn't stop whatever warming is caused by greenhouse-gas emissions; it would just slow it. And it would barely do that. Tom Wigley of the National Center for Atmospheric Research calculated that the full global implementation of Kyoto would prevent 0.07 degrees Celsius of global warming by 2050, an outcome that is all but undetectable. To put a dent in CO_2 levels, you'd need much greater emissions reductions than Kyoto calls for. Jerry Mahlman of the National Center for Atmospheric Research, for example, has called Kyoto a "first step" and said that "30 Kyotos might do the job."

Thirty Kyotos would also come at the price of economic collapse. When it's not even clear that the warming we've seen is hurting us—many argue that it's a boon, citing its benefits to agriculture and its potential to make severe climates more hospitable—such draconian solutions should be unthinkable. And if it turns out that carbon dioxide is hurting the planet, it's probably doing so at such a gradual pace that the best solution is to wait for markets to produce new innovations in energy technology. (And are we finally far enough away from Three Mile Island to utter the word "nuclear"?)

In the meantime, let's stick with what we know—about melting ice, and about global warming generally. We're not sure that we have a problem. If we do, we don't know that we're the ones causing it. But *Time*, Al Gore, the Democratic party, the EU, politically correct scientists, and the entire green lobby want us to throw enormous sums of money at solutions that won't work anyhow.

Good plan, guys.

POSTSCRIPT

Should the United States Fight Climate Change?

The provisions of the Kyoto treaty include the requirement that the treaty would not go into effect until it was ratified by at least 55 countries representing at least 55 percent of the world's greenhouse gases. That requirement was met in October 2004 when Russia ratified the treaty. As a result, it became active in February 16, 2005 without U.S. ratification. By 2008, all ratifying countries are required to begin cutting their carbon emissions and by 2012 industrial nations are required to reach emission reduction targets. Since the United States is the source of approximately 25 percent of the world's carbon dioxide emissions, the U.S. refusal to ratify the treaty is of great importance.

U.S. opposition to multilateral environmental a.ccords and environmental regulations remain despite a 2001 report by an expert working group on climate change, appointed by President George W. Bush, which argued that there is consensus within the scientific community that the earth's temperature is warming and that emissions of greenhouse gases and aerosols due to human activities continue to alter the atmosphere in ways that are expected to affect the climate. This report along with other official U.S. and international reports on climate change, are available on the Web at http://epa.gov/oar/climate change/index.html.

Like most environmental problems, the negative impacts of global warming will be slow to build up and, therefore, are somewhat hard to see. Average temperatures will rise most years in fractions of degrees. Patterns of storms, rain, and other weather factors that strongly govern the climate of any region will also change slowly. Although some coastal cities may disappear and some now-fertile areas may become deserts, that is many years in the future. Besides, other regions may benefit. Marginal agricultural areas in northern regions may someday flourish. To make matters more confusing, the Earth warms and cools in long cycles, and some scientists believe that to the degree there is a general warming, it is all or mostly the result of this natural phenomenon. If that is true, cutting back on greenhouse gases will have little or no effect.

However, if we ignore global warming, there will only be an escalating buildup of greenhouse gases; EDCs will continue to emit them, and emissions from LDCs will rise as part of their modernization efforts. If those who are alarmed about global warming are correct, and we ignore it, there will be many devastating effects that will affect large portions of the globe.

Then there is the matter of the effects of programs to ease global warming. Those who recommend caution in responding to demands that global warming be halted also point out that significantly reducing CO_2 emissions will not be easy. It might well require substantial lifestyle changes in the industrialized countries. For example, cars might have to be much smaller, gasoline prices higher, and electricity production and consumption curtailed. Costs would also be enormous. The Union of Concerned Scientists (UCS) has concluded that a program to cut CO_2 emissions by 70 percent over a 40-year period would cost the U.S. economy $2.7 trillion.

But there will also be benefits. The UCS also projects a $5 trillion savings in fuel costs. Others have pointed to the economic stimulus that would be provided by creating alternative energy technologies. Losses from storm damages would also drop. A stabilization of the climate would stabilize the lifestyles of people in coastal and other areas that would be most strongly affected by global warming.

In the end, the question is this: Should the United States and other countries bet trillions in economic costs that emissions-driven global warming is occurring or bet the atmosphere that it is not occurring? For now, at least, the answer for the United States is the latter. President George W. Bush termed the Kyoto treaty "deeply flawed" and decided not to submit it to the U.S. Senate for ratification on the grounds that the treaty "exempts the developing nations around the world, and . . . is not in the United States' economic best interests," The difficulties are further explored in David Victor, *The Collapse of the Kyoto Protocol and the Struggle to Slow Global Warming* (Princeton University Press, 2001).

Bush's decision was met with strong objections by many foreign leaders. "There is enough scientific evidence to wake us up and allow us to take action," Secretary General Kofi Annan of the United Nations said. "We don't need to wait for the perfect science to be able to act." Taking a similar stand, Margot Wallström, Europe's commissioner of environmental affairs, told reporters, "To suggest scrapping Kyoto and making a new agreement with more countries involved simply reflects a lack of understanding of political realities. We could lose years of work if we were to start from scratch."

An interactive Web site on global warming is available at http://www. environmentaldefense.org/home.cfm. For a more extended view that global warming is a crisis, see Albert K. Bates and Albert Gore, Jr., *Climate in Crisis: The Greenhouse Effect and What We Can Do* (Book Pub, 1990). For a somewhat skeptical review of the evidence supporting the existence of global warming problems, consult S. George Philander, *Is the Temperature Rising? The Uncertain Science of Global Warming* (Princeton University Press, 2000).

ISSUE 19

Is It Realistic for the United States to Move Toward Greater Energy Independence?

YES: Barack Obama, Remarks to the Governor's Ethanol Coalition, (February 28, 2006)

NO: Philip J. Deutch, "Energy Independence," *Foreign Policy* (November/December 2005)

ISSUE SUMMARY

YES: Barack Obama, Democratic senator from Illinois, argues that America's high dependence on oil imports undermines its security by making it rely on unstable and often hostile governments. He argues that the United States can greatly reduce its reliance on oil imports by setting higher standards for auto fuel efficiency and promoting the use of biofuels like ethanol.

NO: Philip Deutch, director of Evergreen Solar and general partner of NGP Energy Technology Partners, a private equity firm investing in energy technology companies, argues that U.S. oil imports are so high that it would be impossible to end them in the next few decades, and that U.S. energy use is likely to continue to grow, as will oil prices, even if energy efficiency and conservation increase.

$\mathbf{A}$nalysts generally agree that the U.S. imports most of the oil it uses, that this creates challenges for American foreign policy, and that in the absence of policy changes the share of U.S. energy use that comes from oil imports is likely to rise. Disagreements arise, however, over how much conservation efforts and programs to stimulate alternative energy sources can reduce this dependency on oil imports, and how soon and at what cost they might do so. As Philip Deutch points out, the United States imports 4 billion barrels of oil a year, over half of the oil it uses. This slows growth in the U.S. economy and hurts the U.S. trade balance when the price of oil rises, as it has in recent years, and it also forces the United States to confront several foreign policy trade-offs.

First, dependency on oil imports, especially those from the Middle East, make the United States vulnerable to any political or military developments that disrupt the production or transport of oil and create demands for U.S. military capabilities and deployments to prevent or reverse any such disruption. Second, research suggests that countries whose economies are dependent on oil exports tend to be less democratic than other countries with comparable levels of GNP per capita. In effect, oil-rich governments are able to buy off a sufficient number of elite supporters to be able to ignore demands from their publics for greater political representation. Thus, payments for imported oil often go to undemocratic governments. Third, high use of oil and many other fuels increases the carbon dioxide emissions that contribute to global warming.

These problems are likely to intensify even if the United States becomes more energy efficient, as growing demand for oil in China, India, and elsewhere may continue to contribute to rising oil prices even if demand in the United States can be reduced below current projections. It remains unclear whether the United States can significantly reduce demand for oil and increase the use of alternative fuels, and whether government policies or market forces are the best ways to bring about these objectives. Rising prices are themselves a powerful mechanism for encouraging conservation, as is evident in the sharp decline of sales of sport-utility vehicles in the United States as gas prices rose above $3 per gallon. Higher prices also make alternative fuels more economically viable. The production of electricity from wind turbines, for example, is presently only about 2 percent of U.S. electricity generation, but is growing rapidly as the rising cost of oil and other energy sources makes the price of wind-generated power more competitive. Even so, Senator Obama sees an important role for the U.S. government in raising auto fuel efficiency standards and creating additional incentives for the production of biofuels, such as ethanol produced from corn and other plants. Philip Deutch, on the other hand, is pessimistic on the prospects for either government policies or higher prices to substantially reduce U.S. oil imports in the near term.

YES ⬅

Barack Obama

Remarks to the Governor's Ethanol Coalition

In this year's State of the Union address, President Bush told us that it was time to get serious about America's addiction to foreign oil. The next day, we found out that his idea didn't sit too well with the Saudi Royal Family. A few hours later, Energy Secretary Bodman backtracked and assured the world that even though the President said he planned to reduce the amount of oil we import from the Middle East, he actually didn't mean that literally.

If there's a single example out there that encapsulates the ability of unstable, undemocratic governments to wield undue influence over America's national security just because of our dependence on oil, this is it.

Now, I could stand up here and give you all plenty of reasons why it's a good idea for this country to move away from an oil-based economy. I could cite studies from scientists and experts and even our own State Department detailing the dangers of global warming—how it can destroy our coastal areas and generate more deadly storms. I could talk forever about the economic consequences of dependence—how it's decimating our auto industry and costing us jobs and emptying our wallets at the pump. And I could talk about the millions of new jobs and entire new industries we could create by transitioning to an alternative-fuel economy.

But all we really need to know about the danger of our oil addiction comes directly from the mouths of our enemies:

"[Oil] is the umbilical cord and lifeline of the crusader community." These are the words of Al Qaeda.

"Focus your operations on oil, especially in Iraq and the Gulf area, since this will cause them to die off [on their own]." These are the words Osama bin Laden.

More than anything else, these comments represent a realization of American weakness shared by the rest of the world. It's a realization that for all of our military might and economic dominance, the Achilles heel of the most powerful country on Earth is the oil we cannot live without.

Oil single-handedly fuels 96% of our transportation needs, and it's also critical to the manufacture of millions of goods and products in this country. As we saw during Hurricane Katrina, this kind of dependency means that the loss of even a small amount of oil and refining capacity for just a few days can

Remarks of Senator Barack Obama, *Governor's Ethanol Coalition,* Washington, D. C, February 28, 2006.

cause economic panic and soaring prices. A serious embargo or permanent loss could cause untold disaster.

It would be nice if we could produce our way out of this problem, but it's just not possible. We only have 3% of the world's oil reserves. We could start drilling in ANWR today, and at its peak, which would be more than a decade from now, it would give us enough oil to take care of our transportation needs for about a month.

As a result, every single hour we spend $18 million on foreign oil. It doesn't matter if these countries are budding democracies, despotic regimes, or havens for the madrassas that plant the seeds of terror in young minds—they get our money because we need their oil.

One need only glance at headlines around the world to understand how dangerous this addictive arrangement truly is.

In Iran, Islamic fundamentalists are forging ahead with their nuclear program, knowing full well that the world's response to their actions will be influenced by our need for their oil. In fact, reports of a $100 billion oil deal between Iran and China were soon followed by China's refusal to press for sanctions against Iran over its nuclear intentions.

In Nigeria, militant rebels have been attacking the country's oil pipelines in recent weeks, sending prices soaring and calling into question the political stability of a country that represents America's fifth-largest source of oil imports.

In Saudi Arabia, Al Qaeda has been attempting attacks on that country's poorly defended oil refineries for years. On Friday, they almost succeeded as a truck full of explosives was detonated by the shots of security guards just before it entered the refinery. Even this minor damage caused oil prices to jump $2 in a single day. But a former CIA agent tells us that if terrorists ever succeeded in destroying an entire oil complex, it could take enough oil off the market to cause economic catastrophe in the United States.

Our enemies are fully aware that they can use oil as a weapon against America. And if we don't take this threat as seriously as the bombs they build or the guns they buy, we will be fighting the War on Terror with one hand tied behind our back.

Now, the good news about the President's decision to finally focus on energy independence after five years is that it helps build bipartisan consensus that our reliance on foreign oil is a problem and shows that he understands the potential of renewable fuels to make a difference.

The bad news is that the President's energy policy treats our dependence on oil as more of a nuisance than a serious threat.

Just one day after he told us in the State of the Union that renewable fuels were the key to an energy independent future, we learned that the President's budget cuts would force layoffs at the National Renewable Energy Laboratory. Last week, this made for a rather awkward situation when the President wanted to use the lab for a photo-op—so awkward that the White House actually re-hired the laid-off researchers just to avoid the embarrassment.

This is only one example, but it tells the story of a larger weakness in the President's energy policy: it's simply not commensurate to the challenge.

There's a reason that some have compared the quest for energy independence to the Manhattan Project or the Apollo moon landing. Like those historic efforts, moving away from an oil economy is a major challenge that will require a sustained national commitment.

During World War II, we had an entire country working around the clock to produce enough planes and tanks to beat the Axis powers. In the middle of the Cold War, we built a national highway system so we had a quick way to transport military equipment across the country. When we wanted to beat the Russians into space, we poured millions into a national education initiative that graduated thousands of new scientists and engineers.

If we hope to strengthen our security and control our own foreign policy, we can offer no less of a commitment to energy independence.

But so far, President Bush seems like he is offering less—much less.

His funding for renewable fuels is at the same level it was the day he took office.

He refuses to call for even a modest increase in fuel-efficiency standards for cars and trucks.

His latest budget funds less then half of the energy bill he himself signed into law—leaving hundreds of millions of dollars in under-funded energy proposals.

And while he cannot seem to find the funding for any of these energy proposals, he has no problem allowing the oil companies to stiff taxpayers $7 billion in royalties that they owe us for drilling on public lands. These are the same oil companies that are currently enjoying the highest profits on record.

Again, this is just not a serious commitment to energy independence. The solutions are too timid—the reforms too small. America's dependence on oil is a major threat to our national security, and the American people deserve a bold commitment that has the full force of their government behind it.

This isn't to lay the blame for our energy problems entirely at the feet of our President. This is an issue that politicians from both parties clamor about when gas prices are the headline of the month, only to fall back into a trance of inaction once things calm down. And so we all need to get serious here. Automakers need to get serious about shifting their technology to greater fuel-efficiency, consumers need to get serious about buying hybrid cars, and Washington needs to get serious about working together to find a real solution to our energy crisis.

Such a solution is not only possible, it's already being implemented in other places around the world. Countries like Japan are creating jobs and slowing oil consumption by churning out and buying millions of fuel-efficient cars. Brazil, a nation that once relied on foreign countries to import 80% of its crude oil, will now be entirely self-sufficient in a few years thanks to its investment in biofuels.

So why can't we do this? Why can't we make energy security one of the great American projects of the 21st century?

The answer is, we can. The President's energy proposal would reduce our oil imports by 4.5 million barrels per day by 2025. Not only can we do better than that, we must do better than that if we hope to make a real dent in our oil dependency. With technology we have on the shelves right now and fuels we can grow right here in America, by 2025 we can reduce our oil imports by over 7.5 million barrels per day—an amount greater than all the oil we are expected to import from the entire Middle East.

We can do this by focusing on two things: the cars we drive and the fuels we use.

First, the cars. For years, we've hesitated to raise fuel economy standards as a nation in part because of a very legitimate concern—the impact it would have on Detroit. The auto industry is right when they argue that transitioning to more hybrid and fuel-efficient cars would require massive investment at a time when they're struggling under the weight of rising health care costs, sagging profits, and stiff competition.

But it's precisely because of that competition that they don't have a choice. China now has a higher fuel economy standard than we do, and Japan's Toyota is doubling production of the popular Prius to sell 1,00,000 in the U.S. this year.

There is now no doubt that fuel-efficient cars represent the future of the auto industry. If American car companies hope to be a part of that future—if they hope to survive—they must start building more of these cars.

But that's not to say we should leave the industry to face these costs on its own. Yes, we should raise fuel economy standards by 3% a year over the next fifteen years, starting in 2008. With the technology they already have, this should be an achievable goal for automakers. But we can help them get there.

Right now, one of the biggest costs facing auto manufacturers isn't the cars they make, it's the health care they provide. Health care costs make up $1,500 of the price of every GM car that's made—more than the cost of steel. Retiree health care alone cost the Big 3 automakers nearly $6.7 billion just last year.

So here's the deal we can make with the auto companies. It's a piece of legislation I introduced called "Health Care for Hybrids," and it would allow the federal government to pick up part of the tab for the auto companies' retiree health care costs. In exchange, the auto companies would then use some of that savings to build and invest in more fuel-efficient cars. It's a win-win proposal for the industry—their retirees will be taken care of, they'll save money on health care, and they'll be free to invest in the kind of fuel-efficient cars that are the key to their competitive future.

Now, building cars that use less oil is only one side of the equation. The other involves replacing the oil we use with home-grown biofuels. The Governors in this room have long known about this potential, and all of you have been leading the way on ethanol in your own states.

This coalition also knows that corn-based ethanol is only the beginning. If we truly want to harness the power of these fuels and the promise of this market, we can and must generate more cellulosic ethanol from agricultural products like corn stocks, switch grass and other crops our farmers grow.

Already, there are hundreds of fueling stations that use a blend of ethanol and gasoline known as E85, and there are millions of cars on the road with the flexible-fuel tanks necessary to use this fuel—including my own.

But the challenge we face with these biofuels is getting them out of the labs, out of the farms, and onto the wider commercial market. Every scientific study in the world could sing the praises of biofuels, but you might still be hard-pressed to find an investor willing to take the risk on a cellulosic ethanol plant or a brand-name petroleum company willing to build an E85 fueling station.

The federal government can help in two ways here. First, we can reduce the risk of investing. We already do this in a number of ways by funding projects critical to our national security. Energy independence should be no different. By developing an Energy Technology Program at the Defense Department, we can provide loan guarantees and venture capital to those with the best plans to develop and sell biofuels on a commercial market. The Defense Department will also hold a competition where private corporations get funding to see who can build the best new alternative-fuel plant. The Department can then use these new technologies to improve the energy security of our own military.

Once we take the risk out of investing, the second thing the government can do is to let the private sector know that there will always be a market for renewable fuels. We can do this in a few ways.

First, we should ramp up the renewable fuel standard and create an alternative diesel standard in this country so that by 2025, 65 billion gallons of alternative fuels per year will be blended into the petroleum supply.

Second, Washington should lead the way on energy independency by making sure that every single automobile the government purchases is a flexible-fuel vehicle—starting today. When it becomes possible in the coming years, we should make sure that every government car is a plug-in hybrid as well.

Third, I'm supporting legislation that would make sure every single new car in America is a flexible-fuel vehicle within a decade. Currently it costs manufacturers just $100 to add these tanks to each car. But we can do them one better. If they install flexible-fuel tanks in their cars before the decade's up, the government should provide them a $100 tax credit to do it—so there's no excuse for delay.

Fourth, there are already millions of people driving flexible-fuel vehicles who don't know it. The auto companies shouldn't get CAF'E credit for making these cars if they don't let buyers know about them, so I'd like to ask the industry to follow GM's lead and put a yellow gas cap on all flexible fuel vehicles starting today. Also, they should send a letter to those people who already have flexible-fuel vehicles so they can start filling up their tank at the closest E85 station.

Finally, since there are only around 500 fueling stations that pump E85 in the country, we recently passed legislation that would provide tax credits of up to $30,000 for those who want to install E85 pumps at their station. But we should do even more—we should make sure that in the coming years, E85 stations are as easy to find as your gas station is now.

Make no mistake—none of these reforms will come easy, and they won't happen overnight. But we can't continue to settle for piecemeal, bite-sized solutions to our energy crisis. We need a national commitment to energy security, and to emphasize that commitment, we should install a Director of Energy

Security to oversee all of our efforts. Like the Chairman of the Joint Chiefs and the National Intelligence Director, this person would be an advisor to the National Security Council and have the full authority to coordinate America's energy policy across all levels of government. He or she would approve all major budget decisions and provide a full report to Congress and the country every year detailing the progress we're making toward our 2025 goal.

In the days and months after September 11th, Americans were waiting to be called to something bigger than themselves. Just like their parents and grandparents of the Greatest Generation, they were willing to serve and defend their country—not only on the fields of war, but on the homefront too.

This is our chance to step up and serve. The war against international terrorism has pitted us against a new kind of enemy that wages terror in new and unconventional ways. At home, fighting that enemy won't require us to build the massive war machine that Franklin Roosevelt called for so many years ago, but it will require us to harness our own renewable forms of energy so that oil can never be used as a weapon against America. From farmers and scientists to entrepreneurs and governors, everyone has a role to play in this effort. In fact, this afternoon I'm sitting down with business and military leaders to discuss this very topic.

Now is the time for serious leadership to get us started down the path of energy independence. Now is the time for this call to arms. I hope some of the ideas I've laid out today can serve as a basis for this call, but I also hope that members of both parties and all levels of government can come together in the near future to launch this serious quest for energy independence.

Thank you.

Philip J. Deutch

 **NO**

Energy Independence

"The West Can Stop Relying on Imported Oil"

Not in this lifetime   When people call for energy independence, they usually mean ending reliance on imported oil. Energy independence, we are told, would avoid dangerous disruptions in supply, ease entanglements in the Middle East, force corrupt petrostates to reform, and dry up terrorist funds. It may be a noble statement of ultimate intentions, but as a practical matter, energy independence is absurd. The amount of petroleum imported by the United States and other countries is so enormous that operating without it over the next several decades will be impossible for any advanced industrialized economy.

The trend lines clearly indicate that Americans are becoming more energy dependent, not less so. In 1973, the United States imported 35 percent of its oil; by 2003, that proportion had jumped to 55 percent. In 2004, the United States consumed an average of 20.4 million barrels of oil per day, more than half of which was imported. Ending dependence on imported oil would mean replacing about 4 billion barrels of oil every year. To put that number in perspective, assuming no major new discovery of oil deposits, the United States would burn through its oil reserves in four to five years without imports. Worse, U.S. demand is projected to grow 37 percent in the next 20 years. At that point, oil imports will likely account for 68 percent of petroleum supply.

The picture is no different if you consider other major industrialized countries. In 2004, Japan consumed an average of 5.4 million barrels a day—almost all of which was imported. Ninety-three percent of Germany's daily oil demand of 2.6 million barrels is imported. And France already imports nearly all of its oil. Energy independence is a distant dream for all of these countries.

"Less Foreign Oil Means Lower Prices"

Wrong   Oil is a global commodity, the price of which is based on worldwide supply and demand. Events influencing supply and demand in one country affect prices in another. In the wake of Hurricane Katrina, gasoline prices in Europe soared as a result of the damage to U.S. refineries, even though those facilities send very little to Europe. Even if the United States did not import one barrel of oil from the Middle East, the price U.S. citizens would pay at the

From *Foreign Policy,* November/December 2005, pp. 20–25. Copyright © 2005 by the Carnegie Endowment for International Peace. Reprinted with permission. www.foreignpolicy.com

pump would still be a function of worldwide supply and demand. Whatever one's opinion about U.S. or European oil policy, all indications are that worldwide demand—and global prices—will climb as China and India continue to grow. China, which imports about half its oil, is expected to double its oil consumption to 14.2 million barrels a day by 2025. India's consumption will likely jump from 1.4 to 5 million barrels a day by 2020. Global demand will cause the worldwide price of petroleum to rise nearly everywhere. No private oil company will sell oil to its domestic market for one penny less than it could realize in foreign markets, and the price that a barrel of oil commands will be based on pressures beyond any one government's control.

"The United States Should Burn Less Coal"

No Many analysts argue that given concerns about global warming and the environment, the United States should avoid burning so much coal. Because the United States has the most technologically advanced energy sector, the argument goes, it should lead the way in giving up its coal habit. But just as independence from foreign oil is virtually impossible in the next two decades, there is no point in pretending that the United States can cease using coal. More important, why should the United States so quickly abandon a natural resource that it has in such abundance?

More than half of the electricity produced in the United States in 2004 was generated by coal. Total U.S. electricity sales are projected to increase at an average annual rate of 1.9 percent, from 3,481 billion kilowatt hours in 2003 to 5,220 billion kilowatt hours in 2025. If you want to begin to imagine reducing U.S. coal consumption, you must first account for how these growing energy needs will be met. The truth is that no other energy source could fill this gap. Wind and solar power now account for less than 2 percent of U.S. electricity generation, and nuclear power only about 20 percent.

Limiting coal also poses a dilemma for those who favor energy independence. True, coal is one of the "dirtier" fuel sources. But, for all its shortcomings, coal is a relatively cheap source of electricity. (It costs four times more to produce a kilowatt of electricity from a solar cell than from coal.) And it is plentiful: The United States has enough domestic coal to last 250 years. If the United States were to cut back on its coal consumption, its current energy needs would require it to import even more oil, reducing the country's energy independence even further.

"Nuclear Power Is Making a Comeback"

Yes, and it's a good thing Concerns about safety, waste disposal, and weapons proliferation are very real. Nevertheless, nuclear power is an important means of diversifying energy supply and reducing carbon emissions. Electricity generated from nuclear power does not produce carbon dioxide, and nuclear energy accounts for almost 70 percent of non-carbon power produced in the United States. Reducing the use of nuclear energy means identifying other clean fuels. A recent British Parliamentary report warned that the planned closure of most of the country's nuclear plants would undermine its goal of supplying 10 percent of Britain's electricity with renewable sources by 2010.

It is because of this calculus that the nuclear power industry is ready to boom again. Last year, 16 countries generated at least one quarter of their electricity from nuclear energy. China and Brazil have plans for the construction of as many as nine new reactors. Twenty-four new nuclear plants in nine countries are under construction, with another 40 in the works. For its part, the last U.S. nuclear plant was ordered in 1973 and completed in 1996. Nuclear energy in the United States is projected to grow over the next 20 years by 9 percent. Given the projected rise in electricity demand, the use of nuclear power, like the use of coal, simply cannot be avoided any time soon. Moreover, as with oil, even if one could somehow end its use in the United States, it would still be a growing source of energy for the rest of the world.

"Energy Conservation Is the Solution"

No chance   Faced with increasing energy demands, some argue that a better alternative is to promote energy conservation. It's worthwhile to try to conserve any natural resource, but we cannot conserve our way out of today's energy bind.

Today's cars use only 60 percent of the gasoline they did in 1972, new refrigerators about one third the electricity, and it now takes 55 percent less oil and gas than in 1973 to generate the same amount of gross domestic product (GDP). Nonetheless, in the United States, national energy use has shot up 30 percent since 1973. This growth is far less than that of the economy as a whole (126 percent), but it is substantial just the same. Consumers are more interested in enjoying the goods and gadgets that require energy than in cutting energy use itself. Few people, for example, decide whether or not to buy a plasma television based on the fact that it uses as much as 10 times the electricity that a standard TV does. Nor can conservation do anything to slow demand in large, growing economies. For example, in 1973, China had an estimated GDP of $140 billion and consumed about 1 million barrels of oil a day. By 2004, China's GDP had ballooned to roughly $7.3 trillion, with demand for oil topping out at almost 6.5 million barrels a day. Thus, in a little more than 30 years, China has become far more efficient in what it gets from the oil it burns, but the needs of its economy swamped these improvements—and the country requires still more oil.

"Customers Are Willing to Pay More for Green Energy"

Prove it   Energy is still a relatively cheap commodity in the United States, but few Americans believed even pre-Katrina energy prices were reasonable. This attitude is puzzling, given that in the early 1980s, U.S. households spent approximately 8 to 9 percent of their income on energy. Today, they spend only 5 to 6 percent. And while post-Katrina oil prices are steep, they are not even close to all-time highs. When adjusted for inflation, the price per barrel of oil in

January 1981 was more than $85. Today's prices would have to remain at this level for three years to have the same economic impact as the earlier oil shocks.

People want and expect cheap energy, and few people would actually pay more for clean power. More than 50 percent of U.S. consumers now have the option of buying electricity generated from renewable energy sources, but only 1 or 2 percent actually do. Hybrid car sales represent less than 1 percent of automobile sales; SUVS account for 25 percent. It is true that residential customers in Europe appear more willing to pay higher rates for green power. (Thirteen percent of people in the Netherlands are said to have chosen green power.) But that is largely a function of the natural resources that are present (such as huge hydroelectric dams) and aggressive government subsidies, which make such power far more affordable. Even with these measures, it's far from clear that a significantly greater proportion of Europeans will pay more.

"The Hydrogen Economy Is Going to Change Everything"

Misleading   The so-called hydrogen economy has many people optimistic about our energy future. The idea is to provide for energy independence from fossil fuels and imported oil by developing technologies such as high-performing fuel cells that will allow clean energy to be produced from hydrogen rather than oil and natural gas. Hydrogen, of course, is plentiful—after all, every water molecule contains two hydrogen atoms. But hydrogen is a fuel that must be created. Hydrogen can be derived from water (through a process using electricity called reverse electrolysis), or directly from natural gas (using a reformer). Even if one assumes fuel cells could be manufactured at a competitive price and that a hydrogen-delivery infrastructure could be constructed (imagine the cost of replacing every gas station with a hydrogen-fueling station), natural gas or electricity produced through coal or nuclear power would still be needed to create the hydrogen. If the electricity to make hydrogen is produced from natural gas imported from Qatar, how is the United States more energy independent? If the electricity is produced by coal plants with high emissions, how is hydrogen any better for the environment? The vision of a hydrogen economy does not solve our energy dilemmas; it obfuscates them.

"New Energy Technologies Will Save Us"

In the long run   Energy independence may be hopeless in the next 20 years, but there is no doubt that emerging technologies will eventually bear the brunt of our energy burden. The cost of producing electricity from wind has fallen approximately 80 percent in the last 20 years, and the cost of solar power has fallen from almost $1 per kilowatt to less than 18 cents. These efficiencies have allowed the wind and solar markets to become multibillion-dollar global markets. The markets for solar, wind, and fuel cells are projected to grow from an estimated $16 billion in 2004 to $102 billion in 2014. For the first time, there are multiple companies selling actual products based on fuel cell technologies. Danish wind manufacturer Vestas Wind Systems had revenues of almost $1.7 billion in the first half of 2005—up 47 percent from the same period in 2004. There are now companies that do nothing but maintain and fuel natural gaspowered vehicles or develop and install solar panels and wind turbines.

Earlier this year, Goldman Sachs bought Zilkha Renewable Energy, a Houston-based wind power developer, believing "wind and other renewable forms of energy will become an increasingly important part of the world's energy mix." The Carlyle Group, one of the world's most successful private equity funds, teamed up with FPL Group, a utility company, to purchase 141 megawatts of solar power in Southern California. MidAmerican Energy, majority owned by market guru Warren Buffet's Berkshire Hathaway, is undertaking a massive wind energy project in Iowa. Goldman Sachs, the Carlyle Group, and Warren Buffet are not in the business of making the world cleaner. They are sophisticated investors who believe that these technologies will offer attractive rates of return.

New energy technologies are beginning to make a difference today, and they will make a bigger difference tomorrow. But clear thinking about changes in energy supply requires a time frame measured in decades and an understanding of the trade-offs that must be made. Jettisoning the loose language about energy independence would be a good start.

WANT TO KNOW MORE?

The National Energy Policy, released by the National Energy Policy Development Group in May 2001, is a good starting point for understanding the trade-offs involved in addressing U.S. reliance on foreign oil. Ending the Energy Stalemate, produced by the National Commission on Energy Policy in December 2004, is an attempt to craft a bipartisan consensus on energy sector reform. The International Monetary Fund's April 2005 World Economic Outlook offers guidance on the interplay between energy and economic growth as well as numbers on oil prices, refining capacity, and inventories.

For a look at how corporations are taking the lead when it comes to energy and the environment, see "In Green Company," by Stuart Eizenstat and Rubèn Kraiem (FOREIGN POLICY, September/October 2005). For a more optimistic view of hydrogen's potential, see "The Hydrogen Economy" (*Physics Today*, December 2004), by George W. Crabtree, Mildred S. Dresselhaus, and Michelle V. Buchanan. A European perspective on the continent's energy future can be found in *Climate Change and a European Low-Carbon Energy System* (European Environmental Agency, 2005).

Those in search of hard data on energy supply and demand should consult BP's Statistical Reviews of World Energy and the Energy Information Administration's Annual Energy Outlook.

POSTSCRIPT

Is It Realistic for the United States to Move Toward Greater Energy Independence?

Future trends in energy dependence and energy consumption will depend on the intersection between market forces and government policies, and the proper roles of the private sector and the U.S. government in the energy market will be a subject of continued debate. Sustained oil prices above $50 per barrel can make ethanol and other alternatives economically competitive even without government subsidies, and encourage higher energy efficiency even in the absence of higher government standards. On the other hand, several kinds of "market failures" can create grounds for government involvement in energy markets. In addition to "negative externalities" like pollution and global warming (see Issue 18), there may be collective action problems that government policies can address. For example, one justification for imposing auto efficiency standards is to reduce the incentives, whether concerns for prestige or a desire for safety, to buy heavier but less efficient cars like sport utility vehicles (heavier cars are safer for their occupants but more dangerous to other vehicles in car crashes).

Another potential market failure arises from the large "economies of scale" that are involved in some energy resources. For example, the possibility of using nuclear fusion to generate electricity requires massive, long-term, and potentially risky investments that the private sector is unlikely to undertake (currently, nuclear power plants use the relatively simpler process of nuclear fission to generate electricity). Indeed, research on fusion technology requires such a large scale of investment that a consortium of states, including South Korea, Russia, China, the European Union, the United States, India, and Japan, agreed in November of 2006 to jointly build an experimental fusion reactor in France. This reactor could begin producing electrical energy in 30 years (see http://news.bbc.co.uk/1/hi/sci/tech/6165932.stm). Alternatively, it could fail entirely, as have earlier efforts to use nuclear fusion to generate more useable energy than it uses up; as many observers have noted, scientists have always seemed to put the prospect of fusion energy 30 years into the future, whether they were writing in 1966 or 2006.

For an analysis of the growing biofuel market, see Adrienne Carter, "Harvesting Green Power," *Business Week*, November 13, 2006, pp. 60–70. For an argument that rising oil prices will by themselves stimulate considerable conservation and investment in alternative energy resources, see Philip Auerswald, "The Myth of Energy Insecurity," *Issues in Science and Technology* (Summer 2006), pp. 65–70. For an argument that various energy resources and conservation measures can substantially reduce America's dependence on foreign oil, see Jenn Baka, Frank Ling, and Daniel Kammen, *Towards Energy Independence in 2025*, at the Web site of the Renewable and Appropriate Energy Laboratory, University of California at Berkeley, http://rael.berkeley. edu. For a report on U.S. energy policy by the National Commission on Energy Policy, a bipartisan group of energy experts, see "Ending the Energy Stalemate," December 2004, at http://www.energycommission.org/site/page.php?report=13. Finally, for an assessment of whether countries whose economies are dependent on oil exports are less likely to be democratic, see Michael Ross, "Does Oil Hinder Democracy?" *World Politics* (April 2001).

Internet References . . .

Bureau of International Organization Affairs

The Bureau of International Organization Affairs of the U.S. Department of State develops and implements U.S. policy in the United Nations, the specialized UN agencies, and other international organizations. On UN issues, the bureau works in cooperation with the U.S. Mission to the United Nations. The bureau also coordinates the U.S. Department of State's involvement in international athletic events.

http://www.state.gov/p/io/

United Nations

The United Nations home page is a gateway to information about the United Nations and its associated organizations. Click on "Human Rights" to explore categories related to human rights around the world, including the UN High Commissioner for Human Rights, the war crimes tribunals for Rwanda and the former Yugoslavia, and the Universal Declaration of Human Rights.

http://www.un.org

Coalition for an International Criminal Court

As its name indicates, the Coalition for an International Criminal Court favors ratification of the ICC treaty and full implementation of the court. This Web site has excellent information, including the full treaty text and up-to-date information on the ratification effort.

http://www.iccnow.org

Amnesty International

One issue related to human rights is the record of those countries with which the United States interacts. Information about the current state of human rights around the world is available at Amnesty International's Web site. The organization is a strong advocate of human rights but has been criticized by some for being too doctrinaire and for being insensitive to what may be acceptable in other cultures.

http://www.amnesty.org

Human Rights Watch

Like Amnesty International, Human Rights Watch is dedicated to preventing discrimination, upholding political freedom, protecting people from inhumane conduct in wartime, and bringing offenders to justice. It investigates and exposes human rights violations and seeks to hold abusers accountable. As stated on its Web site, its goal is to "challenge governments and those who hold power to end abusive practices and respect international human rights law."

http://hrw.org/

The United States and International Rules, Norms, and Institutions

G*lobalization involves a great deal more than the growing economic and environmental interdependence discussed in Part 5. In these areas and in a wide range of others, the United States works with other actors—including states, international organizations, non-governmental organizations, firms, and individuals. International rules, norms, and institutions facilitate these interactions by establishing standards of conduct and shaping expectations about what others will do. As these rules, norms, and institutions evolve, some priorities—like individually based human rights—may come in conflict with others—like the primary right of states to non-intervention as codified in the United Nations charter. Similarly, these rules and norms often change following traumatic events, like the end of a great power war or, some would argue, the terrorist attacks of 9/11/2001. This section takes up two issues that reflect debates over how the United States foreign policy should respond to or perhaps try to change international rules, norms, and institutions.*

- Is it Justifiable to Put Suspected Terrorists Under Great Physical Duress?

- Can Humanitarian Intervention Be Justified?

ISSUE 20

Is It Justifiable to Put Suspected Terrorists under Great Physical Duress?

YES: Charles Krauthammer, from "The Truth about Torture; It's Time to Be Honest about Doing Terrible Things," *The Weekly Standard* (December 5, 2005)

NO: Andrew Sullivan, from "The Abolition of Torture," *New Republic* (December 19, 2005)

ISSUE SUMMARY

YES: Charles Krauthammer, *Washington Post* opinion columnist, argues the lives saved by information provided by those with information about terrorist incidents justify the use of torture to obtain that information.

NO: Andrew Sullivan, senior editor of *The New Republic,* argues against claims of the military utility and necessity of torture.

Conduct regarding the treatment of potential terrorists and those who may be able to provide information about potential terrorists or terrorist activity became a hot legal and political issue following the terrorist attacks of September 11, 2001. There is an extensive body of domestic and international law regarding the treatment of domestic prisoners and prisoners of war—including the Geneva Conventions of 1864, 1929, and 1949, the Hague Conventions of 1908, and the Union Army's Lieber Code of 1863—but these laws pay little attention to terrorists, paramilitaries, and other non-uniformed combatants who were not affiliated with national militaries. This created a gray legal zone in which the debate on the treatment of suspected terrorists after September 11, 2001 evolved.

The salience of this issue intensified in April 2004 following the broadcasting of photographs of abuses by U.S. soldiers of prisoners in the Abu Ghraib prison in Baghdad on nightly news programs. Although the administration asserts that the abuses were carried out by a small number of soldiers acting largely on their own, evidence of the systematic and widespread abuse of prisoners at Abu Ghraib and at prisons in Cuba and Afghanistan soon became a matter of public record.

In addition to the photographs of abuse, several internal executive branch memoranda of interrogation tactics were leaked to the press. These memoranda documented a debate between the Department of Justice, which argued that the Geneva Convention III on the Treatment of Prisoners of War did not apply to the conflict with al Qaeda, and the State Department, which urged the president to reconsider the recommendation. Although the president declared that the conventions did apply, he declared all detainees "unlawful combatants," and therefore beyond the scope of the conventions. Lt. General Ricardo Sanchez later cited the president's comments as justification for some of the interrogation techniques used in prison abuse scandal.

White House counsel (and current attorney general) Alberto Gonzales commissioned a memorandum from the Department of Justice to the president dated August 1, 2002, which provided very specific guidelines for justifying the conduct of interrogations outside the United States and for protecting the CIA from criminal prosecution for breaking U.S. laws prohibiting torture. In the memo, he argued that inflicting pain only constituted torture if it is "sufficiently intense to cause serious physical injury, such as organ failure," or death, or "psychological harm of significant duration, e.g. for months or even years." A Defense Department review board later concluded that this memo led in part to the abuses in Iraq and Cuba.

Several administration's policies were overturned by the Supreme Court in June 2004, including policies that allowed the indefinite imprisonment of American citizens deemed enemy combatants without charge or access to counsel, and the policy that allowed for the indefinite imprisonment of al Qaeda and Taliban prisoners. Just prior to the confirmation hearings of Alberto Gonzales as attorney general in January 2005, the Department of Justice issued a new memorandum denouncing the policies in its previous memoranda on torture, but it left open its earlier position that the president has the authority to declare treaties null and void when he deems it necessary. The controversy continued when statements of presidential support for a congressional amendment to a defence authorization bill prohibiting the inhumane treatment of prisoners written by Senator McCain in December 2005 were followed by a signing statement reserving the president's authority to allow such actions if doing so would forestall another terrorist attack. McCain subsequently negotiated legislation that permitted the president to interpret the meaning and application of the Geneva Conventions as long as the subsequent treatment did not result in "serious" bodily or psychological injury. President George W. Bush signed this Military Commissions Act on October 17, 2006.

Charles Krauthammer argues that the prohibition of torture should not be universally applied and that captured terrorists and those with information about pending terrorist events should not be given the same rights and privileges of ordinary soldiers caught on the battlefield. In contrast, Andrew Sullivan argues that this is an unreliable means of gaining information and is thus unlikely to save lives. Furthermore, it is antithetical to freedom, indeed, the entire structure of American democracy and freedom evolved as a response against the state use of torture.

YES ⤹

Charles Krauthammer

The Truth about Torture

During the last few weeks in Washington the pieties about torture have lain so thick in the air that it has been impossible to have a reasoned discussion. The McCain amendment that would ban "cruel, inhuman, or degrading" treatment of any prisoner by any agent of the United States sailed through the Senate by a vote of 90–9. The Washington establishment remains stunned that nine such retrograde, morally inert persons—let alone senators—could be found in this noble capital.

Now, John McCain has great moral authority on this issue, having heroically borne torture at the hands of the North Vietnamese. McCain has made fine arguments in defense of his position. And McCain is acting out of the deep and honorable conviction that what he is proposing is not only right but is in the best interest of the United States. His position deserves respect. But that does not mean, as seems to be the assumption in Washington today, that a critical analysis of his "no torture, ever" policy is beyond the pale.

Let's begin with a few analytic distinctions. For the purpose of torture and prisoner maltreatment, there are three kinds of war prisoners: First, there is the ordinary soldier caught on the field of battle. There is no question that he is entitled to humane treatment. Indeed, we have no right to disturb a hair on his head. His detention has but a single purpose: to keep him *hors de combat*. The proof of that proposition is that if there were a better way to keep him off the battlefield that did not require his detention, we would let him go. Indeed, during one year of the Civil War, the two sides did try an alternative. They mutually "paroled" captured enemy soldiers, i.e., released them to return home on the pledge that they would not take up arms again. (The experiment failed for a foreseeable reason: cheating. Grant found that some paroled Confederates had reenlisted.)

Because the only purpose of detention in these circumstances is to prevent the prisoner from becoming a combatant again, he is entitled to all the protections and dignity of an ordinary domestic prisoner—indeed, more privileges, because, unlike the domestic prisoner, he has committed no crime. He merely had the misfortune to enlist on the other side of a legitimate war. He is therefore entitled to many of the privileges enjoyed by an ordinary citizen—the right to send correspondence, to engage in athletic activity and intellectual pursuits, to receive allowances from relatives—except, of course, for the freedom to leave the prison.

From *Weekly Standard,* 11:12, December 5, 2005. Copyright © 2005 by Charles Krauthammer. Reprinted by permission of the author.

Second, there is the captured terrorist. A terrorist is by profession, indeed by definition, an unlawful combatant: He lives outside the laws of war because he does not wear a uniform, he hides among civilians, and he deliberately targets innocents. He is entitled to no protections whatsoever. People seem to think that the postwar Geneva Conventions were written only to protect detainees. In fact, their deeper purpose was to provide a deterrent to the kind of barbaric treatment of civilians that had become so horribly apparent during the first half of the 20th century, and in particular, during the Second World War. The idea was to deter the abuse of civilians by promising combatants who treated noncombatants well that they themselves would be treated according to a code of dignity if captured—and, crucially, that they would be denied the protections of that code if they broke the laws of war and abused civilians themselves.

Breaking the laws of war and abusing civilians are what, to understate the matter vastly, terrorists do for a living. They are entitled, therefore, to nothing. Anyone who blows up a car bomb in a market deserves to spend the rest of his life roasting on a spit over an open fire. But we don't do that because we do not descend to the level of our enemy. We don't do that because, unlike him, we are civilized. Even though terrorists are entitled to no humane treatment, we give it to them because it is in our nature as a moral and humane people. And when on rare occasions we fail to do that, as has occurred in several of the fronts of the war on terror, we are duly disgraced.

The norm, however, is how the majority of prisoners at Guantanamo have been treated. We give them three meals a day, superior medical care, and provision to pray five times a day. Our scrupulousness extends even to providing them with their own Korans, which is the only reason alleged abuses of the Koran at Guantanamo ever became an issue. That we should have provided those who kill innocents in the name of Islam with precisely the document that inspires their barbarism is a sign of the absurd lengths to which we often go in extending undeserved humanity to terrorist prisoners.

Third, there is the terrorist with information. Here the issue of torture gets complicated and the easy pieties don't so easily apply. Let's take the textbook case. Ethics 101: A terrorist has planted a nuclear bomb in New York City. It will go off in one hour. A million people will die. You capture the terrorist. He knows where it is. He's not talking.

Question: If you have the slightest belief that hanging this man by his thumbs will get you the information to save a million people, are you permitted to do it? Now, on most issues regarding torture, I confess tentativeness and uncertainty. But on this issue, there can be no uncertainty: Not only is it permissible to hang this miscreant by his thumbs. It is a moral duty. Yes, you say, but that's an extreme and very hypothetical case. Well, not as hypothetical as you think. Sure, the (nuclear) scale is hypothetical, but in the age of the car- and suicide-bomber, terrorists are often captured who have just set a car bomb to go off or sent a suicide bomber out to a coffee shop, and you only have minutes to find out where the attack is to take place. This "hypothetical" is common enough that the Israelis have a term for precisely that situation: the ticking time bomb problem.

And even if the example I gave were entirely hypothetical, the conclusion—yes, in this case even torture is permissible—is telling because it establishes the principle: Torture is not always impermissible. However rare the cases, there are circumstances in which, by any rational moral calculus, torture not only would be permissible but would be required (to acquire life-saving information). And once you've established the principle, to paraphrase George Bernard Shaw, all that's left to haggle about is the price. In the case of torture, that means that the argument is not *whether* torture is ever permissible, but *when*—i.e., under what obviously stringent circumstances: how big, how imminent, how preventable the ticking time bomb. That is why the McCain amendment, which by mandating "torture never" refuses even to recognize the legitimacy of any moral calculus, cannot be right. There must be exceptions. The real argument should be over what constitutes a legitimate exception.

Let's take an example that is far from hypothetical. You capture Khalid Sheikh Mohammed in Pakistan. He not only has already killed innocents, he is deeply involved in the planning for the present and future killing of innocents. He not only was the architect of the 9/11 attack that killed nearly three thousand people in one day, most of them dying a terrible, agonizing, indeed tortured death. But as the top al Qaeda planner and logistical expert he also knows a lot about terror attacks to come. He knows plans, identities, contacts, materials, cell locations, safe houses, cased targets, etc. What do you do with him?

We have recently learned that since 9/11 the United States has maintained a series of "black sites" around the world, secret detention centers where presumably high-level terrorists like Khalid Sheikh Mohammed have been imprisoned. The world is scandalized. Black sites? Secret detention? Jimmy Carter calls this "a profound and radical change in the . . . moral values of our country." The Council of Europe demands an investigation, calling the claims "extremely worrying." Its human rights commissioner declares "such practices" to constitute "a serious human rights violation, and further proof of the crisis of values" that has engulfed the war on terror. The gnashing of teeth and rending of garments has been considerable.

I myself have not gnashed a single tooth. My garments remain entirely unrent. Indeed, I feel reassured. It would be a gross dereliction of duty for any government *not* to keep Khalid Sheikh Mohammed isolated, disoriented, alone, despairing, cold and sleepless, in some godforsaken hidden location in order to find out what he knew about plans for future mass murder. What are we supposed to do? Give him a nice cell in a warm Manhattan prison, complete with Miranda rights, a mellifluent lawyer, and his own website? Are not those the kinds of courtesies we extended to the 1993 World Trade Center bombers, then congratulated ourselves on how we "brought to justice" those responsible for an attack that barely failed to kill tens of thousands of Americans, only to discover a decade later that we had accomplished nothing—indeed, that some of the disclosures at the trial had helped Osama bin Laden avoid U.S. surveillance?

Have we learned nothing from 9/11? Are we prepared to go back with complete amnesia to the domestic-crime model of dealing with terrorists, which allowed us to sleepwalk through the nineties while al Qaeda incubated and grew and metastasized unmolested until on 9/11 it finished what the first World Trade Center bombers had begun?

Let's assume (and hope) that Khalid Sheikh Mohammed has been kept in one of these black sites, say, a cell somewhere in Romania, held entirely incommunicado and subjected to the kind of "coercive interrogation" that I described above. McCain has been going around praising the Israelis as the model of how to deal with terrorism and prevent terrorist attacks. He does so because in 1999 the Israeli Supreme Court outlawed all torture in the course of interrogation. But in reality, the Israeli case is far more complicated. And the complications reflect precisely the dilemmas regarding all coercive interrogation, the weighing of the lesser of two evils: the undeniable inhumanity of torture versus the abdication of the duty to protect the victims of a potentially preventable mass murder.

In a summary of Israel's policies, Glenn Frankel of the *Washington Post* noted that the 1999 Supreme Court ruling struck down secret guidelines established 12 years earlier that allowed interrogators to use the kind of physical and psychological pressure I described in imagining how KSM might be treated in America's "black sites."

"But after the second Palestinian uprising broke out a year later, and especially after a devastating series of suicide bombings of passenger buses, cafes and other civilian targets," writes Frankel, citing human rights lawyers and detainees, "Israel's internal security service, known as the Shin Bet or the Shabak, returned to physical coercion as a standard practice." Not only do the techniques used "command widespread support from the Israeli public," but "Israeli prime ministers and justice ministers with a variety of political views," including the most conciliatory and liberal, have defended these techniques "as a last resort in preventing terrorist attacks."

Which makes McCain's position on torture incoherent. If this kind of coercive interrogation were imposed on any inmate in the American prison system, it would immediately be declared cruel and unusual, and outlawed. How can he oppose these practices, which the Israelis use, and yet hold up Israel as a model for dealing with terrorists? Or does he countenance this kind of interrogation in extreme circumstances—in which case, what is left of his categorical opposition to inhuman treatment of any kind?

But let us push further into even more unpleasant territory, the territory that lies beyond mere coercive interrogation and beyond McCain's self-contradictions. How far are we willing to go? This "going beyond" need not be cinematic and ghoulish. (Jay Leno once suggested "duct tape" for Khalid Sheikh Mohammed.) Consider, for example, injection with sodium pentathol. (Colloquially known as "truth serum," it is nothing of the sort. It is a barbiturate whose purpose is to sedate. Its effects are much like that of alcohol: disinhibiting the higher brain centers to make someone more likely to disclose information or thoughts that might otherwise be guarded.) Forcible sedation is a clear violation of bodily integrity. In a civilian context it would be considered assault. It is certainly impermissible under any prohibition of cruel, inhuman, or degrading treatment.

Let's posit that during the interrogation of Khalid Sheikh Mohammed, perhaps early on, we got intelligence about an imminent al Qaeda attack. And we had a very good reason to believe he knew about it. And if we knew what he knew, we could stop it. If we thought we could glean a critical piece of information by use of sodium pentathol, would we be permitted to do so?

Less hypothetically, there is waterboarding, a terrifying and deeply shocking torture technique in which the prisoner has his face exposed to water in a way that gives the feeling of drowning. According to CIA sources cited by ABC News, Khalid Sheikh Mohammed "was able to last between 2 and 2 1/2 minutes before begging to confess." Should we regret having done that? Should we abolish by law that practice, so that it could never be used on the next Khalid Sheikh Mohammed having thus gotten his confession?

And what if he possessed information with less imminent implications? Say we had information about a cell that he had helped found or direct, and that cell was planning some major attack and we needed information about the identity and location of its members. A rational moral calculus might not permit measures as extreme as the nuke-in-Manhattan scenario, but would surely permit measures beyond mere psychological pressure.

Such a determination would not be made with an untroubled conscience. It would be troubled because there is no denying the monstrous evil that is any form of torture. And there is no denying how corrupting it can be to the individuals and society that practice it. But elected leaders, responsible above all for the protection of their citizens, have the obligation to tolerate their own sleepless nights by doing what is necessary—and only what is necessary, nothing more—to get information that could prevent mass murder.

Given the gravity of the decision, if we indeed cross the Rubicon—as we must—we need rules. The problem with the McCain amendment is that once you have gone public with a blanket ban on all forms of coercion, it is going to be very difficult to publicly carve out exceptions. The Bush administration is to be faulted for having attempted such a codification with the kind of secrecy, lack of coherence, and lack of strict enforcement that led us to the McCain reaction.

What to do at this late date? Begin, as McCain does, by banning all forms of coercion or inhuman treatment by anyone serving in the military—an absolute ban on torture by all military personnel everywhere. We do not want a private somewhere making these fine distinctions about ticking and slow-fuse time bombs. We don't even want colonels or generals making them. It would be best for the morale, discipline, and honor of the Armed Forces for the United States to maintain an absolute prohibition, both to simplify their task in making decisions and to offer them whatever reciprocal treatment they might receive from those who capture them—although I have no illusion that any anti-torture provision will soften the heart of a single jihadist holding a knife to the throat of a captured American soldier. We would impose this restriction on ourselves for our own reasons of military discipline and military honor.

Outside the military, however, I would propose, contra McCain, a ban against all forms of torture, coercive interrogation, and inhuman treatment, except in two contingencies: (1) the ticking time bomb and (2) the slower-fuse high-level terrorist (such as KSM). Each contingency would have its own set of rules. In the case of the ticking time bomb, the rules would be relatively simple: Nothing rationally related to getting accurate information would be ruled out. The case of the high-value suspect with slow-fuse information is more complicated. The principle would be that the level of inhumanity of the measures used (moral honesty is essential here—we would be using measures that are by definition inhumane) would be proportional to the need and value of the information. Interrogators would be constrained to use the least inhumane treatment necessary relative to the magnitude and imminence of the evil being prevented and the importance of the knowledge being obtained.

These exceptions to the no-torture rule would not be granted to just any nonmilitary interrogators, or anyone with CIA credentials. They would be reserved for highly specialized agents who are experts and experienced in interrogation, and who are known not to abuse it for the satisfaction of a kind of sick sadomasochism Lynndie England and her cohorts indulged in at Abu Ghraib. Nor would they be acting on their own. They would be required to obtain written permission for such interrogations from the highest political authorities in the country (cabinet level) or from a quasi-judicial body modeled on the Foreign Intelligence Surveillance Court (which permits what would ordinarily be illegal searches and seizures in the war on terror). Or, if the bomb was truly ticking and there was no time, the interrogators would be allowed to act on their own, but would require post facto authorization within, say, 24 hours of their interrogation, so that they knew that whatever they did would be subject to review by others and be justified only under the most stringent terms.

One of the purposes of these justifications would be to establish that whatever extreme measures are used are for reasons of nothing but information. Historically, the torture of prisoners has been done for a variety of reasons apart from information, most prominently reasons of justice or revenge. We do not do that. We should not do that. Ever. Khalid Sheikh Mohammed, murderer of 2,973 innocents, is surely deserving of the most extreme suffering day and night for the rest of his life. But it is neither our role nor our right to be the agents of that suffering. Vengeance is mine, sayeth the Lord. His, not ours. Torture is a terrible and monstrous thing, as degrading and morally corrupting to those who practice it as any conceivable human activity including its moral twin, capital punishment.

If Khalid Sheikh Mohammed knew nothing, or if we had reached the point where his knowledge had been exhausted, I'd be perfectly prepared to throw him into a nice, comfortable Manhattan cell and give him a trial to determine what would be fit and just punishment. But as long as he had useful information, things would be different.

Very different. And it simply will not do to take refuge in the claim that all of the above discussion is superfluous because torture never works anyway. Would that this were true. Unfortunately, on its face, this is nonsense. Is one to believe that in the entire history of human warfare, no combatant has ever received useful information by the use of pressure, torture, or any other kind of inhuman treatment? It may indeed be true that torture is not a reliable tool. But that is very different from saying that it is *never* useful.

The monstrous thing about torture is that sometimes it does work. In 1994, 19-year-old Israeli corporal Nachshon Waxman was kidnapped by Palestinian terrorists. The Israelis captured the driver of the car used in the kidnap- ping and tortured him in order to find where Waxman was being held. Yitzhak Rabin, prime minister and peacemaker, admitted that they tortured him in a way that went even beyond the '87 guidelines for "coercive interrogation" later struck down by the Israeli Supreme Court as too harsh. The driver talked. His information was accurate. The Israelis found Waxman. "If we'd been so careful to follow the ['87] Landau Commission [which *allowed* coercive interrogation]," explained Rabin, "we would never have found out where Waxman was being held."

In the Waxman case, I would have done precisely what Rabin did. (The fact that Waxman's Palestinian captors killed him during the Israeli rescue raid makes the case doubly tragic, but changes nothing of the moral calculus.) Faced with a similar choice, an American president would have a similar obligation. To do otherwise—to give up the chance to find your soldier lest you sully yourself by authorizing torture of the person who possesses potentially lifesaving information—is a deeply immoral betrayal of a soldier and countryman. Not as cosmically immoral as permitting a city of one's countrymen to perish, as in the Ethics 101 case. But it remains, nonetheless, a case of moral abdication—of a kind rather parallel to that of the principled pacifist. There is much to admire in those who refuse on principle ever to take up arms under any conditions. But that does not make pure pacifism, like no-torture absolutism, any less a form of moral foolishness, tinged with moral vanity. Not reprehensible, only deeply reproachable and supremely impracticable. People who hold such beliefs are deserving of a certain respect. But they are not to be put in positions of authority. One should be grateful for the saintly among us. And one should be vigilant that they not get to make the decisions upon which the lives of others depend.

Which brings us to the greatest irony of all in the torture debate. I have just made what will be characterized as the pro-torture case contra McCain by proposing two major exceptions carved out of any no-torture rule: the ticking time bomb and the slow-fuse high-value terrorist. McCain supposedly is being hailed for defending all that is good and right and just in America by standing foursquare against any inhuman treatment. Or is he?

According to *Newsweek*, in the ticking time bomb case McCain says that the president should disobey the very law that McCain seeks to pass—under the justification that "you do what you have to do. But you take responsibility for it." But if torturing the ticking time bomb suspect is "what you have to do," then why has McCain been going around arguing that such things must never be done?

As for exception number two, the high-level terrorist with slow-fuse information, Stuart Taylor, the superb legal correspondent for *National Journal*, argues that with appropriate legal interpretation, the "cruel, inhuman, or degrading" standard, "though vague, is said by experts to codify . . . the commonsense principle that the toughness of interrogation techniques should be calibrated to the importance and urgency of the information likely to be obtained." That would permit "some very aggressive techniques . . . on that small percentage of detainees who seem especially likely to have potentially life-saving information." Or as Evan Thomas and Michael Hirsh put it in the *Newsweek* report on McCain and torture, the McCain standard would "presumably allow for a sliding scale" of torture or torture-lite or other coercive techniques, thus permitting "for a very small percentage—those High Value Targets like Khalid Sheikh Mohammed—some pretty rough treatment."

But if that is the case, then McCain embraces the same exceptions I do, but prefers to pretend he does not. If that is the case, then his much-touted and endlessly repeated absolutism on inhumane treatment is merely for show. If that is the case, then the moral preening and the phony arguments can stop now, and we can all agree that in this real world of astonishingly murderous enemies, in two very circumscribed circumstances, we must all be prepared to torture. Having established that, we can then begin to work together to codify rules of interrogation for the two very unpleasant but very real cases in which we are morally permitted—indeed morally compelled—to do terrible things.

Andrew Sullivan

The Abolition of Torture

Why is torture wrong? It may seem like an obvious question, or even one beneath discussion. But it is now inescapably before us, with the introduction of the McCain Amendment banning all "cruel, inhuman, and degrading treatment" of detainees by American soldiers and CIA operatives anywhere in the world. The amendment lies in legislative limbo. It passed the Senate in October by a vote of 90 to nine, but President Bush has vowed to veto any such blanket ban on torture or abuse; Vice President Cheney has prevailed upon enough senators and congressmen to prevent the amendment—and the defense appropriations bill to which it is attached—from moving out of conference; and my friend Charles Krauthammer, one of the most respected conservative intellectuals in Washington (and a *New Republic* contributing editor) has written a widely praised cover essay for *The Weekly Standard* endorsing the legalization of full-fledged torture by the United States under strictly curtailed conditions. We stand on the brink of an enormously important choice—one that is critical, morally as well as strategically, to get right.

This debate takes place after three years in which the Bush administration has defined "torture" in the narrowest terms and has permitted coercive, physical abuse of enemy combatants if "military necessity" demands it. It comes also after several internal Pentagon reports found widespread and severe abuse of detainees in Afghanistan, Iraq, and elsewhere that has led to at least two dozen deaths during interrogation. Journalistic accounts and reports by the International Committee of the Red Cross paint an even darker picture of secret torture sites in Eastern Europe and innocent detainees being murdered. Behind all this, the grim images of Abu Ghraib—the worst of which have yet to be released—linger in the public consciousness.

In this inevitably emotional debate, perhaps the greatest failing of those of us who have been arguing against all torture and "cruel, inhuman, and degrading treatment" of detainees is that we have assumed the reasons why torture is always a moral evil, rather than explicating them. But, when you fully ponder them, I think it becomes clearer why, contrary to Krauthammer's argument, torture, in any form and under any circumstances, is both antithetical to the most basic principles for which the United States stands and a profound impediment to winning a wider war that we cannot afford to lose.

◦◉◦

Torture is the polar opposite of freedom. It is the banishment of all freedom from a human body and soul, insofar as that is possible. As human beings, we all inhabit bodies and have minds, souls, and reflexes that are designed in part to protect those bodies: to resist or flinch from pain, to protect the psyche from disintegration, and to maintain a sense of selfhood that is the basis for the concept of personal liberty. What torture does is use these involuntary, self-protective, self-defining resources of human beings against the integrity of the human being himself. It takes what is most involuntary in a person and uses it to break that person's will. It takes what is animal in us and deploys it against what makes us human. As an American commander wrote in an August 2003 e-mail about his instructions to torture prisoners at Abu Ghraib, "The gloves are coming off gentlemen regarding these detainees, Col. Boltz has made it clear that we want these individuals broken."

What does it mean to "break" an individual? As the French essayist Michel de Montaigne once commented, and Shakespeare echoed, even the greatest philosophers have difficulty thinking clearly when they have a tooth-ache. These wise men were describing the inescapable frailty of the human experience, mocking the claims of some seers to be above basic human feel-ings and bodily needs. If that frailty is exposed by a toothache, it is beyond dispute in the case of torture. The infliction of physical pain on a person with no means of defending himself is designed to render that person com-pletely subservient to his torturers. It is designed to extirpate his autonomy as a human being, to render his control as an individual beyond his own reach. That is why the term "break" is instructive. Something broken can be put back together, but it will never regain the status of being unbroken—of having integrity. When you break a human being, you turn him into some-thing subhuman. You enslave him. This is why the Romans reserved torture for slaves, not citizens, and why slavery and torture were inextricably linked in the antebellum South.

What you see in the relationship between torturer and tortured is the absolute darkness of totalitarianism. You see one individual granted the most complete power he can ever hold over another. Not just confinement of his mobility—the abolition of his very agency. Torture uses a person's body to remove from his own control his conscience, his thoughts, his faith, his self-hood. The CIA's definition of "waterboarding"—recently leaked to ABC News—describes that process in plain English: "The prisoner is bound to an inclined board, feet raised and head slightly below the feet. Cellophane is wrapped over the prisoner's face and water is poured over him. Unavoidably, the gag reflex kicks in and a terrifying fear of drowning leads to almost instant pleas to bring the treatment to a halt." The ABC report then noted, "According to the sources, CIA officers who subjected themselves to the waterboarding tech-nique lasted an average of 14 seconds before caving in. They said Al Qaeda's toughest prisoner, Khalid Sheikh Mohammed, won the admiration of interro-gators when he was able to last between two and two and a half minutes before begging to confess."

Before the Bush administration, two documented cases of the U.S. Armed Forces using "waterboarding" resulted in courts-martial for the soldiers implicated. In Donald Rumsfeld's post–September 11 Pentagon, the technique is approved and, we recently learned, has been used on at least eleven detainees, possibly many more. What you see here is the deployment of a very basic and inescapable human reflex—the desire not to drown and suffocate—in order to destroy a person's autonomy. Even the most hardened fanatic can only endure two and a half minutes. After that, he is indeed "broken."

⋰◉⋱

The entire structure of Western freedom grew in part out of the searing experience of state-sanctioned torture. The use of torture in Europe's religious wars of the sixteenth and seventeenth centuries is still etched in our communal consciousness, as it should be. Then, governments deployed torture not only to uncover perceived threats to their faith-based autocracies, but also to "save" the victim's soul. Torturers understood that religious conversion was a difficult thing, because it necessitated a shift in the deepest recesses of the human soul. The only way to reach those depths was to deploy physical terror in the hopes of completely destroying the heretic's autonomy. They would, in other words, destroy a human being's soul in order to save it. That is what burning at the stake was—an indescribably agonizing act of torture that could be ended at a moment's notice if the victim recanted. In a state where theological doctrine always trumped individual liberty, this was a natural tactic.

Indeed, the very concept of Western liberty sprung in part from an understanding that, if the state has the power to reach that deep into a person's soul and can do that much damage to a human being's person, then the state has extinguished all oxygen necessary for freedom to survive. That is why, in George Orwell's totalitarian nightmare, the final ordeal is, of course, torture. Any polity that endorses torture has incorporated into its own DNA a totalitarian mutation. If the point of the U.S. Constitution is the preservation of liberty, the formal incorporation into U.S. law of the state's right to torture—by legally codifying physical coercion, abuse, and even, in Krauthammer's case, full-fledged torture of detainees by the CIA—would effectively end the American experiment of a political society based on inalienable human freedom protected not by the good graces of the executive, but by the rule of law.

The founders understood this argument. Its preeminent proponent was George Washington himself. As historian David Hackett Fischer memorably recounts in his 2004 book, *Washington's Crossing:* "Always some dark spirits wished to visit the same cruelties on the British and Hessians that had been inflicted on American captives. But Washington's example carried growing weight, more so than his written orders and prohibitions. He often reminded his men that they were an army of liberty and freedom, and that the rights of humanity for which they were fighting should extend even to their enemies. . . . Even in the most urgent moments of the war, these men were concerned about ethical questions in the Revolution."

Krauthammer has described Washington's convictions concerning torture as "pieties" that can be dispensed with today. He doesn't argue that torture is not evil. Indeed, he denounces it in unequivocal moral terms: "[T]orture is a terrible and monstrous thing, as degrading and morally corrupting to those who practice it as any conceivable human activity including its moral twin, capital punishment." But he maintains that the nature of the Islamofascist enemy after September 11 radically altered our interrogative options and that we are now not only permitted, but actually "morally compelled," to torture.

This is a radical and daring idea: that we must extinguish human freedom in a few cases in order to maintain it for everyone else. It goes beyond even the Bush administration's own formal position, which states that the United States will not endorse torture but merely "coercive interrogation techniques." (Such techniques, in the administration's elaborate definition, are those that employ physical force short of threatening immediate death or major organ failure.) And it is based on a premise that deserves further examination: that our enemies actually *deserve* torture; that some human beings are so depraved that, in Krauthammer's words, they "are entitled to no humane treatment."

Let me state for the record that I am second to none in decrying, loathing, and desiring to defeat those who wish to replace freedom with religious tyranny of the most brutal kind—and who have murdered countless innocent civilians in cold blood. Their acts are monstrous and barbaric. But I differ from Krauthammer by believing that monsters remain human beings. In fact, to reduce them to a subhuman level is to exonerate them of their acts of terrorism and mass murder—just as animals are not deemed morally responsible for killing. Insisting on the humanity of terrorists is, in fact, critical to maintaining their profound responsibility for the evil they commit.

And, if they are human, then they must necessarily not be treated in an inhuman fashion. You cannot lower the moral baseline of a terrorist to the subhuman without betraying a fundamental value. That is why the Geneva Conventions have a very basic ban on "cruel treatment and torture," and "outrages upon personal dignity, in particular humiliating and degrading treatment"—even when dealing with illegal combatants like terrorists. That is why the Declaration of Independence did not restrict its endorsement of freedom merely to those lucky enough to find themselves on U.S. soil—but extended it to all human beings, wherever they are in the world, simply because they are human.

❦

Nevertheless, it is important to address Krauthammer's practical points. He is asking us to steel ourselves and accept that, whether we like it or not, torture and abuse may be essential in a war where our very survival may be at stake. He presents two scenarios in which he believes torture is permissible. The first is the "ticking bomb" scenario, a hypothetical rarity in which the following conditions apply: a) a terrorist cell has planted a nuclear weapon or something nearly as devastating in a major city; b) we have captured someone in this cell; c) we know for a fact that he knows where the bomb is. In practice, of course, the likelihood of such a scenario is extraordinarily remote. Uncovering a terrorist plot is hard enough; capturing a conspirator involved in that plot is even harder; and realizing in advance that the person knows the whereabouts of the bomb is nearly impossible. (Remember, in the war on terrorism, we have already detained—and even killed—many innocents. Pentagon reports have acknowledged that up to 90 percent of the prisoners at Abu Ghraib, many of whom were abused and tortured, were not guilty of anything.) But let us assume, for the sake of argument, that all of Krauthammer's conditions apply. Do we have a right to torture our hypothetical detainee?

According to Krauthammer, *of course* we do. No responsible public official put in that position would refuse to sanction torture if he believed it could save thousands of lives. And, if it's necessary, Krauthammer argues, it should be made legal. If you have conceded that torture may be justified in one case, Krauthammer believes, you have conceded that it may be justified in many more. In his words, "Once you've established the principle, to paraphrase George Bernard Shaw, all that's left to haggle about is the price."

But this is too easy and too glib a formulation. It is possible to concede that, in an extremely rare circumstance, torture may be used without conceding that it should be legalized. One imperfect but instructive analogy is civil disobedience. In that case, laws are indeed broken, but that does not establish that the laws should be broken. In fact, civil disobedience implies precisely that laws should *not* be broken, and protesters who engage in it present themselves promptly for imprisonment and legal sanction on exactly those grounds. They do so for demonstrative reasons. They are not saying that laws don't matter. They are saying that laws do matter, that they should be enforced, but that their conscience in this instance demands that they disobey them.

In extremis, a rough parallel can be drawn for a president faced with the kind of horrendous decision on which Krauthammer rests his entire case. What should a president do? The answer is simple: He may have to break the law. In the Krauthammer scenario, a president might well decide that, if the survival of the nation is at stake, he must make an exception. At the same time, he must subject himself—and so must those assigned to conduct the torture—to the consequences of an illegal act. Those guilty of torturing another human being must be punished—or pardoned ex-post-facto. If the torture is revealed to be useless, if the tortured man is shown to have been innocent or ignorant of the information he was tortured to reveal, then those responsible must face the full brunt of the law for, in Krauthammer's words, such a "terrible and monstrous thing." In Michael Walzer's formulation, if we are to have dirty hands, it is essential that we show them to be dirty.

What Krauthammer is proposing, however, is not this compromise, which allows us to retain our soul as a free republic while protecting us from catastrophe in an extremely rare case. He is proposing something very different: that our "dirty hands" be wiped legally clean before and after the fact. That is a Rubicon we should not cross, because it marks the boundary between a free country and an unfree one.

Krauthammer, moreover, misses a key lesson learned these past few years. What the hundreds of abuse and torture incidents have shown is that, once you permit torture for someone somewhere, it has a habit of spreading. Remember that torture was originally sanctioned in administration memos only for use against illegal combatants in rare cases. Within months of that decision, abuse and torture had become endemic throughout Iraq, a theater of war in which, even Bush officials agree, the Geneva Conventions apply. The extremely coercive interrogation tactics used at Guantánamo Bay "migrated" to Abu Ghraib. In fact, General Geoffrey Miller was sent to Abu Ghraib specifically to replicate Guantánamo's techniques. According to former Brigadier General Janis Karpinski, who had original responsibility for the prison, Miller ordered her to treat all detainees "like dogs." When Captain Ian Fishback, a West Point graduate and member of the 82nd Airborne, witnessed routine beatings and abuse of detainees at detention facilities in Iraq and Afghanistan, often for sport, he tried to stop it. It took him a year and a half to get any response from the military command, and he had to go to Senator John McCain to make his case.

In short, what was originally supposed to be safe, sanctioned, and rare became endemic, disorganized, and brutal. The lesson is that it is impossible to quarantine torture in a hermetic box; it will inevitably contaminate the military as a whole. Once you have declared that some enemies are subhuman, you have told every soldier that every potential detainee he comes across might be exactly that kind of prisoner—and that anything can therefore be done to him. That is what the disgrace at Abu Ghraib proved. And Abu Ghraib produced a tiny fraction of the number of abuse, torture, and murder cases that have been subsequently revealed. The only way to control torture is to ban it outright. Everywhere. Even then, in wartime, some "bad apples" will always commit abuse. But at least we will have done all we can to constrain it.

⌖

Krauthammer's second case for torture is equally unpersuasive. For "slow-fuse" detainees—high-level prisoners like Khalid Sheikh Mohammed with potentially, if not immediately, useful intelligence—Krauthammer again takes the most extreme case and uses it to establish a general rule. He concedes that torture, according to almost every careful student and expert, yields highly unreliable information. Anyone can see that. If you are screaming for relief after a few seconds of waterboarding, you're likely to tell your captors anything, true or untrue, to stop the agony and terror. But Krauthammer then argues that, unless you can prove that torture *never* works, it should always be retained as an option. "It may indeed be true that torture is not a reliable tool," he argues. "But that is very different from saying that it is *never* useful." And if it cannot be deemed always useless, it must be permitted—even when an imminent threat is not in the picture.

The problem here is an obvious one. You have made the extreme exception the basis for a new rule. You have said that, if you cannot absolutely rule out torture as effective in every single case, it should be ruled in as an option for many. Moreover, if allowing torture even in the "ticking bomb" scenario makes the migration of torture throughout the military likely, this loophole blows the doors wide open. And how do we tell good intelligence from bad intelligence in such torture-infested interrogation? The short answer is: We cannot. By allowing torture for "slow-fuse" detainees, you sacrifice a vital principle for intelligence that is uniformly corrupted at best and useless at worst.

In fact, the use of torture and coercive interrogation by U.S. forces in this war may have contributed to a profound worsening of our actionable intelligence. The key to intelligence in Iraq and, indeed, in Muslim enclaves in the West, is gaining the support and trust of those who give terrorists cover but who are not terrorists themselves. We need human intelligence from Muslims and Arabs prepared to spy on and inform on their neighbors and friends and even family and tribe members. The only way they will do that is if they perceive the gains of America's intervention as greater than the costs, if they see clearly that cooperating with the West will lead to a better life and a freer world rather than more of the same.

What our practical endorsement of torture has done is to remove that clear boundary between the Islamists and the West and make the two equivalent in the Muslim mind. Saddam Hussein used Abu Ghraib to torture innocents; so did the Americans. Yes, what Saddam did was exponentially worse. But, in doing what we did, we blurred the critical, bright line between the Arab past and what we are proposing as the Arab future. We gave Al Qaeda an enormous propaganda coup, as we have done with Guantánamo and Bagram, the "Salt Pit" torture chambers in Afghanistan, and the secret torture sites in Eastern Europe. In World War II, American soldiers were often tortured by the Japanese when captured, But FDR refused to reciprocate. Why? Because he knew that the goal of the war was not just Japan's defeat but Japan's transformation into a democracy. He knew that, if the beacon of democracy—the United States of America—had succumbed to the hallmark of totalitarianism, then the chance for democratization would be deeply compromised in the wake of victory.

No one should ever underestimate the profound impact that the conduct of American troops in World War II had on the citizens of the eventually defeated Axis powers. Germans saw the difference between being liberated by the Anglo-Americans and being liberated by the Red Army. If you saw an American or British uniform, you were safe. If you didn't, the terror would continue in different ways. Ask any German or Japanese of the generation that built democracy in those countries, and they will remind you of American values—not trumpeted by presidents in front of handpicked audiences, but *demonstrated* by the conduct of the U.S. military during occupation. I grew up in Great Britain, a country with similar memories. In the dark days of the cold war, I was taught that America, for all its faults, was still America. And that America did not, and constitutively could not, torture anyone.

If American conduct was important in Japan and Germany, how much more important is it in Iraq and Afghanistan. The entire point of the war on terrorism, according to the president, is to advance freedom and democracy in the Arab world. In Iraq, we had a chance not just to tell but to show the Iraqi people how a democracy acts. And, tragically, in one critical respect, we failed. That failure undoubtedly contributed to the increased legitimacy of the insurgency and illegitimacy of the occupation, and it made collaboration between informed Sunnis and U.S. forces far less likely. What minuscule intelligence we might have plausibly gained from torturing and abusing detainees is vastly outweighed by the intelligence we have forfeited by alienating many otherwise sympathetic Iraqis and Afghans, by deepening the divide between the democracies, and by sullying the West's reputation in the Middle East. Ask yourself: Why does Al Qaeda tell its detainees to claim torture regardless of what happens to them in U.S. custody? Because Al Qaeda knows that one of America's greatest weapons in this war is its reputation as a repository of freedom and decency. Our policy of permissible torture has handed Al Qaeda this weapon—to use against us. It is not just a moral tragedy. It is a pragmatic disaster. Why compound these crimes and errors by subsequently legalizing them, as Krauthammer (explicitly) and the president (implicitly) are proposing?

Will a ban on all "cruel, inhuman, and degrading treatment" render interrogations useless? By no means. There are many techniques for gaining intelligence from detainees other than using their bodies against their souls. You can start with the 17 that appear in the Army Field Manual, tested by decades of armed conflict only to be discarded by this administration with barely the blink of an eye. Isolation, psychological disorientation, intense questioning, and any number of other creative techniques are possible. Some of the most productive may well be those in which interrogators are so versed in Islamic theology and Islamist subcultures that they win the confidence of prisoners and pry information out of them—something the United States, with its dearth of Arabic speakers, is unfortunately ill-equipped to do.

Enemy combatants need not be accorded every privilege granted legitimate prisoners of war; but they must be treated as human beings. This means that, in addition to physical torture, wanton abuse of their religious faith is out of bounds. No human freedom is meaningful without religious freedom. The fact that Koran abuse has been documented at Guantánamo; that one prisoner at Abu Ghraib was forced to eat pork and drink liquor; that fake menstrual blood was used to disorient a strict Muslim prisoner at Guantánamo—these make winning the hearts and minds of moderate Muslims far harder. Such tactics have resulted in hunger strikes at Guantánamo—perhaps the ultimate sign that the coercive and abusive attempts to gain the cooperation of detainees has completely failed to achieve the desired results.

The war on terrorism is, after all, a religious war in many senses. It is a war to defend the separation of church and state as critical to the existence of freedom, including religious freedom. It is a war to persuade the silent majority of Muslims that the West offers a better way—more decency, freedom, and humanity than the autocracies they live under and the totalitarian theocracies waiting in the wings. By endorsing torture—on anyone, anywhere, for any reason—we help obliterate the very values we are trying to promote. You can see this contradiction in Krauthammer's own words: We are "morally compelled" to commit "a terrible and monstrous thing." We are obliged to destroy the village in order to save it. We have to extinguish the most basic principle that defines America in order to save America.

No, we don't. In order to retain fundamental American values, we have to banish from the United States the totalitarian impulse that is integral to every act of torture. We have to ensure that the virus of tyranny is never given an opening to infect the Constitution and replicate into something that corrupts as deeply as it wounds. We should mark the words of Ian Fishback, one of the heroes of this war: "Will we confront danger and adversity in order to preserve our ideals, or will our courage and commitment to individual rights wither at the prospect of sacrifice? My response is simple. If we abandon our ideals in the face of adversity and aggression, then those ideals were never really in our possession. I would rather die fighting than give up even the smallest part of the idea that is 'America.'" If we legalize torture, even under constrained conditions, we will have given up a large part of the idea that is America. We will have lost the war before we have given ourselves the chance to win it.

POSTSCRIPT

Is It Justifiable to Put Suspected Terrorists under Great Physical Duress?

The issue at stake was summarized nicely by Alberto Gonzales during his confirmation hearings for the position of attorney general on January 7, 2004. He argued, "After the attacks of 9/11, our government had fundamental decisions to make concerning how to apply treaties and U.S. law to an enemy that does not wear a uniform, owes no allegiance to any country, is not a party to any treaties and—most importantly—does not fight according to the laws of war. As we have debated these questions, the president has made clear that he is prepared to protect and defend the Untied States and its citizens, and will do so vigorously, but always in a manner consistent with our nation's values and applicable law, including our treaty obligations."

Ultimately, the treatment and interrogation of prisoners involves an interpretation of the spirit as well as the letter of domestic and international law. Even if the narrow definition of torture specified by White House counsel to the president in August 2002 holds up to judicial scrutiny, the brutality of U.S. interrogations of potential terrorists and other nontraditional or unlawful combatants challenges the spirit of existing laws. This suggests that the Geneva Conventions may indeed need to be updated to account for the role terrorists and other nonstate actors play in matters of international security. The practices established by the United States are significant because they may set precedent against which negotiations over such future conventions may take place and against which others may justify their use of various techniques in the interrogation of others—including U.S. citizens and military personnel.

Details and evidence supporting Alan Dershowitz's arguments that torture is appropriate under given circumstances are available in his book, *Why Terrorism Works* (Yale University Press, 2002). A counterpoint is offered by Anthony Lewis in his article, "Making Torture Legal," *New York Review of Books* (July 15, 2004).

The ACLU has posted an extensive collection of records regarding torture that have been released as the result of a request under the Freedom of Information Act. See http://www.aclu.org/safefree/torture/torturefoia.html. Additional materials may be found at http://findlaw.com/ and the National Security Archive, George Washington University at http://www2.gwu.edu/~nsarchiv/nsa/the_archive. html.

ISSUE 21

Can Humanitarian Intervention Be Justified?

YES: Kenneth Roth, from "Setting the Standard: Justifying Humanitarian Intervention," *Harvard International Review* (Spring 2004)

NO: Alan J. Kuperman, from "Humanitarian Hazard: Revising Doctrines of Intervention," *Harvard International Review* (Spring 2004)

ISSUE SUMMARY

YES: Kenneth Roth, executive director of Human Rights Watch, argues that while humanitarian intervention is extremely costly in human terms, it can be justified in situations involving ongoing or imminent slaughter, but that it should only be considered when five limiting criteria are met.

NO: Alan Kuperman, resident assistant professor of international relations at Johns Hopkins University, argues that the benefits of humanitarian intervention are much smaller and the costs much greater than are generally acknowledged because violence is perpetrated faster than interveners can act to stop it and the likelihood of humanitarian intervention may actually make some local conflicts worse.

$\mathbf{T}$he question of whether humanitarian intervention is justified hinges on the nature of human rights and the question of intervention. The United Nations reaffirms "faith in fundamental human rights" and "encouraging respect for human rights and for fundamental freedoms for all" through the 1948 Universal Declaration of Human Rights and a variety of other covenants, protocols, and agreements. There is also a growing number of regional and group-specific human rights commissions and treaties like the European Commission on Human Rights and the World Conferences on Women.

Despite the growing number of agreements on human rights, there is no consensus on what rights constitute human rights and which of these are sufficient to justify intervention if they are violated. The United Nations specifies two fundamental sets of rights as specified in the Covenant on Civil and Political Rights and the Covenant on Economic, Social and Cultural Rights. The

United States and others in the West tend to define human rights in terms of civil liberties including the right to freedom of thought, religion, expression, peaceful assembly, movement, and the right to take part in periodic and genuine elections with universal and equal suffrage. Others emphasize the relative importance of economic, social, and cultural liberties, including rights to food and a standard of living adequate for health and well-being; right to work, rest, and leisure; rights to access to a free education; and social security.

There is also disagreement about whether international human rights agreements should be interpreted as guidelines or moral standards that define good behavior, or whether they provide a regulative entitlement one can demand. The former interpretation provides a much weaker basis for humanitarian intervention than the latter.

Furthermore, there is no global consensus on whose rights are most appropriately considered human rights, nor whose take precedence when they conflict with one another. Indeed, defining human rights in terms of the rights of individuals is a relatively recent phenomenon. The rights of groups and those of states have historically taken precedence over those of individuals. For example, the 1907 Hague Conventions, one of the earliest international agreements regarding human rights, limited what a state could do to foreign nationals, but did not limit what states did to their own people; even slavery was not outlawed by international treaty until 1926. The indictment of "crimes against humanity" was applied for the first time only in 1945–1946 at the Nuremberg War Crimes Trials following the holocaust in World War II.

Despite its support for human rights, the United Nations has historically considered human rights to be the internationally protected prerogative of sovereign states. Article 2(7) denies the United Nations jurisdiction in domestic matters and, therefore, in the way that states treat their citizens. Furthermore, Article 2(4) of the Charter explicitly forbids members from engaging in the threat or use of force against the territorial integrity or political independence of any state except in self-defense. And, should any state pose such a "threat to the peace," Chapter VII of the UN Charter allows for the Security Council to adopt military and economic sanctions against that state if peaceful settlement procedures have failed. Thus, the United Nations prohibits states from attacking others for violations of human rights. International legal scholars like Thomas Franck have justified this prohibition by arguing "in very few, if any, instances has the right [to humanitarian intervention] been asserted under circumstances that appear more humanitarian than self-seeking and power seeking." There are arguable exceptions, however, including U.S. intervention in Somalia in 1992–1993 and NATO intervention in Kosovo in 1997, both of which were clearly motivated by humanitarian concerns.

Despite these difficulties, there is a growing recognition in the United States and the world community that basic human rights are of high moral importance and that states are increasingly using humanitarian grounds to justify or at least bolster their arguments for intervention. Kenneth Roth argues that intervention may be justified, but only under a very limiting set of criteria. In contrast, Alan Kuperman argues that even if practiced under those criteria, humanitarian intervention would be ineffective at best and may even be counterproductive.

YES

Kenneth Roth

Setting the Standard: Justifying Humanitarian Intervention

Humanitarian intervention was supposed to have gone the way of the 1990s. The use of military force across borders to stop mass killing was seen as a luxury of an era in which national security concerns among the major powers were less pressing and problems of human security could come to the fore. Somalia, Haiti, Bosnia, Kosovo, East Timor, and Sierra Leone: these interventions, justified to varying degrees in humanitarian terms, were dismissed as products of an unusual interlude between the tensions of the Cold War and the new threat of terrorism. The events of September 11, 2001, supposedly changed all that by inducing a return to more immediate security challenges. Yet surprisingly, even with the campaign against terrorism in full swing, the past year has seen four military interventions that their instigators describe, in whole or in part, as humanitarian.

In principle, one can only welcome this renewed concern for the fate of faraway victims. What could be more virtuous than to risk life and limb to save distant people from slaughter? But the common use of the humanitarian label masks significant differences among these interventions. The French intervention in the Democratic Republic of Congo in 2003, later backed by a reinforced UN peacekeeping presence, was most clearly motivated by a desire to stop ongoing slaughter. In Liberia and the Ivory Coast, West African and French forces intervened to enforce a peace plan but also played important humanitarian roles. A handful of US troops briefly joined the Liberian intervention, but with little effect. All of these African interventions were initially or ultimately approved by the UN Security Council. Indeed, in each case the relevant government consented, though under varying degrees of pressure.

By contrast, of the various grounds used by the US-led coalition forces to justify the invasion of Iraq, only one—and a comparatively minor one at that—was humanitarian. The UN Security Council did not approve the intervention, and the Iraqi government, its existence on the line, violently opposed it. Moreover, unlike the relatively modest African interventions, the Iraqi invasion involved an extensive bombing campaign and some 150,000 ground troops.

The sheer size of the Iraqi invasion, the central involvement of the world's superpower, and the enormous controversy surrounding the war meant that it overshadowed the other aforementioned military actions. For

From *Harvard International Review*, Spring 2004, pp. 58–62. Copyright © 2004 by Harvard International Review. Reprinted by permission.

better or worse, that prominence gave it greater power to shape public perceptions. As a result, at a time of renewed interest in humanitarian intervention, the effort to justify the Iraq war even in part in humanitarian terms risks giving humanitarian intervention a bad name. If that breeds cynicism about the use of military force for humanitarian purposes, it could be devastating for people in need of future rescue.

Since the Iraq war was not mainly about saving the Iraqi people from mass slaughter, there was little serious pre-war debate about whether it could be justified in purely humanitarian terms. Indeed, if Iraqi President Saddam Hussein had been overthrown and the issue of weapons of mass destruction reliably dealt with, there clearly would have been no war, even if the success or government were just as repressive.

Over time, however, the original justifications for war lost much of their force. More than seven months after the declared end of major hostilities, weapons of mass destruction still have not been found. No significant prewar link with international terrorism has been discovered. The difficulty of establishing stable institutions in Iraq is making the country an increasingly unlikely staging ground for promoting democracy in the Middle East. More and more, the Bush administration's remaining justification for the war is that Hussein was a tyrant who deserved to be overthrown—an argument for humanitarian intervention. The administration is now citing that rationale not simply as a side benefit of the war but as a prime justification for it.

Does that claim hold up to scrutiny? This is not a question about whether the war was justified on other grounds; my organization, Human Rights Watch, is explicitly neutral on that point. Rather, it is a question about whether humanitarianism alone can justify the invasion. Despite the horrors of Hussein's rule, it cannot.

A Time for War

War's human cost can be enormous, but the imperative of stopping or preventing genocide or other systematic slaughter can sometimes justify the use of military force. Human Rights Watch has thus, on rare occasion, advocated humanitarian intervention—for example, to stop ongoing genocide in Rwanda and Bosnia.

Yet military action should not be taken lightly, even for humanitarian purposes. Such force might be used more readily when a government facing serious abuses on its territory invites military assistance from others, as in the three recent African interventions. But when military intervention on asserted humanitarian grounds occurs without a government's consent, it should be used with extreme caution.

Given the death, destruction, and disorder that are often inherent in war and its aftermath, humanitarian intervention should be reserved as an option only in situations of ongoing or imminent mass slaughter. Only the direst cases of large-scale slaughter can justify war's deliberate taking of life.

If this high standard is met, one should then look to five other factors to determine whether the use of military force can be characterized as humanitarian. First, military action must be the last reasonable option. Second, the intervention must be primarily guided by a humanitarian purpose. Third, it should be conducted to maximize respect for international human rights law. Fourth, it must be reasonably likely to do more good than harm. Finally, it should ideally, though not necessarily, be endorsed by the UN Security Council or another body with significant multilateral authority.

Mass Slaughter

The most important criterion in legitimating humanitarian intervention is whether mass slaughter is underway or imminent. Brutal as Hussein's reign was, the deaths being directly caused by his government in March 2003 were not of the exceptional magnitude that would justify humanitarian intervention. Granted, during the previous 25 years of Baath Party rule, the government murdered some 250,000 Iraqis. There were times in the past when the killing was so intense that humanitarian intervention would have been justified—for example, during the 1988 Anfal genocide, in which the Iraqi government slaughtered some 100,000 Kurds. But by the time of the March 2003 invasion, the government's killing had ebbed. On the eve of war, no one contends that Baghdad was engaged in murder of anywhere near this magnitude. "Better late than never" is not a justification for humanitarian intervention, which should be countenanced only to stop mass murder, not to punish its perpetrators, desirable as punishment is.

It might be argued that if Hussein committed mass atrocities in the past, his overthrow was justified as a way to prevent his resumption of such atrocities in the future. However, humanitarian intervention may be undertaken preventively only if slaughter is imminent. There must be evidence that large-scale slaughter is in preparation and about to begin unless militarily stopped. No one seriously claimed before the war that Hussein's government was planning imminent mass killing, and no evidence has emerged that it was. There were claims that the government, with a history of gassing Iranian soldiers and Iraqi Kurds, was planning to deliver weapons of mass destruction to terrorist networks, but no supporting proof of these allegations has yet emerged. There were also fears that the government might respond to an invasion with the use of chemical or biological weapons, perhaps even against its own people, but no one seriously suggested such use as an imminent possibility in the absence of an invasion.

The Last Reasonable Option

The lack of ongoing or imminent mass slaughter in March 2003 was itself sufficient to disqualify the invasion of Iraq as a humanitarian intervention. Nonetheless, in light of Hussein's ruthless past, it is useful to examine the other criteria for humanitarian intervention. For the most part, they too, were not met.

As noted, because of the substantial risks involved, an invasion qualifies as a humanitarian intervention only if it is the last reasonable option to stop mass killings. Since there were no ongoing mass killings in Iraq in early 2003, this issue technically did not arise. But it is useful to explore whether military intervention was the last reasonable option to stop what Iraqi abuses were ongoing.

It was not. At least one other option should have been tried long before resorting to the extreme step of military invasion—criminal prosecution. There is no guarantee that prosecution would have worked, and one might have justified skipping it had large-scale slaughter been underway. But in the face of the Iraqi government's more routine abuses, this alternative to military action should have been tried.

To be sure, an indictment is not the same as arrest, trial, and punishment. A piece of paper will not stop mass slaughter. But as a long-term approach, an indictment held some promise. The experiences of former Yugoslav President Slobodan Milosevic and former Liberian President Charles Taylor suggests that an international indictment profoundly discredits even a ruthless, dictatorial leader. That enormous stigma tends to undermine support for the leader, both at home and abroad, often in unexpected ways. By allowing Hussein to rule without the stigma of an indictment for genocide and crimes against humanity, the international community never tried a step that might have contributed to his removal and a parallel reduction in government abuses.

Humanitarian Purpose

A humanitarian intervention should be conducted with the aim of maximizing humanitarian results, since an intervention motivated by purely humanitarian concerns probably cannot be found. Governments that intervene to stop mass slaughter inevitably act for other reasons as well, but a dominant humanitarian purpose is important because it affects numerous decisions that can determine the intervention's success in saving people from violence.

Humanitarianism, even understood broadly as concern for the welfare of the Iraqi people, was at best a subsidiary motive for the invasion of Iraq. The principal justifications offered in the prelude to the invasion were the Iraqi government's alleged possession of weapons of mass destruction, its alleged failure to account for them as prescribed by numerous UN Security Council resolutions, and its alleged connection with terrorist networks. US officials also spoke of a democratic Iraq transforming the Middle East. In this tangle of motives, Hussein's cruelty toward his own people was mentioned, sometimes prominently, but, in the prewar period, it was never the dominant factor. This is not simply an academic point; it affected the way the US attacks were carried out, to the detriment of the Iraqi people.

Most significant, if invading forces had been directed to maximize the humanitarian impact of an intervention, they would have been better prepared to fill the security vacuum that predictably was created by the toppling of the Iraqi government. It was entirely foreseeable that Hussein's downfall would lead to civil disorder. The 1991 uprisings in Iraq were marked by large-scale summary executions. The Iraqi government's Arabization policy raised the prospect of clashes between displaced Kurds seeking to reclaim their old homes and Arabs who had moved into them. Other sudden changes of regime, such as the Bosnian Serb withdrawal from the Sarajevo suburbs in 1996, have been marked by widespread violence, looting, and arson.

In part to prevent violence, the US Army Chief of Staff before the war, General Eric K. Shinseki, predicted in 2003 that "several" hundred thousand troops would be required. But the civilian leaders of the US Pentagon dismissed this assessment and launched the war with considerably fewer combat troops—some 150,000. Coalition troops were quickly overwhelmed by the enormity of the task of maintaining public order in Iraq. Looting was pervasive. Arms caches were raided and emptied. Violence was rampant.

The problem of understaffing was only compounded by the failure to deploy an adequate number of troops trained in policing. Regular troops are trained to fight—to meet threats with lethal force. But that presumptive resort to lethal force is inappropriate and unlawful when it comes to policing an occupied nation. The consequence was a steady stream of civilians killed when coalition troops, on edge in the face of common but unpredictable attacks by resistance elements, mistakenly fired on civilians. That only increased resentment among Iraqis and fueled further attacks. Troops trained in policing—that is, trained to use lethal force as a last resort—would have been better suited to conduct occupation duties in a humane fashion. But the US Pentagon has not made a priority of developing policing skills among its troops, leaving relatively few to be deployed in Iraq.

Compliance with Humanitarian Law

Every effort should be made to ensure that a humanitarian intervention is carried out in strict compliance with international human rights and humanitarian law. Compliance is required in all conflicts—no less for an intervention that is justified on humanitarian grounds. The invasion of Iraq largely met this requirement, but not entirely. Coalition aircraft took extraordinary care to avoid harming civilians when attacking fixed, pre-selected targets. But the coalition's record in attacking targets that arose unexpectedly in the course of the war was mixed.

As described in Human Rights Watch's December 2003 report, US efforts to bomb leadership targets were an abysmal failure. The 0-for-50 record reflected a targeting method that was dangerously indiscriminate, allowing bombs to be dropped on the basis of evidence suggesting little more than the presence of a leader somewhere in a community. Substantial civilian casualties were the foreseeable result.

Coalition ground forces also used cluster munitions near populated areas, with a predictable loss of civilian life. After Human Rights Watch found that roughly a quarter of the civilian deaths in the 1999 NATO bombing of Yugoslavia were caused by the use of cluster bombs in populated areas, the US Air Force substantially curtailed this practice. But the US Army apparently never learned this lesson. In responding to Iraqi attacks, US Army troops regularly used cluster munitions in populated areas, causing substantial losses of life. Such disregard for civilian life is incompatible with a genuinely humanitarian intervention.

Better, Rather than Worse

A humanitarian intervention should be reasonably calculated to make things better rather than worse for the people being rescued. One is tempted to say that anything is better than living under the tyranny of Hussein, but unfortunately, it is possible to imagine scenarios that are even worse. Vicious as his rule was, chaos or abusive civil war might well become even deadlier, and it is too early to say whether such violence might still emerge in Iraq.

Still, when the war was launched in March 2003, the US and British governments clearly hoped that the Iraqi government would topple quickly and that the Iraqi nation would soon be put on the path to democracy. Their failure to equip themselves with the number of troops needed to stabilize postwar Iraq diminished the likelihood of this rosy scenario coming to pass. However, the balance of considerations before the war probably supported the conclusion that Iraqis would be better off if Hussein's regime were ended. But that one factor does not make the intervention a humanitarian one.

UN Approval

There is considerable value in receiving the endorsement of the UN Security Council or another major multilateral body before launching a humanitarian intervention. Convincing others of the validity of a proposed intervention is a good way to guard against pretextual or unjustified action. An international commitment also increases the likelihood that adequate personnel and resources will be devoted to the intervention and its aftermath. And approval by the UN Security Council, in particular, ends the debate about the legality of an intervention.

However, in extreme situations, UN Security Council approval should not be required. In its current state, the UN Security Council is simply too imperfect to make it the sole mechanism for legitimizing humanitarian intervention. Its permanent membership is a relic of the post-World War II era, and its veto system allows those members to block the rescue of people facing slaughter for the most parochial of reasons. In light of these faults, one's patience with the council's approval process would understandably diminish if large-scale slaughter were underway. However, because there was no such urgency in early 2003 for Iraq, the failure to win the UN Security Council's approval, let alone the endorsement of any other multilateral body, weighs more heavily in assessing the intervenors' claim of humanitarianism.

Of course, the UN Security Council was never asked to opine on a purely humanitarian intervention in Iraq. The principal case presented to it was built on the Iraqi government's alleged position of and failure to account for weapons of mass destruction. Even so, approval might have ameliorated at least some of the factors that stood in the way of the invasion being genuinely humanitarian. Most significant, an invasion approved by the UN Security Council is likely to have seen more foreign troops join the predominantly US and British forces, meaning that preparation for the post-war chaos might have been better.

Failing the Humanitarian Test

In sum, the invasion of Iraq fails the test for a humanitarian intervention. The killing in Iraq at the time was not of the dire and exceptional nature that would justify military action. In addition, intervention was not the last reasonable option to stop Iraqi atrocities. It was not motivated primarily by humanitarian concerns. It was not conducted in a way that maximized compliance with international humanitarian law. It was not approved by the UN Security Council. And while at the time it was launched it was reasonable to believe that the Iraqi people would be better off, it was not designed or carried out with the needs of Iraqis foremost in mind.

Hussein certainly presided over a coercive, undemocratic, and brutal regime, and few shed tears at his overthrow. But in the interest of preserving popular support for a rescue option on which future potential victims of mass slaughter will depend, proponents of the Iraqi war should stop trying to justify it as a humanitarian intervention.

Alan J. Kuperman

NO

Humanitarian Hazard: Revisiting Doctrines of Intervention

No foreign policy seems more inherently benign than humanitarian military intervention. It is rooted in the altruistic desire to protect innocents from violent death. It appears feasible, given the military superiority of Western forces over those in developing countries where most violent conflict occurs. And the only obvious costs are a modest financial commitment and the occasional casualty.

For these reasons, in the wake of the world's failure to prevent violence in the Balkans and Rwanda, US President Bill Clinton declared in June 1999 the doctrine that bears his name: "If the world community has the power to stop it, we ought to stop genocide and ethnic cleansing." In December 2001, a distinguished international panel went a step further and declared the existence of a "Responsibility to Protect"—suggesting that the failure to intervene by those capable of doing so might even breach international law.

But a more sophisticated analysis calls into question the value of humanitarian military intervention, even when judged by its own explicit standard of saving lives. For two reasons the benefits of such intervention are much smaller, and the costs much greater, than commonly recognized. First, most violence is perpetrated faster than interveners can realistically arrive to stop it. Second, as economists could have predicted, but few humanitarians have acknowledged, the intervention regime actually exacerbates some conflicts through what I have labeled "the moral hazard of humanitarian intervention." In light of these two dynamics, an increase in intervention does not save as many lives as commonly claimed. Unless the West adopts a number of reforms outlined at the end of this article, more intervention might actually lead to a net increase in killing.

Killers Are Quicker than Interveners

In the high-profile conflicts of the 1990s, most violence was perpetrated far more quickly than commonly realized. In Bosnia, although the conflict dragged on for more than three years, the majority of ethnic cleansing was perpetrated in the spring of 1992. By the time Western media arrived on the scene later that summer, Serb forces already occupied two-thirds of the republic

From *Harvard International Review*, Spring 2004, pp. 64–68. Copyright © 2004 by Harvard International Review. Reprinted by permission.

and had displaced more than one million residents. In Rwanda, at least half of the eventual half-million Tutsi victims were killed in the first three weeks of genocide. When Croatia's army broke a three-year cease-fire in August 1995, it ethnically cleansed virtually all of the more than 100,000 Serbs from the Krajina region in less than a week. In Kosovo, when Serbian forces switched from a policy of counter-insurgency to ethnic cleansing in March 1999, in response to NATO's decision to bomb, most of their cleansing occurred in the first two weeks, and they managed to cleanse 850,000 Albanians, half the province's total. In East Timor, following a 1999 vote for independence, Indonesian-backed militias damaged the majority of the province's infrastructure and displaced most of the population in little more than a week.

Even less well recognized is the fact that logistical obstacles impose significant delays on military intervention, humanitarian or otherwise, even where a strong political will exists. For example, after Iraqi President Saddam Hussein invaded Kuwait in August 1990, and US President George Bush ordered an immediate deployment to defend Saudi Arabia (Operation Desert Shield), it took nine days for the first unit of 2,300 US troops to reach the area of conflict. Another week was required before the unit was sufficiently prepared to venture beyond its makeshift base. Thus, even with the vital national security interest of oil at stake, it took the United States more than two weeks to deploy and begin operations of a relatively tiny force. The reasons are numerous, but stem mainly from three factors: modern militaries cannot operate without their equipment, their equipment is extremely heavy, and there are limits to the rate at which such equipment can be airlifted to remote countries.

Indeed, the airlift to Saudi Arabia was much easier than a typical humanitarian intervention because the Arabian peninsula is closer to the United States and has better airfields than most conflict zones. Even short-distance interventions can be bedeviled by the combination of poor airfields and weighty forces. For example, when the United States deployed just 24 Apache helicopters from Germany to nearby Albania (Task Force Hawk) for the 1999 Kosovo intervention, it required 17 days. Two factors explain this: poor Albanian airfields and a US Army doctrine that mandated a force of 5,350 personnel and their equipment to operate, maintain, and protect the helicopters. In total, this task force weighed 22,000 tons, necessitating 500 flights of large, modern C-17 cargo aircraft.

Intervening in Africa, where most of today's violent conflicts take place, is even harder due to bad airfields and the farther distance from western military bases. Had the United States tried to stop the Rwandan genocide, it would have required about six weeks to deploy a task force of 15,000 personnel and their equipment. This time estimate is conservative, because analogous past interventions to Haiti, Panama, and the Dominican Republic actually required somewhat larger forces. Unfortunately, this means that by the time Western governments learned of the Rwandan genocide and deployed an intervention force, the vast majority of the ultimate Tutsi victims would already have been killed.

The fact that much civil violence is carried out more quickly than intervention forces can arrive is by itself no excuse for failing to intervene; some lives can be saved even by belated intervention. However, it does mean that the benefits of humanitarian intervention are far smaller than commonly realized. This is important to remember as we turn to the unexpected costs of humanitarian intervention.

Intervention Exacerbates Violence

The most counterintuitive aspect of humanitarian military intervention is that it sometimes may cause the very tragedies it is intended to prevent. The explanation for this starts from the little known but empirically robust fact that genocidal violence is usually a state retaliation against substate groups for launching armed secession or revolution. Most groups are deterred from such armed challenges by the fear of state retaliation. In the 1990s, however, the regime of humanitarian military intervention changed this calculus, convincing some groups that the international community would intervene to protect them from retaliation, thereby encouraging armed rebellions. As events played out, these armed challenges did provoke genocidal retaliation, but intervention arrived too late to save many of the targets of retaliation. Thus, the intervention regime—intended to insure against risks of genocide and ethnic cleansing—inadvertently encouraged risk-taking behavior that exacerbated these atrocities. This is the classic dynamic of moral hazard, which is an inherent drawback of insurance systems.

For example, in the early 1990s, Bosnia's Muslims wanted their republic to secede from Yugoslavia so that they could establish their own state. However, they knew Serbs in Bosnia and the rest of Yugoslavia, who possessed considerably greater military power, opposed secession, so they initially eschewed secession as suicidal. By 1992, however, the international community had pledged to recognize Bosnia's independence if it seceded. This led the Muslims to believe that they had a guarantee of humanitarian military intervention if they armed themselves and seceded from Yugoslavia—which they did (with the support of Croats, who mainly hoped to join Croatia). The Serbs retaliated as expected in April 1992, but the international community did not intervene with significant force for more than three years—by which time an estimated 100,000 Bosnian Muslims had been killed and more than 1,000,000 displaced.

A similar scenario played out a few years later in the Serbian province of Kosovo. There the local ethnic Albanian majority sought independence but prudently had hewed to peaceful resistance throughout the early 1990s. Even after an influx of light weapons from neighboring Albania in 1997, most of Kosovo's ethnic Albanians, including the rebel Kosovo Liberation Army, believed they were no match by themselves for heavily armored Serb forces. However, the rebels expected that if they could provoke the Serbs into retaliating against Albanian civilians, the international community would intervene on their behalf, thereby facilitating independence. The plan played out almost perfectly. The rebels began shooting large numbers of Serb police and civilians in 1997, the Serbs retaliated with a brutal counter-insurgency in 1998, and NATO bombed the Serbs and occupied the province in 1999, establishing Kosovo's de facto independence. As noted above, however, the intervention also compelled the Serbs to initiate last-ditch ethnic cleansing—displacing about half the province's Albanians and killing more than 5,000. After Serbia's defeat, the Albanians took revenge by ethnically cleansing 100,000 Serbs, about half those in the province, while killing hundreds more.

All of this death and displacement on both sides was a direct conse-quence of the promise of humanitarian intervention. Research in both Bosnia and Kosovo, based on interviews with senior Muslim and Albanian officials who launched the suicidal armed challenges, indicates they would not have done so except for the prospect of such foreign aid. The unavoidable conclu-sion is that the regime of humanitarian intervention helped to cause the tragic outcomes it intended to prevent, at least in these two cases.

In the wake of the terror attacks of September 11, 2001, the international community—and especially the United States—has switched its military focus from altruistic humanitarian intervention to a self-interested war against terror-ism and proliferation. One unintended side benefit is that rebels no longer expect that they can attract humanitarian intervention by launching provocative armed challenges against states. In today's security environment, the United States is more likely to view such rebels as international terrorists and to support state retaliation against them. As a result, nascent rebellions by Albanian rebels in Macedonia and southern Serbia have fizzled out, rather than replicating the dynamics of Bosnia and Kosovo. However, when and if the terrorist threat wanes, the international community is likely to pick up the gauntlet of humanitarian intervention once again, and recreate the problem of moral hazard.

A Lesson Learned

The shortcomings of humanitarian military intervention do not mean it should be abandoned as a policy tool. The goal should be to enhance its ben-eficial potential, while reducing its unintended costs. The conflicts of the 1990s present three major lessons: the speed of violence, the moral hazard of intervention, and the limits of coercive diplomacy. Formulating reforms to address these lessons, however, requires a sober consideration of both the costs and the trade-offs.

The first lesson, based on the lightning pace of the recent violence, is that we need intervention forces that can deploy more quickly. Lighter forces, with fewer heavy weapons and less armor, require fewer cargo flights and thus can save more lives by deploying quicker. However, shedding protective armor and weaponry also would increase casualties among the interveners. Such a trade-off cannot be made lightly.

An alternative is to pre-position troops and their heavy equipment at forward bases closer to where they are most likely to be needed for humanitar-ian intervention: in Africa. Interventions could be launched from these bases using small military cargo aircraft, which are more plentiful and better able to land at rudimentary African air fields than wide-body inter-continental mod-els. The cargo aircraft could also make several round-trips per day to an inter-vention from forward bases, rather than one trip every few days from distant US or European bases—radically reducing deployment time from weeks to days. One obstacle, however, is that many Africans oppose foreign military bases as a form of neo-colonialism. An even bigger obstacle is that western states so far have been unwilling to invest in military forces dedicated to missions other than defending their own interests.

In recognition of the West's lack of will to deploy ground troops to Africa, the United States launched a project in the mid-1990s to train indigenous African forces for humanitarian intervention. This initiative had a reasonable premise—that African states would be more willing to risk the lives of their troops to stop conflict on the continent—but it has several shortcomings. First, there has been little provision of weaponry or combat training, so the African forces are suitable only for the permissive environment of peacekeeping after a conflict ends—and even then only so long as violence does not reignite, a common risk. Second, the initiative so far has failed to pre-position heavy weapons, armored personnel carriers, or helicopters at African bases, so that in the event of a crisis such equipment would have to be transported and joined up with intervention forces on an ad hoc, protracted basis. Third, most training has been conducted within national units, so that the few trained forces are unprepared for multi-national coalition operations that would be necessary in any large-scale intervention. In light of these shortcomings, if major civil violence were to break out again in Africa in the future, an all-African force would have little hope of quickly or effectively stopping the killing.

Another option is a UN rapid response capability, as proposed several years ago by an international commission headed by Algerian diplomat Lakhdar Brahimi in 2000. This panel called for expanding UN standby arrangements "to include several coherent, multinational, brigade-size forces and the necessary enabling forces, created by Member States working in partnership, in order to better meet the need for the robust peacekeeping forces." One problem is that the report makes no provision for the coordination of airlift operations. Only the US military has a large, long-haul cargo air fleet; rapid reaction to most parts of the world is impossible unless the United States participates. A further problem is that even if UN member states were willing to commit troops in advance for humanitarian intervention, it is uncertain they would actually deploy them when called upon. Relying on a UN force that might not materialize when needed could prove even worse than today's ad hoc system—in which states at least know that the buck stops with them.

Reduce Moral Hazard

As noted, some sub-state groups have been emboldened by the prospect of humanitarian intervention to launch armed challenges against states, provoking genocidal retaliation. One superficially attractive solution would be for the international community to launch timely humanitarian military intervention in every case of genocidal violence. However, this is unfeasible for two reasons. First, even if the political will for such extensive intervention existed (which it does not), the number of actual cases of such violence would soon exhaust our resources. The 1990s alone witnessed major civil violence in at least 16 areas (some on several occasions): Albania, Algeria, Angola, Azerbaijan (mainly in Nagorno-Karabakh), Bosnia, Cambodia, Congo Republic,

Croatia, Ethiopia, Liberia, Kosovo, Sierra Leone, Somalia, Sudan, Tajikistan, and Zaire (and its successor, the Democratic Republic of Congo). Moreover, by the logic of moral hazard, each instance of humanitarian intervention raises expectations of further intervention and thus encourages additional armed challenges that may provoke still more genocidal retaliation—further overwhelming the international capacity for intervention.

Two means exist to mitigate moral hazard. First, the international community should reward non-violent protest movements, rather than armed rebellions. In Kosovo, it did the opposite, ignoring a non-violent ethnic Albanian resistance for eight years and then rewarding its violent counterpart with military assistance. So long as disgruntled ethnic groups believe they can attract Western intervention with violence rather than with passive resistance, Western states encourage rebellions that provoke genocidal retaliation.

The second solution is drawn from the economics literature on moral hazard, which suggests we should not pay claims that arise solely because of the provision of insurance coverage. In other words, the international community should not intervene on behalf of groups that provoke retaliation in the hope of garnering humanitarian intervention. If the West adopted this policy, and stuck to it, such cynical rebellions would likely peter out fairly quickly. Such a policy still would permit humanitarian intervention on behalf of groups that suffer genocidal violence through no fault of their own—for example, at the hands of leaders like Adolf Hitler or Pol Pot—as the concept originally envisioned.

A policy of not intervening in cases of intentionally provoked genocide is open to criticism as being hard-hearted. This is especially true in cases where the victims of retaliation did not endorse the armed challenge or did not know it would provoke a backlash. However, if the theory of moral hazard is correct, a policy of not intervening in response to deliberate provocations eventually would reduce the number of such cases—and thereby the overall incidence of genocidal violence. If so, such a policy would not be hard-hearted, but actually compassionate, at least from a long-term perspective.

Avoid Pyromaniac Diplomacy

A third lesson is that the international community needs to better coordinate its diplomacy with military intervention. Since the end of the Cold War, the West has tried to coerce authoritarian governments (or rebels) to hand over power to opponents by applying economic or military sanctions. However, in several cases, including Rwanda, the former Yugoslavia, and East Timor, the targets of coercion have responded instead by ethnically cleansing their opponents. To prevent this eventuality, the West needs to preventively deploy robust intervention forces, prior to exercising coercive diplomacy. Unfortunately, most preventive deployments so far have been feeble. When violence breaks out, as in Rwanda and Srebrenica, they provide little protection and then are withdrawn. Such half-hearted deployments lend a false sense of security that encourages vulnerable groups to let down their guard so that they ultimately die in greater numbers, making this type of intervention worse than nothing.

If the West is unwilling to deploy robust forces preventively, it must temper its use of coercive diplomacy aimed at compelling rulers or rebels to surrender power, because of the risk of inadvertently triggering massive violence. So long as the West lacks the will for adequate preventive deployments, its diplomats should focus instead on carrots, rather than sticks—offering incentives to oppressive governments and rebels, including economic assistance, in exchange for gradual power-sharing. The West also should be prepared to offer "golden parachutes"—monetary rewards, asylum, and immunity from subsequent prosecution—to entrenched leaders willing to peacefully yield power. While human rights groups abjure the prospect of cutting deals with leaders who have blood on their hands, in some cases forgiving past crimes may be the price of preventing future ones.

It may be a noble endeavor to use military force to protect victims of genocidal violence. But it is infinitely preferable to prevent the outbreak of such violence in the first place. To do so requires adoption of more enlightened policies of humanitarian intervention, tempering altruistic instincts with the stubborn realities of human nature and military logistics.

TO MOVE A GIANT

Ground forces, while required for effective humanitarian intervention, are the slowest to deploy. The US Army is dependent upon support from US Air Force or Navy units for mobility. Such deployments are subject to availability of transportation, quality of ports or landing zones, and the need for heavy machinery.

While various technological improvements can be made on current transportation methods, a more effective means of facilitating mobilization is efficient prepositioning. Efficient pre-positioning would allow for the rapid transfer of soldiers and equipment as well as expedite the establishment of a base of operations.

Current positioning of US forces is inefficient and could be substantially improved. US forces in Central Europe, for instance, could be transferred to Italy, close enough to assure NATO of US priorities in the area, but also closer to the Mediterranean for quick deployment. Additional forces in the Pacific should be moved onto Theater Support Vessels and placed off the West Coast of Australia and near Japan to support the brigade already in Korea. Coverage of South and Central America could be improved by placing better naval transport options in the Gulf of Mexico.

An examination of the main conflicts involving US troops in 2002 reveals that most occurred as sudden urban conflicts. Since 75 percent of major urban areas are within 150 miles of coastline, a naval pre-positioning such as the one mentioned here could theoretically move a medium brigade anywhere in the world in four days, an entire division in five days, and five divisions in 30 days.

POSTSCRIPT

Can Humanitarian Intervention Be Justified?

The debate over humanitarian intervention is not simply an academic exercise. As Kenneth Roth points out, the preservation of human rights has been offered as part of the justification for the recent U.S. intervention in Iraq. The degree to which that justification is accepted will affect the perceived legitimacy of U.S. actions and, as a consequence, the ease or difficulty with which the United States can build local and international support for its efforts there. Samantha Powers is critical of the United States for not doing more to fight genocide and violations of human rights abroad. See Samantha Powers, *"A Problem from Hell": America and the Age of Genocide* (Harper Collins, 2003). Powers and others have also criticized the United Nations, the United States, and other states for not taking stronger action to stop what they characterize as an ongoing episode of genocide in Darfor, Sudan. For a review of U.S. interventions in general, see Richard Haass, *Intervention: The Use of American Military Force in the Post-Cold War World* (Brookings Institution Press, 1999). The failure of the United States and the international community to take action against genocide in Rwanda was also the subject of a current movie, *Hotel Rwanda*.

U.S. conduct following humanitarian interventions has also been a matter of dispute. In particular, U.S. actions involving the interrogation of prisoners following the terrorist attacks of September 11, 2001, in Afghanistan, Cuba, and Iraq could be interpreted as violations of human rights. If so, these actions could be used to justify the equally poor treatment of U.S. combatants in foreign conflicts. They may also undermine the symbolic role of the United States as the purveyor of civil and political liberties, thereby greatly complicating its efforts to democratize Iraq and other countries. In such instances, nongovernmental organizations like Human Rights Watch (http://www.hrw.org/) and Amnesty International (http://www.amnestyusa.org/) play a key role in monitoring human rights violations and providing documentation of human rights abuses.

Other nongovernmental organizations play a key role in humanitarian interventions. David Rieff provides a critical assessment of humanitarian intervention and the roles played by relief organizations like Oxfam, CARE, and Doctors without Borders. He also rejects "the false morality play" that, in any given conflict, there are victimizers and innocent victims, and that it is always clear who is who. See David Rieff, *A Bed for the Night: Humanitarianism in Crisis* (Simon & Schuster, 2002). In contrast, Martha Finnemore argues that there is a growing norm of humanitarian intervention and an important role played by nongovernmental organizations. She argues that long-term trends suggest the steady erosion of force's normative value in international politics, the growing influence of equality norms in many aspects of global political life, and the increasing importance of law in intervention practices. See Martha Finnemore, *The Purpose of Intervention: Changing Beliefs About the Use of Force* (Cornell, 2003).

Contributors to This Volume

EDITORS

ANDREW BENNETT is professor of government at Georgetown University. He has written or edited books on military interventions, alliance burden sharing, and research methods, and he teaches courses on international relations theory, research methods, and the American foreign policy process. Professor Bennett has also worked as a staff aide in the U.S. Senate, a special assistant to the Assistant Secretary of Defense for International Security Affairs, and a foreign policy advisor on several presidential campaigns. His Web site can be found at: http://www8.georgetown.edu/departments/government/faculty/bennetta/.

GEORGE E. SHAMBAUGH, IV, Ph.D., is an associate professor in the Edmund A. Walsh School of Foreign Service and chairman of the department of government at Georgetown University. He has written numerous articles and taught classes on international politics, foreign policy, international political economy, and the environment. He is author of *States, Firms, and Power: Successful Sanctions in U.S. Foreign Policy,* co-author of *The Art of Policymaking: Tools, Techniques, and Processes in the Modern Executive Branch,* and co-editor of *Anarchy and the Environment: The International Politics of Common Pool Resources.* His articles have appeared in a range of journals including *American Political Science Review, International Politics, Environmental Politics, International Interactions, International Studies Quarterly, The Journal of Peace Research, Review of International Studies,* and *Security Dialogue.* Dr. Shambaugh received a B.A. in government and physics from Oberlin College, an M.I.A. in international affairs, and a M.Phil. and Ph.D. in political science from Columbia University. His departmental Web page is http://explore.georgetown.edu/people/shambaug/?PageTemplateID=156.

STAFF

Larry Loeppke	Managing Editor
Jill Peter	Senior Developmental Editor
Susan Brusch	Senior Developmental Editor
Beth Kundert	Production Manager
Jane Mohr	Project Manager
Tara McDermott	Design Coordinator
Nancy Meissner	Editorial Assistant
Julie Keck	Senior Marketing Manager
Mary Klein	Marketing Communications Specialist
Alice Link	Marketing Coordinator
Tracie Kammerude	Senior Marketing Assistant
Lori Church	Pemissions Coordinator

AUTHORS

SPENCER ACKERMAN is a former associate editor of *The New Republic*. A graduate of Rutgers University, today Ackerman is a senior correspondent for *The American Prospect*. Ackerman's blog, http://toohotfortnr.blogspot.com/, chronicles the author's thoughts and opinions.

HUSSEIN AGHA is senior associate member of St. Antony's College at the University of Oxford. He is the author, with A. S. Khalidi, of *A Framework for a Palestinian National Security Doctrine*. He has been an advisor for the Palestinian delegation in Middle East peace negotiations.

REND AL-RAHIM is the executive director and co-founder of the Iraq Freedom Foundation. Ms. Al-Rahim served as Iraq's representative to the United States and the Iraqi Chief of Mission. She has contributed to numerous reports and books on Iraq, and has written policy papers and reports for the Iraq Foundation. She holds degrees from Cambridge University and the University of the Sorbonne.

BOB BARR is an attorney and a former member of the U.S. House of Representatives from Georgia. Barr represented the 7th District of Georgia, from 1995 to 2003. Barr is now a life member of, and on the National Committee for, the United States Libertarian Party. Barr is a commentator on political and social issues and is chairman of the American Conservative Union Foundation's 21st Century Center for Privacy and Freedom.

DENNIS BLASKO served 23 years in the U.S. Army as a military intelligence officer and foreign area officer specializing in China. Mr. Blasko was an army attaché in Beijing from 1992 to1995 and in Hong Kong from 1995 to 1996. He served in infantry units in Germany, Italy, and Korea and in Washington at the Defense Intelligence Agency, Headquarters Department of the Army (Office of Special Operations), and the National Defense University War Gaming and Simulation Center.

GEORGE W. BUSH is the 43rd and current president of the United States, inaugurated on January 20, 2001 and re-elected in the 2004 U.S. presidential election. Bush is the eldest son of the 41st U.S. president, George H. W. Bush, grandson to Prescott Bush, the former U.S. senator from Connecticut, and older brother to Jeb Bush, former governor of Florida. George W. Bush became the 46th governor of Texas in January 1995, resigning in December 2000, after being elected president.

VICTOR D. CHA holds the D. S. Song-Korea Foundation Chair in Asian Studies in the department of government and the Edmund Walsh School of Foreign Service, Georgetown University and is the Asia director in the National Security Council of the U.S. government. He is the author of *Alignment Despite Antagonism: The United States-Korea-Japan Security Triangle* and has written articles on international relations and East Asia in journals including *Foreign Affairs, International Security, Political Science Quarterly, Survival, International Studies Quarterly, Journal of Strategic Studies, The Washington Quarterly, Orbis, Journal of Peace Research, Security Dialogue, Australian*

Journal of International Affairs, Japanese Journal of Political Science, Korean Studies, and *Asian Survey.*

WILLIAM J. CLINTON was the 42nd president of the United States, serving from 1993 to 2001. Before his election as the president, Clinton served nearly 12 years as the 50th and 52nd governor of Arkansas. His wife, Hillary Rodham Clinton, is the junior United States senator from the state of New York. After leaving office, Clinton created the William J. Clinton Foundation to address international crises such as HIV/AIDS and other humanitarian causes.

DAVID COLE is the legal affairs correspondent for *The Nation* and a professor at Georgetown University Law Center. He is the author of *No Equal Justice: Race and Class in the American Criminal Justice System;* co-author, with James X. Dempsey, of *Terrorism and the Constitution: Sacrificing Civil Liberties for National Security;* and author of *Enemy Aliens: Double Standards and Constitutional Freedoms in the War on Terrorism.*

CHARLI E. COON is senior policy analyst for energy and environment at the Heritage Foundation in Washington, D.C. Before moving to Heritage, she was a research and budget analyst for Republicans in the Illinois state assembly. She earned her M.A. in public administration from the University of Illinois–Springfield in 1976 and her law degree from Loyola University of Chicago in 1992.

MICHAEL CROWLEY is a senior editor at *The New Republic.* Before joining *The New Republic,* he worked for *The Boston Globe* and *The Boston Phoenix.* Crowley has also written for *The New York Times Magazine, The New Yorker, Slate, The New York Observer, The Washington Monthly, New York* magazine, and other publications. He is a 1994 graduate of Yale University.

IVO H. DAALDER is a senior fellow in foreign policy studies at the Brookings Institution, where he also holds the Sydney Stein Jr. Chair in International Security. He has written 10 books including most recently, *America Unbound: The Bush Revolution in Foreign Policy* (with James Lindsay). His other books include *Protecting the American Homeland, Winning Ugly: NATO's War to Save Kosovo, Getting to Dayton: The Making of America's Bosnia Policy,* and *The United States and Europe in the Global Arena.*

PHILIP DEUTCH is a member of the board of directors of Evergreen Solar and is a former board member of Beacon Power Corp., Northern Power Systems and International Marketing Concepts. Mr. Deutch has spoken or been on panels at energy conferences held by Goldman Sachs, Bank of America, Credit Suisse First Boston, Salomon Smith Barney, the American Council for Renewable Energy, Bear Stearns, Montreux Energy, McIntire School of Commerce at the University of Virginia, and the FRA Renewable Energy Finance & Investment Summit. Mr. Deutch served on the Advisory Committee for the 2005 Energy Venture Fair and the selection committees for the 2005 Cleantech Venture Forum and 2005 National Renewable Energy Laboratory Industry Growth Forum.

SYDNEY FREEDBERG JR. covers the military, homeland security policy, and interagency coordination as a staff correspondent for *National Journal*. He has written extensively on military personnel and veterans' issues; on defense "transformation"; on federal, state, and local preparedness for terrorist attack; and on the reorganization of government for the war on terror at home and abroad, as well as a wide range of other security-related subjects. Before joining *National Journal* as a reporter in 1997, Freedberg was a reporter-researcher at *New Republic* magazine. He earned a bachelor's degree, summa cum laude, from Harvard University and a master of philosophy degree from Cambridge University (United Kingdom), both in modern European history.

RONIL HIRA is assistant professor of public policy at the Rochester Institute of Technology and chair of the R&D Policy Committee for the Institute of Electrical and Electronics Engineers, United States of America.

JOSEF JOFFE is editor and publisher of *Die Zeit*, a weekly German newspaper, the Marc and Anita Abramowitz Fellow in International Relations at the Hoover Institution, a fellow at the Freeman Spogli Institute for International Studies and adjunct professor of political science at Stanford University, and an associate of the Olin Institute for Strategic Studies at Harvard University. His essays and reviews have appeared in a wide number of publications including the *New York Review of Books*, *Times Literary Supplement*, *Commentary*, *New York Times Magazine*, *New Republic*, *Weekly Standard*, and the *Prospect* (London). He is a regular contributor to quality daily newspapers in the United States and Britain.

JOHN B. JUDIS is a senior editor for *The New Republic* to which he has been a contributor since 1982. His articles have also appeared in *The American Prospect*, *The New York Times Magazine*, *The Washington Post*, *Foreign Affairs*, *The Washington Monthly*, *American Enterprise*, *Mother Jones*, and *Dissent*. His books include *The Paradox of American Democracy: Elites, Special Interests, and the Betrayal of Public Trust* and *William F. Buckley: Patron Saint of the Conservatives*.

LAWRENCE KAPLAN is senior editor at *The New Republic*, where he writes about U.S. foreign policy and international affairs. A graduate of Columbia University, Oxford, and the Johns Hopkins School of Advanced International Studies, Mr. Kaplan also writes about foreign policy for *Commentary*, *The Wall Street Journal*, *The Weekly Standard*, *The Washington Post*, and numerous other publications. Before coming to *The New Republic*, he was executive editor of *The National Interest*, the foreign policy journal published by Irving Kristol.

CHARLES KRAUTHAMMER is a Pulitzer Prize–winning columnist and neoconservative commentator. Krauthammer appears regularly as a guest commentator on *Fox News*, and his print work appears in the *Washington Post*, *Time* magazine, and *The Weekly Standard*. In 2006, the *Financial Times* named Krauthammer America's most influential commentator.

MARK KRIKORIAN is the executive director of the Center for Immigration Studies (CIS), a think tank that promotes stricter immigration standards and enforcement. Before joining CIS in February 1995, Krikorian was an editor at The Winchester (Va.) *Star*, as well as editor of a publication on marketing via electronic media and of the monthly newsletter of the Federation for American Immigration Reform. Mr. Krikorian is a regular contributor to the conservative publication *National Review* as well as a regular participant of *National Review*'s "The Corner." Krikorian received his B.A. from Georgetown University and his M.A. from the Fletcher School of Law and Diplomacy at Tufts University.

WILLIAM KRISTOL is editor of the Washington-based political magazine, *The Weekly Standard*. Mr. Kristol regularly appears on *Fox News Sunday* and on the Fox News Channel. Mr. Kristol recently co-authored *The War Over Iraq: America's Mission* and *Saddam's Tyranny*.

ALAN J. KUPERMAN is resident assistant professor of International Relations at Johns Hopkins University, based at Bologna Center. He has also served as fellow at Brookings Institution, Harvard University, University of Southern California, and U.S. Institute of Peace; was legislative director for U.S. Representative Charles E. Schumer, legislative assistant to Speaker of the U.S. House of Representatives Thomas S. Foley, and chief of staff for U.S. Representative James H. Scheuer. His publications include *The Limits of Humanitarian Intervention* and articles on genocide and intervention in the *Journal of Genocide Research, Foreign Affairs, The SAIS Review, The Washington Post, The Wall Street Journal*, and *USA Today*.

ROBERT KUTTNER is founder and coeditor of *The American Prospect*. He writes regularly for the magazine about domestic and international economic policy issues. He is also a regular contributor to *Business Week,* the *Boston Globe,* and *The New England Journal of Medicine.* He has taught at Brandeis University, Boston University, the University of Massachusetts, and Harvard University's Institute of Politics.

JAMES LACEY is a journalist who has written for *Time Magazine* and the *National Review,* and was embedded with the 101st Airborne during the war in Iraq.

MARIO LOYOLA is a frequent contributor to *National Review* and *National Review Online.* He has also published in *The Weekly Standard* and *The American Interest.* He focuses on defense policy, diplomacy, and international law. He also covers nuclear nonproliferation and Iran's nuclear program, global security under the United Nations system, and current issues in China, the Middle East, and Latin America. He holds a B.A. in European History from the University of Wisconsin/Madison, and a J.D. from Washington University in St. Louis.

EDWARD LUCE is a writer for the *Financial Times.*

EDWARD NICOLAE LUTTWAK is a senior advisor at the Center for Strategic and International Studies. He is known for his many publications on military strategy and international relations. He has served as a consultant to the Office of the Secretary of Defense, the National Security Council, and the U.S. Department of State. He is a member of the National Security Study Group of the U.S. Department of Defense, and an associate of the Japan Finance Ministry's Institute of Fiscal and Monetary Policy.

MICHAEL MANDELBAUM is the Christian A. Herter Professor of American Foreign Policy at The Johns Hopkins School of Advanced International Studies in Washington, D.C. He is also the author or co-author of 10 books. Mandelbaum writes a regular column for *Newsday*.

JOHN MCCAIN has been a U.S. senator from Arizona since 1987. A graduate of the U.S. Naval Academy, McCain had a 22-year military career. Five of those years were spent in a Vietnamese prisoner of war camp after he was shot down over Hanoi during the Vietnam War. McCain was elected to Congress in 1982, then elected as U.S. senator from Arizona in 1986.

JOHN J. MEARSHEIMER is the R. Wendell Harrison Distinguished Service Professor of Political Science and the co-director of the Program on International Security Policy at the University of Chicago, where he has taught since 1982. During the 1998-1999 academic year, he was the Whitney H. Shepardson Fellow at the Council on Foreign Relations in New York, and in 2003 he was elected to the American Academy of Arts and Sciences. Professor Mearsheimer has written extensively about security issues and international politics more generally.

TIMOTHY NOAH is a senior writer for *Slate Magazine*, where he writes the "Hot Documents" and "Chatterbox" columns. He is also a contributing editor to *The Washington Monthly*. Noah was previously an assistant managing editor at *U.S. News & World Report* and a Washington reporter for the *Wall Street Journal*. Before that, he was a staff writer at the *New Republic* and a congressional correspondent for *Newsweek*. He is a graduate of Harvard University.

BARACK OBAMA is the junior U.S. senator from Illinois. According to the U.S. Senate Historical Office, he is the fifth African American Senator in U.S. history and the only African American currently serving in the U.S. Senate. On January 16, 2007, Obama announced that he had taken the first step toward becoming a candidate for the 2008 presidential election by forming an exploratory committee.

WILLIAM ODOM is a former U.S. Army general and director of the NSA under President Ronald Reagan. He is currently on the faculty of the Center for Peace and Security Studies in the School of Foreign Service at Georgetown University where he specializes in military issues, intelligence, and international relations. He is also a senior fellow at the Huston Institute.

TOM RIDGE became the first Office of Homeland Security Advisor in the history of the United States of America on October 8, 2001. Prior to directing the Department of Homeland Security, Secretary Ridge was twice elected governor of Pennsylvania, serving from 1995 to 2001.

DAVID RIEFF is a contributing editor to *The New Republic*. He has also published articles in *The New York Times, The Los Angeles Times, The Washington Post, The Wall Street Journal, The Atlantic Monthly*, and *Foreign Affairs*. His books have focused on issues of immigration, international conflict, and humanitarianism. He is a senior fellow at the World Policy Institute at the New School for Social Research, a fellow at the New York Institute for the Humanities at New York University, a member of the Council on Foreign Relations, a board member of the Arms Division of Human Rights Watch and a board member of the Central Eurasia Project of the Open Society Institute.

KENNETH ROTH is the executive director of Human Rights Watch. Previously, he was a federal prosecutor for the U.S. Attorney's Office for the southern district of New York and the Iran-Contra investigation in Washington. He also worked in private practice as a litigator. Mr. Roth has conducted human rights investigations around the globe, devoting special attention to issues of justice and accountability for gross abuses of human rights, standards governing military conduct in time of war, the human rights policies of the United States and the United Nations, and the human rights responsibilities of multinational businesses. He has written over 70 articles and chapters on a range of human rights topics in such publications as *The New York Times, The Washington Post, Foreign Affairs*, the *International Herald Tribune*, and the *New York Review of Books*.

TERESITA SCHAFFER joined the Center for Strategic and International Studies in August 1998 after a 30-year career in the U.S. Foreign Service. She devoted most of her career to South Asia and international economic issues. Her publications include "Sri Lanka: Lessons from the 1995 Negotiations," in *Creating Peace in Sri Lanka*; two studies on women in Bangladesh; "Kashmir: Fifty Years of Running in Place," in *Grasping the Nettle*. She has taught in the past at Georgetown University and American University.

JOSEPH SIEGLE is Douglas Dillon Fellow at the Council on Foreign Relations. Dr. Siegle has worked on international development and humanitarian assistance projects in Africa, Asia, and the Balkans. He was the country director for the international NGO, World Vision, in Eritrea from 1995 to 1997 and promoted aquaculture as a Peace Corps volunteer in Liberia in the mid-1980s. His publications include *Democratization and Economic Growth: The Contribution of Accountability Institutions*; "Understanding Food Security: A Conceptual Framework for Programming"; "Operationalizing Reconciliation: Strategies for Rwanda and Burundi"; and "Botswana's Approach to Drought: How Disaster Relief Can Be Developmental."

JACK SNYDER is the Robert and Renée Belfer Professor of International Relations in the department of political science and Institute of War and Peace Studies at Columbia University. His research focuses on international relations theory, Post Soviet politics, and nationalism. Snyder received his BA from Harvard University, his certificate from the Russian Institute at Columbia University, and his PhD also from Columbia University.

JASON LEE STEORTS is a deputy managing editor of *National Review* and is involved with the *National Review Online* and *NRO's* "Out of the Corner" blog.

ANDREW SULLIVAN is a journalist and political commentator. Sullivan is the former editor of *The New Republic,* known for both his unusual personal-political identity (HIV-positive, homosexual, self-described conservative often at odds with other conservatives, and practicing Roman Catholic), as well as his successful and pioneering efforts in the field of blog journalism. He is also the author of three books.

STEVE WALT is a professor of international affairs at Harvard University's John F. Kennedy School of Government. In 1983, he received a Ph.D., in political science, from the University of California, Berkeley. Dr. Walt developed the 'Balance of Threat' Theory, which defined threats in terms of aggregate power, geographic proximity, offensive power, and aggressive intentions.

MURRAY WEIDENBAUM, an economist, holds the Mallinckrodt Distinguished University Professorship at Washington University in St. Louis, Missouri, where he also serves as chairman of the university's Center for the Study of American Business. He has been a faculty member at the university since 1964, and in 1981 and 1982, he was President Ronald Reagan's first chairman of the Council of Economic Advisers. Dr. Weidenbaum earned his M.A. from Columbia University and his Ph.D. from Princeton University. Among his many publications are *Looking for Common Ground on U.S. Trade Policy* (Center for Strategic & International Studies, 2001) and *The Bamboo Network: How Expatriate Chinese Entrepreneurs Are Creating a New Economic Superpower in Asia,* coauthored with Samuel Hughes (Free Press, 1996).

TAMARA COFMAN WITTES is a research fellow in the Saban Center for Middle East Policy at the Brookings Institution where she analyzes U.S. policy toward democratization in the Arab world and the challenge of regional economic and political reform. She has also served as an adjunct professor of security studies at Georgetown University and a consultant for the RAND Corporation, the U.S. Institute of Peace, and the Middle East Institute. Her publications have appeared in *Political Science Quarterly,* the *Weekly Standard,* the *Chronicle of Higher Education,* and *National Security Studies Quarterly.*

Index